Knights

IN HISTORY AND LEGEND

Knights

IN HISTORY AND LEGEND

CHIEF CONSULTANT
Constance Brittain Bouchard

**CHARTWELL
BOOKS, INC.**

This edition published in 2012 by
CHARTWELL BOOKS, INC.
A Division of BOOK SALES, INC.
276 Fifth Avenue Suite 206
New York, New York 10001
USA

Managing Director Chryl Campbell
Publishing Director Sarah Anderson
Art Director Kylie Mulquin
Project Manager Scott Forbes
Chief Consultant Constance Brittain Bouchard
Contributors Constance Brittain Bouchard, D'Arcy Jonathan Dacre Boulton, Lesley Coote, David Cornell, Paul F. Crawford, Stephanie Hathaway, Stephanie Hollis, John D. Hosler, Steven Isaac, Des McNicholas, Stephen Morillo, Richard Scott Nokes, Mark Gregory Pegg, William J. Purkis, Jarbel Rodriguez, Deborah Vess, David Whetham
Commissioning Editor David Kidd
Editors Scott Forbes, Mary Trewby, Dannielle Viera
Proofreader Kevin Diletti
Indexer Margaret Findlay
Cover Design Stan Lamond, Kylie Mulquin
Design Concept Stan Lamond, Kylie Mulquin
Designers Cathy Campbell, Avril Makula, Mark Thacker
Photo Researcher Tracey Gibson
Cartographer John Frith
Production Manager Ian Coles
Rights Manager Belinda Vance
Publishing Assistant Jessica Luca

ISBN-13: 978-0-7858-2954-6

Text © Global Book Publishing Pty Ltd 2009
Maps © Global Book Publishing Pty Ltd 2009
© Global Book Publishing Pty Ltd 2009
181 Botany Road
Waterloo, NSW 2017
Australia
website: www.globalbookpublishing.com.au
email: rightsmanager@globalbookpublishing.com.au

Printed in China
Color separation Pica Digital Pte Ltd, Singapore

JEAN 2

Contributors

CHIEF CONSULTANT

Constance Brittain Bouchard received her PhD from the University of Chicago and is now Distinguished Professor of Medieval History at the University of Akron, in Akron, Ohio, United States. Winner of a Guggenheim fellowship and a Fellow of the Medieval Academy of America, she has written numerous books including *"Strong of Body, Brave and Noble": Chivalry and Society in Medieval France* (1998) and *Sword, Miter, and Cloister: Nobility and the Church in Burgundy, 980–1198* (1987).

CONTRIBUTORS

D'Arcy Jonathan Dacre Boulton is a graduate of the Universities of Toronto, Pennsylvania (PhD), and Oxford (DPhil). He is currently Professor of Medieval Studies at the University of Notre Dame, Indiana, United States, and a Fellow of the Royal Heraldry Society of Canada, the International Heraldic Academy, and the Society of Antiquaries of London. His publications include *The Knights of the Crown: The Monarchical Orders of Knighthood in Later Medieval Europe, 1325–1520* (2000), and (with Jan Veenstra) *The Ideology of Burgundy: The Promotion of National Consciousness, 1364–1565* (2006).

Lesley Coote is a lecturer in the departments of English and Film Studies at the University of Hull in the United Kingdom. Her main interests are prophesy, chivalric romance, and modern cinematic and television medievalisms. She has written extensively on all of these topics, and has also produced a "scholarly but easy-read" edition of Chaucer's *The Canterbury Tales* (2002).

David Cornell spent several years researching the Anglo-Scottish wars of the fourteenth century at the University of Durham, England, and his PhD thesis focused on English castle garrisons of that period and how the English Crown sought to use the castle as an instrument

of war; he is currently extending this thesis into a monograph entitled *The Castle at War*. David is also the author of *Bannockburn: The Triumph of Robert the Bruce* (2009), and has contributed papers to academic journals including the *Scottish Historical Review*.

Paul F. Crawford is Assistant Professor of Ancient and Medieval History at California University of Pennsylvania, United States. He is a specialist in the history of the crusades and the military orders (especially the Templars and Hospitallers), and is the translator of *The "Templar of Tyre": Part III of the "Deeds of the Cypriots"* (2003) and a coeditor of a forthcoming book of articles on the trial of the Templars. He has appeared in several History Channel programs on the Crusades, including the popular *Lost Worlds: Knights Templar*.

Stephanie Hathaway obtained her PhD at the University of Sydney, Australia, and has lectured there in French, Germanic, and Medieval Studies since 2005. She specializes in the *chansons de geste*, Saracens, monastic rules, and chivalry. She has published papers on medieval French and German literature, presented papers at international conferences, and has been a guest speaker on Guillaume d'Orange. She is the coeditor of *Studies in Intercultural Transmission in the Early Medieval Mediterranean* (2009).

Stephanie Hollis is Professor in English and Director of the Centre for Medieval and Early Modern European Studies at the University of Auckland, New Zealand. She completed a PhD at the Australian National University, and has for many years taught Old and Middle English literature and Old Icelandic. Her main field of research is women in England pre-1200; her publications in this field include *Anglo-Saxon Women and the Church: Sharing a Common Fate* (1992) and *Writing the Wilton Women: Goscelin's*

Legend of Edith and Liber Confortatorius (2006). She also coedited *Migrations: Medieval Manuscripts in New Zealand* (2007), with Alexandra Barratt.

John D. Hosler is Assistant Professor of History at Morgan State University in Baltimore, Maryland, United States. He holds a PhD in medieval European history from the University of Delaware and is a specialist on warfare in the British Isles and France during the eleventh and twelfth centuries. He is the author of *Henry II: a Medieval Soldier at War, 1147–1189* (2007) and articles in the *Haskins Society Journal* and *Journal of Medieval Military History*.

Steven Isaac is Associate Professor of History at Longwood University in Virginia, United States. He began his doctoral studies in medieval military history under Randall Rogers, a renowned expert on Crusade-era siegecraft. He has gone on to publish a number of articles on mercenary activity across western Europe in the twelfth century; his full study on medieval mercenaries is forthcoming. Steven's more recent topics of research, and the subjects of future monographs, are the militancy of urban populations and the 1173–74 conflicts that nearly engulfed King Henry II of England.

Des McNicholas is an Australian-based freelance writer and editor, with an extensive publication history in areas such as military history, technology, training, and management. Des holds master's degrees in arts and defense studies and he is a graduate of the Royal Military College of Science at Shrivenham in the United Kingdom. Des's interest in military history grew from his military service in the Royal Australian Artillery, from which he retired in 2002 as a lieutenant colonel.

Stephen Morillo is the Jane and Frederic M. Hadley Chair in History at Wabash College, Indiana, United States, where he teaches world and European history. He did his undergraduate degree in medieval history at Harvard University and obtained his DPhil at the University of Oxford, specializing in Anglo-Norman military and administrative history. He is a specialist in the global history of warfare, especially in the premodern era. His books include *War in World History* (2009), *What is Military History?* (2006), *Warfare under the Anglo-Norman Kings, 1066–1135* (1994), and *The Battle of Hastings: Sources and Interpretations* (1995).

Richard Scott Nokes is Associate Professor of Medieval Literature at Troy University, Alabama, United States. His research has focused on medievalism in popular culture, the use of new technologies in medieval studies, and Anglo-Saxon magic and medicine. His most recent book is *Global Perspectives on Medieval English Literature, Language, and Culture* (2007), and he is writing a monograph tentatively entitled *Medieval America*. He also produces the medieval blog Unlocked Wordhoard.

Mark Gregory Pegg is Professor of History at Washington University in St. Louis, United States. He studied at the University of Sydney and Princeton University. His publications include *The Corruption of Angels: The Great Inquisition of 1245–1246* (2001) and *A Most Holy War: The Albigensian Crusade and the Battle for Christendom* (2007).

William J. Purkis has a BA and MA from Lancaster University and a PhD from the University of Cambridge, and is Lecturer in Medieval History at the University of Birmingham, England. His research interests lie in the history of crusading, pilgrimage, and monasticism, and in the social and cultural history of the Iberian Peninsula. He has published a monograph, *Crusading Spirituality in the Holy Land and Iberia, c. 1095–c. 1187* (2008), and a number of articles on the religious culture of the eleventh and twelfth centuries.

Jarbel Rodriguez is Associate Professor of Medieval History at San Francisco State University, United States, specializing in Spain, Christian–Muslim relations, and captivity and slavery. He is the author of *Captives and their Saviors in the Medieval Crown of Aragon* (2007) and *Exchanges: A Global History Reader* (2008).

Deborah Vess is Professor of History at Georgia College and State University, United States. She holds a PhD in history from the University of North Texas, and her areas of expertise are Church history and medieval monasticism. She has won several awards, including the Board of Regents Hall of Fame Award (2008), and the Ernest L. Boyer International Award for Excellence in Teaching, Learning, and Technology (2008), and was a Carnegie Scholar with the Carnegie Foundation for the Advancement of Teaching (1999). Deborah has published articles in *The American Benedictine Review, Mystics Quarterly, Word and Spirit, The Modern Schoolman*, and has authored two college textbooks on world civilizations.

David Whetham obtained his PhD at the University of London and joined the Defence Studies Department of King's College London in 2003. Based at the UK Joint Services Command and Staff College, David focuses on the ethical, legal, and moral dimensions of conflict while retaining a keen interest in medieval warfare. He has also worked for BBC History and with the Organizations for Security and Co-operation in Europe (OSCE) in Kosovo, contributing to the 2001 and 2002 elections. His book *Just Wars and Moral Victories: Surprise, Deception and the Normative Framework of European War in the Later Middle Ages* was published in 2009.

CONTENTS

Foreword

Five centuries after knights ceased to play a role in Europe's wars, they continue to intrigue us. All over the world, children construct makeshift "castles" and play-fight with plastic swords. Adults reenact medieval battles or take on the personae of fictional knights. Meanwhile, the image of the bold, Christian fighter, absolutely loyal to his lord, gentle to women and the weak, but implacable toward his enemies, is ubiquitous, appearing in video games, novels, and even sports logos. This romantic image inspires many people to find out more about the Middle Ages.

But was there ever a real age of knighthood? Stories of knights in shining armor can be so romanticized that one might easily imagine that knights are as fantastic as the dragons they supposedly fought. Knights *were* real, however. Horseborne warriors, they first emerged in France during the eleventh century and dominated Europe's wars until the fourteenth century, when advances in infantry tactics and the development of gunpowder reduced their effectiveness. They might have often been quick-tempered and violent, coarse and rough, but even their enemies recognized them as superb fighters. And as those of noble blood also began to define themselves as knights, these fighters, encouraged by their lords, ladies, and the church, tried to temper their violence and rude ways by adhering to ideals of honor and courtesy—the concept of chivalry, in other words. Increasingly, too, they enjoyed hearing and reading stories of legendary knights who fought gallantly for God and the ladies they loved—just as we enjoy such stories today.

This book introduces both the history and the legend of medieval knights. In its pages, contributors from North America, the United Kingdom, and Australasia, all experts in their fields, explore the role of knights across the centuries. Knights are seen emerging into history, at the same time as castles were first built, and playing major roles in such events as the Norman Conquest of England in 1066, the Crusades against Islam, and the Hundred Years' War. A knight's youthful training, his horse, his sword and armor, the heraldic symbols that came to identify him, tournaments, the tricky reconciliation of violence with Christian beliefs, and the shifting ideals of chivalry are all detailed. Comparisons are made with fighters in other parts of the world, such as Japan's *samurai*, who were both like and unlike the knights of Europe. Knights are also seen through the lens of literature—both medieval works and modern tales—and through a rich array of illustrations, including images from medieval manuscripts and from nineteenth-century paintings, where representations of the knight reach an apex of romance and glorification. The volume concludes with the continuing appearance of knights in games and movies, and in the titles given to members of modern organizations such as the Knights of Columbus—indicating that, while historical knights may be far in the past, their legend lives on.

Constance Brittain Bouchard

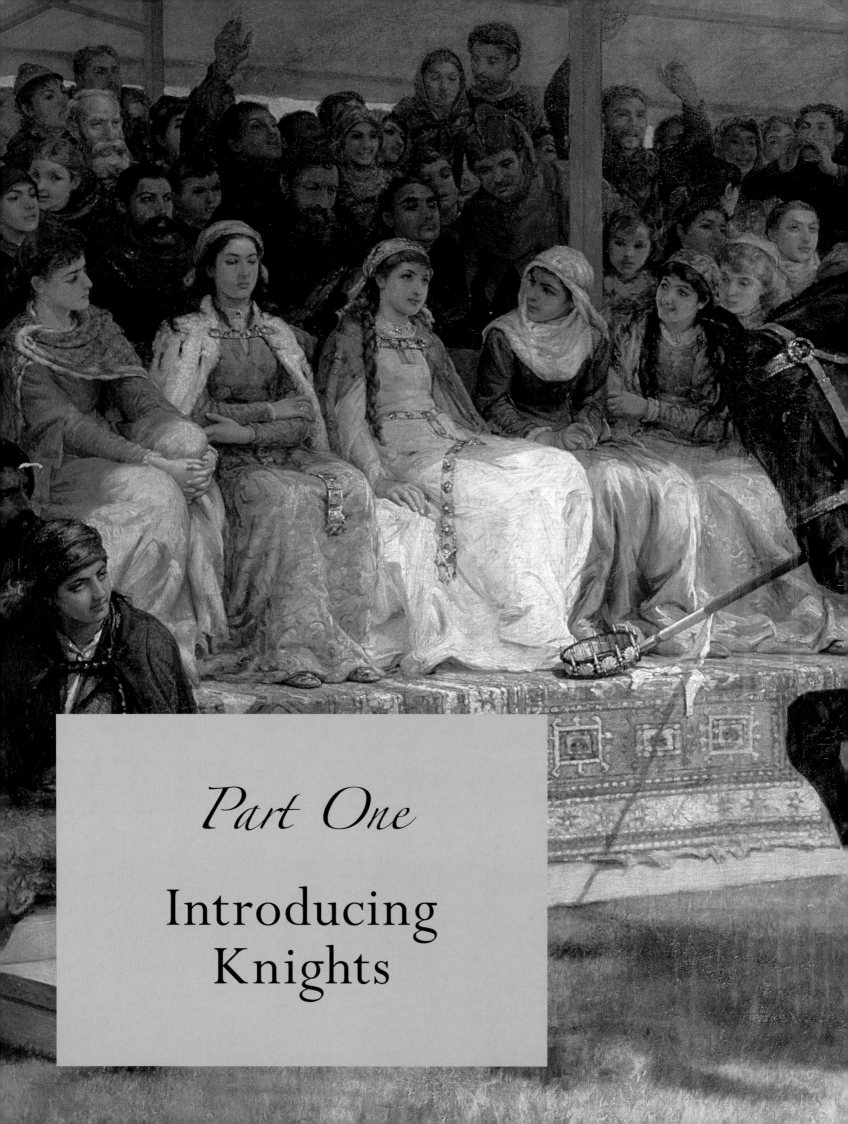

Part One

Introducing Knights

The Origins of Knights

Knights are the emblematic warriors of the European Middle Ages. But knights were not merely professional warriors: knighthood includes the notions of social status, political power, and legal classification, and at the least it implies those cultural expressions of knightly identity—bravery, honor, loyalty, and service to women— that are commonly known as chivalry.

At the most basic level, knights are the European version of warrior elites, a social type that is common across almost every traditional (or pre-industrial) society of a certain level of complexity. Warrior elites combined a profession—or, more accurately, a lifestyle—dedicated to fighting (usually although not always on horseback) with high social status, prestige, and power.

Along with the religious elites and scribal elites, or bureaucrats, warriors were one of the three sorts of men (and, rarely, women) who dominated the traditional political and social structures. The characteristics of individual warrior elite groups might vary in terms of their precise social status, of their relationship to the formal mechanisms of state power, of their styles of fighting, weaponry, and armor, and, above all, in the details of their culture. But beyond being warriors with high social status, different warrior cultures tended to share certain features that were centered around the notions of bravery and honor—however differently those two warrior concepts might be defined in practice.

A SOCIAL ORDER

Yet the unique details of the European form of knighthood matter, and it is at this level that the complexity of the topic of knighthood becomes more apparent. Knights were not merely soldiers. In medieval Europe, many townsmen and even peasants at times served in armed gatherings. Nor did knighthood necessarily encompass all of the better-armed and better-trained soldiers in armies. Medieval armies regularly included well-trained professional soldiers serving both on foot and on horseback. And purely in

LEFT: *The top and sides of this twelfth-century French wooden wedding chest are painted with figures of warrior knights; this side shows a chevalier going to war.*

RIGHT: *Despite its opposition to violence, the church was inextricably linked to the idea of the knight, and clerics educated young knights. This manuscript illumination shows the monk Eadwine working on the Eadwine Psalter, c. 1150.*

terms of their fighting styles, many of the non-knightly soldiers were tactically indistinguishable from the knights.

The distinction between soldiers and knights lay in social status: the knights ultimately became part of the European ruling class. They came to be considered noble, a status that was imbued not just with informal prestige and with social influence, but also, eventually, with definite legal privileges, obligations, and formal authority. Landholding was often associated with knighthood.

Details varied even within western Europe—England differed from much of the Continent in that knighthood never became a closed social class there, whereas in Germany there were some servile (legally unfree) knights—adding to the complexity of the topic.

Knighthood was, in short, a social order, and indeed, it was recognized as such by social theorists of the Middle Ages, who divided society into those who worked, those who prayed, and those who fought. (Medieval theory did not make a place for townsmen and merchants, whose ideals and practices often conflicted with those of both the fighters and the prayers.)

THE KNIGHTLY CLASS

How did this social order emerge in the Middle Ages? Before about the year 1000, Europe was dominated by an aristocracy descended from a mixture of old Roman families and the Romanized Germanic tribes (which were political rather than truly ethnic groupings). This aristocracy had dominated the Roman Empire politically from around the fifth century CE. By 1000, the aristocrats' power was buttressed by the free, arms-bearing men who were their retainers. Increasingly, estates centered on a castle, which gave the lineage its surname and

LEFT: *Simone Martini painted this fresco of a solitary knight riding across a battlefield in 1328. In fact, the knight's very identity was inextricably tied to a social class.*

became the basic unit of political and social power. More individual lineages with castles to garrison meant there was a need for more armed retainers, most of whom lived in the households of their lords at this point. It was these armed retainers of the aristocracy who formed the basis of the knightly social class, and who became defined, in particular, as warriors on horseback.

This emergent class of military retainers, occupying a middle ground between the aristocracy and the peasantry, gained increasing social and legal definition in the century after 1100 as, increasingly, their lords adopted knightly attributes, a process reflected in the development of the formal ceremony of dubbing that marked a young aristocrat's entry into knightly status. These rising warriors also became culturally self-conscious and began to construct a distinct social identity for themselves. In many cases they were rewarded for service to their lord through a practice called *enfeoffment*, the granting of a piece of land, known as

a *fief*. At first, this tended to be given after a substantial term of service in the lord's household, but increasingly enfeoffment preceded the performance of the military obligations that were tied to the possession of the fief, because the grant of a fief proved to be politically useful in establishing ties of political alliance. In fact, it became one of the fundamental contractual ties, along with marriage, that held together the aristocracy, who enfeoffed each other as well as their retainers (although the most militarily useful of whom continued to be unlanded household retainers).

Even though many knights' fiefs were quite small, the possession of land came with legal jurisdiction over the peasants who worked the land. This element of formal authority was the reason for the upward assimilation of knightly status into the realm formerly occupied solely by the aristocracy. By 1200, the knightly class had entered into the nobility. Increasingly thereafter, in most places outside of England, the status of knight came to be defined by inheritance on the aristocratic model.

ABOVE: *By 1200, knights were part of the nobility. The richest aspired to leave grand memorials of themselves, along the lines of these royal tombs in the Cathedral of St. Denis, Paris.*

FEUDALISM?

Knights and knightly service in armies are often associated with the supposed political system known as *feudalism*. The problem with the term *feudalism* is that there are almost as many definitions of it as there are historians. As a result, the term has fallen into disfavor among military historians, whose definitions of feudalism must be so narrow that actual instances can be found nowhere, and among social historians, whose definitions are so broad that it can be found anywhere. Medievalists prefer not to use the term at all, with its universal-sounding *-ism* ending, and instead they restrict the adjective *feudal* to describing aspects of fiefs.

THE DECLINE OF THE KNIGHT

At the same time this was happening, there was a downward assimilation of the aristocracy into knightly status. The success the knightly class had had in appropriating the central ground of warrior identity, and in creating a successful chivalric ideal of behavior to define that identity, drew the aristocracy into defining themselves as knights, too. Even kings identified themselves with knighthood, and they furthered this social order by founding, after 1300, formal orders of knighthood.

An ironic outcome of this double assimilation was to raise the prestige and cost of formal entry into knightly status, as well as the social, legal, and military obligations it entailed. Many knightly families who possessed only small estates found such costs difficult to bear, and as a result the would-be knight tended to delay, sometimes indefinitely, formal entry by dubbing into knightly status, choosing instead to remain a squire. Consequently, the number of knights, as a social group and a proportion of many armies, declined slowly but steadily between 1300 and 1500, the period of knighthood's greatest social and political prominence. By the latter date, the very nature of knighthood as well as the military role of knights were being altered fundamentally by wider developments in politics, society, and warfare.

In sum, knighthood as a social order began to emerge after 1000, continued to develop in sometimes contradictory ways throughout the remainder of the Middle Ages, and was, throughout the period of its existence, a complex and composite slice of medieval society.

KNIGHTLY ETYMOLOGY

The complex and composite nature of this medieval social order is reflected in the terminology employed to identify knights. The English word *knight* derives from the Anglo-Saxon *cniht*, meaning "boy" or "servant", and is related to the Old German *knecht,* a knave—which is a clear demonstration of the low and dependent status of the original retainers who rose to become the knightly class. The fact that the word is a social, rather than a military, descriptor is also significant—*knight* in English does not acquire a clear military connotation until the age of the Hundred Years' War, but by the late fourteenth century it was well established as the English equivalent of the Latin term *miles* (plural: *milites*), meaning "soldier," and also designated the social order described above.

But the Latin *miles* had originally referred specifically to an elite, well-trained, and well-equipped soldier, which in a Roman context had meant a legionnaire and, thus, an infantryman. The word retained this basic meaning of elite soldier well beyond the year 1000, but the changes in the social structure from classical to medieval times meant that the word came to imply a cavalryman rather than an infantryman, as indicated by its use in the phrase *milites peditesque*, meaning "horse and foot."

This emphasis on the mounted nature of knights' usual military role is, in turn, reflected in the French word designating a knight, *chevalier*. Its collective form for the social and military order, *chevalerie*, is distinguished from the purely military term *cavalerie*, which is the the source of the English word *cavalry*. We therefore see that the vocabulary of knighthood reveals the mixture of social status and military function that defined the place of knights in medieval society.

Despite the fact that both the origins and the eventual social composition of the knightly class were complicated and composite, there was some unity to the order of knighthood across large parts of western Europe. This coherence was provided by the cultural construction of a knightly identity that, even though itself complex and contested, created a set of ideals that helped define knighthood: bravery, honor, loyalty, and service to women—collectively known as chivalry.

LEFT: *The king was at the top of the medieval social and political hierarchy—next to God, as in this depiction, from the* Gospel of Henry the Lion, *of the 1168 coronation of Henry the Lion, Duke of Saxony, and his wife Matilda. But he relied on the knightly class to retain his status.*

Chivalric Ideals

The chivalric ideals of knighthood explain who knights thought they were. But, if we are to understand the knights of the Middle Ages from their own perspective, then the modern myths and misconceptions about chivalry—more than any other topic that is associated with knights—must be separated from medieval reality.

The existence of warrior elites in almost all traditional societies was matched by the variety of ideals and of self-conceptions each of these groups developed. Such ideals were influenced by the wider matrix of cultural values within which the warrior group lived. Thus, different religions, social practices, social structures, and political arrangements all shaped the individual warrior cultures.

But some common themes emerge across this cultural variety, themes that are not surprising, given that warfare and fighting placed certain inevitable demands on the behavior of warriors. These included a high value attributed to bravery in combat and loyalty to one's lord; depending on the political environment, however, the latter might often be honored more in word than in deed, and indeed might be emphasized by leaders because such loyalty was difficult for them to maintain. Success in warfare was inevitably central, although the tactics acceptable to achieving success varied, as did the acceptable responses to defeat. Finally, also common was an emphasis on notions of individual honor and the necessity to defend that honor by force. Feuds and bloody contests for status often, therefore, characterized

RIGHT: *In this thirteenth-century Spanish miniature,* The Miracle of the Virgin Acting as a Knight, *the warrior-knight is shown at prayer, fighting, and paying homage to his lord.*

warrior behavior, and they fitted in well with warrior ideals. In short—romantic notions to the contrary—warrior ideals glorified violence.

A CULTURE OF VIOLENCE

The military retainers of the western European aristocracy who emerged as the knightly class were no exception in their violence, even before they developed a coherent self-perception and set of ideals. When they did so, starting in the eleventh century, the result reflected sometimes contradictory influences.

The initial impulse came from the church, led by the bishops, attempting to reign in the violence of the warrior aristocracy and their followers. This took two forms. First was an attempt to limit the impact of warfare through restricting its effects to certain times, places, and people. Second, and more influentially, from 1095 the crusading movement sought to harness warrior energy to church-defined goals.

Both these efforts took place in the context of a larger ideological program of reform, which sought to distinguish between religious and secular power in both theological and practical ways. The reformers wished simultaneously to free the church from secular interference (most notably in the dispute over investiture, whereby a monarch bestowed

ABOVE: *The reality of warfare was far removed from the romanticized view in paintings such as Paolo Uccello's* Battle of San Romano *(1456).* **RIGHT:** *A twelfth-century knight, mounted, with chain-mail armor, shield, and sword, is represented in this ivory chess piece.*

upon a bishop the ring and staff, symbols of religious office) and to subordinate secular to religious authority. The efforts of the church to separate religious and secular authority met explicit ideological resistance from kings and emperors, but they also sparked a broader cultural resistance among warriors.

THE ORIGINS OF CHIVALRY

The warrior aristocracy and their retainers were not resistant to religious ideals per se; however, they refused to accept the church's definition of themselves. The idea that violence was an evil, even if a necessary one that in certain circumstances could be employed for good ends, was simply too restrictive for a group that already saw glory and honor in their participation in war.

These beliefs are evidenced by epic poetry such as *The Song of Roland* (*La chanson de Roland, c.* 1100). Such poems were transmitted by an oral tradition that thrived at least since Carolingian times (late eighth and ninth centuries)

and were being written down from the late eleventh century. This tradition—which at the level of heroic combat has parallels in epics through much of the traditional world of warrior elites—reflected not just the glory of war but also the prereform concept of equal cooperation between the religious and secular powers in maintaining social order. The result was the beginnings of ideals of knightly or chivalrous behavior that were built around the sanctification of violence and its wielders. In short, as "those who fight," knights came to see themselves as a formal part of a social order ordained by God—as an order in themselves whose function of fighting was a just and necessary end in itself. This shift was marked by the creation and elaboration of the rituals of dubbing, which took on the trappings of a religious ceremony, although not one recognized by the church as a sacrament.

But given their origins in resistance to the imposition of the ideological program of the church, chivalrous ideals were never exclusively, or even predominantly, religious in nature. Nor were these ideals codified into actual rules of conduct, at least until much later (near the end of the Middle Ages), and then the process of codification and formalization probably reflected the declining significance of chivalrous ideals and of knights as a social and military class. Instead, chivalrous ideals were constructed and reconstructed constantly in the interplay between the real behavior of knights and literary and artistic representations of knightly behavior.

AN EMPHASIS ON LOVE

It was through literature that chivalrous ideals became entangled with another

set of ideals emerging in twelfth-century France: those associated with love. Embodied in the romance, which supplemented the epic poem as the literary expression of the European secular elite, courtly behavior broadly *(courtoisie)*, and proper behavior toward women specifically, became part of chivalry's broader cultural context. In other words, courtliness encompassed a wider field of ideals and behavior, especially with regard to women, than did chivalry.

For chivalry, at its root, remained a set of ideals for warriors in warfare: it was developed by and applicable to men who fought. It is essential to keep this in mind in order to separate myth, or perhaps elements of the broader courtly culture, from chivalrous reality.

HONOR AND LOYALTY

What behaviors, then, did chivalrous ideals sanction? One place to start is that chivalry frowned on the dishonorable treatment of knightly prisoners, and killing an unarmed prisoner was particularly bad—unless such a move was dictated by military necessity as when Henry V (reigned 1413–22) ordered French prisoners in 1415 killed at Agincourt. Overly harsh imprisonment was also criticized. But there was a clear material motive behind these strictures, because noble prisoners could be ransomed for healthy sums.

At a more ideal level, the fundamental duty of a knight arose from the function that defined knighthood as a social order: to protect those he was charged to protect.

ABOVE: *Knight Geoffrey Luttrell bids farewell to his family as he sets off on campaign, in this illustration from the* Luttrell Psalter *(c. 1340).*

Therefore a chivalrous knight would not abandon the land—and specifically the churches and towns—that was his to defend in the face of the enemy without honorable effort. Retreat or surrender under conditions of military necessity was again acceptable, providing suitable resistance had first been offered. This accounts for the common scenario in medieval wars in which a besieged garrison offered to surrender if no relief were forthcoming within a negotiated period.

The knight's duty to defend specific people overlapped with the duty to obey and support one's lord, since the land, the churches, and the towns that a knight was supposed to defend usually belonged to the lord for whom the knight fought. Loyalty to one's lord was chivalrous.

Outright treachery clearly was not, but there was a substantial gray zone in which a knight could resist and even, to a degree, fight against his own lord. This speaks to the interaction of chivalric ideals with the realities of lordship and vassalage, which were essentially contractual relationships with mutual rights and obligations. Particularly in conditions of multiple lordship (where a knight owed service to several masters), exactly what was chivalrous could get quite complicated. Loyalty as a chivalrous ideal

BELOW: *Courtly love was an intrinsic part of chivalric ideals, as shown in the fifteenth-century* Bible of Borso d'Este *by Marco dell'Avogadro.*

was also conceived of more generally as loyalty to the group. Here, chivalry mediated the conflicted relationship between individual glory-seeking and group discipline. Knights are often thought of as being individualistic and undisciplined glory-seekers, but in fact chivalric ideals saw the abandoning of the group in the midst of battle—for whatever reason, not just cowardice—very unfavorably. Ultimately, it was a combination of peer approval, which was sometimes negotiated on the spot, and an appeal to military success that governed the various interpretations of individual behavior in combat.

THE REALITIES OF WAR

Chivalrous ideals saw nothing wrong with ambushes, trickery in combat, and

BELOW: *This illustration from the fourteenth-century manuscript* The Story of Godfrey de Bouillon (Roman de Godefroy de Bouillon) *shows Godfrey and his men beseiging a castle.*

> *He is no true knight who, for fear of death, or of what might befall, fails to defend the land of his lord, but in truth he is a traitor and forsworn.*
>
> **HONORÉ BOUVET,** *THE TREE OF BATTLES* **(***L'ARBRE DES BATAILLES***, 1387)**

avoiding battle when doing so was the prudent course of action, as it often was in medieval war. Face-to-face combat on an open battlefield between social equals might be the ultimate ideal—and found expression in the tournament, that artificial form of warfare—but it was not to be sought in defiance of military common sense. Chivalry simply recognized the normal patterns of medieval warfare. On the battlefield the realities and popular myths of chivalry were in most conflict.

The common patterns of medieval warfare included, and indeed were dominated by, plundering and pillaging. And chivalric ideals saw nothing wrong with this. It is simply the converse of the duty to protect: knights on campaign had an equal duty to damage the enemy. If that included—as it inevitably did—burning villages, trampling crops, and killing peasants, therein lay the glory.

After all, chivalry was a class- and gender-bound set of ideals. It did not apply to peasants or townsmen, who might quite acceptably be targets and victims, but could not, by definition, behave chivalrously themselves. Nor did it apply to churchmen, who were accorded the respect due to an equal social class but who had their own code of conduct. It only tangentially considered women, and then only when they were noble. Courtliness might idealize love, but in war knights saw women as, at best, an irrelevancy. The reality for peasant and merchant women was often much worse.

The Noble Steed

Central to a knight's ability to do his chivalric duty on the battlefield was his horse. Knightly culture endowed warhorses with their own nobility, and although a knight might, in fact, have to fight on foot as well as on horseback, his cultural identity was mounted squarely on his most noble steed.

Not all warrior elites rode horses, but those that did not almost always either lacked horses altogether, as in the pre-Columbian Americas, or they lived in climates and disease zones in which horses did not survive well, such as the tropics. Everywhere else, the warrior elites rode horses, although they did not always fight on horseback. They rode because horses provided mobility, which was useful strategically and tactically in military terms, and because good warhorses were large and expensive, and therefore symbolically displayed the superior wealth and higher social status of their riders. European knights fit this pattern perfectly.

European warhorses, or chargers, of the early medieval period were not particularly large. However, selective breeding on aristocratic stud farms was increasingly employed to produce superior horses. Fast-running Arabians, for example, were highly valued and often bred into European lines. In the later Middle Ages, the need for horses to carry fully armed knights wearing heavy plate armor led to an increased demand for large and powerful mounts (although still not quite on the scale of Clydesdale or Belgian workhorses of today). Their relative scarcity raised the value of these

ABOVE: *As well as a horse's inherent strength, the great height of the animal gave the mounted knight a distinct advantage over opponents fighting on foot. This illumination of a group of armored knights on horseback is from a French manuscript of the fourteenth century.*

horses and made them clear markers of the economic and political distinctions among the knightly class.

A charger was trained from an early age to respond to its rider's commands, to perform the sorts of maneuvers used in combat, and to become accustomed

to the sounds and sights of the battlefield. This took time: warhorses were at their best between the ages of 8 and 12.

Future knights needed early riding training as well. According to a Carolingian proverb, a boy who had not learned to ride properly before puberty would never learn to do so well.

MOBILITY ON THE BATTLEFIELD

The value of warhorses in time and money, and the increasing use of missile weapons in the late Middle Ages, reinforced the tendency for horse armor to become heavier and more elaborate over time. The most heavily armored cavalry, though, were probably less useful than if they had been more lightly armored, since armoring forced a tactical trade-off in terms of decreased mobility, which was the key to cavalry's effectiveness in battle and on campaign.

The importance of this mobility on campaign is obvious. Mounted troops could cover more ground, pillage more widely, and respond to threats more rapidly than could men on foot. Thus, even the warriors who regularly fought on foot by tactical tradition, such as the thanes of Anglo-Saxon England, rode

LEFT: *A warhorse had to remain steady in the noise and chaos of the battlefield, as in this fifteenth-century manuscript illustration.*

charge—although it was not used in the way that is commonly thought. The tactic did not succeed by multiplying the speed of the charge by the weight of horse and armored knight delivered through the tip of a couched lance—this might be a good tactic in a joust, but against a solid wall of steady infantry, horses would "refuse," or draw up short of an inevitable collision with an object they could see no way around, over, or through.

In fact, the most successful charges were executed at a trot, not a gallop, as this allowed the charging formation to maintain its cohesion. And this, in turn, heightened the essential effect of the battle charge, which was psychological: a good charge presented the image of inevitability, which induced some of the enemy line to break and run, thus opening gaps into which knights could ride, exploiting their superior attacking height.

It should be emphasized that knights often fought on foot. Their elite status, however, gave them advantages in training and equipment, whether they rode or not. But the quintessential knight charged into combat on his noble steed.

horses on campaign. On the battlefield, the cavalry could use its mobility to attack the flank and rear of an enemy line or pursue a fleeing foe; conversely, mounted men had a greater chance of escaping successfully from a battlefield defeat. Indeed, ease of flight sometimes prompted leaders to dismount their

knights to ensure that they fought more stubbornly in defense. Mobility enabled cavalry to feign flight, then turn on the pursuers when they became disorganized.

THE CHARGE

Mobility was the key to the classic battle tactic used by the European knight, the

THE KNIGHT AND HIS HORSES

The largest, strongest, and most expensive chargers, favored for battle and tournaments, were known as *destriers*. But many knights rode less expensive horses called *coursers* and *rounceys*—the former light and fast, and popular on the battlefield, the latter good all-rounders. Poorer knights also had fewer animals overall. A warhorse would not be ridden except in battle. When on campaign, a knight would ride a *palfrey*, the horse most favored for riding, hunting, and ceremonial use, and carry his baggage on a packhorse.

RIGHT: *A knight's status was tied to the quality of the horses he rode to war and, as in this fourteenth-century illustration, at leisure.*

Knights in the Arts

As a socially dominant class in medieval Europe, knights were closely associated with the arts as subjects, patrons, and even as producers. The arts of the Middle Ages, especially literature, reinforced the knights' chivalric image of themselves and today they reveal to us both the ideal and the reality of knightly culture.

European knights again fit into broad patterns in their relationship to the arts. Warrior elites, as elites, consistently integrated violence with sophisticated expressions of their cultural identity. Early in their history, European knights were perhaps unusual only in their low levels of literacy compared with warrior groups in many other parts of the world, at least among sedentary societies. This situation changed steadily between the years 1100 and 1500.

EPIC AND ROMANCE

The literature of the Middle Ages is full of knights. At the start of this period, historical writing was dominated by churchmen. Their accounts of knightly violence were not always flattering, although the close familial associations tying together the European priests and the warriors sometimes mitigated this. William of Poitiers (*c.* 1020–*c.* 1090), chaplain and biographer to William I the Conqueror (reigned 1066–87), was a trained military man before entering the church, for example. Similarly, knights make appearances in hagiographies (saints' lives) in various roles.

By the fourteenth century, Jean Froissart (*c.* 1333–*c.* 1400) and other herald-historians were writing secular histories essentially from the knightly perspective. But in literature the knightly culture reflected broader shifts. Epic poetry—heroic, male-dominated tales about war—was accompanied by romances, in verse and prose, in which women and courtly values played larger roles, arising from and constructing an increasingly literate knightly culture.

At the same time, William IX, Duke of Aquitaine (*c.* 1071–1126), made his reputation not just as a warrior (he was a leader of the First Crusade) but as a troubadour, a vernacular song writer, and was thus the founder of a tradition leading to the works of Dante Alighieri (1265–1321) and beyond.

By the fourteenth century, the variety of types of literature portraying knights is too vast to enumerate. *The Knight's Tale* by Geoffrey Chaucer (*c.* 1342/43–1400) is but one example of a corpus that also included the whole Arthurian tradition. The development of literature of all types for and by the knightly class, including in such mundane forms as government

LEFT: *Edward Burne-Jones's* Dream of Sir Lancelot at the Chapel of the Holy Grail *(1896) is a Pre-Raphaelite view of the knight.*

THE LADY AND THE UNICORN

There are few extant medieval tapestries. Apart from the Bayeux Tapestry depicting the Battle of Hastings, the one best known is *The Lady and the Unicorn (La dame à la licorne)*, a French series of six tapestries of mysterious meaning. The central figures of the lady and the unicorn, on a dark blue island against a red background, are surrounded by flowers and trees, but also by military accoutrements, such as spears, banners, and standards bearing heraldic symbols. The tapestries are believed to have been executed between about 1485 and 1500. They are now in the Cluny Museum in Paris.

LEFT: Taste, *one of* The Lady and the Unicorn *tapestries, includes many of the visual elements that are typical of the series. In traditional sacred images, the unicorn symbolized the incarnation of the Virgin Mary; in courtly terms, it stood for the lover.*

documents, was significant for stimulating the creation of the vernacular languages to be the vehicles for literary expression, thus supplementing (and supplanting) the Latin of the church.

KNIGHTS IN PICTURES

Visual arts in the Middle Ages present an equally rich and varied picture. Manuscript illuminations linked painting to literature. Many of the most vivid portraits of knights in action—in battles and sieges and as ideal types in illustrations of the social orders—come from illuminations. Although it developed later as an independent art, from early in its history painting included portraits of knights. More common, though, were the tapestries that adorned the walls of knightly castles, providing some insulation and scenes of noble bravery and of courtly love from epic and romance; they were also tangible expressions of the owner's wealth and status.

Some of the most striking portraits of individual knights, and some of our best sources for styles of armor, come from sculpture, especially from tombs of famous knights. Knights endowed

ABOVE: *This illustration is from a Caxton edition of the prologue to* The Canterbury Tales *by Geoffrey Chaucer, printed c. 1478.*

churches and built castles, contributing to the architectural history of Europe. And probably the quintessential knightly art form was heraldry, the decoration of shields so that individual knights could be identified in combat.

THE AFTERLIFE OF THE KNIGHTLY CULTURE

The cultural afterimage of the knight has long outlived the Middle Ages, becoming a staple of popular culture. The image of knights may have suffered in the sixteenth to eighteenth centuries—the Don Quixote of Miguel de Cervantes (1547–1616) is emblematic of a class whose relevance fell into question—but by the nineteenth century, when social and military revolutions had made real knighthood extinct, romantic writers such as Alfred, Lord Tennyson revived, or more accurately invented, the modern chivalric image of the slayer of dragons and courteous defender of women.

Painters of the time, notably the Pre-Raphaelites, followed suit. Howard Pyle's magnificent illustrated versions of the Arthurian cycle ushered in a twentieth century overflowing with knightly images in literature, music, and, above all, movies. The romantic image still predominates, whether as inspiration, as in the magnificent armored excess of John Boorman's fantasy film *Excalibur*, or as foil, as in the classic and much-quoted farce of *Monty Python and the Holy Grail*. The plate armor of late medieval knights lives on in the design of futuristic warrior robots in Japanese *manga* comics, ensuring that the afterimage of knights will not fade any time soon.

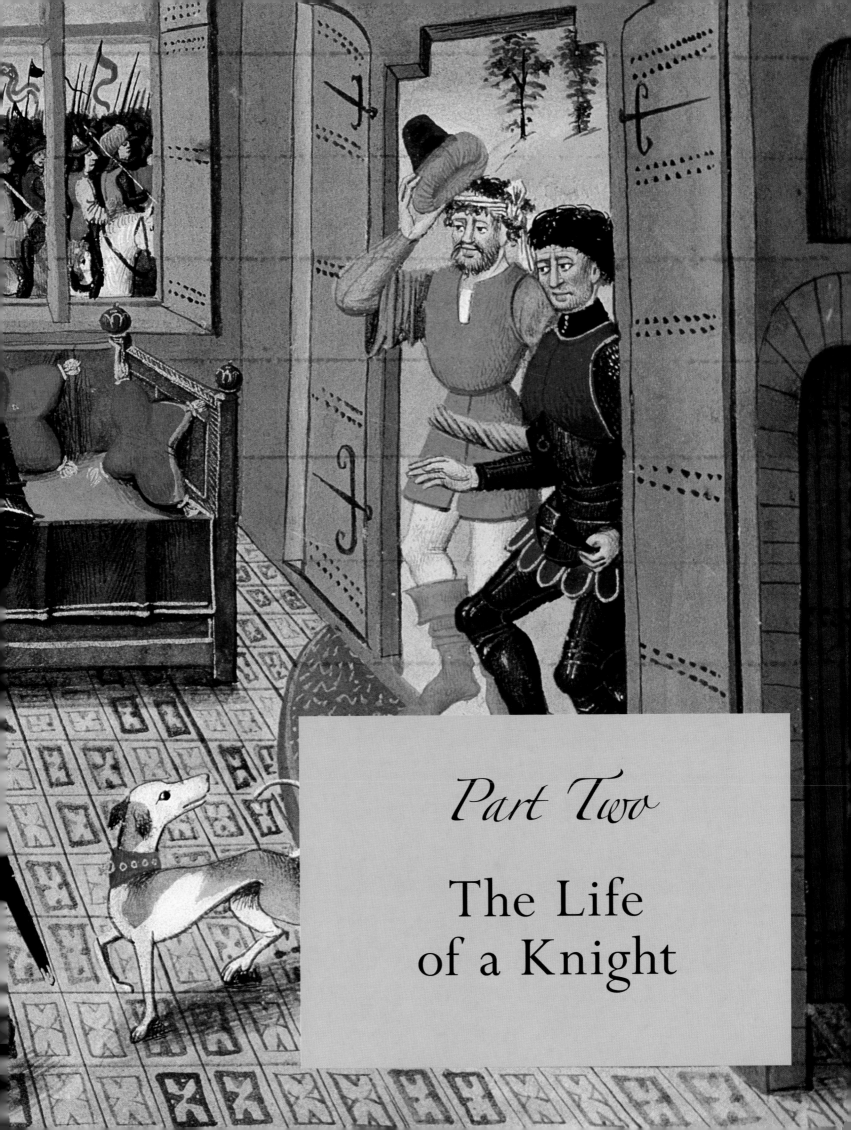

Part Two

The Life
of a Knight

Becoming a Knight

In the beginning, a knight became a knight by virtue of his warrior status and his experience. Over the centuries, however, a complex system of education gradually developed. By the time he formally became a knight, a youth would probably have spent about a dozen years honing his knightly skills.

The first knights, who appeared in France before elsewhere in Europe, fought on behalf of the powerful, but they were not themselves from aristocratic families. It was no coincidence that castles and knights developed at the same time, for the great castellan lords assembled groups of knights around them, men who would be ready to enforce the lords' pronouncements. Those who built castles staffed them with fighters of every sort, including knights who would ride out to fight and then retreat behind the safety of castle walls. The chroniclers of the early eleventh century characterized them as violent and dangerous—nothing like the romantic terms attached to chivalrous knights two or three centuries later. Rather, they were considered rough warriors, who could easily overcome any resistance.

Known as *service knights*, these men would have needed training to be able to fight and ride effectively, but there was no formal ceremony or even regular training method that they underwent. Their horses and their weapons were given to them by their lords, the powerful owners of lands and of castles. Their

subservient status was specially marked in Germany, where many knights were servile during the Middle Ages, officially unfree—who were referred to in Latin as *ministeriales*, or those who served.

By the final decades of the eleventh century, both in France and in England

(which had not had knights at all before the Norman conquest in 1066), nobles increasingly defined themselves militarily, and specifically wanted to be knights. Knights in their turn wanted to be more like the aristocracy. As the two groups sought to adopt each others' attributes and indeed began to intermarry, it slowly became more and more difficult to draw any sharp distinctions between them.

The service knights had continued to fight on behalf of their lords without any special ceremonies or status markers. However, during the twelfth century a set of procedures developed by which a young aristocrat would become a knight.

KNIGHTLY TRAINING

By the time a boy was six or seven, noble parents would normally decide whether he was going to join the church or stay in the world. If they chose the latter, then his knighthood training would begin. To learn to fight well

LEFT: *The king was at the pinnacle of earthly power, as shown in the Manesse Codex (c. 1304). Ennobled knights had a higher status than service knights.*

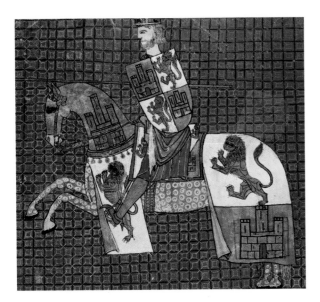

as a knight was a prolonged process, a process comparable to becoming an elite gymnast or a figure skater in the twenty-first century, where training must also begin in childhood. A knight's training was designed to create someone strong and agile, and a superb rider, who could handle the lance and the sword easily while also controlling his horse.

But learning how to become a knight was more than military training. For the young aristocrats, this was inextricably embedded in their overall education, and it indicates how thoroughly the military attributes had become part of noble self-definition by the middle of the twelfth century. This education of the young knight included the basics of reading and writing, as well as learning the proper courtly behavior.

When a youth was said to have been made a knight, it indicated that he had come of age, but it also suggested that he had embraced his moral responsibilities. By the thirteenth century, the knighting ceremony had taken on rich and complex symbolism that suggested a "true" knight would embody all the religious and chivalric values.

LEFT: *Alfonso X the Wise, king of Leon and Castile (reigned 1252–84), seen in this thirteenth-century manuscript, encouraged the development of a distinctive native literary language.*

AWAY FROM HOME

Frequently, noble boys would be sent away from home in order to be trained as knights, sometimes to the court of their fathers' lord, sometimes to the home of an uncle. Maternal uncles were preferred to paternal ones. Because inheritance went preferentially to men, a father's brother could well consider that his nephews were his rivals. But a mother's brother was happy to establish a close relationship with young relatives without entertaining any thoughts that their inheritance ought to be his.

In addition, because young aristocratic women typically married men older than they were—sometimes much older—a maternal uncle would often be closer in age to the boys he was training than would a paternal uncle.

In other cases, a powerful count or duke might have a whole group of young would-be knights training at his court. In the stories of the time, such young men appear at the courts of King Arthur and Charlemagne. At some level, these youths served as hostages for the good behavior of their fathers, men who were supposed to serve the lord but could be suspected of an independent streak. Less ominously, the youths grew up with a close bond to the family to which they would owe loyalty. This training also fostered close connections between all the young men of a region, because boys who trained together would normally grow up to be extremely close friends.

BELOW: *As part of their education, young boys acted as pages at banquets, as shown in this illustration from a fifteenth-century version of the story of Renaud de Montauban.*

THE ELEMENTS OF KNIGHTLY EDUCATION

Mastering all the skills of war—fighting with lance and sword, from horseback, on foot, and one on one—was just one part of the knight's education. His long training was also aimed at producing a literate man with courtly manners.

The boys received a good basic education, learning to read and write, both in the vernacular and, to some extent, in Latin, and also being taught arithmetic. These were skills that they would need when adults—the ability to read and understand contracts and charters, and to be able to keep track of their income and obligations. Like their contemporaries in the church, they were exposed to Classical Latin authors, even if only to excerpts from the works. These pagan authors were considered to offer excellent examples of how someone strong and powerful was supposed to behave in the secular world: with modesty, with restraint, and with self-control—all attributes that must have been difficult to impress on rambunctious boys who could hardly wait to be able to lay about them with a sword.

The boys' literary education was accompanied by religious education, so that they grew up with the rudiments of Christian theology and a good appreciation of the main points of doctrine. A castle chaplain would normally supervise the boys' education. In the twelfth century, when the Cistercian order of monks attracted the conversions of a number of adult knights, these new converts were expected to be able to read Latin in order to be able to participate in the liturgy; it is a tribute to many nameless castle chaplains that few of these knights had any problems meeting this requirement.

LEARNING TO FIGHT ON HORSEBACK

As well as spending part of each day in the classroom, the youths would have spent several hours riding horses and learning to fight. Training as a fighter on horseback was considered the most important goal for a noble boy. To be able to use a long lance and a sword, and especially to do so while galloping, took years of practice. The boys began by riding ponies and fighting with wooden swords, gradually advancing to horses and real blades. To learn to aim the lance, they would practice riding at a ring that was hung from a string, the objective being to thrust the lance through it. They learned to joust by riding at a *quintain*, a stake from which hung a mail shirt, a helmet, and a shield.

Typically, an old knight took charge of the boys' training. When they were young, their exercises were little more than games, but as they reached adolescence their training intensified, as more and more was expected of them. They learned both to ride well and to take proper care of their horses. They got accustomed to wearing armor for hours without becoming exhausted by its weight.

By the time the training was complete, after a dozen years or so, the boys would have turned into formidable fighters and were usually eager to prove themselves at tournaments or in battle. During the

ABOVE: *A boy had to learn to control a powerful charger in the heat of battle. This relief is on the twelfth-century town hall of Fritzlar in Germany.*

RIGHT: *Many of the books used in the education of knights were copied and illuminated by monks, as shown in this fifteenth-century manuscript.*

LEFT: *Learning to fight on horseback was a long process, requiring years of practice. Here, French king Francis I (reigned 1515—47) is in the midst of the Battle of Marignano in 1515.*

The association of warrior elites with hunting was both ancient and almost universal across human societies. Some historians and anthropologists have even seen the origins of warfare in the hunter-gatherer phase of human prehistory, but others dispute this. Although hunting (especially big-game hunting) and warfare call for some of the same skills, it does seem more likely that warfare is a later invention of settled hierarchical societies.

The congruence of skills that are involved in hunting was an important factor in maintaining it as a common warrior activity. Hunting was an important way for small groups of knights—a lord and his household, the basic unit of knightly military organization—to gain experience of riding and wielding arms together. In this context, it is interesting that such hunting in Europe was a small-group activity, unlike hunting among steppe nomadic warriors, whose hunts were organized as vast roundups with hundreds of horsemen surrounding large areas of grassland and driving every wild animal within their cordon into a killing zone. Neither the terrain and fauna of Europe nor the social organization of European knights permitted such hunts. But in their smaller groups, European knights practiced horsemanship, the use of weapons, and how to read terrain. Probably more importantly, hunting cemented social bonds among the group, therefore contributing to the potential cohesion of the group in battle.

He is brave and courtly and skillful, and noble and of a good lineage and eloquent, handsomely experienced in hunting and falconry; he knows how to play chess and backgammon, gaming and dicing.

POET GUILHEM DE TUDELA (FLOURISHED 1199–1214) DESCRIBING THE IDEAL KNIGHT

Crusades, even the Muslim enemies of Western knights had to agree that they were highly skilled and superbly trained.

THE ART OF HUNTING

Hunting was part of the life of every aristocrat, and knighthood training included education in the right way to chase, kill, and cut up the quarry. In addition to it being good practice for warfare in a variety of ways, hunting also created and displayed social status and power, and, of course, it retained its original function of providing food for knightly households.

ABOVE: *Knights were expected to be proficient at chess. In this scene from the* Manesse Codex *(c. 1304), the Elector and Margrave of Brandenburg plays a game with his wife.*
RIGHT: *Knowledge of the latest dances and the ability to sing and play musical instruments were also required of the well-rounded knight. This illustration is from the 1520 Flemish book of hours known as* The Golf Book.

TRAINING IN COURTESY

In addition to a basic Classical education and military instruction, the boys also received extensive training in courtesy. They were expected to know how to behave properly in polite society, which included speaking in a cultured manner, dressing properly, keeping themselves clean—not forgetting their fingernails—and practicing such arts as dancing, music, and poetry. In spite of the brutish violence inherent in fighting and killing with lance and sword, knights always wanted to regard themselves as refined.

A courteous young man would learn to sing and play an instrument, so that long winter evenings could be spent in musical entertainment. Such evenings might also be spent in reading epics and romances aloud. Many of these works were doubtless written by professional minstrels, but knights certainly authored some of them, indicating that they had the background in writing and in poetry to make such compositions possible.

The young men would also learn to play games, especially chess, which has not changed very much since the Middle Ages. This game about bishops, knights, kings, and castles was considered to be especially appropriate for the aristocracy. And, of course, the young knights were expected to be well able to converse with ladies appropriately, without being either coarse or tongue-tied with shyness.

THE RIGHT CLOTHES

Another important part of a young man's training in courtesy would be learning how to dress properly. Clothing, which was always handmade, was very costly by modern standards, and made even more expensive by an aristocratic need

THE LADY OF THE CASTLE

The lady of the castle was the youths' chief teacher in courtesy. She might well have been closer in age to the boys than she was to her own husband, and both romances and memoirs suggest a long-lasting bond was formed between many a youth and his "lady." Although, of course, actual dalliance was completely out of the question, the boys might bring her flowers, practice their poetry on her, and even dream that she might someday return their unspoken love and their desires. Even after they became adults and married, the knights remembered and honored their "lady of the castle."

to display social standing through the use of costly fabrics such as silk and fine woolens, which were given rich colors using rare dyes. Clothes were made with loose sleeves, extra folds, and gores, just to demonstrate that one did not need to stint on fabric. Cloaks and mantles were trimmed or lined with fur. An especially elegant outfit might be decorated with hard-to-find seed pearls. Clothing was usually cut in a way to display a young man's shapely legs. Shoes with long, pointed toes were similarly extravagant. Young men were expected to learn the latest fashions and dress appropriately.

Medieval clothing for all sectors of society was most commonly made of wool, which had to be cleaned, carded, spun, and woven; woolen cloth, both dyed and undyed, was one of the major commodities of trade. Linen, spun and woven from flax, was favored for more lightweight garments. Cotton, from India, reached Europe first in the late twelfth century and was used especially for underwear. Silk, from China, was highly expensive and greatly prized because it could be dyed brilliantly and would not be eaten by clothes moths; only the aristocracy could afford it.

RIGHT: *The quality and quantity of cloth used in clothes, and the richness of its color, were signs of wealth. Caring for clothes was an important task, as shown in the Nuremberg* Kitchen Mastery (Kuchemaistrey, *c. 1490).*

Young knights also learned to style their hair in the newest fashions. For most of the twelfth century, for example, they preferred to wear it in long, curling locks. It is striking that the fierce warrior of the battlefield was supposed to appear almost delicate in a court setting.

Although churchmen mocked such vanity, the knights felt it necessary to look as handsome as possible, both to impress each other and, according to the stories, to attract ladies. Descriptions from the twelfth century suggest that the youths women admired were those with softly curled hair and pink cheeks—young aristocrats were generally clean-shaven—aspects that today are usually considered exclusively feminine. At the time, such an appearance was thought to distinguish the aristocrats from coarser-looking peasants.

SOCIAL CODES AT BANQUETS

This proper appearance was especially expected at banquets, and so was proper behavior. Young men were supposed to be deferential to their elders and to demonstrate restraint. Only the coarse and uneducated would overeat or grab food unceremoniously from the platters. There were even manuals that spelled out in detail exactly how to eat in a suitably courtly manner.

The foods served at an aristocratic feast distinguished the participants from the people of a lower status, who were assumed to eat only simple food—not the game, fowl, white bread, or honey-sweetened puddings of the court. In learning to eat and appreciate such rich meals, the youths were becoming imbued with the social standards that, it was expected, they would continue to uphold when they became knights themselves.

Banquets reinforced the social hierarchy, too, for where one was seated in the hall very much depended on one's status, with the most powerful and honored guests sitting at the head table. There are accounts of fights breaking out when guests felt that someone had been placed above them inappropriately. The young knights-in-training would have learned the way that social standing determined the proper organization of guests—and the best ways of avoiding ugly incidents involving precedence.

FROM PAGE TO SQUIRE

By the thirteenth century, a young man's progress through training for knighthood was marked by specific stages, and a boy would proceed explicitly from page to squire to knight.

Pages served knights while engaged in their own education. In the court, they carried out such tasks as setting up the tables for dinner, carrying messages, and helping knights dress. At a banquet, they provided much of the service for those seated in positions of honor, from spreading the tablecloths to bringing basins of hot water for the guests to wash their hands, and to carrying out the platters of food from the kitchen and keeping the goblets filled. These somewhat menial duties were intended both to inculcate them into the proper functioning of the court and to accustom them to obedience. It is likely that they would have greatly admired the knights they served, and this would have been an inspiration to them to work hard at their training.

As he began to grow into manhood, at a certain point a page would become a squire. Knights went to tournament and to battle accompanied by one or two squires, who helped them with their

LEFT: *The fashions of the day are on display in this scene of the Duc de Berry's household exchanging New Year's gifts, from the* Très riches heures du duc de Berry *(c. 1410).*

Do not put such a large piece [of bread] into your mouth that the crumbs fall out left and right, otherwise you will be considered a glutton … Drink only when your mouth is empty, otherwise you will be regarded as a drunkard.

PETRUS ALFONSI, *DISCIPLINA CLERICALIS* **(TWELFTH CENTURY)**

armor, sharpened their swords, took care of the horses, and gave them new lances when theirs shattered. Essentially, a squire had learned most of what was required to be a knight, but he had not yet undergone the knighting ceremony that allowed a young nobleman to style himself *chevalier*. By the late thirteenth century, that ceremony had became more and more expensive and elaborate. Squires might postpone it indefinitely, and indeed many of them spent a major part of their adulthood living as knights in all but name.

FRIENDSHIPS OF KNIGHTS

Young knights educated together would have established lifelong friendships. In medieval stories, a knight often had one very close friend, with whom he went to tournaments, to festivals, and to war. In some cases, a large group of young men, of roughly the same age, trained together, came to adulthood together, and then they went off together looking for adventures in love and war.

One of the challenges faced by young knights who had completed their training was that they were often not in a position to inherit yet. Being somewhat at loose ends, groups of these knights would set off looking to display their warrior skills.

Tournaments provided an outlet for young knights eager to prove they were the equals of more experienced knights. A major or minor war would attract hordes of young knights. And, likewise, any rumors of an unmarried heiress would bring these youths from far and wide. Many of these groups of knights joined the Crusades in the twelfth century. Even when a knight decided to abandon life in the world and become a monk, he might bring many friends with him—as did Bernard, future abbot of Clairvaux, who was said to have brought 30 knightly companions when he joined the monastery of Cîteaux in 1113.

ABOVE: *At a feast, the social hierarchy required that the most important guest be seated at the high table. A king joins the bride and groom in this fourteenth-century Flemish illumination.*

LEFT: *The young men in the foreground play* jeux-de-paume, *an early form of tennis, while the older pair are engrossed in a game of chess. This illustration, from about 1500, decorates the work of the Classical writer Valerius Maximus.*

THE KNIGHTING CEREMONY

When his training was complete, probably in his late teens, a young nobleman would be ready to be knighted. At first a simple marker that he had successfully completed his education, the ceremony quickly became elaborate and loaded with symbolism. The earliest known example of a fully developed knighting ceremony was held in 1128 for Geoffrey, the future Count of Anjou.

Such ceremonies were only for the sons of noble lords, not for the service knights, who took up their swords and their duties without anything of the sort. Hence, not all knights underwent the knighting ceremony, but it was expected that all nobles would if they were to be considered knights. This coming-of-age ceremony was sometimes called *dubbing*.

THE SYMBOLISM OF THE KNIGHTING CEREMONY

At the heart of the ceremony was the recognition that a youth had attained manhood and his own weapons. The ceremony also reflected the complex and contradictory demands of chivalry.

Swords had always been the sign of lordship, and in the early Middle Ages sometimes the young sons of kings were

LEFT: *In the earliest ceremonies, the knight was simply girt with a sword to indicate he had come of age.*

given their own swords. These swords would often be a family heirloom, not something a boy was expected to use in anger. In the twelfth century, the significance of these swords was expanded to indicate that any aristocratic youth—not just a king's son—had become a man. The sword he was given at the knighting ceremony was intended to be carried into battle. He was also given a set of spurs, which symbolized the knight as a horseman. The ceremony initially might involve little more than a wise old knight giving the youth his sword and spurs, perhaps slapping him on the shoulder or giving him a kiss, and declaring he was now a knight. Such

simple ceremonies persisted throughout the Middle Ages. For the ostentatious, however, this was considered inadequate.

By the thirteenth century, a fully developed knighting ceremony had taken on complex symbolism, and a young man had to go through a series of steps over two or more days, rather than just being given sword and spurs. The symbolism was heavily religious, an assertion by the knights (against the opinion of bishops) that it was possible to follow the ways of knighthood and of Christianity at the same time. The Christian symbolism used is especially striking because, in most cases, priests had no direct involvement or role in the knighting ceremony.

BELOW: *King Richard II (reigned 1377–99) knights Henry of Monmouth, the future Henry V, with a sword, during the Irish campaign of 1399, as shown in the* Histoire du roy d'Angleterre Richard II *(c. 1405), by Jean Creton.*

The youths were commonly dressed in white, to symbolize their purity and to equate them with the white-clad novices of a monastery, and they were instructed to spend the night in prayer before their actual dubbing. They might be encouraged to use a sword, the hilt of which formed a cross with the blade, to meditate on the crucifixion. The white belt they wore was supposed to represent continence. In all of this was the clear message that fighting did not necessarily have to be sinful, and that a young knight devoted to protecting churches, the weak, and the poor was a true *miles Christi*, "soldier of Christ," even if he never joined a monastery or went on crusade.

In the morning, the young men would all take a ritual bath, which had unmistakable parallels to baptism. The old sinful self was washed away and the knight who fought for Christ emerged. They would be clad in armor and given their spurs and sword, as the symbols of their martial role. Some sort of specific act followed, to show that the new knight was crossing the threshold into adulthood. Modern depictions usually show someone receiving a light tap with a blade on the shoulder, but a slap to the cheek was more common. The lord who administered the slap declared the youth a knight, and everyone proceeded to a tournament and feasting.

THE KNIGHTING FESTIVAL

The knighting ceremony quickly became an excuse for a festival that might go on for days. If a group of boys had entered knighthood training together, a dozen years later they might all be knighted together, the ceremony being followed by general feasting and a tournament in which the new knights could display all they had learned.

As for a knight I will make you ... Be ye a good knight, and so I pray to God so ye may be, and if ye be of prowess and of worthiness ye shall be a knight of the Table Round.

SIR THOMAS MALORY, *LE MORTE DARTHUR* (1485)

It was considered an especially great honor to have someone of high stature officially declare the youths as knights, and in the epics and romances squires routinely sought out Charlemagne or King Arthur for the purpose. In practice, though, the honor generally went to the count or the uncle who had supervised the training of the youths. In some cases, if there were a nobleman of higher status or natural leader among the new knights, he might formally knight his comrades after having been knighted himself.

The high cost of the party that came to be a necessary part of the ceremony no doubt gave many proud parents some pause. In twelfth-century England, those who did homage for their fiefs to a lord had to promise they would help pay for the knighting ceremony of the lord's eldest son, indicating that even the most powerful needed financial assistance to pay for this ceremony. Its cost was one of the reasons why, in the late Middle Ages, many men who were fully qualified to become knights remained squires.

Chivalry

In twelfth-century France, a set of idealized behaviors for knights evolved called chivalry (chevalerie in Old French). These were noble attributes that aristocratic knights liked to believe marked them, and which, at least sometimes, influenced their actions in daily life, in relationships, and on the battlefield.

Although medieval authors insisted there were certain ways in which knights should behave, they could never come to full agreement on what the key elements of chivalry were. Had chivalry been a legal category, it would have been rendered in Latin, not in the vernacular. Thus it was never a "code," which would have meant there was a set of rules and regulations on which knights all agreed, whether or not they actually followed them. In fact, chivalry was inherently self-contradictory, so it would have been impossible for a single person to try to follow all the demands and strictures that the different authors claimed made up its necessary elements.

FIGHTING AND COURTESY

In the eleventh century, chivalry was understood simply to mean battlefield virtues: courage, endurance, loyalty to one's comrades, and fighting skill. But during the twelfth century, as young aristocrats began to define themselves as fighters on horseback, the idea of chivalry incorporated a number of other elements. To be chivalrous was always to be admirable. There was extensive debate about which admirable activities were the most important, however. And, as with the knighting ceremony, knights claimed an inherent religious aspect for chivalry, in spite of the quite dubious attitude of church leaders.

ABOVE: *In Wolfram von Eschenbach's romance Parzival (c. 1210), the knight Parzival quests for and finally attains the Holy Grail.*

Courtesy (*cortoisie* in Old French) was the most significant addition to chivalry's basic meaning of fighting on horseback. In the middle of the twelfth century, authors might describe a knight as "chivalrous and courteous," creating (at least temporarily) a clear distinction between the two. But by the late twelfth century, a knight considered chivalrous would also have to be courteous—that meant he was able to function well in a court setting. He would have to converse

LEFT: *Like the idea of chivalry itself, the legend of King Arthur and his Round Table took on more fabulous elements as the Middle Ages progressed. This is an illustration from a fourteenth-century version of the story by Chrétien de Troyes.*

Latin of the church or of the law court. Works written in the medieval versions of German, Spanish, and Italian soon appeared, as well as ones in Old French. These were principally written for and about knights, and were typically told in verse, although modern translations usually render them in prose.

The stories were concerned with knightly adventures, love, and fighting, involving members of the aristocracy, and often included a strong element of the supernatural. Given the contradictory meanings of chivalry, it should be no surprise that the plots of most of the vernacular epics and romances turned on some inherent tension, such as that between love and honor, or between fighting and service to ladies. Authors were not presenting an ideal of a chivalrous knight for their readers to emulate; rather, they were critiquing this ideal—the idea that one person could possibly achieve all that was expected of him.

in a refined manner, be able to dance and sing elegantly, dress well, and keep himself scrupulously clean—all things that the ladies taught the young would-be knights. The chaplains who educated these young men had been imbued with a Classical Roman culture that went back to Cicero, a culture that stressed the Stoic values of honorable behavior and restraint, and they also passed these values on to their pupils.

Scholars have tried to explain how prowess on the battlefield could have developed into an ideal of behaving in an upright, strong, yet gentle manner. But it is not necessary to seek any single explanation: chivalry had many roots besides warfare on horseback. Rather, the multitude of meanings imposed on chivalry by different writers at the time, and by the different social groups (men, women, churchmen, and so on), yielded a truly strange mix of expectations.

Thus, by the start of the thirteenth century, to encompass all the prescribed aspects of chivalry, a knight had to be a ferocious fighter who had slain countless foes; a devout Christian who was always concerned about the wellbeing of the weak and the helpless; a sophisticated charmer who loved to dance and flirt with the ladies; and a proud, stern man who would tolerate nothing that might undercut his honor. Understandably, no one could follow all these contradictory expectations at the same time.

CHIVALRY IN LITERATURE

Much of what we know about medieval attitudes toward chivalry comes to us through the literature of the period. In the twelfth century, starting in France, literary fiction became common for the first time in nearly a millennium. These works were written in the vernacular—that is, in the ordinary language spoken by ordinary people—rather than in the

RIGHT: *The duty to fight evil, represented by dragons, is emphasized in a twelfth-century manuscript of* Moralia in Job *by Pope Gregory I.*

HONORABLE CONDUCT

B ecause chivalry was so clearly an attribute of knights, authors of the Middle Ages routinely called chivalrous behavior the mark of a "true knight," and they even argued for an "order of knighthood" to be made up of those who behaved in certain ways. The difficulty was that every author came up with his own set of definitions. Although in the epics and romances, the characters often

LEFT: *Accused of treason, John Welch fights for his honor in a duel before Richard II in the late 1300s, as shown in a contemporary manuscript.*

speak confidently of what a true knight would do, the characters in different works—and sometimes in the same one—came up with different examples of suitably honorable conduct. Implicitly or explicitly then, each author rejected other authors' versions of chivalry in favor of his own, which is why it is impossible to speak of a uniform code.

For example, in the earliest Holy Grail story, *Perceval, or The Knight of the Grail (Perceval, ou Le conte du Graal)* by the poet Chrétien de Troyes (flourished 1165–80), the mother of Perceval, the hero, sends him off to be a knight with the injunctions always to honor ladies and not to go beyond a kiss, to associate with the wellborn, and to frequently pray. Later, Perceval receives quite a different set of injunctions from a worthy aristocrat, who describes the "order of knighthood" as entailing mercy

to defeated enemies, polite silence in company rather than foolish chatter, consolation and support for ladies who need it, and frequent prayer. Other than the sense that proper treatment of ladies was required and one should pray a lot, these descriptions of a good knight are quite different; both took it so much for granted that a good knight would be an excellent fighter on horseback, however, that they did not mention that aspect.

LIVING FOR GOD
A quite different set of ideals appears in the *Policraticus*, a political treatise by John of Salisbury (1115/20–1180) written about the same time. It consists of a pseudo-historical account of Roman soldiers, who were clearly supposed to represent an ideal version of the knights of John's own day. When being given their "military belt," symbolizing their

BELOW: *The real life of a knight had little to do with romance. Two knights are seen fighting a bloody duel in a fourteenth-century manuscript.*

LEFT: *In this illustration from Jean Fouquet's telling of the story of Roland in* Les Grandes Chroniques de France *(c. 1460), Charlemagne finds Roland's body after the Battle of Roncesvalles.*

entry into a military order, they swear loyalty both to God and to the Roman republic, and then swear to honor priests and avoid hurting the poor. There are no ladies described, but, as in the Perceval stories, the emphasis is on being a good Christian and showing restraint, although this is demonstrated in different ways.

ATTRIBUTES OF CHIVALRY

Several broad themes kept recurring when medieval people spoke of chivalry, however. The starting point was always skills on the battlefield, whether they were exercised in deadly earnest or in the mock battles of a tournament. Nearly as central were the ideals that the bishops had been trying to inculcate in knights since mounted warriors first appeared in the eleventh century: that warriors should not attack the weak and the defenseless, but rather should protect them. This was a message, of course, being given to men whose knighthood training had made them into fighters— who were taught to be violent, quick-tempered, and always ready for battle.

If any speaks better concerning women than I ... [i]t would please me to learn of their great pleasure. From one alone would I withhold my loyal service— having found her unfaithful, my anger towards her does not change.

WOLFRAM VON ESCHENBACH, "APOLOGY," IN *PARZIVAL* (C. 1210)

Slowly, another layer of expectation was added: that true knights would not attack other knights without warning, would not kill helpless men even if they were their foe, and would resolutely maintain all loyalties and promises they had made, no matter what the cost. In the thirteenth century, Louis IX

of France (reigned 1226–70) tried to impose these sorts of restraints on his knights, going so far as to forbid them to wear their swords indoors at his court. Yet Louis never intended to deprive his nobles of their warrior attributes; he needed them fierce and skillful for his crusades. It is indicative of the difficulty of instituting this kind of restrained behavior that it took a highly regarded king to establish it as the norm at his court—and even so the practice did not outlive him.

Knightly honor was always gained by successful fighting. In *The Song of Roland (La chanson de Roland, c.* 1100), the anonymous author lavished praise on his characters for their "chivalry." They were such powerful fighters that they could strike their swords not only through their opponents' helmets and skulls, but often down through their entire bodies, saddles, and horse as well. This writer was ready to admire anyone with this sort of skill, even the Muslims against whom his heroes were fighting; they would have been admirable knights if only they had been Christian, he said several times. As this example indicates, battlefield skills were always admirable, no matter where they were found, and medieval accounts of chivalrous knights always glorified violence.

Loyalty to one's sworn lord was also always admirable. Medieval aristocratic society was bound together by loyalty, which worked both up and down the social scale—that is, the powerful were supposed to be loyal and helpful to those who served them, as well as vice versa. Counts had little way to control the lords of castles in their region other than through their oaths; these castellan lords, in turn, had to rely on the sworn loyalty of their knights. Thus, it is not surprising that descriptions of a chivalrous person always included devotion to his lord as an admirable quality.

Loyalty to one's fellow knights was almost as important. At some level, even enemy knights or knights fighting on the other side in a tournament were one's fellows and a true knight was expected to give a fallen foe an opportunity to rise before slashing him with a sword, wait to attack an opponent until he had donned his armor, refrain from bringing down a knight by targeting his horse, and accept a defeated enemy's surrender without inflicting further damage. It would have been considered dishonorable to take advantage of another's weakness—a sign not of strength but of cowardice. This is why knights in general were supposed to avoid attacking churchmen, merchants, and peasants, because they were in no position to fight back.

MAINTAINING HONOR IN A VIOLENT WORLD

In practice, knights routinely did things that would not, strictly speaking, have been considered honorable. They often, for example, turned a blind eye to the activities of the contingents of pikesmen and archers who traveled with them and who would bring down mounted knights or their horses with little regard for the rules of chivalry. When knights were at war or participating in a tournament, they often inflicted collateral damage on local peasants and their property. Some unscrupulous knights even attacked the caravans of merchants, who had to hire their own knights to defend against

LEFT: *King Ferdinand I of Naples (reigned 1458–94) receives due homage from a knight in his camp, as illustrated in the manuscript* De Majestate *by Juniano Majo (1492).*
BELOW: *The lintel on the Cathedral of St. Peter in Angoulême, France, glorifies the knightly ideals of skill and courage on the battlefield. This is a cast of the stone carved about 1125–35.*

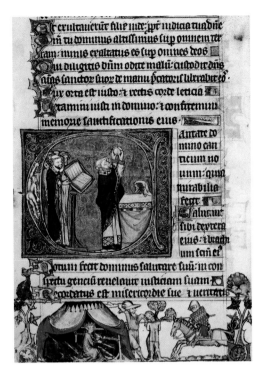

such raids. The attackers, it was widely agreed, were not "true" knights; nonetheless, many *were* knighted men of aristocratic lineage.

The inherent violence of fighting with weapons designed to wound and kill meant that the calm and honorable restraint urged by both churchmen and the authors of the epics could not be counted on. As in all societies, there was not a perfect correlation between what was considered honorable and what those who would have liked to think of themselves as honorable actually did. And, of course, a desire to maintain their honor made many knights touchy,

so that any perceived insults would be answered with threats and violence, unless the friends of the insulted knight could calm him down in time.

CHIVALRY IN THE LATE MIDDLE AGES

Explicit definitions of chivalry, along with manuals on how to achieve it, first appeared in the late Middle Ages, some two centuries after chivalry itself. The most influential, by the Catalan writer Ramon Lull (1232/33–1315/16), was the *Book of the Order of Chivalry (Libre del ordre de cavayleria)*, which was probably written between 1263 and 1276. In this rambling work, which glorified knights as the best of men, Lull created a fairly comprehensive list of all the things a chivalrous knight was supposed to do: defend the church and the weak; keep fit by partaking in tournaments; serve the king; track down malefactors; and avoid lies, lechery, and pride. These ideas were not new, but this was the first time they were pulled together into a handbook.

The fullest development of chivalric honor occurred during the Hundred Years' War between France and England in the fourteenth and fifteenth centuries. This war—in which first contingents of longbowmen stopped cavalry charges, then the development of cannon made such cavalry charges pointless—was also a war in which knights, doubtless in reaction to suffering defeat at the hands of non-knights, exhibited an exaggerated sense of chivalry. One knight, who was commanding a besieged castle, was so awestruck by the honor when he recognized the famous lord who was attacking him that he surrendered the castle at once.

The most striking example of such chivalrous behavior was that of the French king, John II, also known as John the Good (reigned 1350–64), who was captured by the English during the Battle of Poitiers in 1356 and held for ransom. When the ransom was slow to arrive, John headed back to France, first giving his word "as a knight" that if he could not raise the funds within a certain time, he would return to his imprisonment, which, in fact, he duly did.

These extreme gestures reflected a growing belief that a golden age had passed, that the aristocracy's time of glory was gone, and that therefore it was necessary to cling to whatever was left that might validate its position. In the late Middle Ages, reenactments of scenes from the Arthurian legend multiplied, complete with round tables and people calling each other Lancelot, Gawain, and the like. It was also during this period that the chivalric orders were established throughout Europe.

KNIGHTLY VISION

Author of the *Book of the Order of Chivalry*, Ramon Lull was a former knight who had served the crown of Aragon (in northeastern Spain). He played a crucial role in the administration of Majorca, being the seneschal, or steward, for his king's son James, who ruled the kingdom of Majorca. Lull also wrote poetry celebrating knightly deeds and romantic love. But in 1263 he had a series of life-altering religious visions. In the following years he wrote his *Book of the Order of Chivalry*, which emphasized the ideal of the Christian knight. After becoming a teacher at the Franciscan College of Miramar in 1276, he learned the Arabic and Latin languages and wrote a number of works of mystical philosophy. He was killed when, at over 80 years old, he set out to convert Muslims to Christianity.

A KNIGHT AND HIS LADY

The twelfth century, the same period as the ideals of chivalry developed, saw a new interest in romantic love. Although men and women had doubtless been falling in love since the Stone Age, romantic love took on a centrality in literature that it had not had before and, indeed, would not have again until the twentieth century.

Songs and stories from this period generally included a love interest, and in this literature falling in love was treated as a reason why a couple should marry, which was a subversive attitude, given that the aristocratic families of the time normally arranged the marriages of their children. Those who wrote of idealized chivalric behavior also wrote of love, so that a close relationship was established between the two.

At one time, scholars used the term *courtly love*, as though there were some clearly defined way medieval lovers were expected to behave. In fact, love—like chivalry itself—was shot through with contradictions and with conflicting expectations. Everyone agreed that love was a powerful force, but they glorified their own versions of it. Just as authors came up with their own descriptions of a chivalric knight, so they came up with very different lists of proper behaviors for lovers. Scholars who have tried to create tidy descriptions of courtly love, despite the clear evidence that medieval authors disagreed with each other, have not reached a consensus about whether this love was found in adultery, or in the affection between husband and wife, or in chaste yearnings from afar. Thus, the powerful force of love in medieval literature can be better understood if it is not regarded as some concrete code.

BELOW: *A good knight would slay a dragon in order to protect his lady, as in Paolo Uccello's* St. George and the Dragon *(c. 1460).*

LEFT: *Away from the battlefield the knight had to be a man of impeccable manners, as illustrated here in the fifteenth-century* Roman de la Rose. **RIGHT:** *In this illustration from a French book of miniatures (1475), a knight kneels before his lady to demonstrate his devotion and deference.*

SERVICE TO HIS LADY

One central aspect of love—whether the author was discussing adulterous love or (as was more common) the love between a man and woman who might soon be married—was that the knight was supposed to serve his lady. He knelt before her in the same way that a knight knelt before a lord who was granting him a fief—and he hastened to do her bidding at every turn.

A knight who failed to do what his lady demanded, and especially one who tried to force his affections on her when she was not willing, was considered to be grossly dishonorable. Of course, this problem was avoided in the many stories in which a beautiful young maiden, who is aroused to excitement by a knight's manly form, creeps into his bed shortly after meeting him.

The idealized deference to women was especially striking because women rarely held the same power as men in rule or in politics in the real medieval world. Inheritance and authority always went preferentially to men—and the men who made themselves dependent on a woman's whim were behaving in ways that contradicted the normal expectations of medieval society. This contradiction underlined the enormous force of love and it also, at least potentially, made a man appear ridiculous to his male friends, even while it endeared him to the women.

DEVOTION AND DISCORD

A certain aggrieved tone runs through many of the medieval poems and stories—a knight loves a woman and serves her without stint, yet she merely mocks him. In other stories, a lustful woman tries to test a knight's loyalty or chastity by openly offering him her body, even when he is honor-bound not to accept it. Or a man is made foolish by love. In the earliest of the Lancelot stories, for example, the hero kisses the golden hairs that were caught in the comb of his beloved queen and treats them like some sort of religious relic—not realizing he has been challenged by another knight until knocked from his horse, because he is too caught up in thinking of her rosy lips—and then happily fights disgracefully badly at a tournament because she had ordered him to do so, just to test his devotion.

In all these storylines, the poets display a certain distrust of women, even while they agreed that knights ought to serve them. The ladies were doubtless just happy to be offered whatever service was available.

KNIGHTLY LOVE IN ACTION

Many a young knight carried for years the memory of the "lady of the castle" he had served as a youth and sought to honor her, even after he had married someone else. The knight-poet, Ulrich von Liechtenstein (1200–78), recounted in his memoirs, *Service of the Lady (Frauendienst)*, that he had fought countless jousts across central Europe in his lady's honor, an accomplishment which he expected her to recognize by giving him her love—although, according to Ulrich himself, she and her ladies unceremoniously and deliberately dumped him off her balcony. Honor, indeed.

THE ROLE OF RELIGION

Everyone, from bishops to romance writers to knights such as Ramon Lull, believed a truly chivalrous knight had to be a good Christian. Many knights claimed the title of *miles Christi*, "soldier of Christ"—a term used for centuries by monks who fought for God's cause through their prayers rather than with swords. The knights believed that they could pursue the fight equally well with their swords. The difficulty was that most of the attributes of chivalry conflicted with religious teachings. But the knights themselves believed that they were (or could be) excellent Christians, and they pointed to their role in giving protection to churches, to widows, and to the poor. Their dubbing ceremony itself was rich with religious imagery.

In fact, the churches relied on the knights. Their wealth depended on pious gifts. But they would not have needed the protection provided by the knights if they had not had potential enemies in other knights—who were tempted to steal their altar goods or their lands, and were ready to reclaim, by force if necessary, pious gifts made by their relatives. There was a long tradition in the church that equated power and wealth—the attributes of aristocrats—with evil and oppression. Twelfth-century miracle stories frequently told of vile-tempered, greedy knights who seized church property and mocked the saints—and in these stories the villains were more likely to be blasted by an angry saint than corrected by a good, pious Christian knight.

RELIGIOUS PRACTICES

As in other areas of everyday medieval life, variety characterizes the religious practices of European knights. Most of them were conventionally religious, some were undoubtedly genuinely pious; some were hardly religious at all, however. The topic places us at a complex intersection between the public image and private belief of the knight.

> *A knight must be strong and fierce in battle, or ... he should be a monk in one of those monasteries, where they always pray for our sins.*
>
> THE SONG OF ROLAND (*LA CHANSON DE ROLAND*, c. 1100)

In their variety, knights do not seem to have been radically different from other segments of medieval society (including churchmen, to whom the same distribution could be attributed). But their particular expressions of religiosity, of whatever intensity, were influenced by the social status and function of the knightly class. The emergence of chivalry as the ethical model for knights may be usefully considered as a sort of secular religion of a warrior elite. But when considering other forms of religious expression, it is dangerous to draw lines of causation that are too simplistic: the dangers of battle might intensify belief in some, while making cynics of others.

FIGHTING FOR GOD

Of course, fighting was contrary to religious values, and although medieval Christianity supported the idea of a just war and that of fighting to defend the helpless, most knightly fighting looked nothing like a just war. The

LEFT: *In this carving from the abbey of Vézelay in Burgundy, France, an angel strikes down a knight in mail armor.*

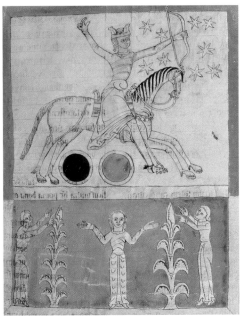

ABOVE: *The "Faithful Knight," mounted on a white horse, leaves to battle Satan, in this illustration from the twelfth-century Portuguese manuscript the* Apocalypse of Lorvão.

all encounters were so predictable, and many knights who were caught in an ambush or unexpected encounter faced death without the solace of confession. In cases where no priest was readily available to serve a mortally wounded knight, the knight would confess to a friend or companion.

One interesting aspect of the intersection of combat, knightly honor, and religion was that, unlike their Roman forebears or their otherwise quite similar counterparts in medieval Japan, European knights almost never "fell on their sword"— in other words, committed suicide to avoid capture or defeat. (Of course, suicidal attacks on vastly more powerful enemy forces were not unknown, but they are a separate phenomenon.) Although it is tempting to see the Christian church's injunctions against suicide at work here, Buddhism discouraged suicide, too. It is more likely that the differences in the political and social contexts of knightly and *samurai* activity were much more important in this respect.

ABOVE: *A knight receives communion before he departs for battle, as depicted in a fifteenth-century manuscript. During the Crusades, priests administered the last rites to dying knights.*

Crusades were offered as opportunities for knights to take out their aggression against the nonbelievers (Muslims), to use all the warrior skills in which they had been trained, and to save (rather than to lose) their souls in the process. The military orders in the Holy Land, the Templars and Hospitallers, were promoted as combining the best of the knightly life, its warrior skills, with the best of the monastic life, progress toward Heaven. Many young knights were inspired to go on crusade, but the majority preferred to stay home, especially once it became clear that one was more likely to die of disease or by drowning on the way to the Holy Land than in battle there, and that salvation came at a very high monetary cost.

HONOR IN DEATH AND LIFE

When armies faced each other and a major battle loomed imminently, priests on both sides would go through each army hearing confession lest any knight die suddenly in combat unconfessed— and so risk not just bodily demise but his soul's eternal damnation. Of course, not

Knights and the church were also at odds over the issue of service to ladies. The church felt that it could lead, at worst, to adultery and, at best, to lustful dalliances that would distract a knight from his religious duties. The writers of several medieval romances tried to get around this issue by suggesting that love could become almost an alternate religion, with its own liturgy and doctrine.

If you bear the cross gladly, it will bear you.

THOMAS À KEMPIS,
OF THE IMITATION OF CHRIST
(DE IMITATIONE CHRISTI, 1418)

The difficulty with this was that an alternative religion to Christianity was, by definition, heresy, which the writers knew perfectly well. As the story of Lancelot was told and retold, increasingly it became a story of sin, in which the knight was not only punished by not being able to reach the Grail, but had to see Camelot itself destroyed by his adulterous love for the queen.

RELIGIOUS ARCHITECTURE

The conventional piety of the knightly class was most often expressed in architectural terms. Most castles of any size included a chapel where the resident chaplain—a regular official in noble households who also travelled with the lord when he left the castle—said Mass. Especially in the earlier centuries of the period, when many knights were still

ABOVE: *The twelfth-century Church of Travanca, near Amarante in northern Portugal, built in the Romanesque style, was a monastic church typical of those endowed by knights.*

illiterate, the chaplain also acted as the household scribe, writing letters and other documents.

Beyond their own residences, often knights further supported the church through endowing particular churches or monasteries with land grants from family estates; entirely new houses were sometimes founded by the noble donors. In such cases, a common expectation was that the monks of an endowed monastery would perform intercessory prayers—prayers for the salvation of the soul of the donor and his family— in perpetuity thereafter.

LEFT: *Bernard of Clairvaux, founder of the Cistercian monastic order, seen in this fourteenth-century painting by Italian artist Giovanni Simone dei Crocifissi, was at one time a knight.*

CONVERSIONS TO THE RELIGIOUS LIFE

As the knights themselves realized, if they were serious about saving their souls and attaining eternal salvation, the only real way to do so was to convert to the religious life, usually by becoming a monk. In the twelfth century, it became increasingly common for young knights, having been educated in Christian values and then having decided that knightly violence was reprehensible, to opt to join the church. Prominent among these converts was Bernard of Clairvaux (1090–1153), the most famous member of the Cistercian Order (founded in 1098). Like most of the new religious orders of the time, the Cistercians found the majority of their monks among young knights.

Even though the majority of knights continued to follow the knightly life into their old age, enough young knights left the world to staff large numbers of religious houses. These conversions were often disturbing to the knights' parents, who had expected their sons to succeed them. But the knights made their decisions with the same determination and boldness with which they had, a short time earlier, rushed into the melee at a tournament or gone to war.

It had long been common for ageing aristocrats to retire from the secular life and enter a monastery once they were widowed and past the age at which they could engage in active combat; as one eleventh-century lord was quoted as saying, he had planned to become monk only "after he had grown weary of arms and satiated with worldly pleasure." In this case, the monastery seemed to have been regarded primarily as a retirement home, but those with great sins on their consciences might also retreat to the religious life, often to a monastery they had founded or which they had endowed significantly themselves.

In living out the rest of their lives, whether for days or years, according to the rhythms of monastic life, knights followed a long-standing tradition. Many of the saints of the early Middle Ages had begun their careers as fighting men, only to convert, becoming "soldiers of Christ." The numerous and popular saints' lives provided a model for this expression of piety by a warrior wishing to cleanse his soul more fully than simply by a deathbed confession. Most of the Lancelot stories have him becoming a hermit once he has realized that his adultery has led to Arthur's death and to the destruction of the kingdom of Camelot. Interestingly, such

RIGHT: *The French Dominican friar and renowned preacher St. Vincent Ferrer (1350–1419) is being revered by knights in this 1465 work by Portuguese artist Nuno Gonçalves.*

late-life conversions also occurred among medieval Japanese warriors, who would, of course, have joined Buddhist rather than Christian monasteries.

THE LAST RITES

A further expression of piety by the knightly class was the provision of a proper Christian burial for deceased knights. This might be located in the grounds of, or inside, a church or a religious house that had been endowed by the knight or his ancestors.

Richer knights provided for tombs, whose carved effigies provide us with one of the best sets of evidence about the appearance of knightly equipment and of the knights themselves.

Everyday Life

Although knights shared a central role as members of a warrior elite, they occupied many different temporal and social positions. Often their roles were more the result of individual taste and opportunity than formal appointments or inherited responsibility.

ABOVE: *The busy fabric market at Ravenna Gate in Bologna, Italy, as seen in a fifteenth-century manuscript, was a center of industry.*

The term *knight* covers a broad segment of the European elite over a span of several hundred years. The responsibilities, routines, and activities of a dependent household knight in late-eleventh-century England, for example, differed markedly from those of a great French nobleman in the fifteenth century. Because daily routines and activities were tied only loosely, if at all, to the fundamental duties of knights as a social class, many factors, some of which were themselves subject to change, influenced the everyday lives of individual knights.

The time period in which a knight lived was important. In general, western Europe became wealthier between 1000 and 1500, although the demographical disaster of the Black Death, which swept through Europe from about the year 1347, complicates that generalization, especially for landlords (who would by then have included most knights), who saw rents decline and the wages of their workers increase. Still, economic development, including Europe's greater ties to Asian trades in luxury goods—which were being imported through the eastern Mediterranean—provided knights with a greater variety of goods and more options in terms of housing. During the Middle Ages, there was also a marked population shift from country to town.

VARIATIONS IN SEASON AND PLACE

Time affected the daily lives of knights in terms of seasonality. In a world with much less insulation from the rhythms of nature than today's world, seasonal changes in temperature, the lengths of days, and so forth, were felt acutely. More importantly, the basic cycles of an agricultural economy meant that late spring through to the early fall was the season for campaigning, when, if he were militarily active, a knight's routine would have been that of the camp and not of his primary residence. Fall was harvest time, which, as landowners, knights would have supervised, though not doing the work themselves.

Geographic or regional variation in culture and in opportunities was also important: Europe encompassed many climate zones, languages, and cultures. For example, Mediterranean Europe was significantly more urbanized than northern Europe, and much more of its ruling class, including knights, lived in towns instead of on rural estates. And the class of knights encompassed a broad

ABOVE: *The* Albelda Codex, *a tenth-century compendium of civil and canon law, shows the governing structure—castle, king, and council members—of the city of Toledo, Spain.*

His steeds were good, but yet he was not gay. / Of simple fustian wore he a jupon / Sadly discoloured by his habergeon; / For he had lately come from his voyage / And now was going on this pilgrimage.

DESCRIPTION OF A KNIGHT, GEOFFREY CHAUCER,
THE CANTERBURY TALES (*c.* 1387–1400)

Finally, knights occupied a range of official offices or none at all. The daily routine of a knight belonging to an Anglo-Norman king's *familia regis* (royal military household) would have been dominated by prescribed duties or ad hoc tasks that a knightly gentleman living in the country would take no account of.

PRIVATE LIVES?

The question of office holding, however, highlights a paradox in the analysis of the everyday life of knights. For a modern audience, the notion of everyday life probably overlaps significantly with the notion of *private* life: the assumed question might take the form, "What did knights do when they were not doing official knightly things?" The answer, which would also be true of many elites (and even of commoners) in many traditional societies, is that in the Middle Ages the notion of a private life was not exactly a natural one.

Especially for those elites for whom social status defined their power and roles, life was lived, nearly constantly, on display. They were surrounded by dependents, by courtiers, and by guests,

among others. Therefore, the performance of their knightly being almost never ceased. They had to act, dress, eat, and live appropriately, for in such conventional societies appearance was expected to conform with—and indeed create—reality. (This dynamic explains in part why honor and shame were such powerful aspects of the knightly ethos.) Nevertheless, knights also engaged in many activities out of human necessity or for their own simple enjoyment.

RIGHT: *The lives of knights were governed by the seasons. In this twelfth-century Romanesque fresco of seasonal activities, farmers pick fruit in September and knock acorns off trees in October to fatten their pigs for slaughter.*

spectrum of economic and social status. Rural knights with tiny estates, if any— the *milites rustici* of some sources—contrasted sharply with the upper levels of the great aristocracy whose lands could include title to entire counties.

Even among knights of relatively equal status, housing options made for clear differences in daily life, and those options reflected broader social settings that varied constantly. A knight living in a castle in a time of war lived differently from one in an estate house in a time (or in a place) of peace—and both of them had different choices from a knight who lived in a fine house in a town or city. Moreover, everyday life is the aspect of knights' lives that was most affected by individual taste and inclination.

HOUSING AND HEALTH

Knights lived dangerous lives in an age of primitive medical care, and they sheltered from a sometimes harsh climate in housing that lacked plumbing or efficient heating. Despite their elite status, their daily lives could be hard. Maintaining health and dealing with illness and injury were constant worries.

THE KNIGHT'S HOUSE

Knights as a class emerged in connection with the spread of the private castle, which helped shape the lineage-oriented family structure of the aristocracy and knighthood. In the early Middle Ages, most private castles were of the motte-and-bailey type, constructed of earth and wood. The central tower topping the motte, or hill, inside the bailey doubled as the key defensive structure and as the residence of the castle's owner. As such, the upper room of the tower served as great hall and sleeping quarters; arrangements for sanitation and the provision of decoration were, at first, ad hoc and primitive.

As time went on and certain castle sites remained occupied permanently, rebuilding in stone was the norm, both the bailey wall and, more importantly from the perspective of housing, the central keep. New construction also employed stone. This allowed more permanent arrangements for sleeping quarters and sanitation: one common architectural feature was a privy built into an outer wall so that the waste would drop directly outside the castle (or into a moat if there were one). But stone construction did little to address the problem of heating such buildings (which, of necessity, had at least some open windows as arrow-slits). Castles usually had large central fireplaces that were also used for cooking, and more affluent knights would hang tapestries on the walls and pile the floors with rugs for insulation as well as decoration.

HOUSES OF MORE HOMELY CHARACTER

Continued economic development, as well as regional political variations, opened up further options for knightly housing. In areas where warfare was infrequent, such as much of England, knightly housing gradually lost much of its military character, moving toward the country estate model, and hunting lodges, such as the one Henry I (reigned 1100–35) maintained at Woodstock near Oxford, increased in popularity.

Knights who chose to live in the prosperous and growing towns of the Middle Ages acquired town houses. But while urban life could provide access to increased cultural opportunities, and to social and political networking, it exacerbated other problems. Medieval towns had no system of running water

BELOW: *The fireplace was the heart of the medieval house, as this illustration from the* Bible Historiale *(1470), by Guyart des Moulins, shows.*

With us ther was a DOCTOUR of phisik; / In al this world ne was ther noon hym lik, / To speke of phisik and of surgerye, / For he was grounded in astronomye.

GEOFFREY CHAUCER, *THE CANTERBURY TALES* **(c. 1387–1400)**

ABOVE: *As the Middle Ages progressed, knights increasingly moved to towns, such as the one shown in this detail from Luca Signorelli's* Martyrdom of St. Sebastian *(1496).*

or arrangements for mass sanitation. They were always unhealthy, and death rates exceeded birth rates within towns, which grew through people moving from fertile rural areas.

MEDIEVAL LIFE EXPECTANCY

What, then, was the life expectancy of knights? This is a difficult question to answer, for the statistics we have are inadequate. Furthermore, we must be aware of certain methodological issues. Average life expectancy in medieval Europe is thought to have risen to the mid-40s by 1340, then dropped back with the coming of the Black Death in 1347 and the regular recurrence of the bubonic plague after that. But this is misleading in the sense that it does not mean that most people, including peasants, died when they were in their 40s. Rather, the very high infant mortality rate, which was followed by a second mortality spike in early puberty,

lowered the average: those people who survived to 20 years of age usually lived on into their 50s or early 60s. Knights probably differed little from the general average because whatever advantage they gained in nutrition and quality of housing from their status was balanced by the higher risk inherent in their profession. The risk of a violent death was, in fact, much higher for all levels of society than we are accustomed to today.

Ironically, the elevated social status of knights may have created another risk factor, especially at the highest levels of knightly society. There is anecdotal evidence that the type and the quantity of food in knights' diets might have contributed to some cases of obesity. William I the Conqueror (reigned 1066–87) was quite corpulent by the end of his life and his son, Henry I, who famously died from eating too many lampreys, was also described as stout. Their contemporary, Louis VI of France (reigned 1108–37), was known as Louis the Fat.

Some nobles from the period drew notice from chroniclers for their weight, including Henry II of England (reigned 1154–89). "In order to reduce and cure, as far as possible, this natural tendency and defect, he waged a continual war, so to speak, with his own belly by taking immoderate exercise," Gerald of Wales noted. Henry's solution must have been the common one. A knight who was active in warfare would have exercised regularly by riding, hunting, and practicing with weapons. On campaigns, the food served would not have been as rich or as copious as that served at home.

KEEPING CLEAN

Another important aspect of everyday health was personal hygiene. Contrary to popular myth, bathing was not thought to be unhealthy in medieval culture. The limitation, especially in winter, was hot water, which had to be heated over a fire and then poured into a large tub in a room in the castle or, in good weather, outside.

Knights living in towns had the option of going to public bathhouses in the earlier centuries of the period. Bathing became less common by the end of the Middle Ages—a shortage of firewood in some areas, and changes in religious morality causing the closing of most public bathhouses, contributed to the trend. So did the Black Death: without knowing about germs, people understood infection, and bathhouses were feared as places that spread disease.

BATTLE INJURIES AND THEIR COMPLICATIONS

Undoubtedly the two biggest threats to knights' lives were combat injuries and disease. The former were, obviously, a hazard of the knightly lifestyle, and veteran knights carried scars, lost digits, and other disfigurements as badges of their bravery on the battlefield. The chronicles tell some harrowing tales of the grisly sorts of wounds that could result from hand-to-hand combat. Jean de Joinville (c. 1224–1317) describes a knight at the Battle of Arsouf during the Fifth Crusade whose nose was sliced nearly off. Despite this, the knight fought on for several hours before dying.

Even when a wound was not fatal, the complications that could result from it, especially infection, might well be. Without the antibiotics we now take for granted, any infection could turn deadly.

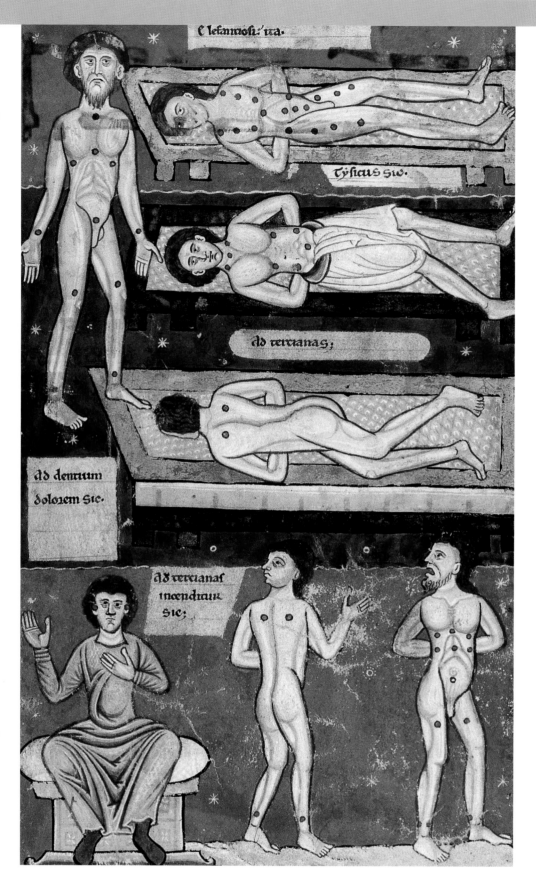

Clean incisions were perhaps the easiest for the medicine of the time to deal with. But puncture wounds, such as those from lances or crossbow bolts, particularly to the body rather than to the limbs, were much more dangerous. Not only could they bring on peritonitis

ABOVE: *In this early-thirteenth-century Latin scientific treatise, the illustrations of human figures are marked with red spots indicating particular parts of the body. Much medieval medical knowledge was derived from the writings of ancient Greek physicians, especially Galen of Pergamon (CE 129–200).*

HENRY V DIES OF DYSENTERY

In 1421, Henry V of England (reigned 1413–22) was not only king in his own realm, but was also married to Catherine of Valois and was the designated heir to the throne of France. In October, while besieging Meaux near Paris, he contracted what most historians believe was dysentery, a common disease among armies camped for long periods without a good way to dispose of their excrement. He gradually declined, and died in August 1422. The hero of Agincourt had been brought low by a microbe. It was not uncommon: more soldiers died of disease than combat in every major war until World War I.

directly if they pierced the intestines, but their depth made them more prone to infection. Richard the Lionheart (reigned 1189–99) was struck by a crossbow bolt while besieging Châlus in Aquitaine, and the bolt could not be removed. The wound became gangrenous, and he died shortly after.

Riding, too, was hazardous. Knights could be thrown, resulting in broken bones and concussions. William the Conqueror died from internal injuries received when he was thrown violently forward onto the pommel of his saddle.

The medical care available to treat combat and other injuries was, as noted, primitive and often did more harm than good. Surgery hygiene was nonexistent and the common method of treating deep incisions was cauterization with hot oil; thus infection was always a danger. Herbal remedies were applied for some wounds and diseases—most monasteries maintained a herb garden—but their efficacy is open to question. Certain medical practices improved over time, some credit for which must go to the assimilation of superior Muslim medical practices through contacts in Spain and in southern Italy.

THE DISEASES OF THE MIDDLE AGES

Disease was the other great killer of knights on campaign, exceeding combat as a cause of death, as was universally true before the twentieth century.

Two sorts of diseases were of most concern: endemic and epidemic.

Of the endemic diseases—diseases that were constant low-level killers—dysentery was probably the most common because it broke out so easily under conditions of siege warfare. But other poxes, infestations, and crowd diseases were also constantly making the rounds: this is why Europeans were so deadly to Native Americans and other indigenous peoples they colonized. Edward the Black Prince (1330–76), the eldest son and heir of the English king, Edward III, predeceased his father, dying from what some historians think was tuberculosis contracted on campaign in Spain. Endemic diseases were often overlooked as a major killer then (and now) because they were so common and so taken for granted as a constant risk.

PLAGUES AND OTHER EPIDEMICS

Epidemic diseases—rapid killers of large portions of a population—were rarer than endemic diseases but thus more noticeable. The most notable example in medieval Europe was, of course, the Black Death, which first struck Europe in 1347 and recurred at irregular intervals thereafter until 1720. Bubonic plague is thought to have been a major component of these epidemics, but a number of killers (including pneumonic plague) must have been involved.

The first outbreak carried off about one-third of the population of Europe, killing indiscriminately among rich and poor, and urban and rural communities (although some areas, such as parts of the Netherlands and Poland, mostly avoided the plague for reasons that are unknown). Thus, knights suffered along with their peasants. Later outbreaks tended to be concentrated in the cities, and the knights who lived in the towns usually tried to escape to their country estates, just like the characters in *The Decameron* (1353), by Italian poet Giovanni Boccaccio.

BELOW: *In this illustration from a fifteenth-century edition of Pedanius Dioscorides's medical treatise* De materia medica, *written in the first century CE, a knight extracts balsam from plants for use in herbal medicine.*

HUNTING AND HAWKING

The leisure activity that is probably most characteristic of the knightly class is hunting, including hawking. Its combination of privilege, physical skill, danger, and expense fits the image and the function of a warrior class perfectly. Hunting was both sport and a way to get extra meat for the table. The aristocracy tried—not always successfully—to keep hunting rights to themselves, rather than allowing peasants to take game.

TYPES OF PREY

The common prey of medieval hunting parties included deer, bear, birds (hunted with hawks and other birds of prey), and wild boar. Of these, the boar was considered the most prestigious catch because it was the most dangerous. Boar hunting typically took place in fall, when the animals fattened themselves on acorns. Because boars could not be stopped with arrows, they were hunted with spears. Knights pursued them on horseback. Sometimes men on foot did the spearing; at other times the final kill might match a charging boar against a lance-armed, mounted knight.

Deer, and particularly mature males called harts, were hunted on horseback with hounds; men on foot accompanied the hunters. The prey was killed with arrows, then field dressed. To show that he was truly courtly, a knight was supposed to know the different methods

RIGHT: *Falconry was a leisure pursuit reserved for the aristocratic class and an activity in which women fully participated. This illustration is from a fifteenth-century French manuscript.*
BELOW: *Hunting wild beasts with a lance and nets is explained in the* Oppiano Codex, *an eleventh-century Greek treatise on hunting.*

of dressing each animal before carrying the pieces home. Whereas a boar might simply be cut into four quarters, a hart was supposed to be dressed in a manner considered to honor it.

Falconry—the hunting of birds using hawks—was an aristocratic sport. Knights and ladies rode out with their hooded hawks perched on heavily gloved wrists. When prey was spotted, the hawk's hood would be removed and the hawk launched into the air. Hawks were specially trained to take the prey and bring it back. However, much of the day could be spent whirling a lure (a bunch of feathers tied together, to which a hawk had been trained to return), trying to recover a recalcitrant hawk.

AN ARISTOCRATIC DISPLAY

One major reason for the popularity of hunting among the knightly class was that it was an ideal way to display social status and privilege. In the most obvious way, hunting was expensive, requiring specially trained animals: not just horses but hounds and various trained raptors. The importance of raptors in projecting images of royal and aristocratic authority is indicated by the common use of the eagle as a royal symbol in heraldry.

Hunting operated in other ways to define and enforce status distinctions. In some times and places, the privilege of hunting was restricted to the king and companions, emphasizing the nobility of the pursuit. In addition, hunting could be constructed as part of the essential function of a warrior elite, involving as it did the killing of wild animals that could pose a threat, at least in theory, to farmers and farmland, allowing knights to exercise their protective role in society (although this never stopped knightly hunters from trampling crops in hot pursuit of prey). Such a function could be further justified by biblical injunctions to exercise dominion over the earth, with wild animals being construed as rebellious members of the natural order.

ABOVE: *Strategies for hunting deer and other prey were described and illustrated in the* Traité de Fauconnerie et de Vénerie, *a 1459 French manuscript on falconry and hunting.*

In other, more concrete ways, hunting legitimated the structuring of space in terms of social power. Nobles often kept parts of their estates forested for hunting (although forest was useful for pasturing domestic pigs, too). At the highest level, designating game preserves resulted in the creation of royal forests, such as the New Forest in England, where King William II (reigned 1087–1100) was accidentally shot in the chest with a crossbow bolt by his companion, Walter Tyrel, and died of his injuries. The social privilege of hunting was enforced by forest wardens, who policed poaching of the deer and other game reserved for the king's sport and for the king's table.

THE RIGHT WAY TO DRESS A HART

After a mature male deer, or hart, was killed, it was laid on its back and the skin split from muzzle to belly. The four legs were flayed and the forelimbs cut free. The hindquarters and haunch were kept together, but separated from the backbone. The breast was also separated from the backbone, but not split. The ribs and flanks on each side were then cut away, thus completing the butchering of the principal cuts of meat. Lastly, the head, heart, backbone, and liver were cut free, and the hounds were fed the entrails. The pieces of the hart were carried home separately, starting with the head.

THE FEAST

Like hunting, feasting, especially the hosting of large feasts, was a universal characteristic of warrior elites—and, indeed, all elites—and an important part of the life of a medieval knight. Feasting created, expressed, and also reinforced the social bonds that held aristocratic societies together. The ability of a lord to support his followers was demonstrated by the provision of food. The feast also created a social setting where the exchange of gifts and the enjoyment of entertainment occurred.

Medieval feasts normally took place in the great hall of a castle and, unlike many other knightly activities (including most forms of hunting), they involved the women of the knightly class. Despite this, the feasts were seldom genteel affairs, but more often raucous and loud. The anonymous poet of the twelfth-century French epic *Raoul of Cambrai* urges his audience, at the beginning of his performance (which was sung, usually after a feast) to "make less noise and listen to the song." And some of the accroutrements of "courtesy," or courtly manners, such as the fork, were only invented later.

The central cultural importance of feasting is indicated by its prominent place in the epics and romances. The horrors in *Beowulf* begin with Grendel's invasion of the Dane's banqueting hall, and King Arthur's Round Table is virtually a character unto itself.

A SYMBOL OF WEALTH AND POWER

The feast was thus not merely a meal; it was also a social occasion and stage for the performance of the appropriate roles of lords, men, and women. The giving of gifts (including the basic gift of a meal) was an act loaded with symbolic significance in this moral economy of reciprocity: the giving of a gift obligated the receiver and bound him to the giver. In a pattern that was common to traditional societies everywhere, lords demonstrated their wealth by giving it away—the distribution of wealth was an investment in the maintenance of the power relationships through which further wealth (and power) could be obtained. Indeed, feasting is generally a sign of a society that is built around power relationships rather than market ones. The element of display of power and status in medieval feasting shows up in the drinking, boasting, and singing of epic tales, and sometimes the fighting that accompanied the meal.

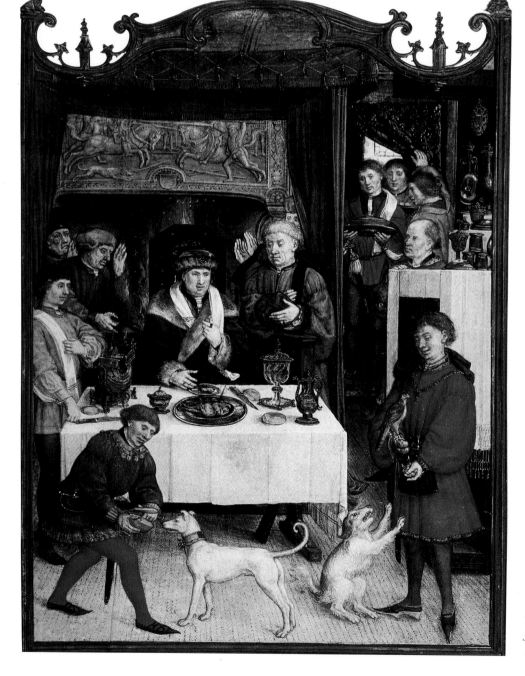

LEFT: *Servants surround the dining table of a wealthy lord in this miniature from a medieval manuscript. The meal was not simply a time for feasting but also for reinforcing social positions and forging new relationships.*

ABOVE: *A court banquet of 1220 is presided over by Alfonso IX of Leon (reigned 1188–1230), as shown in this tiled scene from the Plaza Espana, Seville, Spain.*
LEFT: *A servant slaughters a pig for the banquet table in this illustration from* The Breviary of Love, *a thirteenth-century Provençal codex.*

THE FOOD AND DRINK

The staples of the medieval diet were bread and wine, and, at the lower social levels, which would have included the poorer knights, beer. Food shortages could be a problem, even among nobles—a modern examination of the teeth of Duke William IX of Aquitaine (*c.* 1071–1126) indicated that he suffered malnutrition in childhood. Such problems become less acute (outside of local famines) after 1000, as peas and beans increasingly supplemented diets.

Knights certainly ate legumes and other vegetables at times, but a knightly feast was distinguished by the quantity and variety of meat served, including both domesticated and game animals, plus fish and fowl of all sorts. Greater protein intake was beneficial to elite health generally, and particularly to the health and fitness of warriors expected to perform strenuous physical labor. But the extent to which meat-eating was differentially reserved for the elite relates not to function (farming is hard physical work) but to status distinctions: meat, especially wild game, was noble food.

The preparation and presentation of food reinforced this aspect of feasting.

Extant medieval recipes often feature bizarre (to modern eyes) combinations of meat with dried fruits and exotic spices. Trade in the latter, including cinnamon, cloves, and above all pepper—the expensive spices of the Indian Ocean trade world—provided the cooks of the knightly world with the chance not just to enhance the flavor of their dishes but to display their patron's wealth and connections: spices advertised status.

Cooks went to elaborate lengths to present the beasts whole and decorated, sometimes with large roasts containing successively smaller ones inside each other: as a central social event, a feast had to be a treat for guests' eyes as much as sustenance for their bodies.

DEATH FROM A SURFEIT OF LAMPREYS

Henry I of England (reigned 1100–35), who came to the throne when his brother William Rufus died in a hunting accident, succumbed to feasting. In 1135, after a long day of hunting and riding in Normandy, he sat down to a sumptuous meal of freshly caught local freshwater eels, or lampreys. Never known for the moderation of his gastronomic or sexual appetites, he ate copiously, became ill that night, and the next day was dead, famously, of "a surfeit of lampreys." A succession dispute and civil war followed his death. Feasting, like hunting, could have its dangers.

Castles

The castle was, and indeed remains, the greatest physical monument to the medieval knight. Its importance was more profound than just its fabric of timber and stone; as both fortress and residence, the castle was a singular product of medieval lordship. This unique dual function inextricably associated the castle with the knight.

As warriors, knights manned garrisons in times of war; during times of peace, they frequently resided in the castle of their lord. The wealthy knights aspired to owning their own castles, and the life of almost every knight centered significantly upon the castle. This dominating building retained a powerful hold on the popular imagination; as chronicler Lawrence of Durham commented, "the keep is a queen, looming aloft, mistress of all she surveys."

As a fortification, the castle was of a radically different nature from those that had preceded it. After the demise of the Roman Empire, throughout Europe defenses had taken the form of earthen enclosures of banks and ditches that were reinforced by timber palisades. Encompassing a large area, the castles offered security for the community that was enclosed within them—a community that constructed and maintained the ramparts, and that defended them when attacked. Such fortifications were public in nature, and intended to protect the wider community.

In the aftermath of the Viking raids of the ninth century, against which even well-defended city walls could barely stand, and then the assumption of public power by the counts in the tenth century, a new kind of fortification emerged. During the late tenth century and early eleventh century, first the counts and then lower-ranking landed lords started constructing their own fortresses. Some of these structures were in or adjoining towns, but increasingly they were built in the country, commanding roads or fords, or looking down from hilltops.

BELOW: *This keep, known as Clifford's Tower, in Yorkshire in the north of England, was part of an early-fourteenth-century castle built on top of a motte, the site of two earlier castles of William the Conqueror, the first dating from 1068.*

THE FIRST CASTLES

A castle was essentially a private fortress. Lords constructed castles to secure their lands, exert local authority, and provide refuge for themselves and their households. The principal focus was not on the community but on the needs of the elite. A lord sought to provide a place of safety for himself, his family, and his household: these basic requirements dictated that a castle only needed to occupy a relatively small site.

The earliest common form of castle to appear in northern France and England in the tenth and eleventh centuries was the *motte-and-bailey* castle. The *motte*, a raised earthen mound, was the foundation upon which a wooden tower was built. The summit of the motte was surrounded by a palisade made of timber, with a stairway or flying bridge providing the means of ascent. The motte was positioned at one end of an enclosed area, the *bailey*, which was usually called the *ward* in later stone castles; the perimeter of the bailey was defended by a ditch and by a timber palisade. Domestic buildings occupied the bailey, and, during an emergency, the local inhabitants could seek safety within it, thereby providing the castle with an aspect of public protection. But the castle's strongest defensive structure was the private tower that was perched upon its motte—and this was where the lord and his household would take refuge at a time of danger.

EARLY CASTLE BUILDERS

Such a fortification could only be taken by a determined enemy. Just as importantly, these relatively simple structures of earth and timber were easy to build. Among the most prolific of the early castle builders was Fulk Nerra, Count of Anjou (c. 970–1040). Some of the 27 fortifications attributable to Fulk were motte-and-bailey castles.

ABOVE: *The castle dominated the life of the knights and peasants alike in the Middle Ages. It was often built on prominent hilltops for defensive reasons, and also as a way to reinforce the social status of its owner and his power within the community, as seen in this illustration from the* Très riches heures du duc de Berry *(c. 1410).*

It was the Norman invasion of 1066 that introduced the castle to England. William the Conqueror (reigned 1066–87), the hostile *Anglo-Saxon Chronicle* remarked, "had castles built, and poor men hard oppressed." William constructed motte-and-bailey castles at both Pevensey and Hastings in 1066, in the two weeks between landing in England and the Battle of Hastings. By 1100, the Anglo-Norman kingdom may have contained as many as five hundred castles.

As the Norman lords and knights sought to establish their own authority in new territories, they took the new building technologies with them, constructing castles to consolidate their power; it was said of the expansionist Frederick I, Duke of Swabia (reigned 1079–1105), that he "dragged a castle at his horse's tail."

The Norman occupation of Sicily and the Crusades further distributed this distinctive fortification. In times of rebellion or war, lords were quick to build themselves rudimentary castles. An English chronicler of the civil war that occurred during King Stephen's reign (1135–54) wrote dramatically that "every great man built himself a castle and held it against the king; and they filled the whole land with these castles."

Like the knight, the castle was the inextricable product of the increasing militarization of the aristocracy. It was the most important secular building, an instrument of war, a center, and a symbol of authority, and the dominant feature of medieval life. Although its origins were military in nature, over time the castle evolved into a much more complex institution and an integral feature of medieval politics and society. As its importance and functions increased, so castle building became ever more sophisticated and elaborate.

BELOW: *La Zisa in Palermo, Sicily, was built in the twelfth century in the Arab style, for the Norman conquerors of the island.*

CASTLE BUILDING

Although topography ensured every castle was unique, general trends in the construction and design of the castle are apparent, and throughout the Middle Ages new techniques were continually being trialed and implemented.

The first major transformation of the castle was the replacement of wooden structures with stone. Timber fortifications remained vulnerable to fire, and because they were prone to decay had to be regularly restored. Stone fortifications were much more durable and formidable.

The massive weight of a stone tower, however, was in many cases too great for the unsettled earth of the artificial motte; consequently, it was usually built elsewhere within the bailey. This great tower, the *magna turris*, or *donjon*, became the main defense and residence of the castle. Its strength depended upon the thickness of its walls and its height. The first stone towers—better known today

as *keeps*—date to the later eleventh and early twelfth century, although a fine early-eleventh-century example is Fulk Nerra's great rectangular keep at Loches in Touraine, central France.

William the Conqueror commenced the construction of the White Tower in London in 1078. Fifty years later, in the 1120s, the English king, Henry I (reigned 1100–35), built a similar keep at Falaise in Normandy. Both were massive rectangular stone structures of two or three stories, and they included a great hall and chambers for the king and his household. The rectangular-shaped keep spread throughout feudal Europe and the Holy Land in the twelfth century.

FORM AND DEVELOPMENT
The great tower, however, was only one form of early stone castle. Many a castellan also replaced the timber palisade that encircled the motte with a simple

ABOVE: *The building of a fortified castle at Marseilles, France, required an army of workers, as shown in this fifteenth-century manuscript illumination. The walls and towers were erected using a winch and a wooden platform.*

stone wall. These *shell-keep* castles took two different forms. Domestic buildings or rooms were either built on the ground level within the walls, as at Restormel (*c.* 1100) in Cornwall, England, or, if the motte was sufficiently strong, a stone tower was constructed within the walls, as at Gisors in Normandy, which dates from the twelfth century.

More common than the shell-keep, however, was the replacement of the bailey palisade with a circuit of stone *curtain walls*, which might incorporate several *mural towers*, such as at Richmond in Yorkshire, England (*c.* 1071). Ideally, the towers projected forward from the castle wall, enabling archers to deliver flanking fire. This emphasis on strong curtain walls and mural towers was a feature of most castles of the late twelfth and early thirteenth centuries, leading to the building of "keepless castles," such as Framlingham in Suffolk, England, and Angers in Anjou, France; the walls of the former were defended by 13 rectangular flanking towers.

During this period, the design of the tower, both of the keep and mural tower, underwent further experimentation. Most early stone towers were rectangular or square structures, and their corner angles were vulnerable to the missile fire of siege engines and to undermining. An exceptionally early

BELOW: *The 18-sided polygonal keep at Orford Castle, Suffolk, England, built in the 1160s, was intended to guard against coastal invaders.*

RIGHT: *The castle of Falaise in Normandy was remodeled by Philip Augustus in 1207.*

round keep was built at Fréteval in the Loire in the late eleventh century. King Henry II (reigned 1154–89) oversaw the construction of an extraordinary polygonal keep at Orford in Suffolk, England, in the 1160s.

A keen advocate of the round keep was Philip II Augustus (reigned 1179–1223). The French king consolidated his conquests in Normandy by constructing many substantial round towers: his keep at Falaise was a contrast to the earlier, neighboring rectangular keep of Henry I. At Anjou, the castle's formidable stone walls were defended by 17 round towers. In England, the square keep of Rochester, dating from the early twelfth century, was protected by four square corner towers; when the southeast tower collapsed in 1215 after being undermined during a long seige, it was replaced with a round tower. The apparent advantages of the round tower design did not signify the end of the rectangular keep or tower, however. It was domestic considerations, not military practicalities, that led to its survival, for the rectangular or square keep was far more suited to housing the great hall and chambers a lord required.

THE GOLDEN AGE

During the thirteenth century, the castle reached its magnificent apogee. The most notable development was the *gatehouse*, in which the potential weakness of the main entranceway was rectified by constructing two mural towers close together, flanking the gateway.

The fortified gatehouse became increasingly substantial, and the courtyard-facing sides of some of the towers—many of which were D-shaped—became particularly extensive. Often, they contained the main accommodation of the castle, thus effectively supplanting the keep as the principal fortress and residential suite of the lord.

ABOVE: *At Beaumaris Castle, in Gwynedd, Wales, the matching gatehouses provided a formidable defense against attackers.*

Fronting a gatehouse with walls that comprised a *barbican*, or outer fortification, further transformed the castle's entranceway into a killing ground.

The heavily defended gatehouse was a principal feature of several of the formidable castles the English king Edward I (reigned 1272–1307) constructed in the late thirteenth century to consolidate his conquest of Wales. Beaumaris and Rhuddlan were each provided with two substantial gatehouses that were situated directly opposite one another. Their towered curtain walls were symmetrical and they were protected by a lower, outer circuit of walls, which created inner and outer wards. The development of this concentric defense produced castles designed with fine proportions and technological sophistication.

However, the dual function of the castle, and the unique nature of every

site, ensured that no design predominated exclusively. Caernarvon, built between 1283 and 1323, was the most spectacular of Edward's Welsh castles. Its site precluded a concentric defense, so Caernarvon became an elongated enclosure castle comprising a single curtain wall with projecting mural towers. The castle had a sizable cross wall that divided the bailey into inner and outer wards, the former defended by two elaborate gatehouses. There was no keep, although the proportions of the Eagle Tower are suggestive of a donjon, or great tower.

The castle of Krak des Chevaliers in Syria was transformed in the thirteenth century, with the substantial outer wall and round towers being added to the existing twelfth-century, rectangular-towered curtain wall to create the formidable concentric defense. The majestic Castel del Monte in Apulia, Italy, which was built by Holy Roman Emperor Frederick II (reigned 1215–50) in the 1240s, was a grand residence rather than a fortress, which had eight polygonal towers abutting the corners of its octagonal keep.

RESIDENCE AND SPLENDOR

As well as its defensive function, a major castle was also an aristocratic residence intended for formal occasions and personal comfort. The White Tower in London had three floors. Storerooms and a freshwater well occupied the ground-level basement. The first floor comprised the constable's hall, chamber, and chapel. On the second floor were the Chapel of St. John the Evangelist, the king's great hall, his chamber, and two garderobes.

[I] could hold the castle even it its walls were made of butter.

RICHARD I OF ENGLAND ON HIS SUPPOSEDLY IMPREGNABLE CHÂTEAU GAILLARD

The design of Edward I's Beaumaris Castle suggests there were five separate suites of accommodation, each having its own hall and chamber. Castles without a keep or gatehouse often had a stone great hall built within the ward, such as the late-eleventh-century Scolland's Hall at Richmond in Yorkshire.

Further domestic buildings, built of either timber or stone, also occupied the castle ward, including a great kitchen, a bakehouse, a granary, a grange, and

A "PERFECT" DESIGN

In 1196, King Richard I of England (reigned 1189–99) began construction of a remarkable castle in Normandy. Sited on a 300-foot (90-m) limestone crag that overlooks the Seine, Château Gaillard— the "saucy castle"—was built in just two years, the king lavishing twelve thousand pounds on this great, fortified complex. Comprising an elliptical keep enclosed within an extraordinary curvilinear wall, and surrounded by two additional circuits of curtain walls, it was a defensive masterpiece. Indeed, Richard believed that Château Gaillard was so perfectly designed that it would be impregnable. Following his death, however, it fell to the French in 1204, after a soldier climbed the seemingly unscaleable cliff, got in at night through a chapel window, and opened the outer gates. The form of Château Gaillard suggests the influence of crusader castles in the Holy Land.

RIGHT: *Richard I's "perfect" Chateau Gaillard, at Les Andelys, Normandy, today lies in ruins.*

RIGHT: *Krak des Chevaliers, in Syria, was originally built in 1031 for the Amir of Aleppo. The castle was captured by crusaders in 1110, and substantially rebuilt by the Knights Hospitaller as the largest crusader castle in the Levant.*

stables. A residential castle required a permanent domestic staff, and, consequently, it became the focus of the local community. The revenue and foodstuffs that sustained a castle were produced on the demesne lands, or *châtellenie*, that surrounded and belonged to the castle. The local community worked these lands and their lord's castle dominated their lives. Pleas and lawsuits were heard at the castle, and it was there they went to pay rents and fines. During an emergency, they could seek refuge within its walls.

A SYMBOL OF POWER

A castle was a powerful symbol of royal or seignorial authority, the splendor and the size of its design and fortifications reflecting the wealth and power of its lord. Philip Augustus's construction of a round tower at Falaise next to the rectangular keep of Henry I was a bold political statement about French supremacy over the English. Edward I evoked echoes of imperialism at Caernarvon; its banded stonework was an imitation of the ancient walls of Constantinople.

FUNCTION AND AUTHORITY

As the focus of a lordship, the castle functioned as an administrative center. This was particularly true of royal castles, which effectively constituted "the bones of the kingdom." They served as armories, treasuries, and prisons, as the depositories for archives, and as the headquarters for principal local officials.

The most important castles were vital to the effective exercise of government and authority and were integral to the effective exercise of royal or seignorial authority. For example, by tradition, whoever was in possession of the keep of the castle at Rouen was said to be the legitimate ruler of Normandy; it was not until 1449 that the French finally drove the English from the region. In the twelfth century, the castle of Chinon in Touraine became the center of Angevin power in France. The hub of English administration was the White Tower in London.

URBAN CASTLES

The most significant of the administrative castles were located within towns, rulers having recognized that it was imperative to exercise authority over urban populations. The ramparts dominating Caen in France, like the formidable White Tower in London, were originally built by William the Conqueror. Most of these castles were intrusively implanted within existing urban centers. Of the 37 royal castles established in England prior to 1100, 20 of them were built within or against the walls of a town.

The urban castle also provided the framework by which a ruler sought to implement his authority in the most

BELOW: *Most of the existing castle at Chinon in Touraine, France, was built by Henry II, the Angevin king of England, in the twelfth century. Both he and his son, Richard I, died there.*

populous areas of his domains: it was intended to overawe the inhabitants of the town, and its defenses designed to protect it from both external enemies and any potential internal threat from the townspeople. If it were located on the perimeter of a town, it enjoyed direct access to the countryside. The castle was thus a separate entity within a town or city, customarily enjoying its own privileges—including a separate legal jurisdiction—and accessing local sources of revenue.

DISORDER AND REBELLION

The private baronial castle, however, could pose serious threats to this authority, providing its disaffected lord with a secure refuge. For example, during the turmoil of the reign of King Stephen of England (1135–54), the barons built castles and "filled them with devils and evil men." For a ruler, it was vital to

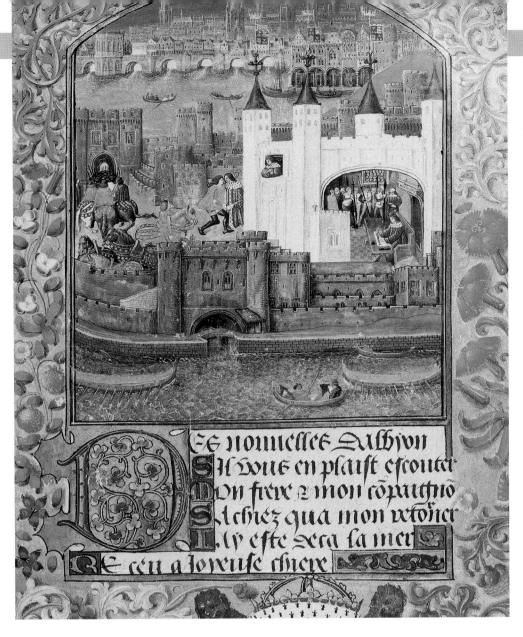

The French kings limited the number of baronial castles in the Île-de-France; the English kings looked to their entire realm. In 1154, the ratio of baronial to royal castles in England was five to one; by 1189, it was almost equal. Henry II achieved this by embarking on a major building program—the royal castle at Orford, for example, was built to offset the regional power of the Earl of Norfolk—and, to counter rebellion in the 1170s, more than 40 royal castles were readied for war. When Henry subsequently confiscated rebel castles, systematically destroying many in England, Normandy, and Anjou, a contemporary lamented, "so passes the glory of the world."

Civil war led kings to besiege rebel castles; King John (reigned 1199–1216) captured Rochester after 50 days in 1215, and Kenilworth Castle capitulated to Henry III (reigned 1216–72) in 1266 after a gruelling six-month siege. These castles were taken because of the extensive resources available to kings. Indeed, as the wealth of rulers increased, so the cost of maintaining a first-rate castle grew beyond the means of many barons, and kings attained the level of control they had long desired.

exercise control over all major castles, but this was difficult to achieve. The resources of rulers were limited, and the prolific castle building that occurred in the eleventh and twelfth centuries was fuelled by the dynamic of kings and dukes encouraging barons to construct fortifications on newly acquired land. This system depended on the interests of the ruler and his barons coinciding.

When Fulk Nerra, Count of Anjou, built a network of castles in the early eleventh century, he made sure that the lords to whom he entrusted them swore oaths of fealty to him, in order to curb any incipient independence they might display. In 1091, William the Conqueror proscribed the construction of fortifications over a certain size, and, more importantly, he declared his right as duke to enter or demand render of all the castles in Normandy. It was through

such *rendability*—a custom by which a lord was expected to surrender his castle to his overlord if requested—that rulers sought to exercise control. In the wars of the 1190s, Philip Augustus agreed on charters of rendability with the French castellans around Normandy, exerting his right to enter or occupy their castle.

A LICENSE OF STATUS

From the late eleventh century, kings increasingly asserted the sole right to license the building of castles, but it is doubtful any ruler actually achieved such a level of control. Although licenses to build castles, or licenses to crenellate, were requested, particularly in the thirteenth and fourteenth centuries, and frequently granted, they did not always result in castles. Many licenses merely permitted the addition of battlements to houses. Some were never acted upon, the license itself being sufficient to satisfy the petitioner's ambitions: few could afford to build castles, but a royal license proclaimed knightly status.

CASTLES AND WARFARE

Despite the variety of functions it adopted, the castle ultimately was an expression of armed force. Militarily, it was among the most important instruments of warfare. Rulers readied their castles for war by providing them with victuals and garrisons. Campaigns often revolved around castles, and the prevalence of the castle largely dictated the character of medieval warfare.

DEFENSIVE FEATURES

The castle itself was repeatedly rebuilt with additional defenses to further increase its ability to withstand attack, the heads of the curtain walls and the towers receiving most attention. Timber platforms, known as *hoardings* or *brattices*, were attached to the outside of the tops of towers or curtain walls, using horizontal beams or stone corbels, to provide added protection and a vantage point for defenders. The platforms were

usually enclosed by paneled timber walls and sloping wooden roofs, which were often covered with damp hides to make them less vulnerable to fire. Slots or holes, called *machicolations*, were built into the floor so that the defenders could drop missiles and liquids onto attackers below. The importance of hoardings and machicolations was such that they were later incorporated into the stonework, becoming part of the permanent fabric of the castle.

Timber barriers were often erected in front of the castle walls, particularly the gatehouse, and wooden palisades were raised to create an outer line of defense, or to enlarge the capacity of the castle for holding troops and stores. To defend Newcastle from the Scots in 1298, the English garrison protected the stonework of the walls by hanging a hundred timber boards at the *embrasures* (the openings in the battlements or

ABOVE: *Raglan Castle in Wales was constructed with a defensive moat. Dating from the late Middle Ages, when Britain was relatively peaceful, the castle nevertheless was besieged for 13 weeks during the Civil War of the 1600s.*

crenellations) of the castle and affixing tree trunks to the walls; a platform was also built for the *springald* (effectively a giant oversize crossbow) they had constructed. Most castles contained siege engines, and some towers were provided with flat lead roofs to act as platforms on which the engines could be placed.

In the thirteenth century, the appearance of arrow-slits in towers and walls increased the capacity of defenders for missile fire. The *postern gate*, a relatively small defensible gateway, enabled a garrison to launch sudden attacks against besieging troops. The postern was an integral defensive feature, and so were the drawbridge, *portcullis* (a sliding iron grating hung over the gateway), and the battlemented walls.

GARRISONS AND PROVISIONS

A large proportion of wartime garrisons comprised mounted troops, including knights, proving that they were intended to operate aggressively beyond the walls. The castle building itself was inherently defensive, but a major wartime garrison was primarily aggressive, using the fortification as a heavily defended forward base from which to dominate the surrounding area. Through the presence of such a garrison, a castle realized its full potential as an instrument of war.

The number of troops within a garrison depended on the size of the castle, and on the resources of its lord.

When Château Gaillard fell in 1204 to Philip Augustus of France, its surviving English garrison numbered 156 men; at full strength, it may have comprised 300, of which 40 were knights. The average garrison size for the Anglo-Norman and Angevin periods has been calculated at approximately 140 troops, a figure similar to the size of the English garrisons installed in Scottish castles during the warfare of the fourteenth century (although a garrison of 300 was based in Roxburgh in 1400). In 1260, the Christian castle of Saphet in the Holy Land contained 430 troops. The rebels besieged in Kenilworth, England, in 1266 numbered about 700 armed men.

The provision of sufficient victuals to maintain the garrison of a castle was of fundamental importance. Fish, especially dried and salted for preservation, was a staple foodstuff, along with meat and livestock. Wheat, flour, oats, and barley were required for the baking of bread, and for feeding horses. Drinking needs were met by wine or beer. A clear-water well within the defenses was essential, as were raw materials, such as coal and iron, to maintain the fabric of the castle, and the armor and weapons of the garrison.

All provisions and supplies had to be worked by skilled hands, and a major wartime castle required the services of a large supporting staff.

RIGHT: *A spear-throwing siege machine, known as a* ballista fulminalis, *was widely used throughout the Middle Ages.*

BELOW: *Besieged repeatedly during the Albigensian Crusade of the early 1200s, Carcassonne in southwest France was regularly refortified.*

In 1260, the crusader castle of Saphet in the Holy Land had 820 workmen and 400 slaves. The English garrison occupying Edinburgh Castle in 1300 had 193 noncombatants supporting it. Sustaining substantial wartime garrisons was an enormous financial drain on a ruler.

AN INSTRUMENT OF WAR

The tactical and strategic purpose of a castle, or a network of castles, was not necessarily constant. Fulk Nerra, Count of Anjou and the earliest prolific castle builder of the Middle Ages, originally constructed a series of fortifications to secure lines of communication between his widespread landholdings in northern and central France, particularly along the Loire. As Fulk's territory expanded, so Anjou became the heartland of his power base, and the castles designed to secure access to newly won lands effectively became a defense in depth that enclosed and protected Anjou. From this fortified base, the counts of Anjou extended their power in the twelfth century.

Similarly, in the mid-twelfth century, the crusaders constructed four castles near the Muslim city of Ascalon in the Holy Land. Their garrisons were to attack anyone issuing from the city. Although the castles were founded as instruments of conquest and expansion,

A GILDED HELM

During the Anglo-Scottish wars of the early fourteenth century, an English knight, William Marmion, was presented by his lady with a gilded war helm, and was challenged to make it famous by venturing to the most perilous place in Britain. William made straight for Northumberland, entering Norham Castle on the Tweed, the borderline between England and Scotland. When the Scots approached the castle, William charged them alone and was unseated from his mount. The Norham garrison sallied on foot, putting the Scots to flight, and rescued and remounted William. The knight had risked all to prove his valor.

in the 1180s when the Muslim leader Saladin (1137/38–93) took the offensive, they became key points in the crusader defense of the Holy Land.

In the reign of King John, Château Gaillard was a critical part of the English defense of Normandy, and its capture by Philip Augustus effectively heralded the loss of the duchy to the French. Yet Richard I had intended Château Gaillard to function as a formidable forward base for his recapture of the Vexin region from Philip: it was part of a complex offensive network that included the construction below its ramparts of the new town of Les Andelys on the Seine and extended back to England and Richard's new naval base at Portsmouth.

A castle, or a network of castles, was most effective when used aggressively to intrusively project military power. On the defensive, a castle and its garrison were at their most vulnerable. If they were left isolated for a prolonged period, even the strongest and the most heavily manned castle would fall eventually. Such a situation enabled Robert the Bruce, king of Scotland (reigned 1306–29), to reduce the major English-held castles in Scotland between 1311 and 1314; after their capture, he destroyed these powerful fortresses to deny the English the ability to "lord it over the land."

It was the operation of a field army in conjunction with a friendly castle that fully realized the fortification's aggressive potential, the castle providing the army with victuals, refuge, intelligence, and reinforcement. The defense of the Kingdom of Jerusalem was led by a field army, but, when it moved against an enemy force, the major border castles provided invaluable support, with their garrisons supplementing the army. In 1187, during the Hattin campaign, the crusader garrisons were stripped to reinforce the field army. In Wales, Edward I's castles were built on a capacious scale so they could house a field army should an offensive campaign prove necessary. By

LEFT: *Siting a castle on the coast, as with Dunluce Castle, in County Antrim, Ireland, limited the possibility of attack from land.*

siting these castles on the coast, Edward ensured they could be provisioned by sea rather than having to rely on supplies taken overland through hostile territory.

TAKING THE CASTLE

Even if it were isolated, the castle had an essential role to play in warfare, in that it held land and provided a refuge for its lord's authority. If a war of conquest were being waged, enemy castles had to be taken or destroyed. The conflict in the 1190s between Richard I and Philip Augustus was fought for control of land between Paris and Rouen, and it was centered on the seizure and occupation of the castles of the region. After victory at Agincourt in 1415, the English king,

ABOVE: *In this fifteenth-century illustration, a group of knights storms the wall of a castle using* escalade, *a tactic involving ladders or siege towers. This allows another attacker to surreptitiously breach the base of the wall.*

Henry V (reigned 1413–22), embarked on his conquest of Normandy by seizing and garrisoning the castles of the duchy.

The taking of a castle could be a difficult operation; consequently, castles often determined the course of campaigns. Defensive technology was always ahead of offensive technology, until the development of cannon, so many castles might go several generations without experiencing a serious attack, but they

always had to be ready. A common siege tactic was for an enemy to ravage the surrounding countryside, destroying land that provided the castle's resources. A besieging army risked being confronted by a relief force, and this could result in battle. In 1187, when Saladin besieged Tiberias in Palestine, the Christians raised a massive relief force, forcing Saladin to do battle at Hattin; Saladin triumphed, however, and soon took Jerusalem. A Scottish siege of the English-held castle of Stirling in 1314, which pinned down Robert the Bruce and his army, led to the Battle of Bannockburn, where an English force was surprisingly defeated by the Scots.

THE DEMISE OF THE CASTLE

The decline of the castle was gradual yet inexorable, and was brought about by fundamental changes in the society that had produced it. By the later Middle Ages, possession of a network of castles had become of vital importance, and a concentration of castles in the hands of individual rulers marked a transition from private to public fortification.

But the expense of maintaining a network of castles, and of garrisoning and provisioning them, was beyond the means of most barons; and with the advent of gunpowder, high walls no longer resisted concerted attack. Soon, the need for a fortified residence was superseded by a desire for comfort, leading to a shift from the construction of castles to the building of great houses.

Armor

The knight in shining armor remains an enduring symbol of the medieval period, yet the classic full-plated suit, providing cover from head to toe, only emerged in the late Middle Ages once new technologies enabled craftsmen to design better-fitting, lighter, and more effective protection for man and horse.

Impressive and effective armor was essential if knights were to carry out their dual roles as social leaders and the decisive element in battle. Knights were obligated to ensure that they and their retinue were appropriately equipped with armor, weapons, and horses. The cost of acquiring and maintaining such a capability was high and most of it had to be borne by the individual knight as part of his service to his monarch or lord. Although a basic set of armor was relatively inexpensive to a man of reasonable means, the quality of the armor was a very visible sign of social status and of wealth, and, importantly, it also increased the chances of survival on a medieval battlefield.

Knights were not the only wearers of armor during the Middle Ages. Even the lowest-ranked foot soldiers would have

LEFT: *Knights in mail armor pay homage to the corpse of St. Louis, the French king (reigned 1226–70) who died on crusade in 1270, as seen in the fourteenth-century French manuscript* Les Grandes Chroniques de Saint-Denis.

worn some form of protection: historical and archaeological evidence shows that armor of one form or another was in widespread use across medieval armies. Men of land and/or property—whether knighted or not—were also often required to maintain arms and armor to enable service to their lord as needed. It was the need to protect knights, though—and the price they were prepared to pay—that drove the development of armor to the remarkable technological and artistic heights that it achieved by the end of the Middle Ages.

Knights, like other medieval soldiers, faced a great many threats in war, including terrible wounds from stabbing and cutting weapons, hails of arrows, deadly crossbow bolts, crushing blows from heavy maces, and, as the age of chivalry came to an end, even primitive handguns. Since knights were employed as the shock troops of most armies, they could expect to be engaged at long range by missile weapons before moving into equally deadly close combat.

In a time when minor injuries could lead to life-threatening infections, even quite slight wounds had to be avoided if possible, and knights needed to be able to continue to fight if injured. Of course,

just getting to the battlefield could be difficult enough in itself and often involved long marches over rough terrain in harsh weather conditions. So protection for man and horse needed to be balanced with other considerations.

THE ARMORER'S CRAFT

The medieval armorers' challenge was therefore threefold: knights needed to be protected from the wide variety of enemy weapons they would encounter in the front line of battle; the armor had to allow for sufficient freedom of movement to wield weapons while mounted or on foot; and the weight of equipment had to be kept to a minimum to increase mobility and reduce fatigue. All of this

BELOW: *Medieval warfare was bloody and relentless. This illustration (c. 1415) shows how a sword could pierce a suit of armor.*

had to be achieved using a combination of handworked craftsmanship and the rudimentary forging and production processes of the day.

Remarkably, the craftsmen excelled in all three areas, gradually improving armor to counter advances in weaponry, and developing close-fitting and flexible armor to cover almost the entire body. Despite myths to the contrary, the armor worn by a knight in battle was relatively light, at 50 to 60 pounds (23–27 kg)—less than the load carried by a modern soldier—so cranes were not needed to lift a knight onto his horse (although, in

---

There is no armour

against fate.

JAMES SHIRLEY, *THE CONTENTION OF AJAX AND ULYSSES* **(1659)**

---

the late Middle Ages, they sometimes were at tournaments, because armor worn there had become heavier and more elaborate). The fact that mounted knights dominated warfare for several hundred years is perhaps as much a testament to the expertise of medieval armorers as it is to knightly prowess.

HEAVIER AND MORE ELABORATE

Peacetime activities brought their own perils for knights, in the form of tournaments and jousting, or *tilting*, matches that were used to demonstrate the skill and courage of participants. Initially established as a means of training for war, the early tournaments saw massed groups of knights engaging in free-for-all battles using real weapons, in which serious injury and even death were not uncommon. From the twelfth century onward, when rules had been introduced and blunted weapons were used in one-on-one contests, tournaments could be

so ferocious that knights began wearing heavier, specially designed armor to reduce risk of injury if they were struck by a lance or thrown to the ground.

As the Middle Ages progressed, a knight's armor also became a symbol of status and wealth: the more ornate and elaborately decorated equipment was worn by the higher social classes. The designers of the day did a remarkable job of reflecting dominant fashion trends in the armor they produced. Costs grew as armor became more elaborate and comfortable, and this further increased the social divide between knights and ordinary soldiers. Long after its usefulness on the battlefield had ceased, ornate armor continued to be worn to denote rank for ceremonial purposes.

BELOW: *In his bronze tomb effigy in Trinity Chapel, Canterbury Cathedral, executed in 1376 (the year of his death), Edward, the Black Prince, wears plate body armor with a chain-mail coif.*

AKETONS AND TABARDS

The *aketon*, a quilted garment worn underneath the chain-mail tunic, or *hauberk*, and body armor, was intended to reduce rubbing and provide a degree of comfort. As the Middle Ages progressed, *surcoats*, more commonly known today as *tabards*, came to be worn over the top of mail or plate armor.

THE AKETON

The padded aketon provided additional protection to the wearer, spreading the shock received by the impact of weapons on chain-mail or plate armor and further slowing the progress of the points of sword, spears, and arrows. It was effective enough in that regard that many of the poorer foot soldiers wore the aketon as their only form of armor, sometimes reinforced with leather or metal strips at key points for added protection.

The term *aketon* was used interchangeably with *gambeson,* although the latter may have been worn over the hauberk rather than underneath it and may, therefore, have been of a more elaborate design. Aketons and gambesons were made of fiber and stuffed with linen, horse hair, or, in the case of those worn by less affluent soldiers, straw, grass, or any other suitable material to hand. No original examples have survived, so our knowledge of them is restricted to the evidence provided in artwork and the historical records of the period. Another term, *pourpoint*, was also used to describe a close-fitting padded garment that was worn under armor, and it seems this item was smart enough in style to be worn in public after a knight's armor was removed.

Given that they were hidden from view, knights' aketons could be relatively plain garments worn in a mix of colors and styles. The length and broad shape were probably determined by the style of hauberk worn. Wide openings would have been provided at the neck and arms to allow maximum freedom of movement. Visual evidence suggests that some aketons had a high collar to protect the neck from slashing weapons. Most seem to have been laced or buttoned at the front. They were probably tight fitting to reduce rubbing and to ensure comfort when worn with the hauberk.

THE TABARD

Hanging to mid-calf and generally open at the sides and sleeveless, the tabard, in

LEFT: *Besides its practical function of protecting armor, the long tabard also offered a way of displaying heraldic emblems, as depicted in this fourteenth-century English book of hours.*

ABOVE: *King Richard I of England (reigned 1189–99) wears a short tabard decorated with the lion of England and the fleur-de-lis of France, in this stained-glass image in the church of Ashby-de-la-Zouch in Leicestershire, England.*

its plain form, was also worn as an outer garment by peasants. For a knight, it not only offered a degree of insulation but also protected his armor from corrosion in wet conditions. Because it was worn on the outside of the armor, it seems likely that knights would have quickly sought to improve the appearance of the garment. Eventually it played an important role in battlefield identification by bearing the coat of arms or other insignia of the wearer, although little real evidence of this exists before the thirteenth century.

The tabard appears to have been in common use among knights on the Crusades from the late eleventh century, probably gaining in popularity because it was a simple and inexpensive means of protecting armor from the elements.

It may well be that this was something the Christian knights learned from their Muslim opponents, who were obviously used to exertion in the tough climatic conditions of the Holy Land. Interaction between Christian knights from different parts of Europe would have spread the fashion and ensured its wider distribution when the crusaders returned home.

Later, more ornate tabards, which were often much shorter, became a common form of dress for knights and the social elite, even when they were not wearing armor. Increasingly, the tabard was also employed as a means of displaying the heraldic emblems of noble families as well as creating uniforms for household staff. Pictorial evidence suggests that some tabards were masterpieces of the medieval fashion designer's art, incorporating rich colors and patterns, elaborate silk or fur linings, and exquisitely detailed embroidery. Tabards are still worn in

ABOVE: *Tabards (two at right) were worn over armor. The knight at left is wearing a padded aketon under his mail armor. Also shown are chain-mail shirts and coifs (hoods), breastplates, gauntlets, helmets, shields, spurs, and weapons.*

many countries today as ceremonial uniforms, and some modern examples are equally ornate. Often, particular designs and materials are employed to indicate the role or status of the wearer.

BODY ARMOR

Much like the weapons it was intended to defeat, body armor developed relatively slowly until the fourteenth and fifteenth centuries. The most effective component, used in various forms by knights throughout the Middle Ages, was the mail shirt, or *hauberk*. Worn over the padded aketon, it was an improvement on the relatively inexpensive and easily constructed *lorica hamata* mail shirt worn by Roman legionnaires in the third and fourth centuries as their primary protection against the weapons of the day, and on the more expensive and robust Roman cuirass, formed by linking large strips of bronze or iron with leather straps. The Romans had also used "scale armor," manufactured by threading scales of bronze or iron together.

Medieval chain mail was probably more efficient than any of these forms of Roman armor. Hauberks of the Middle Ages would have offered reasonable protection from blows with sharp-edged weapons such as swords, and could even damage those sharp edges. Additionally, they helped spread the shock received from blunt weapons such as maces and hammers.

MAKING CHAIN MAIL

Chain mail was constructed from thousands of iron rings, each of which was linked to four others, arranged in rows. The rings—with average diameters varying between ¼ and ½ inch (6–12 mm)—were most commonly made from beaten wire. They were joined by riveting, a process that remained essentially unchanged throughout the medieval period in Europe.

Solid rings—disks with the centers punched out—possibly formed from a sheet of metal, might also have been used by medieval armorers, although little evidence of this exists and, unless they were simply threaded onto cloth, riveted rings would still have been needed to join them together. It seems unlikely that two methods of manufacture would have been sustained in Europe for any extended period, and riveted rings certainly seem to have

BELOW: *In this anachronistic illustration from a fourteenth-century French manuscript, Charlemagne (c. 742–814) and his army wear armor from the High Middle Ages.*

been the dominant form. (Oriental mail shirts, on the other hand, were often made without linking the rings, an approach that most likely limited their effectiveness.)

Unlike many other components of a knight's armor, which required high levels of craftsmanship, chain-mail rings could potentially have been manufactured by relatively unskilled laborers under the supervision of an experienced armorer. The ability to produce large quantities of chain-mail armor at a reasonable cost was no doubt important to rulers in an age in which military clashes were frequent.

The hauberk was improved throughout the Middle Ages. Longer sleeves were added, together with mail stockings to protect the mounted knight's dangerously exposed legs, which were at just the right height for a foot soldier to attack with sword or pike—serious leg injuries would have made it very difficult for a knight to fight on if he were unhorsed. Splits were provided at the front and rear of the hauberk for easier riding, and links or laces were used to ensure a tight fit and necessary connections to helmets and other equipment. Mail gloves or mittens were provided for the hands, and a mail hood, or *coif,* was worn to protect the neck, face, and head.

THE PROS AND CONS OF MAIL ARMOR

In addition to its relatively simple construction, the hauberk had the benefit of being easily shaped to the human body through the simple method of addition or subtraction of rings, and field repairs were straightforward. These would have been important considerations for knights, who spent large sums on armor for themselves and their retinues and who would often wish to pass the armor on to their sons and other family members. The

ABOVE: *This fifteenth-century mail hauberk would have been worn underneath plate armor to provide extra protection.*

drawbacks of chain-mail armor included its relatively heavy weight and its limited effectiveness against arrows, spears, and thrusting weapons. However, the fact that it remained in service for so long suggests it was considered superior to any of the alternatives available in the mid to late Middle Ages.

Hauberks were also effective as an extra layer of protection under other materials. Indeed, even when plate

armor became commonplace, the hauberk was still worn underneath it to provide added protection and as a means of covering any areas of the body that were left unprotected by the plate—for example, at joins in the armor—and therefore might be particularly vulnerable.

PLATE ARMOR

The advent of plate armor in the thirteenth century was a major technological breakthrough. Although it had been known in various forms since ancient times, plate armor had fallen into disuse during the early Middle Ages and it probably only reemerged in response to the twin drivers of advanced manufacturing processes and the need to defeat an improved mix of battlefield weapons, which included the deadly crossbow and, eventually, firearms.

Correctly shaped plate could deflect cutting and slashing weapons and missiles such as arrows, and was far more effective than mail. Like today's Kevlar and steel body armor, medieval plate gave a tremendous advantage to those who could afford to employ it. Troops that were well led and well protected were difficult to defeat. Indeed, the medieval "arms race" was about capitalizing on weaknesses in the enemy armor and, at the same time, protecting one's own troops better.

Progress in the development of plate armor was slow, however. Initially, it was used to protect only small areas of the body, such as the elbows and knees, though later it was also used to cover the hands, lower legs, arms, feet, and head. In the early period, plates were sometimes attached to the inside of leather coats to provide a sturdy and overlapping "coat of plates" worn over the hauberk, a solution that probably proved effective enough until articulated plate armor was developed in the late

ABOVE: *This 1618 portrait by Peter Paul Rubens shows the Holy Roman Emperor Maximilian I (reigned 1493–1519) wearing an elaborately decorated suit of armor.*

The armourers, accomplishing the knights, / With busy hammers closing rivets up, / Give dreadful note of preparation.

WILLIAM SHAKESPEARE, *HENRY V,* **ACT 4, PROLOGUE (1599)**

thirteenth and early fourteenth centuries. As with any overlapping armor, the wearer was vulnerable at the gaps and joins, and getting a tight and comfortable fit was difficult.

During the fourteenth and fifteenth centuries, new construction methods and the need to protect soldiers against new, more deadly weapons led to the development of fitted breastplates, backplates, and, ultimately, the full suit of armor. Plate could be fitted rigidly where necessary, and the use of hinges and other ingenious mechanisms allowed a good degree of movement.

ARMOR AS A FASHION STATEMENT

Well-made plate armor eventually became a clear indication of the social standing and importance of its wearer. It also provided an opportunity to mix art and fashion in a knight's attire. Fashionable armor reflected the tastes and clothing styles of the day. Ridges, grooves, and patterned edges were incorporated. Some such features, however—embossing, for example—could weaken the plate, so although ornate armor was undoubtedly worn on the battlefield, the most elaborate items were usually reserved for ceremonial functions. Such was the case, too, with Classical-style armor, modeled on the armor worn by ancient Greek and Roman soldiers, which became popular in some countries.

Plate armor continued to be worn ceremonially by the social elite long after its usefulness on the battlefield had passed, following the introduction of effective firearms in the fifteenth and sixteenth centuries. Even today, many armies have special units that dress in suits of plate armor for ceremonial functions.

RIGHT: *Englishman Gilbert de Clare, who was knighted on the eve of a battle, wears early plate armor in this thirteenth-century stained-glass window at Tewkesbury Abbey, Gloucestershire, in southwestern England.*

THE COMPONENTS OF PLATE ARMOR

Having donned their aketons and full or partial hauberks, medieval knights readying for a battle began the more complex and time-consuming task of fitting a full suit of armor. Although this was a less cumbersome task than some histories suggest, knights still needed assistance to dress fully for action.

Equipment varied across medieval Europe, but the key components were broadly the same for all well-financed knights, and styles would have passed fairly quickly across state borders. What worked would have been copied, whereas less effective equipment would have been discarded over time by those who could afford to.

FOOT AND LEG PROTECTION

Dressing from the ground up, knights first placed their *sabatons* on their feet. Essentially plate shoes, sabatons were articulated along their length to allow movement of the foot. Heel sections might be hinged on the side for ease of fitting. Some sabatons came to a long point at the toes, although these were probably better suited to ceremonial activities than battle. The overall shape and size of sabatons would have been limited by the need for them to fit comfortably into stirrups. Those knights who were unable to afford sabatons probably continued to wear mail or hardened leather shoes on their feet to provide protection while mounted.

Greaves were shaped plates that pro-tected the front and rear of a knight's lower legs. Generally hinged on one side and closed with hooks on the other, they would normally be attached directly to the accompanying sabaton. Chain mail would protect any area exposed at the join.

Although the hauberk might extend down to cover the thighs, a strike from below could slip underneath it and do considerable damage. Positioned by leather straps, *cuisses* were shaped to

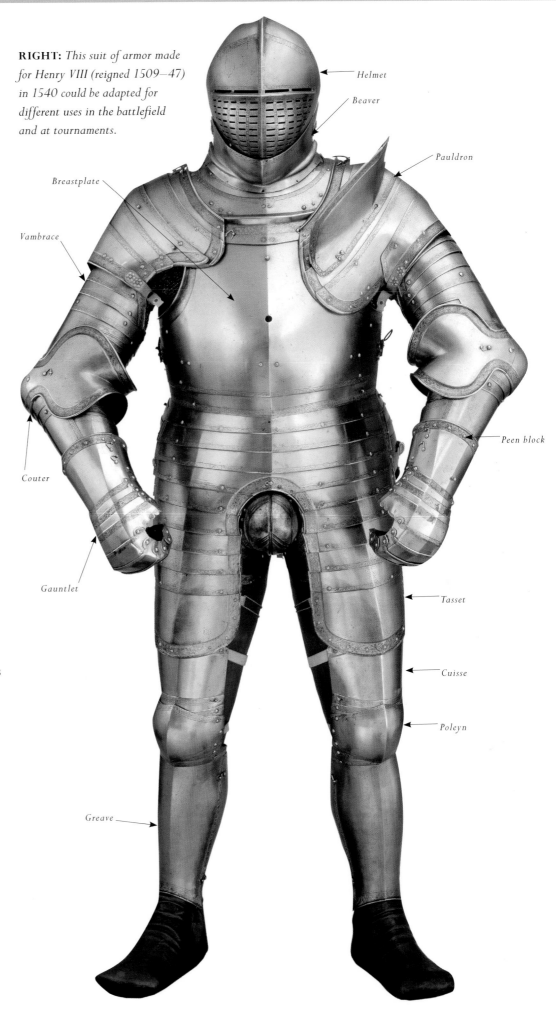

RIGHT: *This suit of armor made for Henry VIII (reigned 1509–47) in 1540 could be adapted for different uses in the battlefield and at tournaments.*

Helmet

Beaver

Pauldron

Breastplate

Vambrace

Peen block

Couter

Gauntlet

Tasset

Cuisse

Poleyn

Greave

LEFT: *Tassets designed to cover the front of the wearer's thighs are attached to this sixteenth-century breastplate by leather straps. Each tasset is made of* lames *(strips of plate) that are linked together by moveable rivets.*

the thigh and covered at the knee by a set of articulated plates called a *poleyn*. This arrangement provided protection while mounted and allowed some reasonable bending of the knee when the knight was fighting dismounted. The hauberk would continue to provide some protection for those areas that could not be covered by the cuisses.

PROTECTING SHOULDERS, ARMS, AND HANDS

Protection and freedom of movement were perhaps even more important for a knight's arms than they were for his legs, because he had to be able to wield a variety of weapons in close combat. *Pauldrons* were fitted to protect the shoulders—which were particularly vulnerable to a downward strike from a sword or a mace. Arms were protected by *vambraces* in much the same way as the legs were protected by cuisses. Articulated *couters* performed a similar function to poleyns, protecting the elbow while still allowing a knight to bend his arm.

Protecting the hands was obviously important in battle, and throughout the Middle Ages knights used a variety of means to do so—from simple leather gloves to the well-known *gauntlets* made of plate which combined high levels of protection with excellent flexibility. Before plate became widely available, chain mail was used to cover the backs of the hands, often as an extension of the sleeve of the hauberk in what were known as *mufflers*.

BREASTPLATES AND BACKPLATES

The knight's now familiar *breastplate* was first introduced toward the end of the fourteenth century. It was progressively extended in length to cover both chest and torso. Later versions were attached by straps to two articulated plate *tassets*, which protected the thighs and afforded reasonable movement at the waist.

A solid *backplate*, which was similar to the breastplate in design and construction, was connected to the latter with straps, to provide protection at the rear.

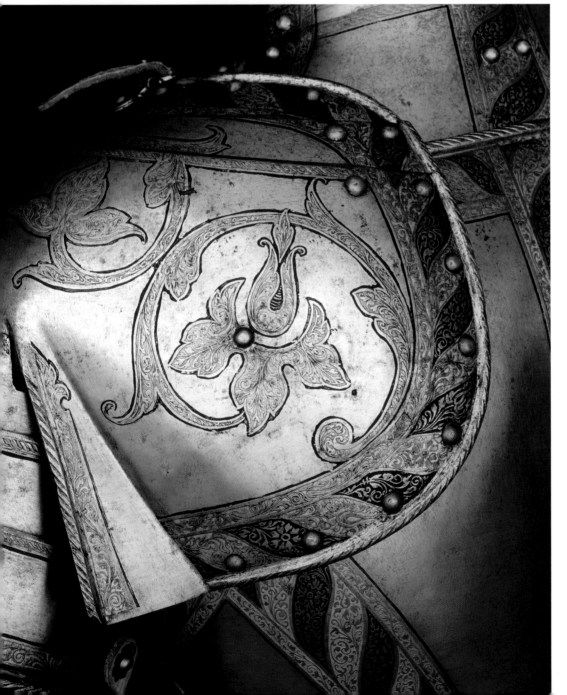

LEFT: *The elaborate, stylized blackened and gilt decoration on the pauldron, or shoulder armor, of this German field and tournament plate armor, dating from around 1590, displays the superb craftsmanship of the armorer's art.*

Unsurprisingly, given that it was the largest and the most prominent piece of armor worn by a knight, the breastplate benefited from further developments over time. One key improvement was the addition of a lance rest, or *arrêt*, on the right-hand side, which helped a charging knight hold his lance couched under his right arm and prevented it from slipping backward on contact; the rest was hinged so that it could be folded out of the way when it was not needed. Another significant development to the breastplate was the addition of riveted bars below the neck and on its arm openings to deflect weapons before they could strike the vulnerable areas of the body.

HELMETS

Protecting the knight's head was one of the more difficult challenges facing medieval armorers: they had to balance protection with providing a reasonable degree of visibility. Thin slits in a helmet, or helm, might protect the eyes from an arrow, for example, but that was not much use if the knight had no peripheral vision and thus was vulnerable to a surprise attack from the left or right. Unfortunately, a wide field of view could only be achieved at the cost of reduced protection for the head and face—a vulnerability that was well understood by an opponent.

The Bayeux Tapestry suggests that a basic conical helmet, similar in design to the *spangenhelm*—which was in use from the late Roman period, long before 1066, the subject of the tapestry—was commonly worn by the Norman knight. The helmets illustrated in the tapestry probably would have been shaped out of leather or metal (although historians are not sure), and they have a noseguard protecting the front of the face. It is clear from some of the images in the tapestry, however, that the neck was protected by a mail coif worn under the helmet and extending below its base at the front and rear.

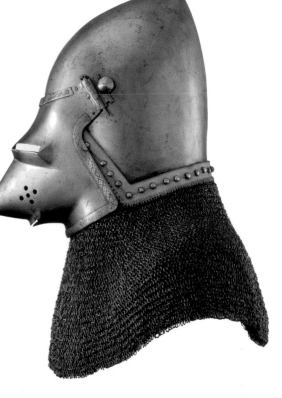

LEFT: *Early medieval helmets would have been similar to this example from a seventh-century burial site at Sutton Hoo, Suffolk, England.*
BELOW: *In this pointed helmet, known as a bascinet, which was made in northern Italy, the steel skull and detachable visor are each forged from single pieces of steel.*

Helmets were slowly improved to provide more protection for the cheeks and face, culminating, before the advent of articulated plate armor, with the large, heavy, flat-topped helm so well-known in medieval legends. The development of plate armor eventually allowed armorers to make elaborate visored helmets, which could be closed or opened as needed.

Some historians believe the opening of the visor was a sign of friendly intent between knights and that this was the origin of the salute used in many armies today, although little contemporary evidence can be found for this theory. There is no doubt, however, that ornate, and occasionally fearsome, helmet designs were used to identify important figures and intimidate their opponents on the battlefield and in tournaments.

A THRIVING INDUSTRY

The manufacture of high-quality plate armor led to the emergence of a major industry that combined superb craftsmanship with the basic elements of early mass production. Based primarily in northern Italy and southern Germany, but common throughout Europe, family-owned companies produced tailored individual armor for wealthy knights, as well as less expensive equipment for ordinary foot soldiers. Each region developed its own distinctive style of design and decoration which influenced armor technology and fashion across Europe. Many kings retained their own armorers at court and history even shows evidence of mail-order purchases.

HORSE ARMOR

A powerful warhorse was essential if a knight were to be effective on the battlefield, and riding the better breeds, such as destriers and coursers, further demonstrated a knight's social standing and wealth. Warhorses were costly to purchase and maintain. A well-equipped knight needed several to fulfill his responsibilities. Three seems to have been the minimum number to allow for injuries and exhaustion, but some accounts show four or more horses for knights and similar numbers for their squires. As a result, feed for the horses was often a greater logistical challenge than supplying the men who rode them.

Given the high cost of horses, the knight's vulnerability when dismounted, and the fact that cavalry would have been a prime target for enemy archers and other missile troops, it is surprising that horse armor did not appear until the late twelfth century. Whether horse armor was gradually improved in response to some particular advance in weapons or tactics is unclear. Tournaments, rather than the demands of battle, may well have driven the design of horse armor in the late Middle Ages, with designs becoming more complex, ornate, and heavier to complement the increasingly elaborate attire of the rider.

AN UNCERTAIN HISTORY

It is difficult to track the development of horse armor because much of what was worn was covered by a large cloth *caparison*, which obscures the detail in contemporary illustrations. (A warhorse's caparison would often bear the rider's colors or coat of arms, like the knight's tabard or quilted gambeson; presumably, it also provided the horse with some degree of insulation from the weather.) It does seem unlikely, however, that horse armor was used in the early Middle Ages—none is illustrated in the Bayeux Tapestry—although conclusive evidence is difficult to find and the tapestry itself is still the subject of much heated debate.

From the thirteenth century, mail *trappers* were used to protect the front of the horse, with leather used on the sides and flanks. It is also likely that leather was used to protect others parts of the

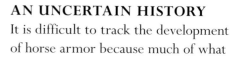

LEFT: *In this illustration from Jean Marot's* The Conquest of Genoa (1507), *Louis XII of France (reigned 1498–1515) leaves the city of Alessandria, in northern Italy, which he has just taken. His surcoat and horse's caparison bear his royal emblem of a beehive surrounded by bees.*

FIT FOR A KING, GIFTED BY AN EMPEROR

Horse armor became increasingly elaborate in the late Middle Ages, and more and more a feature of ceremonial functions than of serious battlefield equipment. A surviving *bard*, given as a gift to Henry VIII by Holy Roman Emperor Maximilian I to mark the English king's marriage to Catherine of Aragon, for example, is beautifully decorated and was originally silvered and gilded at great expense. Unfortunately, wear through constant cleaning and the passage of time has diminished some of its original splendor. Such a gift was clearly not intended for the battlefield, and Henry presumably used it only on important state occasions.

LEFT: *Henry's bard, probably made by Italian or Flemish craftsmen, is covered with the badges of the houses of Aragon and Tudor, and the initials of bride and groom are intertwined at the base of the skirt.*

horse, including the head. In some cases, quilted padding or even coverings similar to the knight's "coat of plates" may have been used. Some medieval images show a full coat of mail, which, if these records are accurate, must have been an extremely heavy load for even the strongest of warhorses.

In the mid-thirteenth century, progress came with the introduction of plate armor. Plate brought the same advantages to the protection of warhorses as it did to the knights who rode them, along with the same need for ingenious design and first-rate craftsmanship. Plate for man and horse must also have given mounted knights another brief period of superiority on the battlefield: they and their chargers were relatively safe from missile fire and unstoppable at close quarters.

MEDIEVAL BATTLE TANKS

Resting on a padded garment or lined with fabric to reduce rubbing and assist in weight distribution and shock absorption, a full set of horse plate armor, known as a *bard*, included a *shaffron* to cover the horse's head and face, a *crinnet* to protect the back of the neck, a *peytral* to cover the vulnerable chest, *flanchards* over the mid-section, and a *crupper* to protect the flanks and rear. Freedom of movement was

obviously an important consideration, and a horse's plate armor—like that of a knight—was not as heavy as it looked.

As a complete unit, a group of knights on chargers was a formidable battlefield weapon. Protected from most threats, the mounted warriors could move, reasonably unmolested by missile weapons, into positions from which they could launch devastating charges—which often proved to be decisive.

In addition to the armor worn by the horse and rider, the saddle provided extra protection to the knight through a high pommel at the front and a high cantle at the rear, both of which also helped the rider to stay seated when in action. Stirrups, originally introduced in the tenth century, would have provided a stable platform for the knight during a charge and reduced the likelihood of him being unhorsed in battle. Without doubt, mounted knights were the battle tanks of their day.

LEFT: *A fully armored knight and horse proved to be one of the most devastating weapons in the medieval arsenal. This armor was made by Joerg Seusenhofer in Innsbruck, Austria, about 1500.*

Weapons

The two weapons most commonly associated with medieval knights are the lance and the sword. However, from a very early age, the knight was also trained in the use of a wide range of other weapons and he would have been equally at home with daggers, spears, and maces.

The warcraft of medieval knights is often reduced to the myth that combatants crudely bludgeoned each another or hacked and slashed savagely with no technique or skill. But the sophistication of the training required for the range of weapons employed is borne out by the fighting manuals that have survived, particularly those of the fifteenth century. Books by such masters as the Friulian Fiore dei Liberi (published *c.* 1410), Sigmund Ringeck (*c.* 1440), and Hans Talhoffer (1467), have left detailed testimony of the complex range of moves and actions required to use many of these weapons effectively. For example, the fifteenth-century German school of fighting explored by Talhoffer in his *Fight Book (Fechtbuch)* of 1467 includes: judicial and personal combat; armored and unarmored techniques, using poleax, dagger, sword, long sword, and buckler; wrestling;

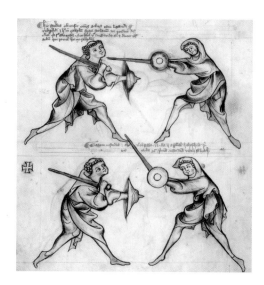

mounted combat with long swords, a long sword against a lance, and a lance against a crossbow; and mounted hand-to-hand fighting.

Many of the illustrations demonstrate the brutal nature of the fighting—the two adversaries are locked together in a life-and-death embrace from which

LEFT: *Two men fence with sword and buckler in this illustration from the late thirteenth-century German* Tower Fightbook. *Each page of this manuscript is divided into two scenes illustrating different guards and methods of attack.*

only one emerges alive. Because of the inherently violent nature of society in the Middle Ages, there was often no distinction between the civilian and the military application of the martial arts.

LANCE AND SWORD

The spear was popular throughout the Middle Ages. It was different from what we would think of as the lance, even when used from horseback. A spear is a thrusting or throwing weapon. When it was employed from horseback, the horse became a platform from which to fight and thrust down from at opponents. When a spear was couched under the arm of the mounted knight, however, it had a different effect altogether; used this way, it became what is generally regarded, from the eleventh century onward, as the lance. To suit the new technique, the weapon became longer and heavier. But even after the spear and lance became distinct weapons, knights might resort to cutting down their lances in length and fighting with what were effectively spears if they found themselves on foot rather than horseback.

The sword is the most celebrated of the knight's weapons. Due to its high cost, in the early medieval period only

HAND-TO-HAND COMBAT

Wrestling was an important skill for a knight to acquire, because it taught positional sense and defensive skills and because the moves learned formed the basis of many different fighting techniques with weapons. Once two people were engaged in melee combat, grapples could be used to disarm an opponent or to throw him to the ground while keeping one's own footing— which was a vital requirement on a crowded, chaotic battlefield. If a knight became disarmed, a good knowledge of wrestling might be enough to save his life, even against an armed opponent. However, wrestling in armor was certainly a skill that needed to be practiced.

the aristocratic classes could afford fine examples. The sword was the weapon of leadership, a ceremonial object, and a deadly tool. It was the symbol of law and order, just as the dagger was the symbol of thievery and lawlessness.

OTHER BATTLE WEAPONS

The shield was an important defensive weapon rather than a piece of armor. It evolved through the period and, at least in some of its forms, could also be used offensively in combat.

The warhorse can also be considered, and was certainly used as, a weapon; indeed, it was possibly the most important piece of military equipment the knight possessed. Improvements in

ABOVE: *Medieval warfare was not the romantic escapade of valor and chivalry depicted in the literature. It was bloody, brutal, and chaotic. In this fifteenth-century illustration, mounted knights stab each other with swords and run each other through with lances, while infantry engage in deadly hand-to-hand combat.*

warhorses came about following the introduction of new technologies and as a result of generations of selective breeding that produced the destrier: fast, strong, aggressive, agile and, most importantly, a horse that was capable of carrying an armored knight in battle.

Dagger fights were often quick and deadly for both opponents. Knowing

how to use and defend against a dagger were essential knightly skills. Although it was not one of the primary weapons on the battlefield, the dagger developed in such a way as to make it ideally suited to piercing armor. As such, it was often employed for the deathblow.

The ax proved to be an extremely valuable weapon for some knights in the medieval period; a light version designed specially for use on horseback evolved. Blunt weapons, such as clubs and, later, maces, could inflict serious injury on an opponent and remained popular throughout the Middle Ages. They found particular prominence in tournaments and judicial contests, as did the halberd and, its later form, the poleax.

LEFT: *In the Bayeux Tapestry, the Normans are shown using kite-shaped shields at the Battle of Hastings against the Anglo-Saxons.*

SHIELDS

Often in the Middle Ages the most effective defensive armament was the shield. It was produced in a number of different shapes, sizes, and materials, depending upon what it was likely to be defending against. The shield could also be employed in an offensive way, either in combination with another weapon, or even, in some circumstances, on its own. One of the marks of a warrior, the shield was commonly buried with its user. And it might be used to carry his injured or dead body from the field of battle.

SHIELD DESIGN

Carolingian shields were generally large, round, concave, and made from covered wood. By the eleventh century, the shield was often kite shaped. On horseback, this narrower shield was more maneuverable, and its greater length provided the horseman's legs with some protection. This shape also benefited the knight when on foot because its sharp bottom edge could be "planted" in the ground, while its wider part was overlapped with

a shield on either side, thus producing a shield wall—a favorite, effective tactic used against cavalry. Kite-shaped shields can be seen being used by Norman knights in the Bayeux Tapestry. They were probably made in a similar way to the large rounded shields used by the Anglo-Saxons (also noted for their shield walls), with a wooden frame being covered with leather and a metal boss, and possibly trimmed with a metal rim.

This kite shield dominated warfare until the start of the thirteenth century. At that point, the shield began to evolve into a shorter and wider triangular shape. This reflected the development of more effective leg armor, which meant there was no need to use the shield to protect the lower body to the same degree.

By the early fifteenth century, the shield had fallen out of favor as knights became increasingly well armored and were almost always mounted. However, metal versions did continue to be used for the joust. Some late medieval shields had a *bouche*, or notch, in the top right-hand corner to support the lance. This meant that the shield did not have to be lowered quite as far during the charge, and thus it maintained its maximum defensive effectiveness.

In the fifteenth century, infantry, too, began to adopt a range of different shield designs. One of these was the *pavise*, a large oblong shield that provided protection for the whole body. It was popular with crossbowmen, who could prop it up with a wooden brace, allowing the shield to stand on its own while they sheltered behind it to reload their weapons. It was the lack of pavises (they were still with the baggage carts)

THE SHIELD AS DEADLY WEAPON

The shield was not simply about defense. For example, Hans Talhoffer's *Fight Book* (1467), one of the most influential and lavishly illustrated fighting manuals of the fifteenth century, has substantial sections dedicated to the use of various types of shield in combination with different types of weapon. One section demonstrates the use of the specialized dueling shield—an oblong made of wood approximately 6½ feet (2 m) tall, slightly concave, with a rectangular boss allowing room for the hands to grip a central pole that ends in a sharp spike at either end. The graphic illustrations show exactly how deadly the shield could be in the right hands.

ABOVE: *This mid-fifteenth-century pavise bears the arms of Zwickau and Saxony in Germany. Made of wood, it is covered with painted gesso.*
BELOW: *In the eleventh-century Greek* Scylitzes Chronicle, *the soldiers of the Byzantine emperor, Basil I (reigned 867–86), bearing long shields, desert their general in the face of Arab forces, who carry round shields.*

> *The two combatants stand in their guards with shields and wooden clubs, according to the Frankish law. God grant them good fortune.*
>
> **HANS TALHOFFER,** *FIGHT BOOK (FECHTBUCH, 1467)*

that probably contributed to the defeat of the Genoese crossbowmen fighting for the French by English archers at the Battle of Crécy in 1346.

Other foot soldiers used the *targe*, or *target*, a fairly large, concave shield that came in a variety of shapes, although it was often round. It was equipped with *enarmes*, or leather straps, which allowed it to be attached to the left forearm and gripped with the left hand.

SWASHBUCKLING

The buckler was a smaller, often concave, round shield with a large boss that looked like an inverted bowl protruding from the center. On the battlefield, its smaller size meant that it was less useful as a defense against missile fire, but, if used properly, it was effective protection against weapons such as swords and maces. Its small size and light weight had advantages: it was easily carried and therefore could form part of the everyday armament of a knight even when not fighting on the field of battle.

The buckler was often made from *cuir bouilli,* or boiled leather, but also wood enforced with metal (particularly for the boss). It was gripped by a single crossbar or handle on the inside of the boss—rather than being attached to the forearm with straps, as were many of the other types of shield of the period. It was used in conjunction with a single-handed weapon, often a sword.

This small shield was very versatile: it could be used to protect the sword hand, to deflect bladed attacks, to mask the position of the sword hand from the view of the opponent, or as a metal "fist" to punch with the boss or the rim, or to "bind" the opponent's arm and/ or weapon and thus disarm him. This sword and buckler combination was popular across Europe from the twelfth century onward, and it is the source of the term *swashbuckler.*

SWORDS

The most celebrated of the knightly weapons was the sword. Its symbolism was powerful, and often a sword would be passed down through a family for many generations. The sword was the knight's constant companion.

MAKING A MEDIEVAL SWORD

The sword was a costly item, reflecting the huge investment required to produce a fine weapon. But as the Middle Ages progressed, swordmaking techniques improved and swords became cheaper.

To begin, the swordsmith needed a bar made of strips of iron and/or steel, twisted together, then forged to ensure the right blend of hardness and tensile strength. This was heated until red-hot, and hammered again and again to reduce its thickness. The *fuller*, the groove that runs down the center of the blade to decrease its weight while retaining its strength, was shaped at this stage.

Once this long hammering process was completed, the edges of the weapon were ground by successively finer stones and files until the desired sharpness was achieved. Below the blade, but part of the same piece of metal, a *tang* extended. To this, the *quillon* (crossguard), grip, and *pommel* were added. Finally, the blade

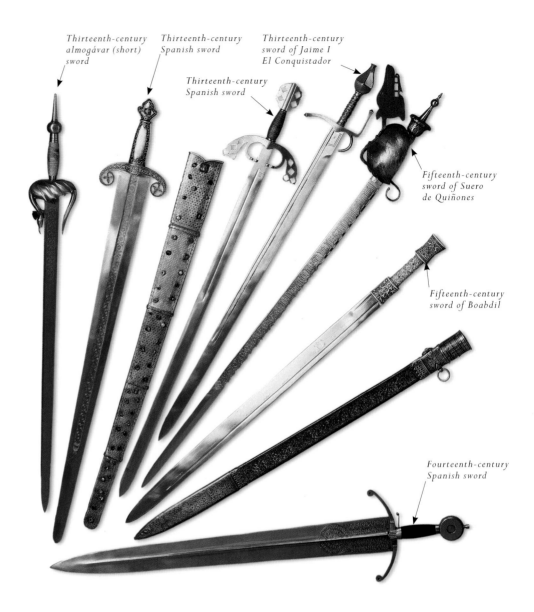

Thirteenth-century almogávar (short) sword

Thirteenth-century Spanish sword

Thirteenth-century Spanish sword

Thirteenth-century sword of Jaime I El Conquistador

Fifteenth-century sword of Suero de Quiñones

Fifteenth-century sword of Boabdil

Fourteenth-century Spanish sword

ABOVE: *Like armor, medieval swords changed over time. These Spanish swords were made between the thirteenth and fifteenth centuries.*

was polished. The swordmaker often inscribed his name on the weapon. Modern attempts to replicate these swords have proved extremely difficult, reflecting the high level of craftsmanship of the period.

USING THE SWORD

Due to its expense, the sword was associated with knights rather than ordinary soldiers. Thus, from the twelfth century on, it was primarily used by the cavalry. A knight needed a heavy blade carrying momentum to slash at an opponent from horseback: the sword of the High Middle Ages was thick and parallel sided with

sharp edges so it could slash through armor. Partly as a response to improvements in armor, the sword blade began to be made more pointed, and with a taper that gradually increased over time. This had the effect of shifting the point of balance of the weapon back toward the hilt, providing the user with far greater control. In turn, this changed the way a knight used his sword, from forceful, occasionally wild, slashing to more sophisticated and subtle movements and thrusts. The sharper point of the later style of sword was more effective in piercing plate armor.

LEFT: *This illustration from a mid-fourteenth-century chronicle shows the king of France killing his opponent with his arming sword.*

SWORDS WITH FANTASTIC PROPERTIES

In the Arthurian legends, the sword Excalibur had magical powers and was associated with the rightful king of England. When it was first drawn, the blade blinded Arthur's enemies with a light that was as bright as 30 torches. The scabbard of the sword also protected its wearer from wounds. Excalibur was returned to the Lady of the Lake as Arthur lay dying.

In the twelfth-century *Song of Roland (La chanson de Roland)*, Count Roland's sword, Durendal, is said to contain holy relics within its golden hilt. At one point, Roland attempts to destroy the sword to prevent it from being captured by the ambushing Saracens, but Durendal proves to be indestructible, so he tries to protect it by lying on it as he dies.

RIGHT: *Siegfried, the hero of Norse mythology, slays the dragon Fafnir with his sword, Nothung.*

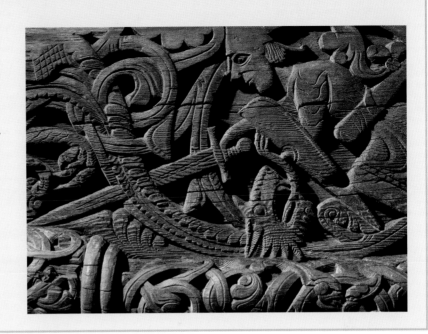

TYPES OF SWORD

When does an arming sword (the typical single-handed sword of the medieval knight) become a long sword, or a great sword, or a two-handed sword? Instead of defining swords by length, it is useful to distinguish between them according to how they were held.

An arming sword's handle can only comfortably fit one hand. A long sword (also known as a "bastard" or "hand-and-a-half" sword) can fit two hands, but it remains light enough to be used with just one hand. But the two-handed, or *great sword*, has a handle and mass that clearly requires both hands.

Typically, the arming sword, used with a shield or buckler, was the knight's standard military sword (often, ambiguously, called a "war sword") until the late thirteenth century. A knight would wear it even when not in combat.

Longer weapons were made possible as steel-working technology developed. The long sword was an extremely versatile weapon. Worn as a sidearm off the battlefield, it was the longest weapon that could reasonably be drawn in one movement from a belt-slung scabbard. It was

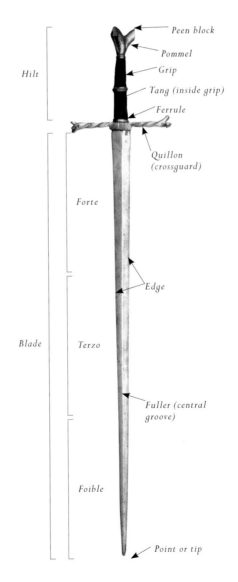

Peen block
Pommel
Grip
Hilt
Tang (inside grip)
Ferrule
Quillon (crossguard)
Forte
Blade
Terzo
Edge
Fuller (central groove)
Foible
Point or tip

LEFT: *In this German-made sword of the fifteenth century, the pommel and quillon are of gilt bronze and the wooden grip is carved.*

maneuverable enough to provide a strong defense, meaning there was no need to carry a shield or buckler, yet was sufficiently light to allow the other hand to engage in disarms, locks, and throws. In battle, it would often be used with one hand on the hilt and the other three-quarters of the way up the blade. As firearms made heavy armor increasingly redundant, this type of sword became lighter, and it evolved into the thrusting weapon we know as the rapier.

The big two-handed great sword is associated with some of the German *landnechts*, the mercenary foot soldiers of the late fifteenth and sixteenth centuries. These swords were too large to be used from horseback, but on the battlefield the foot soldiers used them to provide tactical assistance to the more numerous pikemen, causing confusion and disorder among the opposing pike formations by knocking them aside and hacking the points off their weapons.

SPEARS, JAVELINS, AND PIKES

The spear, a popular Roman weapon, retained its popularity well into the Middle Ages. The right to carry a spear was, for a long time, the mark of a free man. The javelin, a specialized type of spear, was much used by the Romans as well. By the fourteenth century, other spear variations—the halberd, poleax, and pike—were formidable weapons.

THE SPEAR AND JAVELIN

Carolingian knights were required to use the spear as their predominant weapon on foot or horseback. The spear was versatile: a line of infantry armed with spears and, most importantly, the discipline to remain firm in the face of a charge, could see off a cavalry attack. The spear could be employed defensively also—against cavalry, for example, it could be thrust, used from horseback, or it could be thrown as a missile weapon. At the Battle of Stirling Bridge in 1297, for example, the Scottish leader, William Wallace, defeated the English knights led by John de Warenne and Hugh de Cressingham by employing *schiltrons*, disciplined spear-wielding infantry. This favored Scottish technique allowed Robert the Bruce to again show what lowly spearmen could do against armored knights, when he defeated the English army of King Edward II (reigned 1307–28) at Bannockburn in 1314.

Medieval spearheads were made in many shapes and sizes, including angular, triangular, leaf shaped, lozenge shaped, and barbed. If they were designed to be thrust rather than thrown, spears might have "wings" to prevent the tip penetrating too far. This meant that they could then be retrieved easily from a body and used on the next opponent.

The Roman legions used a javelin they called a *pilum*, weighted at its tip to aid its range and penetration. If it found its target, the pilum could stick in a shield and the design of its head meant it could not be removed quickly, thus making the shield impossible to use. If the pilum hit a man, its long, thin head allowed it to penetrate armor, but if it missed completely, the same iron head would often bend, making it difficult to throw back. The weapon could also be employed defensively against cavalry. Specialized javelins were not widely popular once the Roman era had passed. However, throwing a spear remained an option.

THE HALBERD AND POLEAX

The halberd emerged in the early fourteenth century and was probably inspired by agricultural implements such as billhooks. It combined the spear and the ax into a single weapon—an ax with a spike on the side opposite the head. In many ways, it looked like a giant tin opener, and this was precisely what it was designed to do: its shape allowed a soldier on foot to hook a knight from his horse and then pierce his armor. The poleax, which developed from

BELOW: *The lethal heads of medieval spears, lances and halberds were extremely varied in shape, their design depending on whether they were designed to be thrown or thrust. The halberd is second from left.*

LEFT: *The pike-wielding Spanish infantry attacking Muslim-held Granada in 1343 face a similar formation of Moorish soldiers, in this illustration painted by the Master of Mary of Burgundy (flourished 1469–83).*
BELOW: *Mounted knights hold their spears up, ready to attack the enemy, in this battle scene that has been attributed to Niccolò da Bologna and was painted about 1380.*

the halberd, was very similar, except that its axhead was smaller and, instead of a spike on the opposite side, there was a hammer for crushing armor.

Because both weapons were also, in effect, spears, they could be used to keep cavalry at bay. Such weapons were also effective against other infantry, whether they were armored or not; particularly in the poleax form, they became popular weapons for dismounted knights, who prized their offensive capabilities.

The halberd was used to devastating effect by the Swiss infantry against the Austrian knights, who were fighting for the Habsburg duke Leopold I at the Battle of Morgarten in 1315. Halberds also caused massive casualties in the fifteenth-century Wars of the Roses, a dynastic struggle for the English throne fought by the rival houses of Lancaster and York between 1455 and 1485.

THE PIKE

In the fourteenth and fifteenth centuries, the infantry spear lengthened significantly to become a pike. This weapon was often 15 to 18 feet (4.5–5.5 m) long. An individual standing alone with a pike was very vulnerable, because it was such an unwieldy weapon. However, once a block of soldiers was armed with pikes—each one held with its butt on the ground, steadied by a foot, and the end pointing toward the enemy with the weapon tips overlapping—the result was a strong defensive formation that was very difficult to penetrate.

This porcupine effect was especially effective against cavalry. From about the late fifteenth century, having moved away from the halberd, the Swiss gained fame for their disciplined organization, which allowed their pike blocks to maneuver efficiently without losing their

cohesion. The pikemen would assume formations such as a hollow square or circle with the pikemen facing outward. These formations in turn increased their army's tactical options. In particular, they offered additional offensive capabilities, as they effectively created highly maneuverable but almost impenetrable blocks of men. Charles the Bold, Duke of Burgundy (1433–77), trained his infantry to combine pikes with archery, the pikemen kneeling on command to allow the archers to shoot over their heads.

With the introduction of firearms in the late Middle Ages, guns were also mixed into the pike formations. A wall of pikes provided a safe haven behind which the gunners could take the time they needed to reload their weapons. Used in this or a similar way, the pike continued to dominate infantry warfare until well into the eighteenth century.

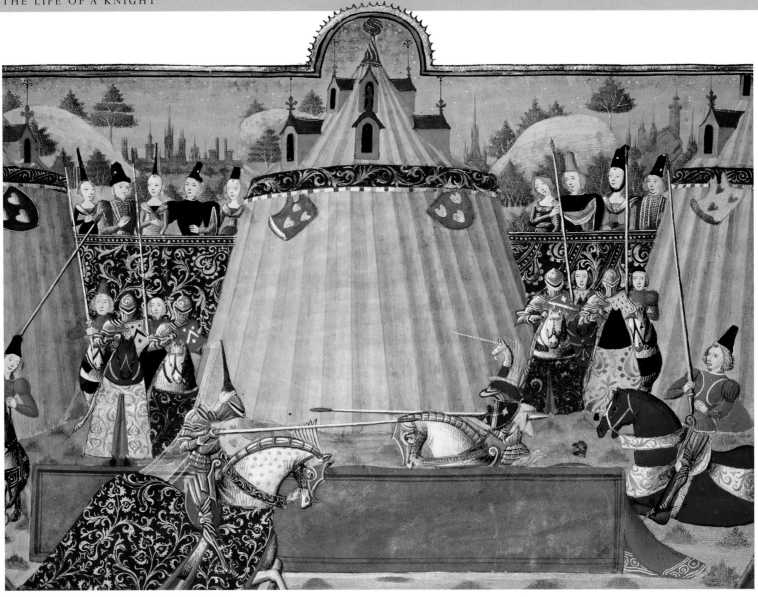

LANCES

The weapon that a mounted knight is most often associated with is the lance. When the lance was held couched firmly under the armpit, a blow from it combined the weights of the lance, the knight, and the horse, which produced an effect far greater than a spear thrust.

The introduction of the stirrup into western Europe in the tenth century helped the knight remain on the horse during combat. An equally important development was the adoption of a deep saddle that acted like an anchor to the horse. A single knight charging was an impressive sight, but, to be truly effective in a battle, a charge needed to be delivered to the enemy en masse. This required coordination and practice.

It was not until the eleventh century that the shock charge really emerged as an effective tactic. The Bayeux Tapestry shows riders with couched lances and some using the weapon over the arm.

By the middle of the twelfth century, the couched lance was employed across Europe. It was the principal weapon of the crusading knights in the Holy Land: their first attack was always a mounted cavalry charge. As well as hitting the opponent, the knight charging with a lance was able to ride through enemy ranks so as to make them panic and flee.

HISTORICAL DEVELOPMENT

Until about 1300, the knight's lance was really a simple pole. Cyprus wood or ash

ABOVE: *The lance was the principal weapon in jousting contests at tournaments, as shown in this early-twentieth-century illustration based on a medieval manuscript illumination.*

was often preferred and the length was about 10 to 12 feet (3–3.5 m), with the end often tipped with a metal head. It grew longer, heavier, and thicker with time and a handguard was incorporated. As the lance became heavier, even though it was designed to be carefully balanced in weight, the weapon became more exhausting to hold in the required position for more than a few moments. It was normal, therefore, to hold the lance upright, resting upon a *fewter*, or felt rest, on the horse's saddle until the last possible moment, when it would be brought down into the couched position. The knight would take aim by maneuvering the whole horse and, if necessary, his body in the saddle to ensure the tip of the lance was on target.

A support for the weapon began to be incorporated into the knight's actual armor. This was called an *arrêt* and was riveted to the solid breastplate to help take some of the massive impact of the strike. As it became more sophisticated, the arrêt could be attached to a spring mechanism so that it clipped shut when it was not in use.

In order to prevent the weight of the lance combined with the force of the blow unbalancing the knight by focusing it all on the right-hand side, the lance point was held to the left of the horse's head, across the body of the knight, and the lance base was held firmly under the knight's right armpit.

TRAINING

The term *quintain* refers to the targets employed by knights when practicing the use of a lance. Common types included a shield, a board, and even a mannequin on a pole. The knight would ride toward the object and attempt to strike it with the point of his lance.

The tournament was where the use of the lance in formation with other knights could be practiced. Contests could involve large numbers of knights fighting in teams; jousts were the one-on-one version of such fights.

Such games used the same lances as for war, but with the sharp lance head replaced with a blunt *coronal* to prevent the tip from actually piercing the armor of an opponent (although the force of the strike could still be enough to knock him from his saddle). However, if the

ABOVE: *Henry VIII's cavalry, armed with lances and arquebuses (early firearms), defeat the Irish in the 1530s, as seen in this illustration from* The Image of Irelande *by John Derricke (1581).*

tournament was to be fought *à outrance*, or "without limits," then it was expected to closely imitate the battlefield and the sharp metal tip remained.

THE LANCE IN COMBAT

The lance had certain limitations. In a tournament, a broken lance could be replaced relatively easily, but this was not necessarily a simple matter in the heat of battle. Charging knights also required a safe place to regroup, reorganize, and catch their breath, thus making coordination with infantry an essential part of their employment.

A knight could also use a lance when he was on foot, in which case it would be cut down to about 6 feet (1.8 m) to make it easier to control and give it more rigidity. The French knights did this before the Battle of Poitiers in 1356, when it was decided that they would be attacking the English position on foot. Effectively, this turned the lance back into the sturdy spear from which it had developed; however, the French strategy at Poitiers proved to be unsuccessful.

LEFT: *In battle, the lance was more effective against infantry than other mounted knights. This English illustration of opposing forces of knights dates from about 1500.*

DAGGERS

Although rarely used in battle, the dagger was the ultimate weapon of last resort. It was also the simplest and most easily carried weapon, both on and off the field of battle.

Mastery of dagger fighting required a great number of wrestling and grappling moves (moves which were the basis of many of the knight's martial arts, not just dagger combat). To use it well, one needed to know how to use the dagger to shield against stabs, how to grip the blade with the other hand to create a lock on the opponent's weapon, how to block an attack with either hand or arm, and how to grapple. Many of the core techniques used in dagger combat could be applied to other weapons.

TYPES OF DAGGER

The dagger called the *misericord* gained its name as a pun on "act of mercy." The weapon itself was a long, narrow knife

RIGHT: *This dagger belonged to William Walworth, the Mayor of London, who used it to kill Wat Tyler, the leader of the English Peasants' Revolt, in 1381.*
BELOW: *This illustration of a dagger fight is from the fifteenth-century French Book of Good Morals.*

often used to deliver the deathblow or to put someone out of their suffering—the mercy stroke. The blade of this dagger could be used against an opponent's face, or it could be thrust through the weak points or gaps in armor, such as beneath the armpit.

The *rondel* had a long triangular or diamond-shaped stiff blade made of steel and a round, tubular grip with flanges at the top and bottom to protect the hand. Developed from the misericord, it was popular from the fifteenth century. It became standard for knights to wear it fixed to the belt with a chain, on the side opposite to their sword. Such a blade or spike could pierce through mail armor or be used to puncture plate armor—sometimes the only way to kill a heavily armored knight.

Other variations on the rondel included the long *baselard*, popular in Switzerland, and the *ballock knife*, or *bollock dagger*, which was widely used in England, Scotland, and Flanders. The latter name was derived from the distinctively shaped guard, in the form of two ovals at the base of the blade.

These weapons were often carried by civilians as well as knights. In *The Canterbury Tales* (c. 1387–1400) by Geoffrey Chaucer, several of the characters are armed with one: the Yeoman, the shipman, Simkin, the murderers in "The Pardoner's Tale," and even the Monk.

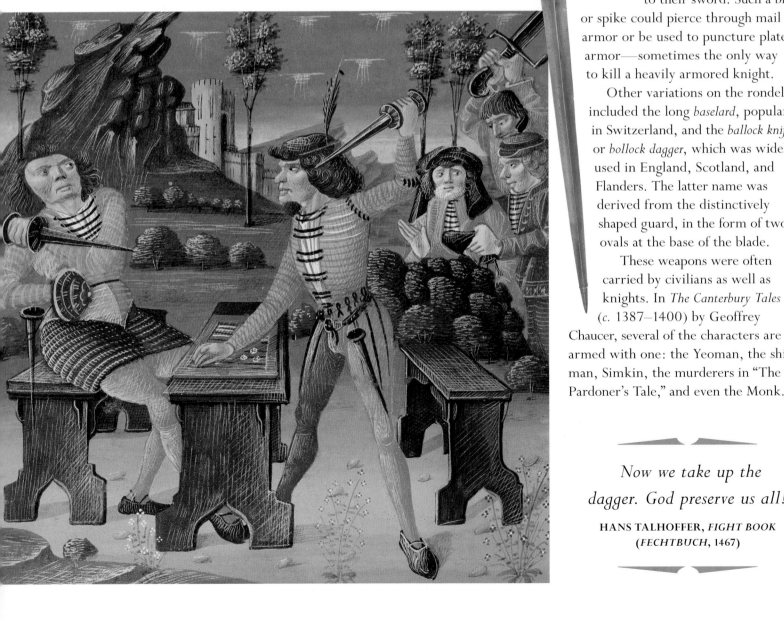

Now we take up the dagger. God preserve us all!

HANS TALHOFFER, *FIGHT BOOK* (*FECHTBUCH*, 1467)

AXES

Axes come in a variety of different lengths, shapes, and weights, and have the advantage of being useful tools as well as fearsome weapons. Probably popularized by the Vikings, the battle-ax was also the weapon of choice for Anglo-Saxon warriors. In 1066 at the Battle of Hastings, the ax was the principal weapon carried by both the Anglo-Saxon *housecarls* and *thanes* (household troops and retainers) and the ordinary foot soldiers making up the *fyrd*, or levy. It also appears to have been familiar to the Norman knights: in the Bayeux Tapestry, William the Conqueror (reigned 1066–87) is shown wielding an ax, although it was not the Norman knight's weapon of choice.

Whether it was short or long, the ax was never acceptable for use in tournaments, probably because of its destructive nature. However, it did retain a level of popularity throughout the medieval period, particularly in the north and east of Europe, although its use as a missile weapon died out.

TECHNICAL DEVELOPMENTS

As armor improved in thickness and in quality, the ax blade started to become thicker in order to be able to penetrate it. By the fourteenth century, however, the halberd and the poleax had replaced the ax for infantry use. Obviously, both of these weapons incorporated the ax into their design, so it certainly did not disappear from the battlefield.

At the same time that the ax was being adapted in one direction as an infantry weapon, the cavalry found a new role for a smaller, lighter ax that could be wielded in close combat. This reserve weapon, called the horseman's ax, had a small head with a curved blade on one side and a hammer on the other side. Its length was comparable to the mace and war hammer.

ABOVE: *The Scottish leader, Robert the Bruce, wields a battle ax in this statue commemorating his 1314 victory over the English at Bannockburn.*
BELOW: *These Viking battle axes and spears (with handles added) dating from the ninth century were found in the Thames River at London Bridge. They may have been left after a battle. An alternative theory is that they were thrown into the river as an offering to the gods.*

GAWAIN STRIKES THE FIRST BLOW

An ax plays the role as the weapon of challenge in the Arthurian tale, *Sir Gawain and the Green Knight*. Gawain accepts a challenge from a mysterious warrior, who offers to allow Gawain to strike him with his ax as long as Gawain will take a return blow in a year and a day from the same weapon:

The head of the big blade over
   a yard in length,
The spike of green steel and
   wrought gold,
The blade brightly polished,
   with a broad edge
Beautifully cast to bite keen
   as a razor …

Gawain beheads the warrior in a single blow, only to have the Green Knight stand up, pick up his head, and remind Gawain to meet him again at the appointed time next year.

BLUNT WEAPONS

A club is a remarkably simple weapon employed for its percussive effect. It could be made out of any material, although wood, fire-hardened or not, was the most common. The mace was obviously descended from a club, but its added head made it more lethal.

THE CLUB

The Bayeux Tapestry depicts clubs being carried by some of the Norman knights and the Anglo-Saxons at Hastings. One is used as a missile weapon. Another is depicted in different colors to the others,

BELOW: *This wooden chest, known as the Courtrai Chest, depicts the Battle of the Golden Spurs in 1302, at which the Flemish citizen militia used* goedendags *against French knights.*

perhaps indicating it was of a different design and thereby showing the start of its transformation from the simple club to the mace. Club and shield was a common combination for use in judicial combats. The *kolben*, a wooden club, was used in Germany for this purpose until at least the end of the fifteenth century.

THE MACE

The mace head was produced in a wide range of shapes and sizes, but two were popular. The first had a head formed by up to seven flanges, or wings, spaced around a central core, which were sharp enough to penetrate chain-mail armor. The second type of head was designed to smash, not penetrate. This mace, which had a knobbed head, was particularly effective against shields and plate armor.

The mace probably was an infantry weapon before being refined and used by the cavalry. When used from a horse, the mace needed to be relatively light in weight and was often made from bronze. Otherwise, iron or steel was used. For battlefield use, the mace sometimes had a spike or spikes added to enhance its deadliness. Without the additional spikes and in a more refined role, it was often used in formal ceremonies, where it was the precursor of the scepter. Such maces were sometimes made from valuable metals such as silver and gold. The mace was also considered an appropriate weapon for use at tournaments.

There is a commonly held idea that priests could use the mace rather than the sword because they were prohibited from spilling blood. However, this is

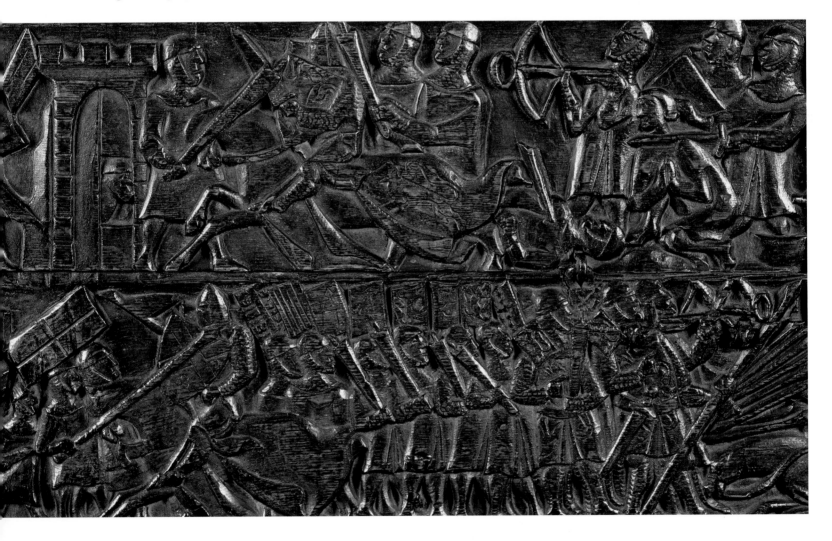

LEFT: *Giuseppe Sabatelli's painting (c. 1839–42) shows Farinata degli Uberti, of the Ghibellines, deflecting a mace attack at the 1262 Battle of Serchio between rival Florentine factions.*

unusual name most likely derived from its resemblance to a star. The war hammer, as distinct from the long-handled poleax, was not widely used in the Middle Ages, but did find popularity in the Hundred Years' War. Like the ax, the war hammer could be a tool or a weapon. It had a short handle, a flattened, metal head for striking with, and sometimes it also had a spike on the back of the head.

unlikely to have been the reason priests might have adopted the mace, and the idea owes more to folklore than the realities of the period. Even when it was used simply as a percussive weapon, the mace would have produced blood. In any case, there is no clear evidence that priests were forbidden from specific weapons in this way. The association of ecclesiastics with the mace is probably best explained by the fact that a mace was also often used as a symbol of office.

VARIATIONS ON THE MACE

The *goedendag*, or "good-day," was a very long mace used by the Flemish. It had a long handle, like the halberd, but was a combination of spear and mace (rather than spear and ax). With it held in two hands, infantry could use it to pull down a knight from his horse and then crush his armor. It was used to deadly effect at Courtrai in 1302 by Flemish citizen militia fighting French knights under Robert of Artois. The battle became known as the Battle of the Golden Spurs because the victorious Flemish took seven hundred pairs of spurs as trophies from dead knights.

The *morning star* was another type of long-handled mace. Its head looked a little like a spiky pineapple, and its

RIGHT: *These nineteenth-century illustrations of blunt instruments employed in the Middle Ages show (from left) a spiked club, a mace, and two versions of a morning star.*

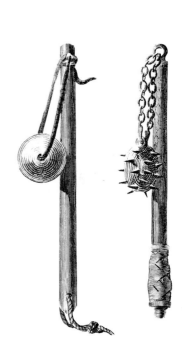

BATTERED BY BLUNT WEAPONS

After a tournament in which the famous English knight William Marshal (1147–1219) was singled out by the assembled nobles for his bravery, it was decided that he was to be awarded a prize. Squires were sent to find him and he was eventually located with his helmeted head resting on a blacksmith's anvil. His armor had received so many blows during the tournament that it was impossible to remove without the aid of the blacksmith. Once the helmet was removed, William received his prize.

THE WARHORSE

The warhorse was possibly the most important piece of military equipment possessed by a knight. A knight would be expected to own a horse for military engagements and, in addition, different mounts for jousts and tournaments. The expense was high, of both purchase and upkeep, and reflected the knight's status in medieval society. The support of infantry should never be underestimated, but the mounted knight dominated the battlefields of Europe from the eleventh century to the start of the fourteenth century. Even when infantry started achieving some notable victories against mounted knights, cavalry remained the most important part of most medieval armies.

THE RISE OF HEAVY CAVALRY

Horses had been used in war by both the ancient Greeks and Romans, but in their armies cavalry was usually regarded as secondary to infantry. It tended to be employed for movement purposes or for skirmishing. Horses might be employed as very mobile missile platforms, as well, with the riders armed with short bows. Such horses needed to be fast but since they were not actually used in sustained close combat, they did not need to be particularly highly trained.

Heavy cavalry began playing a significant part in medieval warfare from the tenth century and had become the most important part of the medieval army by the end of the eleventh century. This

ABOVE: *This miniature, attributed to the Croatian painter Giulio Clovio (1495–1578), depicts the defense of Vienna against the besieging Ottomans in 1529. The Holy Roman emperor Charles V (reigned 1519–56), on the left, helps drive the Ottomans from the field.*

rise in influence came about with the introduction of the knight's high saddle, the stirrup, and the horseshoe.

TECHNICAL INNOVATIONS

The stirrup, introduced into Europe in the tenth century, allowed the horse to be controlled to a greater degree than before, while providing some stability for the rider. This stability made the

horse a better, more secure platform from which to fight with weapons. When, from the late eleventh century on, stirrups were used in conjunction with the high saddle, this stability was greatly increased: the tall, wraparound cantle at the back of the saddle and the high pommel at the front anchored the knight securely to his mount, while also protecting his lower body. This made it possible for the knight to use the lance couched under his armpit, therefore combining the force of lance, knight, and horse, without the impact of the thrust dislodging him from his mount.

In hot climates, because the ground is hard, the horse hoof remains hard and is therefore better suited to moving over rough or rocky terrain. However, in a damp climate, such as that of northern Europe, horse hooves can become soft

and, as a result, easily worn or even broken, thus making the animal lame. By the start of the Crusades, the nailed horseshoe was in widespread use; it allowed horses to travel longer distances over rocky terrain, and at greater speeds even when the weather was wet. This greatly expanded the potential for using horses in warfare.

TYPES OF HORSES

As the technology associated with horses improved, knights became more selective when choosing their mounts. Breeding programs were established to produce faster horses and, as the weight of armor steadily increased, larger, stronger ones.

The word *charger* was used to describe any type of horse ridden by a knight in battle, and there were several different types of horse within this category. The best known of the medieval horses was the *destrier*. This impressive animal was renowned for its battlefield abilities. It was well trained, strong, yet also fast and agile. The destrier was often called the "great horse" in medieval sources due to its size and reputation.

The destrier was probably quite rare, however, and many knights, squires, and soldiers of lower social standing would have ridden smaller, less expensive horses such as *coursers* and *rounceys*. Coursers were light, fast, and strong; they were popular in warfare and in the hunt. Although they were valuable, coursers were not as expensive as destriers. The rouncey was more of a general-purpose mount that could be trained for war or used simply as a riding horse.

It appears the stallion was the preferred horse for

RIGHT: *Knights on crusade are seen in this fifteenth-century manuscript illumination.*

knights, who prized its natural aggression (although mares and geldings could also be damagingly aggressive). Of course, a horse can bite and deliver a devastating kick. Furthermore, pain, rather than distracting it or deterring it, actually spurs it on. This meant that wounds received in battle, unless they crippled the animal, roused its aggression further.

TRAINING THE HORSE

A warhorse had to be trained to move absolutely straight—a crooked mover was impossible to direct in battle. It was important that the horse was extremely responsive, able to instantly answer any instruction from the rider. Another vital requisite was that the horse could be trained to wait while being mounted, and to stand patiently if the rider was thrown so that the knight could then remount. This was a very important requirement on the battlefield.

Great attention was also paid to the pace of the horse. A strong gallop was required for the jousting charge, at a pace between a fast gallop and a slow canter. This allowed the optimum combination of speed with control. The warhorse also needed to become accustomed to wearing armor, and would be trained initially using cloth covers.

Tournaments

Tournaments first became popular at the beginning at the twelfth century and retained their great appeal throughout the rest of the Middle Ages—and, indeed, well into the sixteenth century. All knights considered the tournament to be an important part of what defined them.

Medieval knights were trained to fight and kill, but both society and the church were highly concerned by the prospect of unrestrained violence. By the middle of the eleventh century, bishops began preaching that Christians should not kill other Christians at any time. The knights never completely agreed with this prohibition, but by the end of the century two alternatives were created to channel their violence: the Crusades and tournaments. Churchmen much preferred the Crusades, where knights would use their warrior skills to fight the Muslims in the Holy Land. Knights embraced tournaments with such gusto, however, that those who missed one were assumed either to be wounded or seriously disturbed.

SPORT AND SPECTACLE

A tournament was a mock battle, combining sport and spectacle, in which mounted knights would fight each other, using all their warrior skills and ability, but with the intention of disarming and capturing their opponents, not killing them. Thus, tournaments were usually fought *à plaisance*, meaning with blunted weapons, rather than *à outrance*, with regular sharpened weapons.

The first tournaments were held in the French kingdom (including the area now considered the Low Countries), beginning around the year 1100—they were assumed at the time to be French in origin and, indeed, were referred to as *conflictus Gallicus* in England—and

ABOVE: *The German crusader-poet of the late twelfth-century, Hartmann von Aue, rides to a tournament wearing his heraldic arms, as shown in the* Manesse Codex *(1305–40).*

became common throughout Europe within the next few generations. Any great event or festival could become an excuse to hold a tournament.

The memory of the tournament—who had been present, who had fought brilliantly, who had lost—was always important. By the thirteenth century, every tournament had *heralds*, men who recorded all the chief events and kept track of the coats of arms worn by the various knights so that they would be easily recognized next time. The

heralds were specialists, with extensive memories of the knights of a region. They also tried to create rules for the coats of arms, and came up with the precise terminology to describe the different kinds of images used.

POPULAR APPEAL

The popularity of tournaments was such that, according to one thirteenth-century writer, one was held every two weeks in northern France. Although this may well be an overstatement, it is indicative of their popularity. Participation in tournaments was considered necessary to develop and maintain one's skills as a fighter, as well as being exciting. French knights on the Second Crusade of 1147 mocked the German knights who joined them, saying that they rode "like girls," which they attributed to the infrequency of tournaments at the time in Germany. One thirteenth-century romance has King Arthur calling for a tournament because there were scarcely any "adventures" in his kingdom anymore, and he "did not want his companions to cease bearing arms." Tournaments became a normal occupation for a knight, to the extent that giving them up could be a form of

RIGHT: *The tournament was an ambiguous affair, its pomp and ceremony contrasting with the violence and chaos of the fighting. This image is from a late-fifteenth-century French manuscript,* Le Jouvencel, *by Jean de Bueil.*

penance. A lord might take his men to tournaments, to win glory for his rule.

Tournaments served as opportunities for knights to learn what other knights were doing elsewhere, and they led to a general uniformity in armor, weapons, and chivalrous behavior. They were also opportunities to show off one's prowess.

By the late Middle Ages, they had also became places to flaunt one's aristocratic status, as by then only the wellborn were allowed by participate. The spectators always included ladies, and, according to the romances, the knights were inspired to greater feats by admiring smiles and, indeed, might even win hearts through their jousting skills.

Even more so than real knights, the legendary knights of the romances were enthusiastic participants in tournaments. From their beginnings, the Arthurian stories were full of these events, even though the legends on which the stories were based date back some six centuries before the development of tournaments. Lancelot was always portrayed as an enormously skilled tournament fighter, as well as the queen's lover. Knights all wanted to emulate these great heroes of legend. In the late Middle Ages, a real tournament might even have the participants wear Arthurian garb and take the names of the Round Table knights.

ORGANIZATION

Tournaments were typically held on a Monday, after the rest period of Sunday. They were announced ahead of time to allow the participants to prepare their weapons and armor and arrive ready to fight and show off.

BELOW: *Heralds oversaw every aspect of a tournament. In this scene from the* Tournament Book of René d'Anjou *(c. 1460), which outlined the rules governing tournaments, the heralds inspect the knights' helmets.*

Boasting and individual challenges led up to the beginning of the tournament.

By the thirteenth century, notable fighters, who would add luster to the contest by their presence, might be sent special invitations. A large tournament would attract knights from a number of different regions—even from different countries—and, some sources indicate, it could draw over three thousand participants; allowing for hyperbole, these would have been major affairs.

At the beginning of a tournament, knights would hang up their shields in front of their tents to call attention to themselves. By the late twelfth century, heralds noted who was in attendance by the emblems on the shields.

The tournament was a very popular entertainment. The crowds assembled and the tournament grounds were full of food sellers, jugglers, and weapons makers, eager to earn some money from the knights.

WINNINGS AND LOSINGS

A well-organized tournament offered a prize to the knight who had fought the best. Medieval authors indicated that often this was some sort of wild or semi-wild animal, such as a bear or a pig (pigs were rarely penned and instead foraged for themselves in the woods). As fierce creatures, these worked symbolically to reward the fiercest and most dangerous fighters—and a pig was always welcome as a source of meat. It is less clear what a knight would do with any bear he won, especially if he was a frequent victor. The romance *Parzival* (c. 1210) by German poet Wolfram von Eschenbach, has a heathen queen offer herself in marriage to the man who won the tournament that she organized, a story that may have inspired a later real tournament in which a prostitute was awarded to the winner.

From the twelfth century onward, tournaments became places where a knight could make a respectable profit, for a victorious knight could claim his opponent's armor, weapons, and horses, or the loser might ransom them back. William Marshal (1147–1219), who came from a relatively undistinguished knightly family, gained prominence on the tournament circuit. At the end of his life William calculated he had captured five hundred knights over the years and they all had to pay to retrieve their possessions. William's superior skills won him the attention of the English crown—he became the companion and

LEFT: *In this illustration from a facsimile of the* Manesse Codex *(1305–40), a victorious knight receives a ring from a maiden. Women played a vital role in the tournament—as witnesses of the chivalric behavior of the knights.*

tutor to the heir to the throne, Prince Henry, son of Henry II (reigned 1154–89), and eventually the regent and first Earl of Pembroke.

Tournaments could also be ruinously expensive. The horses, armor, and weapons required were all costly, as were the entry fees charged at the prestigious tournaments. A knight would also be embarrassed to appear at a tournament without fine clothing and supplies. The knight who successfully unhorsed many opponents might leave the tournament substantially richer, but those knights he had unhorsed would have left much poorer. Moneylenders attended tournaments, and the stories carry hints that

many a young knight squandered everything his father had given him—and then some—on the tournament circuit, and that mature knights often had to explain to their wives that to pay tournament debts they had mortgaged their lands. Indeed, the knight who had lost his wealth in a tournament became a stock figure in medieval literature.

CHIVALRY ON DISPLAY

Tournaments were expected to be loci of chivalry. Fighting skills and courtesy toward the ladies, and solid Christian values (at least as the knights themselves understood them)—all the things that constituted chivalry—were on display. Tournaments were thus more than sporting events. They were essential to

BELOW: *The moneylender was a ubiquitous presence at tournaments. This 1514 painting of one is by the Flemish artist Quentin Massys.*

LEFT: *Knights of the Round Table joust in a tournament, watched by King Arthur and Queen Guinevere. This is an illustration from a fifteenth-century French manuscript of Chrétien de Troyes's retelling of the Arthurian legend.*

the aristocracy's self-definition, from the twelfth century onward. Chivalry was what set knights apart and many believed it could be best demonstrated at tournaments.

At a time when real wars in Europe were infrequent, tournaments were the main opportunity for many knights to show themselves as brave and ferocious. The chronicler Roger of Hoveden (died c. 1201) commented on the need for tournaments to prepare men in case a real war did break out: "He is not fit for battle who has never seen his own blood flow." Not surprisingly, as tournaments became more orderly and regulated, with fewer serious wounds and loss of teeth, older knights said disparagingly that the younger generation had grown soft—perhaps being more interested in booty than in battle—and would never have survived the youth of their time.

THE WOMAN'S PLACE

Women, of course, never took any part in tournaments. They had no opportunities for knighthood training and lacked the necessary upper-body strength, just

as today most sportsmen and women participate in separate leagues. Because tournaments were seen as manly exercises, the men would have been extremely disturbed to see a woman seeking to step outside her proper gender role and enter the lists.

However, women were a necessary section of the audience, and they were expected to watch admiringly, inspiring the fighters with their presence, and, sometimes, to help announce the winners. The romances are full of men who received tokens from their ladies to wear in a tournament. Sleeves were the most common tokens, and were attached to the top of a knight's helmet in place of a plume (sleeves were detachable, and sewn into place each day). A maiden

would be distraught to see her favorite wearing someone else's sleeve.

In the thirteenth century, knights would set out on long circuits, with the intention of attending every tournament they could reach and challenging other knights to fight along the way, for the ostensible purpose of honoring a lady. The most famous of them was Ulrich von Liechtenstein (1200–78), whose *Service of the Lady (Frauendienst)* recounts his triumphs and travels from Italy to Bohemia. Ulrich created a nearly life-size representation of his lady's upper half and mounted it on his helmet; this was certainly a demonstration of his devotion, although it must have seemed as bizarre in his time as it does to us today. Parts of Ulrich's account prompt skepticism—for example, that he broke three hundred spears in jousts in just one month. But clearly Ulrich thought his contemporaries would admire his enormous skill and strength, as well as a devotion to his lady that led him to force defeated knights to bow to the four corners of the earth in her honor.

THE TOURNAMENT IN THE LATER MIDDLE AGES

More and more, tournaments became markers of social status. The increased regulation of the events in the thirteenth

A MYSTERIOUS CHALLENGE

One of the more elaborate late medieval tournaments was held at Chalon-sur-Saône in France, in 1449–50. A knight, Jacques de Lalaing, erected a pavilion on an island in the river Saône with statues of a lady and a unicorn—the lady was apparently drenched in tears and the unicorn had three shields around its neck, colored white, violet, and black—representing, respectively, ax, sword, and lance. On the first of the month, knights who wished to challenge Jacques were invited to come and touch a shield to indicate which weapon they would use. After a herald verified that all four of the challenger's great-grandfathers were noble knights, a day was set for the fight. Jacques proudly defeated all of the 22 challengers who presented themselves over a year, and then celebrated with all of them at a great feast, at which the centerpiece was a scale model of the pavilion, lady, and unicorn. He sent each of the losers off wearing a golden bracelet, which supposedly only a mysterious lady could unlock.

ABOVE: *Before a tournament event, the knight, at the center of the platform, receives tokens from a lady, which he wears to demonstrate his devotion; an illustration from the* Manesse Codex *(1305–40).*

*"Look!" [the ladies] said. ...
What a perfect body he has!
How evenly those magnificent
legs of his move together! How
tightly his shield stays glued
in its place! How well the
spearshaft graces his hand!"*

GOTTFRIED VON STRASSBURG,
TRISTAN AND ISOLDE (c. 1210)

tournaments. The aristocratic knights, though, often argued that "mercantile" knights were more interested in financial gain than prowess (which, in fact, many of the aristocrats were, too).

Some late medieval tournaments, desperate to prove their social status, announced that only those with two grandfathers and four great-grandfathers who had been formally knighted could participate. However, if enforced, this bar also excluded many nobles. Some of the townsmen retaliated against these kinds of restrictions by organizing their own tournaments. At one urban tournament held in northern France at the end of the thirteenth century, the bourgeois knights fought so well that the heralds reported their prowess to the king and to the Count of Flanders, who felt compelled to ennoble the winners.

Without doubt, the tournament was the great entertainment of the Middle Ages. In his story *Lancelot, or The Knight of the Cart*, the poet Chrétien de Troyes (flourished 1165–80) described one tournament where "the most magnificent, the largest, and the most splendid viewing stands ever seen had been built there on the tournament field, since the queen and her ladies were to be in attendance. All the ladies followed the queen onto the platform … eager to see who would do well or poorly in the combat."

century was intended, at least in part, to exclude those who were considered riff-raff. Because only aristocratic boys generally had the leisure or wealth to undertake the extensive training needed to undergo the knighting ceremony, the ceremony often became a criterion for admission into the tournament.

The heralds made lists of the ancestry and the coats of arms of knights participating in tournaments, with the purpose of ensuring that the lowborn did not attend. The insistence on formal dubbing

could exclude landless service knights, often excellent fighters (possibly because their training had been rougher), but it would also exclude the young noblemen whose families were unable to pay for an elaborate knighting ceremony, and thus were still officially squires.

Somewhat ironically, such a system opened up opportunities for rich non-aristocrats. A wealthy townsman might pay for a son's years-long training and knighting ceremony so that he became eligible for even the most exclusive

TOURNAMENT FIGHTING

There were several different versions of the tournament, each with its own form of fighting. The *joust*, the kind most commonly depicted in modern films, was a formal contest between two knights, usually armed with lances. In contrast, the *melee* was an open fight between two teams. Both might take place at the same tournament.

Originally, tournaments were quite loosely organized. In the excitement of the clash, tempers often flared, so that friendly mock battles became vicious and bloody. Especially if old enemies found each other on opposite sides in the melee, the tournament could become the opportunity to settle old scores.

Areas called *refuges* were set aside, in which knights could arm themselves with the help of their squires or to which they could retreat once defeated. It was widely agreed that knights must not attack squires in the refuges, nor could the squires of opposing knights harm a knight who came into a refuge to catch his breath. However, the frequency with which such occurrences were deplored in contemporary accounts suggests they were far from rare. Indeed, the failure to enforce such rules, combined with an absence of time limits on fights, meant that early tournaments were often more like real battles than sporting events.

ABOVE: *For young knights, the tournament was an opportunity to impress with their courage and their skills on horseback and with weapons. This tournament, illustrated in the fifteenth-century English* St. Alban's Chronicle, *is taking place in front of King Richard II.*

Tournaments were normally fought in full armor and the lance and sword were the principal weapons. Other weapons that might be employed during real battles—such as axes, throwing javelins, and bows (both longbows and crossbows)—were forbidden. These were typically infantry weapons and, as such, were not thought suitable for

LATE MEDIEVAL JOUSTING

Long after the development of gunpowder and cannon had made individual contests between knights nearly irrelevant for the purposes of real battles, knights loved to joust with long lances. The light, fast-running horses that had carried knights in tournaments and into battles in the twelfth and thirteenth centuries were replaced by large, heavy steeds that could support the massive weight of late medieval armor. Knights continued to joust in the manner developed in the twelfth century until well into the sixteenth century—by which time, tournaments had become thoroughly nostalgic, shot through with a longing for a lost golden age—which of course had never existed.

conflict between mounted knights. Furthermore, the bow was considered to be a coward's weapon, in that it inflicted damage from afar, and thus was not thought appropriate for an event that was designed specifically to show off the skills and courage of knights in combat at close quarters.

THE MELEE

A melee might rage on all afternoon and across a large area—aside from the refuges, no areas were officially off-limits, which resulted in frequent damage to land and crops. The aim of the melee was to unhorse as many of the opposing team's knights as possible.

An unhorsed knight, or one who was too wounded to fight on, was supposed to surrender, but if he refused to yield, then the opponent who believed he had defeated him fairly might attempt to drag him back forcibly to the refuges with the help of his squires.

The two sides in the melee might be determined by territorial origin, such as the Angevins, the Flemish, or the French, or they could be given arbitrary names, such as the "Inners" or the "Outers." The leaders of the two sides were the highest-ranking lords present, and other lords with their knights were ranged below them. A great deal of negotiation went into making sure that the two sides were

evenly matched, with equal numbers of knights and an equivalent ratio of more- and less-experienced fighters. Individuals would fight each other as a part of the general battle, but overall it was a team effort. Distinctive coats of arms, usually displayed on shields, allowed fighters to recognize those on their side even when helmets hid their faces.

A team that worked well together was much more successful than one in which the knights sought only individual glory. One technique was for a team to charge in a tight group—forcing their opponents to do the same—and then suddenly spread out, having the knights at the outer ends of their line close in around their opponents' flanks. Another was to feign rapid retreat, then abruptly wheel around, causing panic and confusion among the pursuers.

Such techniques, of course, required discipline among knights eager to show that they were better riders and fighters

ABOVE: *In this illustration from the German Manesse Codex (1305–40), two teams take part in a melee, as noble spectators look on. A melee could last for a whole afternoon.*
LEFT: *René, Duke of Anjou (1409–80), and his courtiers and nobles preside over a melee, as illustrated in the* Tournament Book of René d'Anjou *(c. 1460).*

than even the other members of their team, and the opposing team would, of course, be alert to such strategies. When they worked, however, they were effective and greatly admired. At one famous tournament, a group of knights from Flanders announced that they had come only to watch a melee, not participate. Then, when everyone in the melee was exhausted, they mounted up and quickly overcame the remaining knights. Interestingly, this was not denounced as unfair; rather, the other knights agreed that it was an excellent trick.

Sometimes it could be difficult to say which side had won at the end of a fight. Generally, it was whichever side had the most men still mounted when general exhaustion closed the event. The close of the day was marked by baths for all, by a general binding up of wounds and a setting of broken bones, and by a series of accountings and discussions, as defeated knights arranged to buy back any equipment they had forfeited when unhorsed. A generous, courtly, and successful knight might distribute some of his booty at the end of the tournament to these squires and to the heralds—or, at least, the squires and heralds thought that he should.

THE JOUST

With the advent of heavier armor, the melee gradually fell into disfavor, and by the late Middle Ages the joust was the principal form of fighting at tournaments. A more formal event than the melee, the joust took place on a *list*, a long, narrow strip of ground marked with two parallel tracks, often separated by a fence or other barrier. Armed with long lances, the knights would charge toward each other on opposite sides of the barrier. The aim was to strike the opponent's shield with one's lance and topple him from his mount. If both knights managed to stay in the saddle, they would charge again, either three or five times. If neither was unhorsed by the end of the contest, it was up to the judges to determine the winner. When both knights fell off their horses at the same time, they drew their swords and fought on foot. Horses were specially trained to move out of the way when a swordfight commenced.

A tournament lance was usually blunted and had "wings" placed just behind its tip so that it would not penetrate the opponent's armor. The knight held his shield and reins in his left hand and his lance in his right, in a couched position—tucked under the right armpit—and crossed in front of the saddle, above the horse's neck, so that it pointed ahead and to the left of his body, toward his opponent. He would use his stirrups and saddle to brace himself for the strike.

Sometimes, a tournament would take place as a result of a knight proffering a challenge to meet all comers (individually, of course) in a series of jousts. At other times, a melee, or even a battle, might consist of a number of jousts occurring at the same time—in *The Song of Roland* (*La chanson de Roland*, c. 1100), the momentous battle that took place at Roncesvalles in Navarre, France, in CE 778 between the Christian and Saracen armies is described as essentially a series of jousts.

LEFT: *In this French manuscript illustration dating from 1470, the knight in the left foreground has just unseated his opponent and will thus win the joust. The contest is being watched by a king, queen, and nobles, as well as heralds and musicians.*

ABOVE: *Like every other aspect of the knightly life, the joust was glorified in medieval writings. This illustration from a late-fifteenth-century French treatise on heraldry shows knights in a ring, not on parallel tracks as in a real joust.*

THE BOHORT

A third kind of tournament fighting was the *bohort*, a somewhat milder version of the melee, which appears to have had its origins in Germany, rather than France, in the twelfth century. The bohort was fought with short, blunt lances between mounted knights who wore padded leather garments or even their regular clothing rather than armor. Instead of charging each other at full gallop, the knights thrust about in all directions with their lances, here, too, attempting to unhorse their opponents.

Some accounts suggest bohorts might also have been fought with nothing more than shields, which were used as both offensive and defensive weapons. If the romances are to be believed, it was a sign of ostentatious wealth to wear one's best clothes into the bohort, where they could be torn to shreds. A bohort might be fought on the evening before the real tournament began, as a chance to weed out those who were truly unskilled and to allow the best fighters to intimidate their future opponents. It might also be an impromptu event—for example, if high spirits among a group of young knights led to a full-scale fight.

TRIAL BY BATTLE

The ubiquity of tournaments meant that they were even used to resolve judicial matters. Closely related to the joust in the twelfth century was trial by battle, in which two knights sought to defeat each other in order to prove which one was in the right, or, more commonly, which one was fighting as the champion for those who were in the right. God, it was believed, would make sure that the right side won.

The fighting took the same form as a joust: an initial charge with lances, followed by a sword fight on foot when the lances were broken. However, unlike a tournament fight, the trial by battle was fought with sharpened weapons and, despite encouragement to yield, knights would sometimes fight to the death. Churchmen who initially objected to tournaments, accepted and, indeed, presided at trials by battle, even though some pointed out that forcing God to reveal his position was highly problematic. Laymen also noted that it was possible for someone in the wrong to win such a trial by hiring the most skilled champion. After the Fourth Lateran Council of 1215 convened by Pope Innocent III (reigned 1198–1216) forbade trials by battle, as well as other forms of trial by ordeal, they fell into disfavor and eventual disuse.

RIGHT: *In a joust, if both knights were unhorsed, they would continue the fight on the ground. In this illustration from the French manuscript* Le Jouvencel, *by Jean de Bueil, the knights are sparring with their lances.*

ATTITUDES TOWARD TOURNAMENTS

Tournaments were not universally approved of. People could be, and were, killed in them. A weapon that is blunt can still inflict fatal wounds, and a fall from a galloping horse can be deadly, especially when the rider is weighed down by armor.

The Anglo-Norman kings of the twelfth century forbade tournaments in England, fearing their potential for deadly violence, even though the king's sons routinely attended tournaments on the Continent. Geoffrey, son of King Henry II (reigned 1154–89), was killed in a tournament in Paris in 1186, clearly demonstrating just how dangerous they could be. But when Henry's other son, Richard I (reigned 1189–99), became king, he once again authorized them in England, although he was also the first to lay out specific regulations as to how they were to be conducted.

CHURCH OPPOSITION

Perhaps even more serious than this royal opposition was church opposition. Bishops preached against tournaments repeatedly. They argued that if knights wanted to engage in warfare, there were

RIGHT: *This armor for Henry VIII (reigned 1509–47) was constructed from several older pieces, in preparation for the Field of Cloth of Gold, a grand Anglo-French summit and tournament held near Calais, France, in 1520.*

a great many Muslims left to fight. They were particularly aggrieved at returning crusaders celebrating their safe return by participating in tournaments, and suggested that the knights had not dissipated all their aggression against the infidel on crusade.

Churchmen not only objected to the aggression inherent in tournaments and the possibility of a Christian being killed by another Christian, but also saw these events as invitations to knights to practice all manner of other vices, including anger, vanity, avarice, and lust. Pope Innocent II (reigned 1130–43) called such activities "detestable," and forbade tournaments, a ruling knights routinely ignored but which pleased the bishops.

On occasion, all the participants in a particular tournament might be excommunicated. That meant that if a knight died at that tournament, he would have to be buried in unconsecrated ground, unless his family could pay a substantial sum to have the excommunication reversed. If they failed to do that, the knight's soul would be destined for damnation. In the French story of the early thirteenth century, *Aucassin et Nicolette*, a young knight says that he might not mind going to hell, for at least there he could associate with "fair knights who are killed in the tourney"—ecclesiastical censure did not diminish the popularity of the tournament.

It was especially difficult for churchmen to oppose tournaments that were sponsored by powerful temporal rulers.

When emperor Frederick I Barbarossa (reigned 1152–90) held a great tournament in Mainz to celebrate the knighting ceremonies of his two sons in 1184, all the bishops of his realm were spectators.

BYPASSING THE CHURCH

The approval of God, and thus the attainment of Heaven, was still important to knights. Most adopted a pragmatic approach to the ecclesiastical opposition to tournaments by appealing directly to God. The twelfth-century biographer of Count Charles the Good of Flanders (c. 1084–1127) noted that the count participated in tournaments despite the church's opposition, and explained this behavior away by saying that Charles made it up to God by extra almsgiving.

BELOW: *Two knights are depicted jousting, in this Romanesque bas-relief over the door of St. Zeno Church in Verona, Italy.*

Knights told each other stories in which God and the saints approved of tournaments. In *Erec* by Hartmann von Aue, dating from about 1185, the hero prays to God during a tournament and entrusts "to Him most fully his knightly fame, that He should deign to nourish it." One late-twelfth-century account related how a knight stopped on his way to a tournament to pray at a hermitage and ended up spending the whole day there, then was surprised to learn that he—or a knight who looked just like him—had been the victor of the whole tournament. God, seeing his devotion, had provided a "substitute." A version

Erec was so in love with [Enide] that he cared no more for arms, nor did he go to tournaments … he wanted to enjoy his wife's company … All the nobles said that it was a great shame and sorrow that a lord such as he once was no longer wished to bear arms.

CHRÉTIEN DE TROYES (FLOURISHED 1165–80), *EREC*

of this was soon incorporated into the cycle of stories known as *Miracles of the Virgin*, in which the Virgin Mary herself fought in the lists disguised as a knight. This must have been a startling story, yet it was retold and recopied by clerics.

At no point do knights seem to have understood the church's criticisms, and they continued to consider themselves good Christians. Indeed, every tournament began with Mass, which all were expected to attend, and tournaments were sometimes used to recruit troops for a crusade. By the thirteenth century, knights were even attaching all sorts of Christian symbolism to their swords. In other words, they created their own version of Christianity, in which tournaments were appropriate. This helped counter the criticism, and by the fourteenth century the church had officially abandoned its opposition to tournaments.

BELOW: *This sixteenth-century engraving by Flemish artist Franz Hogenberg shows King Henry II of France (reigned 1519–59) being wounded in a joust at a tournament. The king died of his injuries ten days later.*

Knights and War

Medieval people genuinely believed that God could and did intervene in human affairs. All events, not just those involving conflict, were perceived as an insight into a divine purpose above and beyond that which was being played out in the world. Nowhere was this clearer than on the field of battle.

Today we are used to the idea that war is a terrible thing that should be avoided. However, that was not the view that prevailed in the Middle Ages. In his 1387 book *The Tree of Battles* (*L'Arbre des batailles*), the monk Honoré Bouvet (*c.* 1340– *c.* 1410) explained at great length that it could not be that war itself was a bad thing, as its aim was to "wrest peace, tranquility, and reasonableness from him who refuses to acknowledge his wrong-doing." How could war itself be a bad thing when the very first war took place in heaven when Lucifer and his followers were cast out? War was only wrong when it was fought for the wrong reasons or caused a lot more suffering than the initial reason justified.

THE REASONS FOR WAR

While it is easy to see the desire for wealth as the primary motivation for medieval warfare, at heart it was usually about justice. For example, the main conflict of the later medieval period, the Hundred Years' War, was about different interpretations of rights and obligations. Although the king of England owned parts of France, he still owed the king of France certain

obligations, including military duty. This interfered greatly with the king of England's affairs and became intolerable. The conflict became about who had the right to the French throne, because this was the only way of resolving the discordant rights and duties. Both camps claimed that justice was on their side, and that there was no accepted way of resolving the dispute other than by fighting for their beliefs.

THE CONDUCT OF WAR

In theory, there was a clear distinction between a public war carried out on behalf of a prince or king, and a private war carried out between individuals to

ABOVE LEFT: *Inspired by Honoré Bouvet's* The Tree of Battles, *this fifteenth-century allegorical illustration of medieval society shows the discord between the different social classes.*
ABOVE: *This fourteenth-century manuscript highlights the importance placed on prayer before battle. A knight kneels before the house of God in the hope that God will grant a favorable outcome.*

settle personal quarrels or feuds. What one was permitted to do in each type of war was vastly different. For example, in a private war, one was not supposed to employ fire as this was considered arson. If, however, one had sufficient authority from one's royal leader to fight a public war, fire could be legitimately employed as an effective weapon. Making sure that one had the correct authority for one's actions was a very important part of medieval warfare.

Battles were often very ritualized, with both sides settling on a specific time and location in advance. Pre-battle preparations included praying and religious observations, and, in a tradition passed down through the ages, the winner was expected to remain on the battlefield after the fight to proclaim the victory.

DIVINE INTERVENTION

The general understanding that God's will was being played out on Earth had a profound effect on the way that warfare was understood. In a conflict, it was assumed that God would grant victory to the side that was most just. In a holy war such as a crusade it was obvious, to Christians at least, which side was the "just" side; however, in normal warfare, things were much less clear. Moreover, pitched battles, whereby both sides agreed to a time and place for a fight, were considered subject to the judgment of God—they were ordeals, or trials by battle. And even though combatants might believe themselves to be fighting for a just cause, they were aware that God could choose to use the outcome of the battle to punish one of their number for something completely unrelated to the conflict, or that he might inflict defeat simply to test someone's faith. As a result, pitched battles were seen as highly risky affairs for both sides, to be avoided whenever possible. This explains why they were such a rare

RIGHT: *Portrayed in the fifteenth-century* Chronicle of Normandy (Chronique de Normandie), *William the Conqueror's overwhelming victory at the Battle of Hastings in 1066 was due to the skill and organization of his army as much as God's will.*

War without fire is like sausages without mustard.

HENRY V (REIGNED 1413–22)

thing in the Middle Ages. For example, the whole of the Hundred Years' War saw only three trials by battle with royalty present on both sides.

The famous victory of William the Conqueror (reigned 1066–87) over Harold Godwinson at Hastings in October 1066 was explained as God's will by the Norman victor. The English never recovered from this defeat, and William was crowned in London at the end of the same year. The Treaty of Brétigny in 1360 ceded a third of France to the English King Edward III (reigned 1327–77). It was a direct consequence of what was thought to be a divinely

ordained English victory at Poitiers in 1356 and the capture of the French king. The 1420 Treaty of Troyes may have taken some time to negotiate (and required a little more persuasion), but it still came as a direct outcome of, and was thoroughly shaped by, the judicial decision of God at Agincourt. The treaty proclaimed Henry V (reigned 1413–22) and his future sons as the rightful heirs to the French throne, although the deaths of both the French and English kings within a short space of time and the lack of suitable heirs meant that this failed to end the Hundred Years' War.

THE REALITY OF MEDIEVAL WARFARE

While pitched battles are the events that tend to capture our imagination, the vast majority of the fighting that took place in the Middle Ages was on a smaller or less spectacular scale. Sieges were an essential part of medieval warfare, as it was through the possession of castles and fortifications

that surrounding land was controlled. For example, England's King Richard I (reigned 1189–99) was involved in no more than two or three battles in his entire career, but he was constantly involved in sieges.

To enforce his victory at Hastings in 1066, and to prevent further rebellions throughout England, William the Conqueror defeated the disorganized resistance piecemeal with his knights and other troops. He then undertook the systematic destruction of stores of seed, grain, animals, and agricultural tools in the north of England. This caused widespread famine and refugees, but this "harrying of the north" also put an end to resistance by creating dead zones, incapable of further resistance and unattractive to other potential invaders. The key to maintaining control in the longer term was a combination of a field army and the construction of a network of fortifications.

During the Hundred Years' War, various English kings used *chevauchées* to undermine the strength and prosperity of France, and to show the weakness of the French monarchy. A *chevauchée* involved a military force—usually mounted—moving through the lands of an enemy and causing as much damage as possible. This was not a raid or plundering expedition (although this was also a result of the strategy), but was actually a means of forcing the other side to accept one's argument without having to go into battle.

THE DEVELOPMENT OF WEAPONRY

The knight was trained in the use of many different weapons, with different ones becoming more or less popular over the course of the medieval period. For example, the Anglo-Saxon housecarls and thanes at Hastings in 1066 preferred the battle-ax as their primary weapon, while the poleax—combining spear, ax, and hammer—was a popular weapon with armored knights fighting on foot in the fifteenth century.

The sword and lance are the weapons most often associated with the medieval knight. However, both of these weapons, and indeed many others, underwent

ABOVE: *In Sir John Gilbert's atmospheric nineteenth-century painting* King Henry V at the Battle of Agincourt (1415), *knights await the order to charge, when their upright lances will drop into the "couched" position.*

significant changes in their design and in the way that they were used over time. The lance was simply a spear at the start of the Middle Ages—used overarm to strike down from horseback at people on foot. By the end of the period, it was longer, thicker, and stronger, and was used "couched" under the knight's armpit as a devastating impact weapon. The knight's sword began the medieval period as a slashing weapon for use from horseback, and ended primarily as a thrusting weapon that, depending upon the length of the blade, could be employed with or without a shield.

The longbow is one of the best-known weapons of the Middle Ages. It was powerful, but it needed to be used in the right way to be truly effective. As the knight's armor became better designed and better made,

ARCHERS ALL AQUIVER

A monk at Saint-Denis probably spoke for the whole chivalric class when he indignantly described archers as "men of no value" following the French defeat at Crécy. However, a distaste for this weapon of the peasantry did not stop the French nobility from employing crossbowmen and other archers, sometimes in high numbers (for example, the French were supposed to have had twenty thousand Genoese crossbowmen at Sluys in 1340). The English armies of the Hundred Years' War were effective precisely because of the high number of archers fighting alongside the knights and men-at-arms.

RIGHT: *This c. 1400 illustration shows Bertrand du Guesclin attacking Pestivien Castle, Brittany, in 1364, ably assisted by numerous archers.*

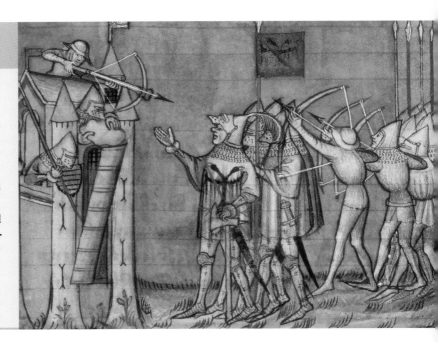

the type of arrowhead used against it changed, as did the way the weapon was actually employed. The key to the longbow's success was the large volume of arrows that could be fired into a target area—each longbowman could shoot up to 15 arrows per minute. It only took one arrow not to be deflected or stopped by a knight's armor to cause a fatal injury. Knowing this, the psychological effect of arrows clanging off one's armor must have been significant, helping to break up the cohesion of an attack. This was in addition to the physical effect on those who were unfortunate enough to actually suffer a penetrating hit. However, for all its effectiveness, massed archery had one major drawback—it depended upon one's enemy attacking a defensive position. Therefore, reliance upon it meant handing the initiative to the enemy. Actually winning with this strategy required the enemy to bungle its attack as well.

Knights were professionals and, as such, had to have a pragmatic appreciation of the value of archery in the right circumstances. However, that did not mean that archers had to be treated as equals. An archer could expect little mercy if captured during a battle by a knight. Death or mutilation was a standard way of dealing with such people.

ABOVE: *Although not as chaotic as a medieval battle would have been, the scene in this 1473 illustration shows how little life was valued on the battlefield. While two opposing armies face each other, with rows of archers in front of cavalry, a knight spears to death two other men.*

BATTLE TACTICS

It was thought by academics for some time that medieval armies had very little idea about military strategy or tactics. It was widely held that medieval warfare was not particularly organized, and that any planning undertaken was rudimentary at best. However, it is now acknowledged that both strategic and tactical thinking were actually highly developed in this period. Princes and kings were expected to study the practice of war using a variety of different books as well as practical experience. For example, Vegetius, a late Roman author, wrote *De re militari* in the fourth century CE, and it was enthusiastically translated, copied, adapted, and read throughout the Middle Ages due to its detailed advice on conducting military affairs.

The benefits of advantageous terrain, surprise, and the use of scouts were all appreciated during the Middle Ages, as was the importance of training, shown in the many popular tournaments of the period. A recently unearthed document shows that the French did have a detailed plan for how to fight the English at Agincourt, even if they chose to ignore much of it on the day. While mistakes were made, and some military leaders may have lacked the ability or experience to apply tactics successfully, the conduct of medieval warfare was generally at least as sophisticated as that of the periods before or after.

A KNIGHTLY CHARGE

The key battle tactic associated with the mounted knight was the shock charge with a couched lance. The heavy lance was held firmly under the armpit, meaning that the weight of the horse was added to the weight of the knight—leading to a greater physical force. This type of charge required both stirrups and a deep saddle to keep the knight from sliding off his horse, and really only developed during the eleventh century.

To be effective, the charge had to be delivered by a coordinated mass of stampeding knights. This took more than simple technology: it also required quite complex social organization, and venues such as tournaments in which to

ABOVE: *In addition to Vegetius's work, De re militari was also the name of a 1472 book by Roberto Valturio, which featured the first technical illustrations of weaponry, siege warfare, and other military techniques of the time.*
RIGHT: *Jousting—which, unlike this romantic image, usually involved a one-on-one contest—was a popular event at tournaments in England and France for knights who wished to practice or flaunt the skill of charging with a couched lance.*

A mounted Frank is irresistible; he would bore his way through the walls of Babylon.

ANNA COMNENA, BYZANTINE PRINCESS AND HISTORIAN (1083–*c*. 1153)

practice the technique. The impact of a well-delivered charge by a group of knights could be absolutely devastating.

THE ARRANGEMENT OF MEDIEVAL ARMIES

Knights fought not as individuals, but as part of armies that were composed of smaller tactical units. These units were formed along kinship or feudal lines. The basis was often the household, or a lord to whom military service was due. Because of the extensive family and feudal networks in place, a ready-made reserve of military units and command structures existed.

The largest of these units were called *battles*. A typical army would have three to five battles, each under the command of a leading noble, with the whole army under the overall command of the king. One battle could be the rear guard, while one could be the vanguard. Smaller groups within the main battles were called *conrois,* and were made up of between ten and twenty knights. Often they were family groups or the followers of a particular lord. Even smaller tactical groups were called *lances*. The lance was a group of men who served under a knight.

Such subdivisions allowed a good degree of tactical flexibility on the battlefield, and they changed somewhat over time. For example, in the mid-fourteenth century, a lance consisted of one heavily armored knight plus several mounted archers. By the fifteenth century, a lance could be made up of a knight and his page, an armed sergeant, three mounted archers, a crossbowman, a pikeman, and even a handgunner. While the knight could fight on foot or on his mount, archers and others used their horses only for movement.

Each tactical subdivision would be represented by a standard or flag. This provided a signal flag for group maneuvers and also a highly visible rallying point. The standard often represented an individual lord or prince, and its loss during battle meant disgrace.

Because many accounts of medieval battles only refer to the knight in each lance, the importance of the many other people involved is easy to miss. However, while the mounted knight in full armor catches the imagination and is often used to represent the warfare of the period, other types of soldier were

ABOVE: *While knights attracted all the glory in battles, it was the infantry who protected the all-important baggage train. If an army lost control of its food resources and other supplies, no amount of knightly skill would save it from starvation and insufficient weaponry.*

also numerous and indispensable—for instance, foot soldiers could often outnumber the knights by five or even ten to one. At least until the end of the Middle Ages, the role of foot soldiers was often defensive, providing a base from which the knights could organize themselves into a charge formation, or to which they could return to catch their breath and recover after a charge. The infantry were also vital for protecting the baggage train, containing all of the army's supplies and loot.

SIEGE WARFARE

To control a region, it was necessary to subjugate the fortifications within that territory. Therefore, gaining control of castles or other protected constructions, from small towers or forts all the way up to walled towns and cities, was often a key objective of a military campaign. Sieges played an important part in this process throughout the medieval period.

The early motte-and-bailey castles favored by the Normans were fairly rudimentary affairs that nevertheless provided a safe haven for the garrison, which could retire behind the wooden walls and await relief. They were not invulnerable, but they were intimidating, overawing many potential rebels. The late eleventh century saw a technical explosion in castle building, whereby great stone towers such as the White Tower in London and the keeps

at Rochester and Colchester rose to new and forbidding heights. Next came multiwalled fortresses, eventually producing the intricate concentric designs that were favored by Edward I (reigned 1272–1307), such as those at Caernarvon or Conway. Each development in defensive technology led to new innovations to try and defeat them.

STRIKING THE STRONGHOLD

During a siege, the quickest method of attack was to storm a castle. Scaling the walls using ladders was a dangerous job and made the attackers very vulnerable. As castle walls got higher, this became even harder. In the eleventh century when wooden motte-and-bailey castles were still common, fire was an obvious weapon to employ. Fire became less effective when stone replaced wood as the building material of choice, but it

ABOVE: *Jehan de Wavrin's fifteenth-century illustration of the siege of Mortagne (1340) shows how the French town was besieged and attacked using a variety of different weapons, from crossbows to early cannon and firearms.*

could still be used against the wooden gates. This led to the introduction of iron guards called portcullises, which were placed in front of the gates, as well as the use of drawbridges and murder holes positioned above gates, through which the defenders could throw down stones and other objects onto their attackers. Arrow slits situated in walls provided safe positions from which archers and crossbowmen could shoot.

Siege towers—wooden constructions on wheels—were known from Roman times and were used throughout the medieval period to get close to castle

A COLOSSAL CATAPULT

The trebuchet was a counterweight throwing engine that emerged in the twelfth century and remained the most important siege weapon until the development of effective cannon. A container that could be filled with a heavy material such as earth was placed at one end of a pole, while a sling to hold a stone was placed at the other end. The pole was mounted on a pivot. When the sling was winched down and released, the stone could be propelled over a considerable distance and could cause substantial damage when it struck high castle walls.

RIGHT: *Trebuchets are depicted here at a siege, c. 1340. Stones weighing hundreds of pounds could be thrown relatively quickly using these machines.*

walls. They allowed attackers to shoot down upon the defenders and to get onto the tops of the walls. Testudos and mantlets were types of roofed protection for besiegers. These could be brought up close to the castle walls so that mining operations could be undertaken or battering rams could be used against doors to force an entry. Breaching the wall by flinging stones at it from a siege engine was also a successful technique.

If a mine could be successfully dug under a wall, it could be collapsed deliberately by burning its supporting timbers, which would bring the castle wall above it tumbling down. However,

water-filled defenses called moats made it difficult to get close to the walls and also made mining under the walls very problematic. Storming a breach was a deadly affair, and the attacker could expect heavy casualties in the process.

NEGOTIATION, STARVATION, AND TREACHERY

The dangers and difficulties of taking a castle by force, especially if the attackers did not have the element of surprise on their side, meant that alternative methods were often employed. The most common of these was negotiation. The rules of siege warfare were well developed and were based on the principles set out in the Bible. Deuteronomy 20 stated that, if a castle fell after resisting attack, all males could expect to be put to the sword and the loot divided among the attacking army. This harsh rule meant that an early surrender was often an attractive prospect. However, if a captain surrendered a castle too early, he risked the charge of treachery from his own lord, who would then have him put

LEFT: *Many medieval castles had a wooden drawbridge that could be raised during a siege to block access. The moat surrounding the castle may have been a dry ditch or filled with water, which acted as a further barrier to the besiegers.*

to death anyway. The result was that both parties often agreed upon the length of the siege. If the lord was unable to come to the castle's aid within a set amount of time, the garrison was permitted to surrender without risking the charge of treason.

Simply cutting a castle off from its supplies and starving the garrison out was another option. However, this could be a time-consuming activity, and the bad hygiene associated with a static military camp meant that the risk of disease was real for both the attacking and the defending force. If storming, mining, negotiation, and starvation all failed, treachery was also a popular method for gaining entrance to a castle.

THE RISE OF THE CANNON

From the end of the fourteenth century, the use of cannon changed the dynamics of siege warfare and threatened to take the advantage away from the defense. The high stone walls designed to stop people climbing them were particularly vulnerable to heavy artillery. Concentrating gunfire on a single, low point on a wall could have the same effect as mining. As a response, walls were lowered and thickened, moats were widened, and earthworks were added. Defensive artillery was also employed to keep the attackers at a distance.

MERCENARIES

Mercenaries formed the core of many medieval armies. It is problematic to define what exactly counted as a mercenary in the Middle Ages, as pay for knights was often provided in addition to or instead of feudal obligations. The most useful way of thinking about mercenaries is as bands of self-employed soldiers who were generally foreigners in the area in which they worked and who received pay from their captain. The captain would represent the whole company and would offer their services to the highest bidder. While some mercenaries gained bad reputations for their greed or cruelty, working as a mercenary could also be a respected profession for a knight. However, many nobles found mercenaries, who were often of low social origins, difficult to accept, perhaps recognizing a threat to the established social order.

It is difficult to say precisely when mercenaries became significant in war, but they were certainly used in the eleventh and twelfth centuries. For example, William the Conqueror hired knights for his harrying of the north of England in 1069–70, and Robert de Bellême employed them in his rebellion at the start of Henry I's reign (1100–35).

Mercenaries remained popular with employers, if no one else, to varying degrees until the end of the Middle Ages.

Certain areas produced different types of specialized mercenaries. For example, Genoese crossbowmen or Welsh and English archers were often employed by the French for their specialist services. Toward the end of the Middle Ages, Swiss infantrymen became popular due to their deadly effectiveness. Knights who found themselves working as mercenaries were often younger sons who would not inherit their family estates, or nobles who through the fortunes of war had somehow lost their possessions.

THE PROS AND CONS OF HIRING MERCENARIES

Mercenaries were useful for kings and princes who needed to raise an effective army quickly. It made sense for them to ensure that the numbers were on their side in any conflict; the royal commander did not want to run the risk of not hiring additional forces, just in case his opponent did choose to augment his army. This meant that money had to be found to pay the mercenaries, so more sophisticated methods of raising revenue were required.

Political complexities could sometimes be avoided by hiring troops. Subjects might expect ongoing favors

AN ENGLISHMAN IN ITALY

Originally from Essex in England, Sir John Hawkwood (1320–94) became one of the most famous and successful captains (known as *condottieri*) of the Italian mercenary troops. He fought for the Black Prince, probably at Crécy and Poitiers, before becoming a mercenary captain following the Treaty of Brétigny in 1360. He found service with the White Company, and was later employed by the cities of Pisa and Milan, and also by the papacy. Once employed by Florence, he remained in the service of the city for the rest of his life. He won many victories, often employing the English tactics of dismounted knights combined with longbowmen.

LEFT: *Hawkwood was probably the son of a tanner, and may not have been a knight at all. But, through skill and valor, by the time he died he was a wealthy military commander of Florence's army.*

LEFT: *Paolo Uccello (1397–1475) portrayed the Battle of San Romano (1432) between Florence and Siena, in which famous Italian* condottiere *Niccolò da Tolentino (c. 1350–1435)—seen here on his white horse—played a central role.*
BELOW: *As illustrated in this 1375 French illumination, the town of Burgos, Spain, surrendered to Bertrand du Guesclin in 1366. The French knight led the* compagnies *(mercenaries) into Spain in 1366 to aid Henry of Trastámara.*

or rewards for their service, but a mercenary was simply doing a one-time paid job. If a king was unpopular, mercenaries might also be trusted more than native knights and soldiers. To ensure continued employment, mercenaries needed to demonstrate their abilities and build their reputations. Their constant practice in their chosen profession meant that they were often very good at what they did.

Of course, the ability of those with an effective reputation to find employment anywhere that a lord was hiring could also cause problems, too. During the Hundred Years' War, the French did their best to find a suitable response to the English use of massed archery. Mercenaries, such as Genoese crossbowmen, were used in large numbers, and other nationalities were also employed, such as the Scots at Verneuil in 1424. There is no doubt that there were English and Welsh archers in the employment of the French crown, too, meaning both that there were fewer archers for the English to call upon,

and that the English risked facing their own, very capable archers on the field of battle. This state of affairs was considered such a serious problem by the English that a royal proclamation was issued in 1365 forbidding archers to leave England without special permission.

THE RENEGADE *ROUTIERS*
Another serious problem was what to do with unemployed mercenaries. Once peace returned, there was no longer any need to employ mercenaries—but the newly unemployed soldiers could often become a real nuisance.

The *routiers* were bands of mercenaries who roamed throughout France during the Hundred Years' War. Most were former knights and soldiers who were no longer required as a result of various truces and peace treaties, or military action moving to another area, but who had no desire to return home. Due to their backgrounds, they were well organized and often well trained.

It was usual for an invading force to live off the land that it was occupying. This could supplement supplies and pay sent from home. As occupations went on, ransacking was replaced with ransoming of whole areas. Effectively, protection money was paid by the inhabitants to allow normal life to carry on. The apparent ease with which the captains of war could make their fortunes attracted others to try the same thing. So, when the "official" war moved on to another area or a royal truce stopped the use of ransoms, the *routiers* often took the place of the departing armies. Some even had their own uniforms and employed secretaries to divide up their spoils. They were also ruthless in their actions, pillaging, raping, and looting indiscriminately.

HEROIC DEEDS

As knights emerged as an elite, self-selected group, distinctly different from simple warriors on horseback, chivalric notions institutionalized the cult of heroism into the formal conduct of its members. Knights and princes often exposed themselves to more danger than was strictly necessary in order to maintain or enhance their heroic reputations or to avoid the possibility of appearing less than honorable to their peers. Promises to perform heroic deeds provided additional motivation for knights to prove themselves and helped ensure group cohesion, for example, by making individual retreat a decidedly *unheroic* option that could destroy a knight's reputation.

It is clear that chivalric ideals had a real impact on medieval warfare. For example, Henry of Trastámara, king of Castile from 1366–67 and 1369–79, was situated in a strong position on the top of a hill before the Battle of Nájera in 1367, but he gave up his advantageous position, against the advice of his captain,

so that no one could accuse him of acting unchivalrously. Unfortunately, he then lost the battle! Heroic deeds, and the expectation that they would be carried out without hesitation, were right at the heart of what chivalry meant to people in the Middle Ages.

The famous French knight Geoffrey de Charny (*c.* 1300–56) wrote in his acclaimed *Book of Chivalry* (1350) that noble responsibilities ranged from giving people good government and serving God to administering justice tempered with pity and mercy where appropriate. A noble ruler must "be the first to take up arms and to strive with all their might and expose themselves to the physical dangers of battle in defense of their people and their land." A contemporary, English chronicler Geoffrey le Baker (flourished 1326–58), described de Charny as "a knight more skilled in military matters than any other Frenchman," so de Charny was obviously a good source of advice in these matters.

THE HEART OF A LION

From an early age, Richard I—known as Richard the Lionheart—showed significant political and military ability. He became noted for his chivalry, heroism, and courage as he fought to control the rebellious nobles in his territories.

Richard had many opportunities to demonstrate his heroic temperament throughout his military career. In the late twelfth century, the fortress of Taillebourg was considered impregnable. Richard destroyed the farms and lands surrounding the fortress, leaving its defenders no prospect of reinforcement and no possibility of retreat. With the defenders forced to come out and fight, Richard quickly seized the castle, achieving his first great military success. During the siege of Acre (1189–91), Richard was taken ill but insisted on picking defenders off the city walls with a crossbow while lying on his stretcher.

BLINDMAN'S BLUFF

John the Blind, king of Bohemia (reigned 1310–46), died at Crécy demonstrating that neither youth nor eyesight was a requirement for heroic deeds. Although he was unable to see his enemy, he did not allow this to put him off taking part in the great battle, and he asked his companions for assistance. Froissart the Chronicler recorded that he requested that they help him get close enough to the enemy so that he could "strike one stroke with my sword." So that they would not lose him in the press of bodies in the battle, his companions tied their horses together and went

LEFT: *At the Battle of Nájera (1367)—seen here in a fourteenth-century illustration—Henry of Trastámara, supported by the French, fought heroically but unsuccessfully against his brother, Peter the Cruel, who was aided by the English under Prince Edward of Woodstock.*

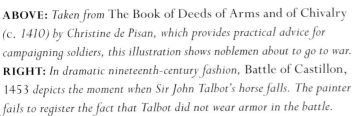

ABOVE: *Taken from* The Book of Deeds of Arms and of Chivalry *(c. 1410) by Christine de Pisan, which provides practical advice for campaigning soldiers, this illustration shows noblemen about to go to war.*
RIGHT: *In dramatic nineteenth-century fashion,* Battle of Castillon, 1453 *depicts the moment when Sir John Talbot's horse falls. The painter fails to register the fact that Talbot did not wear armor in the battle.*

forward into the fight. The blind king accomplished his desire, striking around him at his enemies until he himself was struck down. The next day, the king and his companions were found among the dead, their horses still tied together.

In the same battle, Prince Edward of Woodstock (1330–76), known later as the Black Prince, was at the center of some of the fiercest fighting. When his father, King Edward III, was informed of the danger his 16-year-old son was in, he refused to send help, exclaiming "let him win his spurs." The prince fought at the front of his division, killing knights, helping his comrades, and encouraging all those around him with his heroic deeds. He only ceased his struggle when

the enemy retreated behind the mound of their dead. After the battle, Edward remained on the battlefield in order to pay his tribute to the blind king of Bohemia. He was deeply impressed by the late king's heroism, and, as a gesture of respect and admiration, he took the motto from the king's arms (*Ich Dien*, meaning "I serve") and incorporated it into his own badge.

A RASH DECISION

In another example of a heroic deed, Sir John Talbot (*c.* 1390–1453), Earl of Shrewsbury, was seeking to recover Bordeaux for the English in 1453, when he came across some French knights on a hill. As he had made an oath not to take

up arms against the French again, but was duty bound to fight for the English, Talbot refused to wear armor in the engagement. He unfurled his banner and charged the knights before fully appreciating the strength of the enemy force facing him on the other side of the hill. He would have been an obvious target with his white hair, purple hat, and scarlet gown. When it became obvious that he was actually facing a fortified camp protected by artillery, it would have been sensible for him to withdraw in the face of the overwhelming numbers. However, Talbot heroically chose to continue the attack and was killed in the engagement, which became known as the Battle of Castillon.

Heraldry

Among the most enduring aspects of the chivalric culture that emerged in northern France in the twelfth century was the use of a new type of emblem, called the arms *from 1170, or* coat of arms *(in English) from 1490. At first used simply to identify knights in battles or tournaments, it soon came to serve as a mark of noble status.*

The coat of arms was the first of several related types of visual emblem that would be invented by the nobles of western Europe betweeen the twelfth and fourteenth centuries. Because these emblems came to be closely associated with the profession of men called *heralds*, since 1610 all such emblems have been described as *heraldic*, and associated closely with the term *heraldry*—originally and still properly the name of their profession as a whole.

HERALDRY AND THE HERALDS

Heralds originated in northern France as minstrels specializing in the praise of knights in tournaments, and they learned to recognize and describe emblems in order to distinguish the combatants in those mock battles. Between 1270 and 1330, they were converted both in France and in England into royal and lordly *officers of arms*, charged with a growing set of duties as proclaimers, messengers, masters of ceremonies, and the like. From the beginning, however, one of their principal functions was to record the arms of the nobles of their territory, and eventually (by 1458 in England) royal heralds were also charged in some kingdoms not only with registering existing arms, but with granting new arms and associated emblems to those they recognized as noble. Even the royal heralds lost many of their other functions between 1530 and 1630, but

they usually retained their emblematic functions, and since then have been identified almost entirely with them.

Although *heraldic* remains a convenient general term for nobiliary emblems, the emblems are more precisely represented by terms derived from the word *arms*. These include *armories* (the signs of this set in general), *armorial* (pertaining to armories), *armiger* (an entity legally possessing armories), *armigerous* (possessing armories), and *armigery* (the possession and use of armories).

LEFT: *The tomb-plate of Geoffrey Plantagenet (1113–51), Count of Anjou and father of King Henry II of England, is the oldest known colored representation of a shield of arms.*

THE NATURE AND DIFFUSION OF ARMS

The heraldic arms that first appeared on seals in the 1130s soon came to consist of a stylized design, always including a background, or *field*, and often including one or more figures, or *charges,* set against it. Both field and charges were assigned fixed colors that could be arranged in any of a growing set of standard patterns, normally involving two different colors, chosen from a limited set of seven. The number, arrangement, and other characteristics of the charges also came to be fixed, in such a way as to make the whole design both completely distinctive and easy to recognize from a distance when displayed prominently on shields, flags, and horse trappings (caparisons).

No doubt because this new, stable, all-purpose type of emblem was so effective, armigery spread rapidly among the kings, princes, barons, and other great lords of the central regions of Latin Europe—what may be called the *Primary Armorial Region*—who had a practical need for such an emblem as the leaders of military forces and tournament teams. By 1230, virtually all such lords had become armigerous. The immediate successors of the first

armigers of this period usually retained their fathers' emblems with little or no modification, thus converting them into stable signs of their dynasty as a whole, and of its civil and military authority.

Between approximately 1180 and 1250, armigery also spread widely among the landed simple knights of the same region, and by 1270 almost every

knight and every adult squire of knightly birth in that region had become armigerous. The primary motivation for armigery among simple knights and squires was almost certainly their desire to raise their kindred into the Noble Estate. To do this they had to take on the distinctive characteristics of that estate, of which the most important was patrilineage, marked by a common hereditary surname and by common hereditary arms. By 1250 or so—when knighthood in the Primary Armorial Region was restricted to the descendants of knights—the landed knights had been

ABOVE: *This fourteenth-century illustration of the legendary Battle of Roncesvalles in Spain (CE 778) reflects the contemporary use of arms as a means of identification in battle.*

collectively received into the nobility. After about 1280, indeed, admission to that Estate was increasingly effected by a formal grant from a king or prince of the right to be knighted, and from the 1330s this was increasingly accompanied in many lands (and in England replaced from 1458) by a grant of arms as a formal sign of noble status.

BELOW: *This grant of arms, dating from 1569, awarded noble status to Sir Nicholas Bacon. It bears the signatures of the royal heralds, or kings of arms, based in London.*

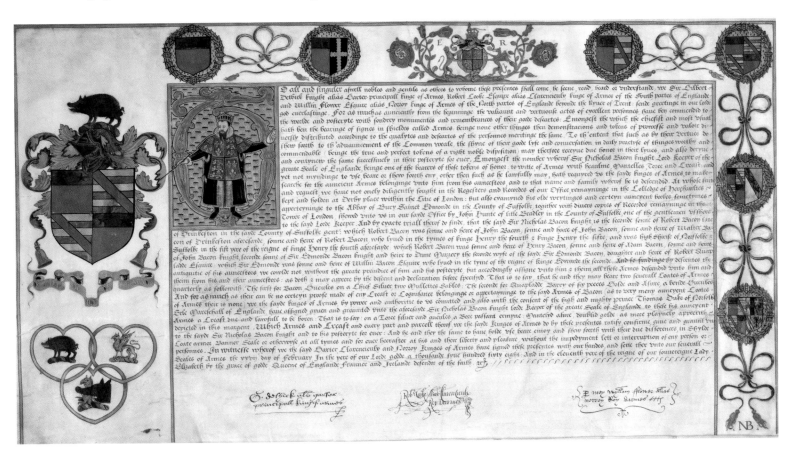

THE COAT OF ARMS

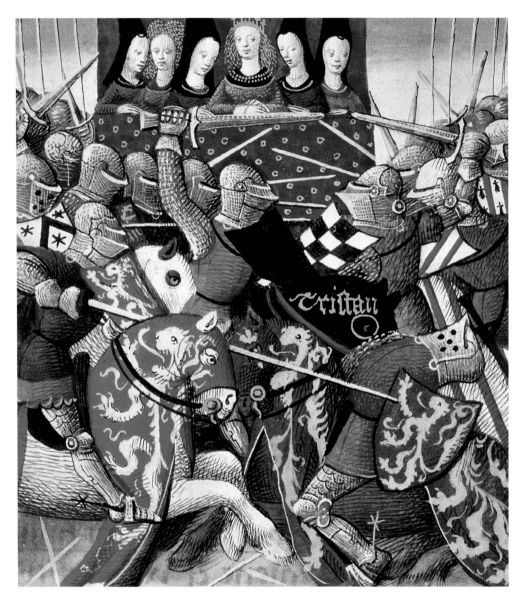

ABOVE: *Distinctive designs for arms helped spectators recognize individual knights in the melee of a tournament, as shown in this fifteenth-century illustration from* Le Roman de Tristan.

The art of the heralds is to devise arms, [and] the colors and the properties that are found in arms. First you shall say the colors ... and then the device of the heralds, as I have learned.

ANONYMOUS, *THE DEAN TRACT* **(1341–45)**

in written *armorials* or *rolls of arms* recording the arms of a large set of knights—in a manner precise enough to permit anyone familiar with the language to produce a technically correct representation. In English a description in this language has been called a *blazon* since 1586, and the act of describing has been represented by the verb *to blazon*.

DESIGN AND COLOR

No limit was set on the kinds of charges that could be employed in the design of a coat of arms, but in practice the vast majority of lay armigers before 1500 chose either purely geometrical types, or charges drawn from a rather small set of beasts, birds, natural objects, and artifacts, often associated with the noble activities of fighting and hunting, or, as with the many forms of cross, with Christianity. Some charges were chosen to play on the surname of the lineage— bows for Bowes and moorcocks for Mo(o)res—or to represent the function

By 1330, the design of arms had become both more precise and fixed, and subjected to a growing set of conventions that constituted a distinct armorial code that varied in detail from country to country. These conventions governed what sorts of patterns and geometrical partitions could be used (especially on the field); what sorts of purely geometrical charges could be set on the field; what sorts of outlines these partitions and figures might have; and what sorts of representational charges might be set on them, with what particular attributes, in what colors, attitudes,

orientations, numbers, and arrange-ments, and in what kinds of relationship to the field and one another.

By 1250, the heralds had established both the basic vocabulary and basic syntactic conventions of an evolving technical language that permitted them to describe concisely all of these aspects of armal design—at first orally, at jousts, but from 1250 increasingly

RIGHT: *An ordinary was a roll of arms arranged by charge. Dating from 1340 and the oldest ordinary in existence, Cooke's Ordinary, a section of which is shown here, catalogued 644 arms.*

it indicated—cups for Butlers, hunting-horns for Fo(r)(e)sters. However, most arms had designs devoid of symbolism.

Down to about 1500 all of the charges were represented in a more or less stylized form, and could be in any of the standard set of seven colors or pair of colors, arranged in any standard pattern. By 1250, the seven colors, or *tinctures*, had been effectively divided into two *metals* (yellow or gold and white or silver), five colors (red, blue, black, green, and purple), and three dichromatic patterns based on and called *furs* (*ermine*, *vair*, and *vairy*), which were treated as equivalent to either a metal or a color. A convention was also established that, for ease of visibility, metal should not be set on (or, in patterns, next to) metal, or color on (or next to) color.

OWNERSHIP, TRANSMISSION, AND DIFFERENCING

Rules also emerged in this period governing the ownership, transmission, and alteration, or *differencing*, of the original or so-called plain arms of a patrilineage. Arms came to be regarded as the legal property of the armigers and their patrilineages, and while they were therefore associated with the common surname of the members of the patrilineage, unrelated patrilineages bearing the same surname (a common occurrence everywhere) were obliged, like all other such lineages in each kingdom or province, to bear unrelated arms.

Transmission customs within patrilineages varied on the basis of regional succession practices. In the lands east of the Rhine and much of northern Italy, the older custom of dividing

noble property equally among sons persisted, so arms were transmitted there to all members of the lineage without alteration. In Britain, France, and other lands west of the Rhine, however, where succession to noble property was governed by primogeniture, the plain arms was regarded as the property of the "chief of name and arms" of the patrilineage—the eldest son of the eldest son (and so on) of the founder. All other male descendants (called *cadets*) were obliged to difference the arms of their father, either permanently or—in the case of the eldest sons of both chiefs and cadets—until their father's death.

Such differencing was never done in a systematic way, and down to about 1330 cadets might either fuse the arms of both of their parents in some way, or adopt a completely different coat, perhaps modeled on that of another relative. After 1330, however, the normal method of

differencing everywhere was to add to the paternal arms a "mark of difference," or *brisure*—initially a large one such as a *label* (a horizontal ribbon with three or more pendants, like those still used in the British royal family) or *bordure* (a colored or patterned border, still used in royal houses and in Scotland), but increasingly, from around 1400, a much smaller one, such as a crescent or star shape (known as a *mullet*), or similar. Such "minor" brisures are still used in nonroyal English lineages.

COMBINING ARMS

Both plain and differenced arms could be used in a "simple form"—that is, not combined with any other—and down to 1450 that was the most common form of display. From 1230, however, and more commonly from around 1340, some armigers combined, or *marshaled*, the arms of their father and their mother (or some other female ancestor) in a single design, to represent the fact that the female ancestor in question had become the heiress of her father or grandfather, and had transmitted to her husband or sons her own ancestral estate (which might include one or more kingdoms or principalities).

Several methods of marshaling were invented. In those called *dimidiation* (involving the right half of one coat and the left half of the other) and *impalement* (involving two or three complete coats set next to one another), the field was divided into two or three

LEFT: *Complex marshaling and the family insignia of coronet and collar feature in the dynastic achievement of Ferdinand I, Archduke of Austria (1521–64) and later Holy Roman Emperor (1558–64).*

monochromatic seals, but from about 1230 they were represented in every imaginable context and scale, often in their full set of tinctures.

It was in the context of several medium-sized escutcheons that arms were normally set on knightly surcoats before about 1330, though they had occasionally been displayed in that context in the primary mode used on flags and horse trappings from 1230 or so. From around 1330 to about 1410 (when the surcoat was temporarily abandoned), and again from about 1430 to about 1500 (when the surcoat in the open-sided form called a *tabard*, still retained by the heralds, was definitively abandoned), the arms were displayed in the primary mode on that coat—from which, in 1490, the emblem took its longer English name.

vertical panels. In that called *quartering per saltire* (peculiar to Spain), it was divided into four triangular partitions. In the most common method, called simply *quartering*, the field was divided both vertically and horizontally into at least four rectangular "quarters," which through subdivision or multiplication could include 16 or more coats.

MODES OF DISPLAYING ARMS

Down to about 1400, arms continued to be displayed in their original contexts—the knightly shield, flag,

and horsecloth—over whose surfaces the whole design was always displayed in full color, in what may be called the *primary mode*. From their first recorded appearance, however, arms had also been displayed in a *secondary mode*, on the surface of a representation of a shield or banner, usually on a significantly smaller scale. Termed *escutcheons*, these representational shields were first set alone on

LATER HERALDIC EMBLEMS

Between 1210 and 1390, armigers in different kingdoms created additional types of emblem, all simpler and less fixed in their characteristics than the arms, but taking a great variety of different forms, and capable of being combined with one another in a similar variety of ways. Two of the new types of emblem, the *crest* and *supporters*, were essentially supplements to the arms for use in particular contexts, were subjected to the same armorial code, and soon formed part of the compound armorial emblem called the *achievement*. The use of a crest (and therefore an achievement) also spread rapidly and widely after 1330 in Latin Europe.

The other new types of emblem, however (including the supporters), were always restricted to the greater armigers, who adopted most of them— the *badge*, *motto*, *device*, *cypher*, and *livery colors*—to mark their servants, allies, and military retinues. As the form and use of these five types of emblem were subjected to a set of conventions quite different from those of the armorial code, they are best described as *para-armorial* emblems.

TYPES OF CREST

The armorial emblem known from 1290 as the crest came into general use in Germany around 1210—more than a century before it did in the rest of Europe. The Latin source-word *crista* had long designated a decorative addition to the summit of a helmet of any kind, and the armorial type probably originated in the representation of

ABOVE: *The wide range and elaborate forms of medieval crests are reflected in this late-fifteenth-century German armorial, the* Hyghalmen Roll, *which also shows how the colors and patterns of the arms were incorporated in the crest design.*

the arms on the initially decorative crest frequently set atop the new form of helmet that evolved between 1180 and 1220: the all-enclosing (*great*) *helm*, which was worn by most knights down to about 1380.

The earliest crests took the form of a fan set at the point of the helm with its flat surfaces at the sides. Many such crests continued to be covered with the arms or one of its charges, but they were increasingly assigned a distinctive emblematic design. The original flat form of crest was the only one used before 1260, and persisted to perhaps 1350, but after about 1260 in Germany, and 1295 elsewhere, it was gradually superseded in most cases by a form molded or constructed in the round in some light material. The new form came to represent a much wider variety of phenomena—especially all or parts of beasts, birds, and human figures—normally arising from a *crest-base* in the form either of a *torse* or *wreath*, or from a decorative *coronet* or *chapeau*. This became the classic type of crest, still in use today, and normally granted along with arms.

THE ACHIEVEMENT

From about 1275 in Germany and 1295 in the rest of western Europe, armorial emblems were increasingly represented pictorially in a formal assemblage called, by 1548, the achievement. The earliest form taken by this compound emblem used by knights and lay lords consisted of a representation of a shield of the arms, over which was set a helm supporting a crest in the current style. From the time of its introduction, this basic form of achievement was sometimes represented on seals between a pair of figures. These figures were originally decorative space-fillers, but from about 1330 they were increasingly distinctive and represented as holding up the shield and helm, thus becoming part of the achievement. In this role they were eventually called supporters.

From 1360 to 1530, supporters frequently took the form of the para-armorial badge of the armiger, but they remained conceptually distinct, and in England from 1508 could be granted as such. From 1350, the achievements of kings and great lords were also increasingly augmented with representations of their crowns or coronets, while those of knights of chivalric orders were augmented with the badge or collar of their order, and those of prelates with insignia of their dignities.

MODERN ARMIGERY

By 1530, the display of arms in the primary mode had fallen into disuse on all social levels except at funerals. Nevertheless, armigery in the secondary, representational mode continued to spread, and the display of armories continued to flourish on all social levels down to about 1690, when it began a long decline. Since about 1870, however, the number of individuals seeking grants of armories, and employing them on their seals, bookplates, china, silver, and the like, has grown steadily in many countries, and armigery has become much more common among corporate bodies—including schools, universities, municipalities, and businesses.

ABOVE: *The London Midland and Scottish Railway Company's achievement combines a shield bearing the arms; supporters; a helmet with torse, crest, and mantling; and a scroll bearing a motto.*

PARA-ARMORIAL EMBLEMS

The most important of the para-armorial emblems was the badge, which was a freestanding figure taking the form of an object, plant, or beast. Many great lords possessed numerous badges. Badges were frequently associated with mottoes, expressing some sentiment, and set on small scrolls. The device was a combination of a badge and a motto, while the cypher consisted of letters representing either a secret motto or personal names. In their distinctive contexts, these emblems were often strewn over a field of livery colors, which could number from one to five, and were usually displayed in panels.

BELOW: *Henry VIII rides a horse displaying his marital cypher and device, alongside servants in livery uniforms. The stand at the rear bears the king's livery colors and badge of a red rose.*

Crusading Orders

Out of the Crusades emerged a form of knightly order now referred to as a crusading order, military monastic order, or religious order of knighthood. Combining the secular ideals of knighthood with the religious ideals of monasticism, it gave rise to military forces that were larger and better disciplined than those of any prince or baron.

LEFT: *Painted c. 1505 by Sodoma, this fresco adorning the cloister of the Abbey of Monte Oliveto Maggiore in Tuscany, Italy, shows Benedict of Nursia, founder of the Benedictine monastic order, eating with his followers.*

Christian monasticism first emerged in the deserts of Egypt in the fourth century CE, primarily to maintain the original heroic form of Christian life during the rapid transformation of the church from a persecuted minority sect into a religion that was not merely tolerated but strongly promoted by the Roman state. The earliest "monks" were hermits who dedicated themselves to a radically world-rejecting lifestyle, but groups of monks were soon united in communities under a strict rule for daily life, and the governance of an abbot. Such monks were normally

required to swear to live in perpetual poverty, chastity, and obedience to their superiors, and to divide their days between prayer and labor.

By CE 486, when the last region of the Latin-speaking Western Roman Empire came under the control of Germanic kings, this form of monasticism had become the dominant type, and by around the year 700 hundreds of monastic communities had been established. The earliest such communities were endowed with a variety of different rules, but by 800 the most common was the Benedictine Rule, composed around 515 by the abbot Benedict of Nursia (c. 480– c. 547), and by 1100 it was the norm.

Significantly, monks soon came to be thought of as *milites Christi*— "soldiers of Christ"—who through their collective prayers fought against the forces of darkness, and protected any laymen who managed to secure a mention in those prayers. This idea gave rise both to the foundation of new monasteries by kings and magnates, and to a continuous stream of generous donations of lands, money, and personnel to existing monasteries by all who could afford to do so.

THE EMERGENCE OF MONASTIC ORDERS

Down to 910, monasteries were all essentially autonomous communities, and recognized no monastic authority higher than those of their own abbot and chapter (general assembly). The foundation in that year of the Abbey of Cluny in southern Burgundy, however, soon led to the formation of the first of what would come to be called monastic *orders*: federations of dozens or even hundreds of monasteries.

Not surprisingly, the most important of these new orders before the proclamation of the First Crusade in 1095 was that of the Cluniacs, but monks of yet more austere inclinations saw even the Cluniacs' achievement as inadequate, and several new orders were founded

BELOW: *The headquarters of the Cistercian order, the Abbey of Cîteaux, near Dijon in France, was almost destroyed during the French Revolution. It was restored to the order in 1898.*

to impose a stricter form of life. The most influential of the new Benedictine orders of the latter type was certainly that based in the Abbey of Cîteaux in northern Burgundy, founded in 1098, and soon in control of numerous daughter houses owing obedience to its abbot. Its members, called Cistercians, emphasized a life of serious manual labor and apostolic simplicity in remote locations. Their communities also incorporated for the first time men called *lay brothers*, who were not required to take full monastic vows, but nevertheless lived within the monastery and carried out many useful tasks for the salvation of their souls. Not surprisingly, the Cistercian version of Benedictine monasticism became one of the principal models for the orders that were not only monastic but also military.

SEMIMONASTIC RULES
Other models were also created in the same period. The monastic state came to be regarded as the spiritual ideal, and many who for various reasons could not embrace a full monastic lifestyle sought to take on whatever elements of it they could. This led to the invention of new semimonastic rules, including the so-called (Third) Augustinian Rule,

ABOVE: *Part of a cycle depicting the Life of St. Augustine painted in 1465 in the monastery of Sant'Agostino, San Gimignano, Italy, this fresco shows Augustine passing his rule to his followers.*

composed anonymously shortly before 1100, on the basis of a letter written by Augustine of Hippo (CE 354–430), and designed for people who had to perform some function in the secular world. It was soon adopted by bodies of *hospitallers*, attendants of hospitals, which at that time were hostels for pilgrims and travelers as well as institutions for the sick. Some hospitallers were priests, but the majority were either clerics in minor orders or simple laymen, so the Augustinian Rule, like the Cistercian, soon proved useful for organizing people of different conditions and functions in the same community.

THE TEMPLARS AND HOSPITALLERS

The combination of the monastic and military ideals of the age in a single body could not have been effected if the absolute moral prohibition of homicide—long maintained by the leaders of the Catholic Church—had not been lifted by the papal proclamation of the First Crusade in 1095. That proclamation had implicitly made homicide not only licit for the first time, but also praiseworthy if committed by a man bound by the vows and living the quasi-religious life of a crusader—as long as those killed were not Christians.

THE FIRST MILITARY ORDERS

The new doctrine allowed crusaders to claim for themselves in a literal sense the traditional monastic title *miles Christi* (*miles* being the singular of *milites*), either in the general sense of "soldier of Christ," or—among those of knightly vocation—in the more particular sense of "knight of Christ." It was on the basis

of these new ideas that the orders of crusading knights were founded.

The first two orders approached the union of monasticism and knighthood from opposite directions: one imposed a monastic rule of Cistercian type on a recently created body of crusading knights, while the other introduced a class of knights into a well-established order of Augustinian hospitallers. This effectively established two quite different models for military orders, one purely military, and the other combining military with charitable

RIGHT: *The Knights Hospitaller fought long and hard to retain the Holy Land, leading the final, unsuccessful defense of Acre, depicted in this 1845 painting by Dominique-Louis Papéty.*
BELOW: *Twelfth-century frescoes in the Chapel of the Templars at Cressac-sur-Charente, near Angoulême, France, depict Templars at the Battle of Bocquee, in modern-day Syria, in 1163.*

*Take this sword; its brightness stands for faith,
its point for hope, its guard for charity.
Use it well.*

THE RITE OF PROFESSION OF THE HOSPITALLERS OF ST. JOHN

activities associated with the care of the sick. Almost all of the later orders would emulate one model or the other, with modifications to suit their particular circumstances.

KNIGHTS OF THE TEMPLE

The first purely military order was founded around 1120 in Jerusalem by a small group of lay knights led by Hugues de Payens (*c.* 1070–1136), a nobleman from Champagne in France. Hugues and his followers took the usual monastic vows of poverty, chastity, and obedience, but also undertook the unusual task of defending the pilgrims then flocking to the Holy City. From the name given to their headquarters, they came to be known as the Knights of the Temple of Solomon, or Templars. By 1129, they had undertaken to contribute to the defense of the kingdom, and lacked only a distinctive rule to make them a true order. Almost inevitably, Hugues turned to Bernard (1090–1153), Abbot of Clairvaux in Champagne, who probably helped to compose the new rule the knights received from the Council of Troyes in 1129, and certainly wrote for them *In Praise of the New Knighthood* (*De laude novae militiae*, *c.* 1130), a tract that justified the foundation of a religious order dedicated to military activities.

The new order, which adopted the formal name of the Order of the Poor Knights of Christ of the Temple of Solomon, appealed immediately to the knightly nobilities of Latin Christendom, and was soon showered with privileges and properties in almost every kingdom, making it one of the largest, richest, and most widespread monastic orders of its time. It was also given a number of key fortresses in the crusader states of the Levant, and soon became a vital element of their defensive system.

KNIGHTS OF THE HOSPITAL

The Order of the Hospital of St. John of Jerusalem grew to be a military order in a completely different way. It started as a body of hospitallers, attached to a hospital in Jerusalem founded around 1080. Its services impressed the crusaders who conquered Jerusalem in the First Crusade, and it was erected into a separate order under the Augustinian Rule in 1103. Under the government of its first Master, the Blessed Gerard (*c.* 1040–1120), other privileges and donations quickly followed, and after 1130 the order developed along the same general lines as that of the Knights of the Temple, acquiring a large number of properties scattered throughout Latin Christendom.

The order began to take in knights as brethren by 1123, probably recruiting from the same pool as the Templars, and they soon carried out military duties similar to those of the Templars,

defending castles and serving as major units in the army of the Kingdom of Jerusalem. By 1150, the Hospitallers rivaled the Templars in the number and importance of their military possessions, and by 1190 in the number of their military brethren—several hundred knights. Nevertheless, the order continued to devote a significant part of its resources to its original charitable functions.

MILITARY ORDERS FOUNDED AFTER 1130

Between 1198 and about 1250, the militarization of the Hospital of St. John seems to have inspired that of three comparable bodies of hospitallers, one founded in Jerusalem by 1142 as a hospital for lepers, the others founded (or refounded) in Acre in 1191 to serve German and English pilgrims respectively. The German body, originally founded around 1120, and militarized around 1198 as the Order of the Teutonic Knights of the Hospital of St. Mary, was the first to take on this character, and the only one of the three to achieve any military or political importance. Both the English Order of the Hospital of St. Thomas of Acre, militarized only in 1227–28, and the Order of the Hospital of St. Lazarus of Jerusalem remained too small and too poor to play a significant part in the defense of the Holy Land.

THE IBERIAN ORDERS

Even before the beginning of the Third Crusade in 1188, four military orders modeled loosely on that of the Temple had been founded to support the Iberian Reconquista, which had been declared to be a crusade by Pope Eugenius III in 1147. Three of these were affiliated with the Cistercian Order: the Order of Calatrava, founded in 1158; the Order of St. Benedict of Évora (later of Avis), founded at Évora in Portugal in 1166; and the Order of St. Julian of Pereiro, founded in León by 1176 and from 1218 known as the Order of Alcántara, after it was granted that town. The fourth great Iberian order, that of St. James (or Sant'Iago) of Compostela in Galicia, was created in 1170 by imposing a semimonastic rule on an older military confraternity.

LEFT: *Military orders were at the forefront of the long campaign to oust the Moors from Spain, depicted in this late-thirteenth-century Spanish manuscript illustration.*

These remained the greatest Iberian orders, but four lesser ones would be founded on that peninsula between 1173 and 1280, and two others would be founded there to replace the local province of the Templars shortly after the suppression of the order in 1312. As a result, after 1170 the peninsula had the highest concentration of military orders of any region in Latin Christendom. All of its orders played a role in the reconquest of Spain from the Moors.

THE BALTIC ORDERS

In the years between the Third and Fourth Crusades to the Holy Land (1192–1204), a third front opened on the frontier between the Christian Germans and their still pagan neighbors—the Baltic Prussians, Lithuanians, and Latvians, and the Finnic Estonians—along the shores of the Baltic Sea. This gave rise to three distinct orders.

RIGHT: *A black cross adorned the shield and surcoat of the Teutonic knight, as shown in this twentieth-century artist's impression.*

A crusade against the Baltic pagans was first undertaken in the far north in 1202 by a new German order officially called the Knighthood of Christ of Livonia, whose members were called the Brethren of the Sword. By 1230, it had succeeded in conquering most of what was called Livonia, corresponding to what is now southern Estonia and most of Latvia. In or shortly before 1228, a Polish bishop founded the Order of Dobrzyn on the same model, to conquer the pagan Prussians at the western end of the region. In the meantime, however,

ABOVE: *Now part of the Polish town of Malbork, Marienburg Castle was the headquarters of the Teutonic Order. Ruined during World War II, it has since been carefully rebuilt.*

in 1225 the Duke of Mazovia in Poland had offered to the Teutonic Order the Culmerland district if they sent a force to fight the Prussians. The Teutonic Order was still based in Acre, but a branch of the order soon took possession of Culmerland, establishing a branch of the Teutonic Order under a new Master of Livonia. In 1235, they absorbed the weaker Order of Dobrzyn, and in 1237 amalgamated with the Order of the Brethren of the Sword.

The Teutonic knights of Livonia quickly made themselves the collective lords of their peculiar order-state, which by 1309—when the Grand Master, driven in 1291 from Acre, established the order's headquarters at Marienburg, modern-day Malbork in Poland—included what is now northern Poland, Lithuania, Latvia, and Estonia.

A CONSISTENT HIERARCHY

Military orders were usually based on the Cistercian model, with houses and provincial commands under a central government. From 1200, the dominant class in every order was composed of *brother knights*, who from about 1250 were drawn entirely from the new knightly nobility of Latin Christendom. Most orders included a second class of military brethren, called *brother sergeants* or *brother sergeants-at-arms*, whose fathers were either landless knights or simple freemen. All orders also included a small number of men in holy orders called *brother chaplains*, and a larger class of

nonprofessed servants of humble birth called *brothers-of-work* or *brother sergeants-of-office*. Some also maintained associated lay confraternities, whose members (*confratres* or "fellow-brethren") were admitted to the order's spiritual privileges in return for donations and vows of protection and occasionally fought in campaigns for a season or two.

The supreme government of each order was vested in a chief officer, the *magister* (master) or *magnus magister*, (grand master). Elected for life, he oversaw the administration of the order, led its forces, and presided over the *chapters general*, meetings of its officers.

It seems that a new knighthood has recently appeared on the earth. It ceaselessly wages a twofold war both against flesh and blood, and against a spiritual army of evil in the heavens.

BERNARD OF CLAIRVAUX,
IN PRAISE OF THE NEW KNIGHTHOOD (DE LAUDE NOVAE MILITIAE, c. 1130)

MILITARY ORDERS SINCE THE CRUSADES

The decline in the fortunes of all of the orders other than the Hospitallers after the failure of the Crusades at the end of the thirteenth century was due to a number of factors, especially the success or failure of the original enterprise, a destructive rivalry among the orders, and the decline of the monastic ideals they represented. In addition, the complete reorganization of national armies effected in the fifteenth and sixteenth centuries removed even the potential utility of most of the surviving orders as military units.

LEAVING THE HOLY LAND

The retaking in 1291 of Acre and Tripoli by the Mamluk sultan of Egypt forced the four military orders that had stayed in the Holy Land to fall back to Christian Cyprus, regroup, and decide what to do next. All but the Templars withdrew from Cyprus as soon as they could find somewhere else to settle. The knights of St. Thomas moved to England, those of St. Lazarus to Italy and France. Neither order played any further role in the Crusades. The former was suppressed for religious reasons by Henry VIII. The Italian branch of the latter was joined with the revived Savoyard Order of St. Maurice in 1572, and its French branch was similarly joined with the new royal Order of Our Lady of Mount Carmel in 1608. The Teutonic Order was obliged to fall back on its Livonian lands, abandoning the Mediterranean completely, but continuing its northern crusade.

ABOVE: *This dramatic oil painting by Belgian artist Gustaf Wappers (1803–74) portrays the Hospitallers defending Rhodes against a Muslim attack in the early fourteenth century.*

The Hospitallers of St. John moved westward in 1310 to the island of Rhodes, where they soon established an order-state, comparable in nature, if not in size, to that of the Teutonic Knights in the Baltic. From there the "Knights of Rhodes" maintained a continuous naval war against the Muslims until 1527, when they were obliged to surrender the island to the Ottoman sultan, following a furious siege. In 1530, Emperor Karl V granted them the island of Malta and its archipelago, and as the "Knights of Malta" they carried on a continuous war against the Muslims in the Mediterranean until dispossessed by Napoléon Bonaparte in 1798. The main, Catholic branch of the order finally moved its seat to Rome in 1831, and survives today as a semimonastic order dominated by knights of the modern, honorific type. Secularized branches of the order also either survived or were revived in a number of Protestant countries, including Britain and its former empire.

The fate of the Templars was uniquely disastrous. They were unable to adjust to their new situation after 1291, and soon fell victim to the ambitions of Philip IV of France (reigned 1285–1314), who accused them of engaging in blasphemous initiation rites. After a trial that resulted in the public burning of the order's last grand master, Jacques de Molay, the Templars were suppressed in 1312 by Pope Clement V, who granted the order's confiscated estates to the Hospitallers. Since 1317, the order has survived only in its reconstituted Portuguese and Aragonese branches, though many other groups have claimed its heritage.

SECULAR CONTROL

Like the four older Iberian orders that survived after 1319, those of Christ and Montesa played an active part in the

LEFT: *The Templars plead before Philip IV and Pope Clement V in this illustration from the fourteenth-century* Chronicles of France.

defense of the peninsula led by Alfonso XI of Castile from 1325 until his death in 1350. Thenceforth, these six Iberian orders had few chances to fight the Moors, and devoted their energies to quarreling, both within and among themselves, and interfering in regnal politics. Like monks in general, their brethren also became increasingly worldly in outlook and behavior. For these reasons, the Iberian kings sought to control the orders within their domains, at first by securing the election of one of their sons or brothers as master, and then, after the completion of the Reconquest in 1492, by annexing the masterships to their own crowns. With hiatuses under republican regimes, all of the major orders have been maintained in this condition, and are treated as elements of the Spanish system of honors for members of the old nobility.

ABOVE: *This early twentieth-century image shows members of the Teutonic Order at the Elizabeth Church, Marburg in Germany, which was built by the order in the thirteenth century.*

The fate of the Baltic orders was similar, but resulted from a different sequence of events. The essential purpose of the Teutonic Order—to bring Catholic Christianity to the Baltic pagans—was finally achieved when Grand Prince Jogaila of Lithuania converted in order to marry the heiress of Catholic Poland, but the ruler of Poland–Lithuania seized control of both eastern and western Prussia and divided the domain into two parts. What was left of Prussia became a fief of the Polish crown, and passed out of the order's control in 1525, when the reigning high master, Albrecht von Hohenzollern, became a Protestant and ruled it as a duke. Livonia remained under the control of the (newly independent) Brethren of the Sword until 1561, when their high master also became a Polish vassal as the Duke of Courland. The Teutonic Order was then restricted to Germany proper, and later Austria, where it persisted as a knightly fraternity until 1929.

Asian Knights

European knights were part of a wider phenomenon of warrior elites in traditional societies. An examination of some of the most prominent "knights" from other cultures—Japanese bushi, *Indian* kshatriya, *and Chinese* yóuxiá—*provides a comparative perspective on the lifestyle and culture of European knights.*

The members of a warrior elite practiced warfare as a lifestyle or duty of their social class—they were raised into it. They were therefore very well trained, at least in the familial and small-group contexts prevailing within their class. Whether formal training in larger groups and centralized military discipline formed part of their experience depended on the relationship of the elites to the central state, and was not a common occurrence. Warrior elites were not, therefore, professionals in a technical sense.

Rather, their privileged social position obligated them to and was maintained by their specialized military function.

WARRIOR ELITES OUTSIDE EUROPE

Warrior elites are probably best considered a phenomenon of sedentary or agricultural societies. Nomadic warriors of the Central Asian steppes, such as the Turks and Mongols, had class distinctions, but these were less vast than among farming communities, and were further attenuated by the fact

that every member of a steppe tribe was a warrior. As a group, steppe nomads might be seen as a warrior elite in waiting (waiting, that is, on conquest of a neighboring sedentary society), but are in truth a separate phenomenon. Conversely, renowned warrior elites who lacked horses, such as the Incas and Aztecs, are comparable to knights in social status and function, even if the lack of horses makes for an odd match. But the most direct comparisons are to the horsed elites of other Eurasian societies.

ABOVE: *With knightlike courage and chivalry, Saladin famously battled Richard the Lionheart and his crusader army throughout the Holy Land.*
LEFT: *This thirteenth-century* CE *stone relief depicts Seljuk warriors in armor reminiscent of the helmets and chain mail of European knights.*

RIGHT: *The Mongol Invasions Scrolls (c. 1293) were commissioned by Japanese warrior Takezaki Suenaga to celebrate his bravery against the Mongol invaders of 1274 and 1281. In this image, Suenaga attacks a Mongol bowman.*

In this context, the cavalry forces of Southwest Asia, which formed the heartland of the medieval Islamic world, are anomalous. The cavalries of the early Arab expansion (CE 632–*c.* 680) were small (infantry predominated), and were less well armed than European knights; their horses were lighter, and they came from a tribal and seminomadic culture. After the rise of the Abbasid Caliphate in 750, and even more after the coming of the Seljuk Turks into the area during the late eleventh century, Central Asian steppe nomads formed the core of Islamic states' military forces. In addition, for a variety of complex political and cultural reasons, these elite warriors were predominantly slaves, dependent on the political leader who owned them. Thus, they meet the definition of a warrior elite militarily, but fall about as far outside the "social elite" aspect of the definition as possible.

Their servile status is an aspect of the idiosyncratic separation of medieval Islamic states from their own societies. At times, as in thirteenth-century Egypt, these slaves, or Mamluks, dispensed with the sultan altogether and ruled the state directly, choosing one of their own as ruler. But even then they cannot be considered a true social elite, because they existed as a closed caste separate from the society that they ruled, foreigners still in their own land. The greatest Islamic leader of the age, Saladin (1137/38–93), earned a well-deserved reputation for being a chivalrous warrior, even among the crusaders whom he defeated, but the image cannot plausibly be extended to his armies. Outside of the Islamic world, the cataphracts of tenth-century Byzantium are fairly comparable to western knights,

Victory is changing the hearts of your opponents by gentleness and kindness.

SALADIN (1137/38–93)

but the strength of the Byzantine central government complicates the comparison in a number of major ways.

AN ASIAN TRIUMVIRATE

While most of these groups display similarities to European knights, three Asian examples offer particularly informative and interesting comparisons. The Japanese *bushi*, or warrior class, are strikingly similar to knights in enough ways as to throw the differences into revealing high relief. The *kshatriya* of Hindu India are a warrior caste for whom the emphasis on their social position carries significantly greater weight than the details of their warrior function. Finally, the Chinese tradition

of *yóuxiá*, or wandering warriors, is a group with a military function and chivalrous(ish) ethos similar to that of the European knights, but detached from elite social standing.

For the sake of a consistent set of comparisons, each group will be considered in terms of four important characteristics. First, social status: where did the group fall in the society's social structure in terms of prestige, influence, and legal privileges? Second, relationship to the state: did warriors dominate the state, or vice versa? In a sense, this is a measure of the influence of the warrior aristocracy over the formal mechanisms of state power, separate from the informal influence of warriors in society. Third, tactics, armor, and weaponry: what were the group's main fighting styles, their preferred weapons, and the other material trappings of their function and status? Fourth, culture: what were the main features of the group's constructed identity in terms of things such as notions of honor, acceptable techniques in war, their attitude to death, and so forth, and the relationship of these factors to religion?

BUSHI AND *SAMURAI*

The *bushi* (warrior class) of Japan originated as the provincial dependents of and enforcers for the Kyoto-based court aristocracy of the Heian period (*c.* CE 794–1185). When court politics became factionalized in the later twelfth century, so did the country's warriors, and a major civil war, the Gempei War (1180–85), resulted in the founding of the first shogunate (military government) under Minamoto Yoritomo (1147–99). This warrior government existed at first alongside the civil government in Kyoto, from which it derived its legitimacy, but by the fourteenth century had displaced it entirely; from this point the *bushi* were the dominant social class in Japan.

The dependents and retainers of the main military families were called *samurai*, derived from the verb "to serve,"

which closely parallels the origin of the word *knight* (which comes from the Anglo-Saxon word *knecht*, meaning "servant"). In the Kamakura period (1185–1333), family relationships dominated the social organization and loyalties of the *bushi*, but this broke down during the fourteenth century, and in the later fifteenth century *bushi* relationships were reconstructed around lordship and pay. This was when the term *samurai* rose in prominence, and corresponded with significant changes in Japanese warfare similar to those in Europe at the same time.

Thus, from roughly 1185 to 1500, the *bushi* corresponded closely to the European knightly class: they rose as the dependents of an older aristocracy to a position of social dominance. This position was more complete in Japan

ABOVE: *Illustrated here by Richard Gordon Smith in 1908, a fourteenth-century Japanese folk tale relates how Murakami Yoshiteru, servant of Prince Morinaga, bravely committed* hara-kiri *to distract the enemies while his master escaped.*

than it was in Europe, as the Japanese warriors had no centralized church or unified priestly order to rival them. The warriors also dominated the operations of the Japanese state under the figurehead of the emperor. But in both social and institutional terms, the *bushi* were for most of this period less firmly connected to and in control of peasant production and village social relations than were knights, receiving assigned shares of income from specific estates, but no proprietorship or legal jurisdiction over those estates.

LEFT: *Although Minamoto Yoritomo, founder of the first shogunate, was a great warrior, he was killed in a simple riding accident.*

TOOLS AND TECHNIQUES

As elite warriors, the *bushi* owned and rode horses that, like knightly steeds, were large, specially bred, and expensive. For most of this period the *bushi* were equally likely to fight on foot as on horseback, with no prestige advantage attaching to either mode, but skill at horsemanship was admired. Warriors wore various forms of body armor, usually sewn together and consisting of multiple panels. The chief weapons were the sword and the bow, and the latter definitely dominated: skill at shooting defined warrior prestige, in contrast to

European knights, who found bows dishonorable. Indeed, *bushido*, meaning "the way of the warrior," was also known as "the way of the horse and bow."

The *bushi* dominated warfare, as lower-class troops were close to useless until the late fifteenth century. Battle seeking was more common than in European warfare, and battles featured an odd mix of ritualistic elements— warriors called out their own names and lineages before battle to advertise their prestige, and they shot whistling arrows to formally initiate combat. Killing of *bushi* by *bushi* was common, while taking prisoners was rare. The practice of *hara-kiri*, or ritual suicide, came to characterize the *bushi* approach to honor.

CULTURE AND RELIGION

More generally, warriors aspired to the cultural standards of the court aristocracy and eventually replaced them as the arbiters of Japanese culture. Literacy was thus a constant feature of the warrior class. Mixing historical and literary elements, war tales both reflected and shaped warrior identity. Interestingly, these tales usually focus on the

losing side (or the losing faction from the winning side), as tragic defeat appealed to warriors more than triumphalism. This may have resulted from the philosophical outlook of Buddhism, the religion (along with Shinto) of the *bushi*.

In the thirteenth century, the particular form of Buddhism known as Zen became especially popular among warriors. Its stress on enlightenment as a state of immediate apprehension of reality and on the transitory nature of existence seemed to fit particularly well with a class that faced death in combat. The cherry blossom, which blooms briefly but gloriously, became the symbol of the Japanese warrior class. *Bushido*, even more than chivalry, was about warrior identity and not about social justice or defending the weak.

BELOW: *Utagawa Kuniyoshi (c. 1797–1861), a master of woodblock prints, depicts Lord Odai Matarokuro (Yorisada) during his sixteenth-century war with Takeda Shingen.*

THE CULT OF THE SWORD

Perhaps the best-known aspect of medieval Japanese warrior culture is also the most mythic. The cult of the sword was largely an invention of the Tokugawa period (1603–1867). Swords as a symbol of *samurai* identity came into their own then for several reasons. First, the musket displaced the bow as the main missile weapon during the sixteenth century, undermining the latter's cultural centrality and emphasizing the shock role of the cavalry. Second, the Tokugawa shogunate consciously promoted the cult of the sword as part of its efforts to eliminate firearms and identify and close off the *samurai* as a social caste.

DIVINE WARRIORS OF INDIA

The *kshatriya*, the warrior class of India, had its origins in the Aryan migration into the subcontinent sometime around 1500 BCE. The Aryans were Indo-European peoples led by chariot-riding elite warriors. Although they lost their preeminent social position to the Brahmin (the priestly class) during the course of the Vedic Age (1500–600 BCE), they remained the second highest of the four great social classes sanctioned by the creation myths of the Vedas, a class consisting of kings and warriors charged with defending society and ruling justly. Warfare was considered their divine duty.

For the *kshatriya*, therefore, their unique social status was, unlike that of European knights, high from ancient times and much more secure. Especially as the caste system developed and hardened in the post-Vedic Age after *c.* 500 BCE, the hereditary status of those in the *kshatriya* was cemented into the Indian social hierarchy and became a given of Hindu culture. So secure was their place within society that a strong state structure proved unnecessary for fostering or maintaining it. Thus, in relation to states, Indian elite warriors not only dominated state structures but virtually superseded them, meaning that, unlike in both Europe and Japan, warrior rule did not lead to the development of stronger state mechanisms over time.

On the other hand, warrior prestige and social power were always in competition with and limited by the superior prestige and

LEFT: *In the First Battle of Panipat on April 21, 1526, the Timur Babur (1483–1530) was victorious over the Sultan of Delhi, Ibrahim Lodi (died 1526), beginning the Mughal rule of India. This c. 1590 Persian illumination was created to accompany the autobiography of Babur.*

Surrendering completely all activities unto Me ... without any desire for gain, free from proprietorship, fight without grief.

KRISHNA TO ARJUNA,
BHAGAVAD GITA, **CH. 3, VERSE 30**

legitimating authority of the Brahmins. By the medieval period, India was divided into many small kingdoms whose *kshatriya* rulers fought among themselves constantly for prestige. So ingrained were their rivalries that they were incapable of uniting in the face of a number of Islamic raiders after CE 800; by the twelfth century, raid was turning to conquest, and Hindu princes often ended up subordinated to Islamic rulers.

A MAMMOTH IMPACT ON WARFARE

The conservatism of an entrenched social class showed in the patterns of Indian warfare and the role of the *kshatriya* in it. Though the Aryans had entered India as a chariot-riding (and thus horse-using) elite, the climate was unfavorable for the breeding of horses, and the elephant became the supreme status symbol of Indian warrior elites. Elephants—huge, dangerous looking, and capable of carrying many warriors at once—were even better than horses for displaying status on the battlefield, and made magnificent parade animals for demonstrations of royal majesty. But they were unpredictable in battle, as liable to rampage and damage friendly forces as they were to break an opposing

BELOW: *An action-packed illustration from* Akbar-Nama, *the biography of Mughal emperor Akbar the Great (1542–1605), shows an elephant creating havoc on the battlefield.*

ABOVE: *In a scene from the* Mahabharata, *an epic Sanskrit poem from the fifth century* BCE, *a king rides in a horse-drawn carriage, possibly driven by a god. They are accompanied by mounted warriors and elephants with* mahouts.

line; their *mahouts*, or drivers, carried steel spikes to drive into rampaging elephants' brains in such circumstances. And though the smell of elephants panicked horses that were unaccustomed to it, horses trained to face elephants were steady and far more controllable and maneuverable in battle.

The individual arms and tactics of Indian warriors also failed to develop much beyond classical models, with the simple bow seen as the most prestigious weapon. From 1100 onward, Indian armies found themselves at a severe disadvantage when facing the mounted archery of Islamic steppe warriors, who dominated Indian warfare until the eighteenth century.

THE PHILOSOPHY OF THE *KSHATRIYA*

Kshatriya culture, already imbued with a sacred mission to defend society, contributed two major elements to Indian political and ethical philosophy. The first was a classic text of practical political philosophy, the *Arthashastra*. Dating to the height of the Mauryan Empire (*c.* 321–185 BCE), this remarkable work details the duties and virtues of a good ruler. The second, and far more widely influential right down to the present day, was the warrior contribution to Hindu ethical thinking. This derives mainly from the *Bhagavad Gita*, an epic poem that forms part of the even larger *Mahabharata*, a central text of Hindu scripture. It tells the story of Arjuna, a great warrior who, in a dynastic war in which his cousins are his enemies, faces a conflict of *dharmas*, or sacred duties: the warrior's duty to fight and the general duty not to kill one's relatives. As time and the action pause just before the battle, his charioteer Lord Krishna, an incarnation of the god Vishnu, teaches him how to work through this dilemma and arrive at the proper decision—to do his duty as a warrior and go into battle—based on the *yogas*, or disciplines, of Selfless Action, Knowledge, and Devotion.

Through this tale, warfare is seen as an allegory for any struggle an individual or group might face, and Krishna's advice to Arjuna becomes the foundation of Hindu ethical philosophy.

At a more general level, the *kshatriya* as the dominant ruling class, though not necessarily as warriors, produced some of the world's greatest religious figures, as both Siddhartha Gautama, who became the Buddha, and Mahavira, the founder of Jainism, were *kshatriya*. But their particular careers and teachings moved them well away from any ruling and warrior function, illustrating that as a warrior elite the *kshatriya* were, in comparison with European knights, much more elite in status and much less warrior in function.

CHINA'S WANDERING BLADES

In contrast with the *kshatriya* of India, the Chinese social group that is most comparable to European knights, the *yóuxiá* or "wandering blades," shares some functional similarity with knights, especially in the ethos of *xiá* (their code of behavior), but almost none of the social status. The disparity rests in the very different early histories of the Indian and Chinese warrior elites.

THE RISE AND FALL OF THE *YÓUXIÁ*

The earliest Chinese states and dynasties were dominated by a chariot-riding warrior elite who fought for status and glory, much like the chariot warriors of early India and ancient Southwest Asia. During the Spring and Autumn period of the Zhou dynasty (c. 770–476 BCE), the *yóuxiá* emerged, much like European knights, as a warrior class situated between the aristocracy and the common people. But changes in Chinese warfare and statecraft during the Warring States period (c. 475–221 BCE) fundamentally altered the context for the *yóuxiá* and thus their character. The Warring States period saw the emergence of strong, centralized, and bureaucratic states whose armies of mass infantry aimed not at glory but at permanent conquest and the elimination of rival states.

The number of Chinese states steadily shrank until, between 256 and 221 BCE, the western state of Qin finally unified all of China. Inspired by the tough philosophy of Legalism, which stressed absolute state power and saw "mercenaries" (including the *yóuxiá*) as one of the "five vermin" who undermined state authority, the Qin and their Warring States rivals gradually ground an independent warrior elite out of existence.

The Han dynasty solidified the social order that emerged from the Warring States period, an order in which scholar-bureaucrats (increasingly trained in Confucian ethics, though still running a basically Legalist structure) dominated, and the army was a state creation whose generals were office holders, rather than aristocrats, and whose common soldiers lacked social status. Only during the Tang dynasty (CE 618–907), whose rulers were connected to the warriors of the steppes, did a warrior elite temporarily reemerge in China, only to disappear in the civil wars that brought down the dynasty. The subsequent Song dynasty (960–1279) was aggressively civilian, and Confucian bureaucrats reasserted their control over the Chinese state and Chinese culture.

THE DIFFERENCE BETWEEN KNIGHTS AND *YÓUXIÁ*

In this context, "wandering blades"—warriors who were adept at swordplay and, increasingly, individual martial arts—still existed, especially during times of dynastic struggle or when China was divided among several states. But they differed from knights in several crucial respects. First, they lacked social status: after the Warring States period, service in the government was the only sure path to social advancement. And given the absence of an independent aristocracy, they lacked even bonds of attachment to or patronage from the powerful.

The *yóuxiá* were neither a threat to nor closely associated with the state; indeed, Chinese governments tended to lump "wandering swords" and bandits together as one group. The *yóuxiá* preferred to fight on foot, as they

LEFT: *Daggers and spearheads used by warriors of the Eastern Zhou dynasty during the Warring States period, c. 475–221 BCE, were made from bronze. Swords were also cast in bronze, and the blades were sometimes intricately carved with patterns.*

The unusual glorification (by Chinese standards) of warfare and military men under the Tang dynasty expressed itself in Chinese art, particularly in the ceramics whose production Tang artisans perfected. One of their most impressive subjects was the warhorse. Many were modeled on the great "blood-sweating" horses bred in the Ferghana area of Central Asia that were imported into China in great numbers, since China itself proved less than ideal for horse breeding. But while such horses were as valuable as any European charger, their riders did not attain the independent social status of European knights.

BELOW: *This fired clay horse from the Tang dynasty (CE 618–907) stands 17 inches (43 cm) high.*

lacked the resources to obtain and maintain expensive warhorses. Their numbers were never vast, and their unofficial nature and informal organization kept the size of their bands relatively small, with the individual swordsman probably most common.

ABOVE: *Qin Shihuang (259–210 BCE) was the First Emperor of China, reigning from 221 BCE until his death in 210 BCE. During his life he created a magnificent tomb at Xi'an, where modern archaeologists have unearthed over seven thousand terracotta warriors.*

A COMMON WAY OF THINKING

The *yóuxiá* resemble the image of knights in at least one way, however. Their guiding philosophy, *xiá*, stressed protection of the poor and the righting of social injustice, much as chivalry (or more correctly the Romantic image of chivalry) did. Like chivalry, *xiá* was not a formal philosophy but a practical guide, and unlike chivalrous knights its practitioners might well operate outside

or even against the law: the sense of justice that informed *yóuxiá* actions derived from personal convictions and ethics, not from formal adherence to legalities or proper social order. This reflected the fact that the injustices that the *yóuxiá* corrected were likely to arise from official oppression and corruption—in this, *yóuxiá* most resemble not knights but Robin Hood and other similar figures, responding to the overwhelming power of the Chinese state. But again, like

knights, the romantic image of the *yóuxiá* has inspired countless folk tales, stories, and even modern movies based on their exploits, becoming in fact a cornerstone of Chinese popular culture. In this sense, the *yóuxiá* are as heroic as any knight—perhaps more so, to the extent that the image of their social mission conformed to reality.

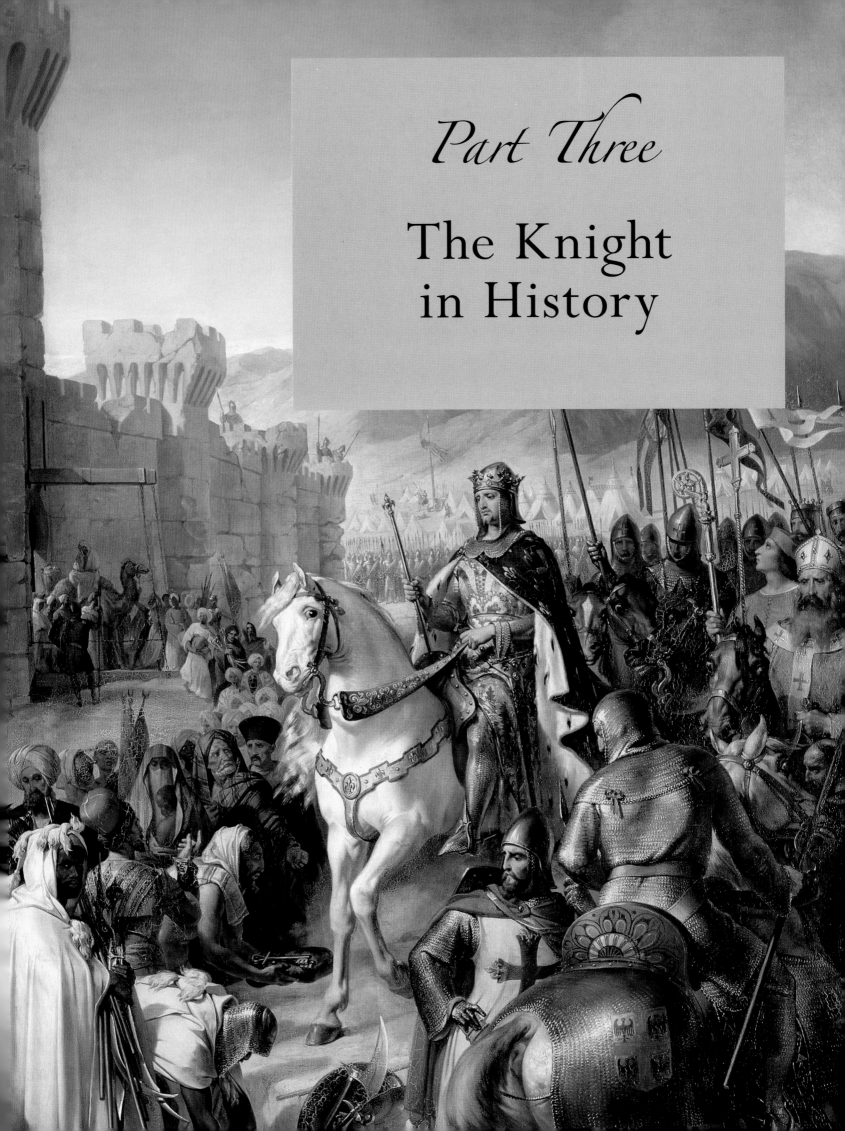

Part Three

The Knight in History

The Rise of Knights

The rise of a knightly order in medieval Europe is the story of a group that slowly emerged from obscure origins to form a social caste that would eventually control the resources and shape much of the politics of the entire continent.

Numerous developments, social and technological, had to occur for knights to rise to prominence. These included improvements in the manufacture and supply of weaponry; sophistication in the breeding, selection, and use of horses; the advent of the private castle; accommodations with the church over the legitimacy of violence; and the creation of ideals of chivalry. Though most of these changes did not take place until at least the late tenth century, others were underway during the reign of Charlemagne, King of the Franks

LEFT: *Along the borders of the Roman Empire, legionnaires and Germanic warriors regularly did battle, as depicted in this second-century CE Roman relief.*

(reigned CE 768–814) and "Emperor of the Romans" (reigned 800–14). Furthermore, the relationships that eventually underpinned knighthood—based on loyalty between a chief and his warriors—were forged much earlier.

ANCIENT LEGACIES

Medieval Europe was born from the collision and union of the Roman Empire and the Germanic peoples. Writing at the end of the first century CE, during the heyday of Roman power, the historian Tacitus showed a deep fascination with the ethos of the Germanic war band, to which he gave the Latin designation of *comitatus* (armed group). He praised the loyalty of these warriors, noting that they faced no greater shame than to outlive their leader or lose a battle.

This admiration is not surprising given that Roman society, too, stressed

BELOW: *Led by Thorismund, the Visigoths turned the tide of the Battle of Châlons in France in CE 451, helping their Roman allies achieve a vital and decisive victory over Attila's Hun army.*

*On the field of battle
it is a disgrace to a chief
to be surpassed in courage by his
followers, and to the followers
not to equal the courage
of their chief . . .
The chiefs fight for victory,
the followers for their chief.*

TACITUS, *GERMANIA* (CE 98)

RIGHT: *The network of relationships that held together medieval society—between farmer and landowner, courtiers and lords—is reflected in this Bohemian fresco, painted around 1400.*

loyalty to leaders. Those of the great senatorial families normally had clients who depended on their patronage and who were ready to back them up whenever needed. Generals received the unswerving support of the legions, to the extent that a number were able to become emperors with military backing.

As Rome went through the crises that would bring about its devolution in the west, Germanic peoples were able to enter the empire, sometimes by agreement, often without. By the fourth century, they had cut deals that recognized their military value to the fading Roman authorities and saw them incorporated in the Roman forces as *foederati* (allies) or *laeti* (a more complicated term that seems to have involved some kind of indentured status). However, once they began to move into the empire more on their own terms, in the fifth century, they often availed themselves of a system called *hospitalitas*, which involved expropriating territory in return for "protection." Across Aquitaine, Burgundy, Spain, and northern Italy, the Ostrogoths, Visigoths, Franks, and Alamanni acquired up to two-thirds of Roman landholders' estates in this way.

In England, which the Romans abandoned around 450, the late-fifth-century Germanic invaders, the Angles, Saxons, and Jutes, quickly seized the upper hand and had even less of an impulse toward accommodation. The retinues that followed Anglo-Saxon kings and heroes, as seen in *Beowulf*, reflected the legacy of the *comitatus*.

A WEB OF LOYALTIES

The personal ties that were so important in the Germanic and Roman systems became even more significant with the disintegration of the empire. The Frankish kings who ruled Gaul (the region that became France) from the fifth century onward governed through counts (*comites* in Latin), men who were their trusted allies and companions. Treaties and allegiances were as much personal as political.

Bonds of loyalty characterized religious practice, too: by the sixth century, when all great churches were dedicated to a saint, that saint was treated as the patron of his or her town and region, as well as church. Even peasants were part of this web of loyalties. Many former slaves became free peasants with the breakdown of the Roman agricultural slavery system in the sixth century, but at the same time other formerly free peasants commended themselves to landlords in order to have a place to live and land to work. Obligations ran both ways: peasants took on heavy agricultural duties, but in return their lords were expected to protect them, both against outsiders and against the dangers of starvation.

When knights first became numerous in the eleventh century, therefore, they took their place in a system of personal ties and loyalties that had been developing for a millennium. They were defined at the most basic level as men who fought on horseback, but their underlying ethos was always one of loyalty: to their lord and to each other.

THE FRANKISH REALM

Among the Germanic peoples who sought first to emulate Rome, then to replace it, the Franks were latecomers. But their success, particularly during the reign of Charlemagne, in conquering rivals, acquiring immense wealth, gaining authority over the church, and briefly establishing a stable realm did much to pave the way for the development of military elites.

BELOW: *In Charles Auguste Steuben's 1837 painting of the Battle of Poitiers (CE 732), the Frankish fighters are portrayed as the defenders of Christianity against the Muslim onslaught.*

RIGHT: Pepin the Short, King of France *(1791), by Marie Champion de Cernel, portrays the influential Carolingian ruler Pepin III, son of Charles Martel and father of Charlemagne.*

The Carolingian family first came to power as Mayors of the Palace for the kings of the Merovingian dynasty founded by Clovis (died CE 511), a post that they parlayed effectively into a type of prime minister's portfolio. The first such Mayor, Pippin of Landen, operated from 613 to 642. Pippin of Herstal (died 714) cemented the family's position by eliminating other rivals in 688, and his son, Charles Martel (*c.* 688–741), claimed further power and prestige for the family by halting the Muslim advance from the Iberian Peninsula into the Frankish kingdom at the Battle of Poitiers (also called the Battle of Tours), near modern-day Tours, France, in 732.

CHURCH AND STATE

Charles's victory also raised the Carolingians' profile as protectors and patrons of the church. This was more than a little ironic since Charles habitually took land and revenues from the church, as well as from laymen he defeated. Following his death, several councils, headed by Charles's oldest son Carloman, met to try to recover the lost lands and revenues for the church, but without substantial success. After Carloman withdrew from temporal affairs to become a monk, his younger brother and heir, Pepin III, also known as Pepin the Short (c. 714–68) continued to exercise control over the Frankish churches—interestingly, while also presenting himself as a valiant protector and advocate of the Christian religion.

Despite these issues, Pepin managed to obtain church support for his campaign for the throne. In 751, he asked Pope Zacharias (reigned 741–52) whether it was proper to call king one who had no real power; the pope responded positively by saying he who wielded actual power should have the title as well. With papal legitimation to bolster his support among the nobles, Pepin dethroned his Merovingian king, Childeric III (reigned 743–51), and took the crown himself. Three years later, Pope Stephen II (reigned 752–57) anointed Pepin as king, thereby adding a Christian sacrality to Frankish kingship.

Pepin was succeeded in 768 by his sons Charles and Carloman, who divided up the kingdom relatively evenly according to the usual Frankish inheritance customs. The brothers apparently spent three wary years as corulers, but any potential problems were abruptly erased by the illness and death of Carloman in December 771. Charles, who would go on to become better known as Charles the Great or Charlemagne, quickly secured sole rulership of the kingdom and launched the first of many famed campaigns.

CHARLEMAGNE'S WARS

In the summer of 772, Charlemagne's forces crossed the Rhine and inaugurated the Saxon Wars, which would last for the next three decades. The opening campaign went almost wholly to Charlemagne's satisfaction, his forces taking the pivotal fortress of Eresburg and then breaching the pagan sanctuary of Irmunsul, burning down the sacred tree that, according to pagan beliefs, held up the sky.

Charlemagne's ability to marshal and bring significant forces to bear on the Saxons spelled almost inevitable victory in each campaign; however, whenever he appeared distracted by affairs in the rest of his empire, the Saxons rebelled. Thus, the king and his army returned in major campaigns in 782, 785, 792–3, and 798–803, and smaller expeditions in other years. Charlemagne's repeated successes came in part from strategic depth. He built fortresses, utilized waterways to keep his forces supplied, and used a combination of rewards and atrocities to bend the Saxon elites into genuine submission, and eventually even amalgamation with his empire.

ABOVE: *The green boundary extending from modern-day France east into Germany and south to Italy indicates the extent of Charlemagne's empire at the time of his death in* CE *814.*

The 790s also witnessed another lucrative success for Charlemagne when he and his magnates ended the Avar Khanate, a powerful state in eastern Europe. Two successive penetrations of the Avars' main encampment, called the *ring*, led to unprecedented wealth being carted away by the Franks.

The territory, loot, and glory acquired in these campaigns allowed Charlemagne to reward his loyal supporters, binding them more tightly to his cause. They, in turn, could of course reward their own followers, thus continuing the legacy of patronage noted by Tacitus among the Germanic war band and also practiced in the Roman legions. In addition, Charlemagne's victories against pagan armies vindicated his reign, confirmed his religious credentials, and promoted the idea that violence was acceptable if used to defend or advance the cause of Christianity.

THE EMERGENCE OF A MILITARY ELITE

Elpanetlos senetre mamtenat.
hout les baros entoz le Roi tursat.
Glen pere tegint ive espirt.
Dos guans te maille neit formet manoiat
Aiquies legante si fent chieçtinant.

LEFT: *Under Charlemagne, mounted warriors gained a more prominent strategic role and greater social prestige. This fourteenth-century manuscript illustration shows Charlemagne granting a soldier the status of cavalryman.*

Most of the Frankish populace were farmers, so the majority of the fighters in Charlemagne's army, particularly in the early days, had only rudimentary arms and likely no mount. However, the emperor's capitularies—a set of administrative or legislative decrees that set out imperial policy—make it clear that by the early ninth century CE he was beginning to expect minimum standards of weaponry.

The expectation that soldiers were to carry better arms may well have been prompted by a resurgence of mining and technological improvements in the acquisition of metal ores and in metalworking during Charlemagne's reign. Or it may just as likely have worked the other way round, with the demand for improved military equipment being the impetus behind the push to find new ore deposits.

STANDARD KIT

Charlemagne demanded that foot soldiers appear not only with a club: bows and arrows were expected at the least. Nobles were ordered to supply their men with spears and shields. Mounted troops had to provide a more extensive kit: shield, lance, long sword *(spatha)*, short sword, and bow and arrows. The richest horsemen were also required to bring and wear their own *brunia*, or "byrnie," a leather jacket supplemented with chain or scale armor. At the same time, the Carolingian law codes forbade the export of these byrnies, clearly so as to maintain a technological advantage over less well-equipped foes.

These comparatively well-heeled mounted warriors were often magnates of the Frankish kingdoms or their immediate retainers. Their weaponry naturally gave them advantages in battle, but their mounts and gear also had a circular social effect: because of their privileged position, they were expected to have and use more powerful combat gear; at the same time, simply by having better weapons and physically dominating the scene from horseback, their social prominence was enhanced.

HORSEBORNE WARRIORS

Most descriptions of battles of this period were compiled by contemporary authors, mainly monks or clergy, who wrote to please a patron or impress their

A MANUAL OF WARFARE

The Roman military handbook, *De re militari* by **Vegetius** (flourished fourth century CE), was hugely influential in the Carolingian era. Many new copies were made, and Hrabanus Maurus, a scholar at Charlemagne's court, reworked it into a handbook of his own, noting the similarities and differences between Roman and Frankish fighting styles. Like Vegetius, Hrabanus stressed the value of the phalanx, the tightly packed rows of infantrymen that underpinned the Roman legions' success and Charles Martel's victory at Poitiers in 732. He noted, too, as did Vegetius, that men who rode into battle usually fought best when dismounted. But he also discussed the use of the Frankish long sword *(spatha)*, describing it as good for slashing, as well as the short sword *(gladius)*, a highly effective thrusting weapon when used by soldiers in phalanxes.

own literary peers. Consequently, they focus more on style than content and reveal relatively little of the actual tactics used by Charlemagne and his forces. However, it is clear from some accounts that the Frankish leader was developing the use of cavalry, and the speed with which he and some of his troops responded to threats leaves little doubt they must have been horseborne.

These mounted warriors adopted specialized fighting techniques: archery, feigned retreats, and carefully held lines during a charge. To learn such skills, younger mounted warriors increasingly had to invest in a form of apprenticeship with older fighters. A common proverb of the day claimed that by adulthood it was too late to start training a horseman in the necessary skills.

A NEW PROFESSIONALISM

Charlemagne's requirements regarding weaponry, his employment of horses, and his increasingly complex maneuvers on the battlefield brought a new degree of professionalism to his forces. Yet the bulk of his armies, those of his foes, and almost all of those of the contemporary Anglo-Saxon kingdoms, remained infantry. Moreover, much time was spent in sieges, not in charges, and it has been repeatedly shown that even the mounted warriors dismounted to fight on foot as often as not.

Certainly, Charlemagne's cavalry had not yet fully developed the mounted shock techniques that would become the basis of cavalry's claim to being indispensable on Europe's battlefields— the current wisdom seems to place that transition between the 1060s and 1090s. Furthermore, although the Carolingian mounted warriors were becoming an evermore elite group, they had yet to take on most of the recognizable social or military trappings of later knights.

IRONWORKING

Since a knight's dominance rested on the very arms and armor that marked him apart from others in the Middle Ages, an understanding of who and what else lay behind those metallic resources is key to appreciating the whole picture of knighthood. It is hard, however, to see clearly the activities of miners and blacksmiths: they rarely earned mentions by contemporaries, and usually then only in complaints about the noise, smoke, and rowdiness coming from their neighborhoods. To no small extent, we must thank archaeologists for bringing these parts of the story back into view.

The downfall of Rome had major and immediate metallurgical consequences: the bureaucracy that oversaw the extraction and transformation of ores into tools faded, and without imperial needs to push it, the industry also declined. As a result, the number of blacksmiths in operation dropped off, and most mining endeavors closed down. In one remarkable case, the legendarily productive mines of Rio Tinto in Spain were lost for nearly a thousand years. With the overall recovery that occurred under Charlemagne came a revival of mining and ironworking—Carolingian expansion eastward opened up new areas to exploit, such as the Rammelsberg mines near Goslar, Germany, and Hungarian mines that Charlemagne exploited with captive laborers. Despite this, weapons manufacture still had a long way to travel in order to regain the quality of Roman weapons.

MINING THE IRON

Mining is still backbreaking work for everyone involved, but one can only marvel at what medieval miners endured to extract ores. The growing appetite for iron meant that surface deposits were rapidly used up. As shafts went deeper to reach ore, various problems had to be surmounted.

LEFT: *A quarry proprietor oversees miners searching for surface ores and minerals in this fifteenth-century illustration from Belgium.*

LEFT: *The harvesting of trees for fuel and building materials led to significant deforestation in medieval western Europe.*

Providing ventilation and preventing flooding were the main aims. Thus, the work multiplied since extra shafts had to be cut to provide air inflow and direct water outside. With only human power behind the chisels and picks, it was rare to drive forward more than 8 inches (20 cm) per day. When a dig reached below the drainage shafts, workers had to carry water-buckets up ladders to the shafts. And, of course, the ore itself had to be carried up, too.

Fire and smoke were constant companions in the mines: firstly to light the shafts but also because large fires were built at the rock face to heat up the ore and help fracture it. It was common for the miners to spend six days a week underground, having Sunday at home while the bonfires burned down.

PROCESSING THE ORE

This same period saw advances in how much iron could be smelted into a usable form from the extracted ores. Since time immemorial, simple *bloomery hearths*, formed by a ring of stones, had been the means of yielding small iron blooms—irregular lumps of metal with minimal impurities that could be knocked off or worked out with further refining. These small operations continued, but in the eighth century, a new furnace was developed in Catalonia that had a shaft that dramatically increased both the purity of the iron bloom and the overall yield. As the technology spread into Austria, Saxony, and along the Rhine valley, this kind of furnace, called *stückoven* after its distinctive tall chimney, grew to heights of 16 feet (5 m) and could produce up to 0.4 tons (350 kg) per operation by the 1300s.

The amount of labor and resources necessary to produce workable iron demonstrates a whole other level of meaning to the description of medieval Europe as a "society organized for war." Up to one-fifth of the expenses of a blacksmith might go just to the small gang of workers needed to operate the bellows that kept the furnace hot enough to make the ore workable. In general, a day of operation required that 1 acre (0.4 ha) of forest be harvested to provide the wood that had to be first turned into charcoal for the smelting. In no time, lumber resources near metal furnaces retreated to a distance that further drove up expenses. The fact that the *Domesday Book* records mills being allowed to pay their rents in blooms further attests to the value placed on iron.

RIGHT: *A blacksmith tests a sword on an anvil, in a scene from a Nordic legend carved in the thirteenth-century Setesdal Church in southern Norway.*

FROM IRON TO STEEL

The iron that resulted from these processes was still far from perfect, however. And so the blacksmith became the third integral part of the refining process. His importance by the early twelfth century is attested by the *De diversis artibus* of Theophilus Presbyter, which gives a picture of wrought-iron products in fabrication, and not least of all, the techniques that were developed to transform brittle iron into harder but tensile steel.

This process was, like all the rest, labor-intensive. The carbon element necessary for steel would be produced by heating iron in a charcoal fire, and then shaping it through seemingly endless, repetitive folding and hammering of the iron. For the finest weapons or tools, the metal would be further improved by the process of tempering, whereby it was repeatedly heated and cooled rapidly. Knives, swords, arrow and spearheads, innumerable rings for chain mail, helmets, bridles—in short, the knight's panoply of war—all this equipment represented a staggering investment of the material and human wealth of the Middle Ages.

CENTRALIZED POWER

Charlemagne's military successes, in conjunction with his family's alliance with the papacy, not only increased the Frankish realm vastly, but also resulted in him being crowned "Emperor of the Romans," in Rome, on December 25, CE 800, by Pope Leo III (reigned 795–816). Even if, as emperor, Charlemagne was still quite distant from the actual nature of classical Roman power and authority, his position as both a Germanic war leader, once combined with the imperial mantle, gave him a clear monopoly on legitimate, state-sanctioned violence. Because of his effectiveness on the battlefield, this claim was real, not theoretical.

With an interest in providing good government as a mark of his legitimacy, Charlemagne oversaw numerous law codes that further sought to forestall feuds among his followers and the enacting of private justice. He granted authority over regions of his realm to counts, powerful nobles who were also his trusted agents. These grants were made *in benefice*, meaning that they were held at the "good will" of the king. At the same time, Charlemagne regularly dispatched royal officials to monitor the behavior and agendas of these regional rulers, and he routinely recalled counts and assigned them to other territories to prevent them from establishing local power bases. These strategies helped

LEFT: *Albrecht Dürer's opulent 1512–13 portrait of Charlemagne was commissioned by the Holy Roman Emperor Maximilian I (reigned 1493–1519).*

check the powerful centrifugal forces that would pull his empire apart not long after his death.

ANGLO-SAXON ENGLAND

In England, the situation was less clear, but ultimately not much different. The fierce rivalry that characterized the

relationships between the Anglo-Saxon kingdoms that emerged in the wake of the fifth-century settlement of England—East Anglia, Essex, Kent, Sussex, Wessex, Mercia, and Northumbria—might have opened up conditions for private initiative, especially in a culture that prized the heroic virtues of a Beowulf or Beorhtnoth. However, although the bravery, even foolhardiness, of the warrior-hero was celebrated in Anglo-Saxon culture, the majority of the populace were stolid agriculturalists who, when called up in the national levy, or *fyrd*, came out to defend their lands, but were not ones to seek out violence as a step to enrichment.

Furthermore, although the aristocrats of Anglo-Saxon England experienced no shortage of the feuds and rivalries that marked later politics in mainland Europe, the reign of King Alfred of Wessex (reigned 871–99), which united the Anglo-Saxon kingdoms, was notable for the *public* nature of the king's authority. One of his most significant acts was the creation of the *burhs*, or boroughs, fortifications that were meant to shelter not just a privileged elite, but the whole populace. Alfred also enacted legislation to protect weaker members of his society from corrupt judicial rulers.

Be truthful to your lord, my son William.
Be vigilant, energetic, and offer him ready assistance.

ADVICE FROM THE NOBLEWOMAN DHUODA TO HER SON (*c. CE 841*)

RIGHT: *King Alfred of Wessex, portrayed here in stained glass in Bath Abbey, Somerset, England, encouraged a revival of learning, even translating several Latin works into English himself.*

SEEDS OF A FUTURE HARVEST

Nevertheless, the personal and private bonds that had characterized Germanic and Roman societies remained strong. In addition, both Carolingian and Anglo-Saxon lands had long since accepted the hierarchical principle in political and religious arrangements: the Anglo-Saxon kings had earls or ealdormen as agents, while the Franks knew counts, viscounts, and margraves as representatives of the king. Furthermore, princes of the church often came to operate as secular magnates themselves, further blurring the line between religious authority and secular governance. Just because there was a hierarchy, though, did not mean that all the members of the system meekly accepted their position, or that of the next person for that matter.

When the sense of a public power—the monarchy, in other words—faded, the resulting vacuum invited trouble. In England, though the great lords would prove hard to manage at times (witness the self-serving career of Earl Godwine, father of Harold II), they generally had little opportunity to achieve autonomy. But in the Frankish Empire, once the later Carolingian rulers proved unable to hold the empire together or to defend it against new invaders, the combination of circumstances gave the counts and dukes their chance for independence.

BELOW: *The cathedral of Aachen, in Germany, houses the Palatine Chapel, where Charlemagne was buried in CE 814. From 794 until then, the town was the main residence of the imperial court.*

THE CONTINUITY QUESTION

Charlemagne's title of "Emperor of the Romans" was an echo, if not a replication, of the former Roman title. The abiding interest in Roman institutions raises the thorny question of continuity: in other words, how much of Rome's institutions survived? The answer is, a perhaps surprising amount. Christianity itself was of course created within the Roman Empire, and the dioceses that bishops headed replicated the *pagi,* the old units of Roman provincial administration; medieval counties, too, in the west, used the boundaries of the *pagi.* Roman roads, Roman aqueducts, and Roman walls continued to be used throughout the Middle Ages, as of course did Latin, the Roman language. Charlemagne's armies also fought in a manner closer to that of the Roman legions than to that of the knights of the twelfth and thirteenth centuries.

NORTHERN AND EASTERN INVADERS

In CE 793, medieval Christians were horrified by the sack of Lindisfarne Abbey in northern England by Vikings. Six years later, Vikings raided the Carolingian coastlands, prompting Charlemagne to order a defensive fleet prepared. Over the next decade, signs of Scandinavian restlessness grew as piracy made the English Channel unsafe, and Charlemagne's Slavic allies around the Elbe suffered Danish incursions.

Although he was approaching his seventies, Charlemagne prepared an expedition in 810 to subjugate Denmark. But he then cancelled the invasion upon hearing that the troublesome king, Godefrid, had been assassinated. Denmark fell into civil war, and Charlemagne assumed this northern threat would subsequently fade. His descendants doubtlessly wished more than once that he had carried through the invasion.

THE EMPIRE DIVIDED

By the time of Charles the Bald's reign (840–77), Norse raids on the Western Frankish kingdom had become an almost annual trouble, and the Carolingian Empire was in the process of devouring itself. Ongoing disputes between Charlemagne's grandsons led to the Treaty of Verdun in 843, under which the empire was divided into three separate realms. Lothair I (795–855) retained the imperial title and Francia Media, a band of territory stretching from the Low Countries to Italy; Louis the German (king of Germany 840–76) gained the land east of the Rhine; and Charles the Bald received Francia Occidentalis, much of modern-day France. With the Viking raids continuing, however, central government was widely shown to be unequal to the task of providing meaningful protection.

The Viking raiders had no compunctions about despoiling churches and monasteries and the denizens thereof, and were capable of occasionally awful brutality. Moreover they were extremely mobile, using their longships to traverse oceans and move far up Europe's river systems. Isolated rural estates were easy pickings, but towns garnered unwanted attention, too, and many important centers were looted: Rouen, Angers, Nantes, Lincoln, Exeter, Oxford, and more. All too often, royal forces showed up after the Vikings had left.

If force and authority are means by which to channel profits, then the Vikings were a particularly naked application of this principle. Yet Frankish and Anglo-Saxon monarchs were seldom loath to do business with these brutal foes. Sometimes they offered a bribe to be left alone, but there were numerous cases, too, when a king paid Viking raiders to go plague one of his rivals.

Behold, the church of St. Cuthbert spattered with the blood of the priests of God, despoiled of all its ornaments.

ALCUIN OF YORK DESCRIBING THE VIKING DESECRATION OF ST. CUTHBERT'S MONASTERY ON THE ISLAND OF LINDISFARNE, CE 793

VIKING LEGACIES

Viking successes in Britain led to the end of the rival Anglo-Saxon kingdoms. Only Wessex was left standing, if only barely, and under King Alfred a rebound began that led to his unusually centralized monarchy. At first the Vikings kept political control over the northeastern reaches of England in an area called

LEFT: *In the early ninth century CE, Vikings from Denmark launched attacks on southern England, striking at East Anglia, Channel ports, and deep into the Thames and Severn estuaries.*

RIGHT: *The victory of King Otto I of Germany over the Magyars at the Battle of Lechfeld in CE 955 encouraged the Magyars to settle, forming in turn what would become the state of Hungary.*

RIGHT: *The victory of King Otto I of Germany over the Magyars at the Battle of Lechfeld in CE 955 encouraged the Magyars to settle, forming in turn what would become the state of Hungary.*

the Danelaw, centered on York. As they settled in, however, they slowly became incorporated into the kingdom of Alfred's heirs.

On the Continent, a similar scenario played out as the Carolingian ruler Charles the Simple (reigned 893–922) reached an accord with the Viking leader Rollo (*c.* 860–*c.* 932) in 911, allowing Rollo and his followers to settle in and control Upper Normandy (half of the future duchy) in return for an agreement not to wage further war and to help Charles keep other Viking raiders at bay. In both cases, once the Vikings came to stay, a process of conversion to Christianity began.

One of the most significant legacies of the Viking invasions was that they boosted the standing of local potentates. Many of those who had succeeded in negotiating with or repelling the Vikings in the absence of centralized defenses saw their clout begin to eclipse that of a distant monarch. For instance, Count Odo's vigorous defense of Paris through the winter of 885–86 with no real help from Charles the Fat (reigned 884–87) led to the latter's deposition and Odo's reign as king from 888 to 893. Charles the Simple, the Carolingian ruler, was crowned in 893 but had to battle Odo for the throne until the latter's death in 898.

THE MAGYARS ARRIVE

A similar threat emerged from the east after 862, when the seminomadic Magyars raided the eastern Frankish marches. By the 890s, the Magyars had moved into and occupied the Hungarian Plain. As with the Vikings, they came to operate among the Frankish lands often as temporary allies of Charlemagne's feuding heirs. By the 900s, however, the Arpad dynasty had established itself

over the Magyars and begun nearly annual summer raids across the heart of the Germanic lands, even into France, Denmark, and Italy. Loot was the draw for these horseborne archers.

Here, too, the lack of a response from a centralized authority helped local military elites within the affected regions to tighten their grasp on power and hone the techniques that would

bring them military and social dominance. When, for example, the dukes of Saxony checked the Magyars in 933 and again, more famously, in 955 at the Battle of Lechfeld, Germany, their future was assured. Their crowning moment would come (literally) when Otto, Duke of Saxony and king of the Germans (936–73), was crowned Emperor of the Romans in 962.

LORDS AND VASSALS

LEFT: *First built in the tenth century, the castle of Foix in southwestern France was from 1034 the seat of the counts of Foix, who ruled their own independent realm until the fifteenth century.*

A s public order broke down in the former Frankish lands during the late tenth century CE, many lower-ranking, untitled landed lords secured their power by building fortresses and, from 1100 or so, castles. The first castles were far from elaborate and almost wholly constructed in timber. Yet they allowed their owners, known as *castellans*, to assert their military control over the surrounding area. Soon the castellans turned this control into political and judicial authority. They began to command and to judge in their neighborhoods, and this right, often referred to as the *ban*, and increasingly accepted by those under their protection, continued to elevate the position of these enterprising magnates. This was especially

the case in what would become France; in England, Alfred's boroughs at least provided some public refuges.

LOCAL POWER BASES

Castellans were served by fighters on horseback, men known as *milites*, or, in modern English, *knights*. Recent advances in such technologies as horseshoes, the stirrup, and the saddle meant that these

RIGHT: *The basic form of the homage ceremony would endure for centuries. Here, Jean de Sainte-Maure makes a vow of fealty to René, Duke of Anjou, in 1469.*

mounted warriors were much better equipped to fight than the horse contingents of Charlemagne's armies. Furthermore, although knights generally lacked the noble blood and wealth of the elites who had governed western Europe for five hundred years and were often men of humble origins, by serving the increasingly powerful castellans, they soon rose to positions of authority.

High walls and fierce warriors gave the castellans an independence that the counts, the hereditary regional rulers of the Frankish realm, considered dangerous. The counts had been the chief political leaders of the Continent for most of the tenth century, ever since the weakness of the late Carolingians had become clear, and they were not about to yield that authority. One method they adopted to control the castellans was to institutionalize the ties of loyalty and obligation that had long been taken for granted into something more concrete, the granting and receiving of *fiefs*. Loyalty of course had a very long history, and the Carolingian kings had made temporary grants of counties *in benefice*, but fiefs were something new.

THE GRANTING OF FIEFS

A fief, at the most basic level, was a piece of property (such as a castle) that one noble, in this case a count, granted to another, in this case the castellan. He who granted was the *lord*, he who received the *vassal*. In return for the fief, the vassal swore an oath to support his lord loyally and do nothing against his interests. As long as the vassal remained loyal, the fief was his for his lifetime (unlike the earlier benefices). On the

had always done. Initially, knights were not involved either. But in the late eleventh century, some castellans began to reward veteran knights—men in their forties or fifties who were considered too old to fight—with fiefs, usually a small piece of property on which the knight could build a house, and on which he might put a miniature tower in imitation of a castle. These retired knights formed a body of tried and trusted men upon whom the castellan could rely; they would appear regularly at the castellan's court, and their sons would usually follow their fathers in becoming knights.

THE OATH OF LOYALTY

Oaths were always at the heart of the granting of fiefs, although the earliest descriptions of the ceremony involved date from the twelfth century. The ceremony was called *homage*, as the vassal was swearing to become the man *(homo)* of the lord. The vassal went on his knees to his lord, holding up clasped hands to him, in what later came to be considered the proper attitude of someone in prayer. The lord in return reached down, put his own hands around his vassal's, drew him up, and kissed him on both cheeks.

The ceremony thus both symbolized the dependency of the vassal and the rough social equality of the parties—who were, after all, usually both aristocrats. Although the vassal initially promised nothing but loyalty, by the middle of the twelfth century it was common for the vassal to promise also to help out financially with the wedding of the lord's oldest daughter or the coming-of-age ceremony for his eldest son, and the generalized promise to fight for his lord was often specified as for no more than 40 days a year.

other hand, because the agreement was made between two individuals, it had to be renewed every generation.

Some counts, such as Fulk Nerra, Count of Anjou, controlled the building of many of the castles in their regions in the early eleventh century. When they granted them to castellans—since they could not be in every castle at all times—they demanded oaths of loyalty in return for these fiefs. Counts who saw local strongmen building their

own castles were also quick to assert that these would-be castellans could only proceed if they accepted that the castles were fiefs held from the counts.

At this point, kings did not hold or grant fiefs, though this would change in the late eleventh century after William the Conqueror divided his new kingdom of England among his loyal followers. Peasants were never involved with fiefs, continuing to hold their lands in return for rents and work obligations, as they

THE PEACE AND TRUCE OF GOD

The rapid spread of well-armed fighters on horseback in the decades around the year 1000 led to widespread anxiety about the violence they could cause, and, not surprisingly, a reaction set in. It came initially from commoners who lived in fear of these warriors, but was soon being led by religious leaders who saw the terror as an affront to the ideals of Christianity.

PROTECTING THE POWERLESS

In CE 990, three church synods, or councils, were organized in central-southern France, at Charroux, Narbonne, and Le Puy, at which ecclesiastics began preaching against the depredations

of their own regional lords. This gave rise to the movement known as the Peace of God. The central idea of this movement was that the powerful should not hurt the powerless. It was not just violence that had the clergy and people so upset; the newfound ability of local lords to insert themselves into formerly royal prerogatives like the ban meant that they could institute all sorts of new exactions, tolls, and customs—innovations that invariably earned condemnation as "evil."

Bishops brought spiritual weapons to bear, threatening those who harmed clergy, peasantry, merchants, or the physical institutions of the church with

ABOVE: *In Eugène Delacroix's* Two Knights Fighting *(c. 1825), heavily armed mounted warriors clash ferociously. The growing potential for such violence in the early eleventh century alarmed commoners and clerics alike.*

excommunication or the vindictive wrath of saints. Further councils were organized in Provence, Burgundy, and Aquitaine, which were attended not only by church leaders, accompanied by the reliquaries of their saints, but also, increasingly, by secular leaders and their knights, who, presumably, soon realized that the movement was directed mainly against *them*.

ENFORCING THE PEACE

How were unarmed people to force reputedly evil knights to behave well? In 1038 Aimon, the bishop of Bourges, France, formed a Peace League, mandating that every male over the age of 15 had to join and suppress anyone who contested the Peace of God's provisions. Although described as unarmed (*inermes*), this multitude apparently succeeded in routing several groups of knights and razing their castles. In the end, though, the one unyielding castellan of the region, Odo of Déols, and his knights, after being cornered, decimated the league's participants, who themselves had dressed up as knights in a last-ditch ploy to cow their opponents.

ABOVE: *Dating from about 1150, this silver reliquary from the Abbey of St. Maurice, Wallis, Switzerland, bears the image of St. Maurice, patron saint of soldiers. A number of chivalric orders were established in the saint's honor.*

The Peace of God spread to Catalonia and central France, and thence on to the German lands in less than a century. In many places, gatherings had to take place in fields outside towns in order to hold all the attendees; shouts of "Peace, peace, peace!" testified to the frustrations of the populace who, with hands upraised, invoked a covenant with God. Sermons were preached against the "invaders, despoilers, ravagers, and oppressors"—otherwise known as knights and castellans.

Caught up in this dynamic, knights who could not avoid such meetings took oaths to abide by the principles of the movement, swearing on relics carried for this purpose by monks or priests. One peace oath of 1023 included the following assertions: "I will not invade a church for any reason … I will not seize villeins of either sex, or servants or merchants, or their coins, or hold them for ransom … I will not attack merchants or pilgrims or take their possessions unless they commit crimes."

LIMITS ON VIOLENCE

In the 1020s, a further development occurred in northern France when a council declared that knights who put aside their arms during Lent would be protected the same as those who usually fell into the unarmed category. This became known as the Truce of God. A council at Arles around 1024 legislated that knights should shun fighting from Thursday through Monday morning to honor the Passion of Christ, and on major saints' feast days and during the Advent season. These Christian limits on violence came to a logical endpoint within a decade, when the next council forbad intra-Christian warfare—though the idea that Christians should not kill Christians did not gain much momentum until the emergence of tournaments and the start of the Crusades at the end of the century.

In essence, the Peace and Truce of God sought to eliminate the private warfare that seemed always to attend the knights. How effective the movements were is a hard question to answer. Given the energized frustration at some of the gatherings, and the role of churchmen and saintly relics in focusing this discontent, one can imagine local knights being either cowed or genuinely swept up in the tide. But the need for repeated councils probably says more about how often the Peace and Truce provisions were violated rather than obeyed.

The Peace and Truce nonetheless became part of the conceptual structures surrounding the private exercise of violence. They also continued a Christian accommodation with violence that went back to Charlemagne's external campaigns against pagans, and culminated not just in the call for knights to go on Crusade, but as well in the papal declaration that the Peace and Truce would apply over France during the armed pilgrimage.

LEFT: *Three different classes of medieval society are represented within this illuminated letter C: cleric, knight, and peasant.*

The Norman Era

The emergence of the Normans as a major military force during the tenth and eleventh centuries not only ended Anglo-Saxon rule in England and altered the political map of Europe, it also spread Norman military culture, with its traditions of knight service and castle-based warfare, across the continent and beyond.

Although William the Conqueror, Duke of Normandy and king of England (reigned 1066–1087), became the most famous Norman of them all, he was preceded by men instrumental to the development and political rise of the duchy itself. Norman history really began in CE 911, when the Carolingian king, Charles the Simple (reigned 893–922), unable to repel Viking coastal attacks from the north, granted Upper Normandy (east of the Seine) to Rollo the Viking (c. 860–c. 932) in exchange for an oath of loyalty and peace. Over time, the traditions of the Viking settlers meshed with Frankish culture, the conversion to Christianity was made, and the Norman "race" emerged.

There is some debate over the political standing of Rollo and his successors. Called "counts of Rouen" (Rouen being the capital of Upper Normandy) and "dukes of Normandy," they seem to have had an administrative role within the hierarchy of the Carolingian kingdom. However, most knowledge of Rollo is legendary and was written down a hundred years after the fact. More is known about the rule of his son, William I Longsword (died 942). He went to war against Arnulf of Flanders (died 942), by whom he was said to have been murdered; thereafter, the Normans became more involved in politics in western Europe.

ABOVE: *This 1289 relief of William the Conqueror adorns the cloister of the church of the Santissima Annunziata in Florence, Italy.*

THE DUKES OF NORMANDY

Rollo and William Longsword were the first in a hereditary ducal succession that stayed within family lines until 1135.

LEFT: *It is said that on pledging his loyalty to Charles the Simple, Rollo, the Viking leader, refused to kneel to Charles, instead lifting the king's foot to kiss it, and deliberately tipping him backward.*

The fourth Duke of Normandy was Richard, who had two children who would play significant roles in both Norman and English history. One was his daughter Emma, who was married to two kings of England, first the Anglo-Saxon Ethelred II, also known as Ethelred the Unready (reigned 978–1016), then the Dane Canute (reigned 1016–35). The other was his son Robert the Magnificent. Robert produced a son who became known as William the Bastard because his parents were not recognized as legitimately married. In 1035, William the Bastard managed to claim his father's title and become the sixth Duke of Normandy.

Queen Emma can be credited with the interjection of the Normans into

English royal politics. In 1042, she intervened to ensure that her half-Norman son Edward, later known as Edward the Confessor, was crowned king of England (reigned 1042–66). Edward in turn appointed a small group of Normans advisors to ecclesiastical and political positions.

THE SUCCESSION DISPUTE

Although Edward had a wife, Edith, he took a vow of chastity and their union produced no children. He therefore had to select an heir, and there were two clear candidates. The first was the powerful Harold Godwinson, Earl of Wessex and Edward's brother-in-law through Edith. Edward and Harold had a rocky relationship initially, but they reached a friendly accord by 1063. The second candidate was Edward's cousin, William the Bastard. The Duke of Normandy had visited England in the winter of 1051, and, according to Norman sources, was at that time made heir. The Anglo-Saxon sources are silent

on the issue, however, so the validity of William's claim to the throne has been disputed for centuries.

Matters were complicated in 1064–65 when King Edward sent Harold to Normandy as an ambassador. The purpose of his mission is unclear, but when Harold landed he was arrested and taken hostage by Guy, Count of Ponthieu, who then turned him over to Duke William. According to the Norman sources and the imagery on the Bayeux Tapestry, Harold then pledged his fealty to William by swearing an oath upon holy relics. If this was true, Harold's actions upon returning to England could be construed as traitorous.

HAROLD MAKES HIS MOVE

In January 1066, Edward the Confessor died of illness. English sources relate that before expiring he made Harold Godwinson his royal heir in a deathbed whisper. As a result, the night Edward died, Harold was immediately crowned King Harold II. The deliberate nature

and speed of Harold's actions have persuaded the majority of medieval historians to accept the Norman version of events: he had committed a coup and seized the English throne illegally.

Duke William at once began preparing for war. He sent letters of protest to both Harold and Pope Alexander II (reigned 1061–73). To the latter, he made the case that Harold was an oath-breaker and in return received permission from the pope to wage war against a fellow Christian. Although some of William's magnates had doubts about the invasion's chances of success, the duke allayed their fears and mustered support in Brittany, Maine, Poitou, Burgundy, and Anjou, among the Normans of Italy, and even from the Paris region.

BELOW: *The Bayeux Tapestry shows Harold Godwinson (center) swearing to support William's claim to the English throne. Anglo-Saxons denied this had ever happened, and would have seen the image as a retrospective rewriting of history.*

THE NORMAN CONQUEST OF ENGLAND

Harold II's accession to the English throne was contested not just by William the Bastard, Duke of Normandy, but also by Harold Haardrada, king of Norway (reigned 1046–66), who claimed that his family had been promised the English crown by King Canute's son Hardecanute (reigned 1028–42). Soon, Harold II was faced with not one but two invasions.

Deeming the Normans more threatening, Harold massed his army in the south. But southerly winds prevented the Normans from sailing and were, conversely, favorable to Harold Haardrada, who landed on the northeast coast of England near Newcastle with three hundred ships on September 25, 1066. King Harold hurriedly marched his army north and overwhelmed the Norwegians at the battle of Stamford Bridge. It was a brilliant victory, but two days later the Channel winds shifted and Duke William's fleet set sail. Once again the Anglo-Saxon army embarked upon a forced march, this time back south, and arrived at the place now called Battle, near the port of Hastings, exhausted and faced with a second pitched battle in less than three weeks.

THE BATTLE OF HASTINGS
As well as being a turning point in English history, the Battle of Hastings, which took place on October 14, 1066, is one of the most famous of all battles.

TOP: *Penny coins bearing the image of William I were minted in England soon after his coronation, no doubt to reinforce the legitimacy of his rule.*
RIGHT: *The last Anglo-Saxon sovereign of England, Harold II's term as ruler lasted only nine months, from January to October 1066.*

Although there remains a degree of controversy about some of its aspects, it is possible to describe and reconstruct most of the action.

Harold arrayed his infantry along a ridge running west to east. This gave him an unencumbered view downward at the Normans, who would have to ascend a gentle slope, rising about 100 feet (30 m), to address his position.

The duke returned to the battlefield, found a scene of carnage which he could only look at with pity, even though the victims were wicked men and it is glorious and praiseworthy to kill a tyrant.

WILLIAM OF POITIERS, *THE DEEDS OF WILLIAM, DUKE OF THE NORMANS AND KING OF THE ENGLISH* **(1071)**

Along this ridge Harold's men formed their famous shield wall: between five and six thousand men in tight formation with their shields interlocked. Mounted troops were still not part of Anglo-Saxon military culture, strictly speaking; influenced by Scandinavian methods of fighting, Anglo-Saxon forces consisted for the most part of foot soldiers wielding swords, spears, and axes, operating in conjunction with missile troops.

Duke William arrayed his army, of probably between seven and nine thousand, in a tripartite formation. His Breton troops took the left wing, his mercenaries and French troops the right, and his mounted Norman knights the center; heavy infantry preceded these knights, and missile troops fronted the entire formation in loose order. William's use of cavalry highlighted the clear distinction between the Anglo-Saxon warrior ethic and the knightly practices of the Continent.

A GREAT VICTORY
The battle began at nine o'clock in the morning with William's army slowly moving up the slope toward Harold's shield wall. It initially held against Norman missile fire, much of which passed above the heads of the Saxons, and also against the infantry attack. The Bretons on the left wing faltered, and the Saxons made a sudden counter-attack that sent them fleeing en masse in a panicked retreat. Their withdrawal exposed the flank of the Normans, who also began to fall back, and in the tumult William was thrown off his horse and disappeared. Rumors then spread that the duke had been killed.

RIGHT: *This suitably bloody but otherwise fanciful depiction of the Battle of Hastings comes from a fifteenth-century manuscript, the* Historical Mirror of France.

But just as the battle seemed lost, William dramatically reappeared and rallied his men. Their morale boosted, the Normans made another assault up the slope and enacted a feigned retreat: pretending to flee, they enticed some of the Saxons to abandon the shield wall and give chase, whereupon the Norman cavalry wheeled around and cut down their pursuers in the open field.

The sources are unclear as to whether the Normans used this tactic once or twice; in any event, the left wing of the shield wall had been greatly weakened. William ordered a final assault up the hill and the Saxon line finally broke. Harold was killed in the melee, either trampled by a horse or struck in the eye with an arrow—the spot where he supposedly died is today marked with an inscription.

BELOW: *William vowed to build an abbey on the site of his great victory, and Battle Abbey was consecrated in 1094, after his death. Little remains of the original structure; the grand gateway shown here was added in 1338.*

The battle had lasted approximately nine hours. Though its outcome had been by no means assured, the opposing armies having been evenly matched for much of the grueling engagement, it proved to be a great victory for William, who would henceforth be known as William the Conqueror.

THE ANGLO-NORMAN REALM

After the battle, William moved northward, to Dover, Canterbury, and, finally, the capital, London, crushing latent resistance and awaiting the submission of the English earls. He was crowned on Christmas Day of 1066 at Westminster Abbey, and the Anglo-Norman realm was created: William was now King William I of England.

The dominions of William the Conqueror were vastly enlarged and enhanced, but his borders were far from secure. On the Continent, Breton and French threats were constant concerns, and in England the new king had the Welsh and Scottish marches with which to contend. In the west, he created three new earldoms to check the Welsh,

and to the north he sent forces to chase away not only Danish incursions (the "harrying of the north") but also to compel the allegiance of King Malcolm III of Scotland (reigned 1058–93).

The Norman conceptualization of knight service and obligation was soon exported to England and either replaced

LEFT: *While the Anglo-Saxon and Norman armies are at times hard to distinguish in the Bayeux Tapestry, some crucial differences are highlighted, including the Norman use of cavalry and the Anglo-Saxons' defensive shield wall.*

or was integrated into existing Anglo-Saxon economic, legal, and military traditions. William distributed lands in England to those men willing to offer their military service to him in times of need. Knights became principal members of elite society in many cases, and cavalry units featured prominently in Anglo-Norman armies thereafter.

William also commissioned a wide-ranging inquest in order to document the extent and resources of his new kingdom, with the results being tallied in the famous *Domesday Book*, the earliest surviving census in world history. While it does not record knight-service agreements, the census gave the crown a precise account of taxable property held by or granted to the magnates and knights. To protect his new lands, resources, and wealth, William constructed scores of castles, primarily in the Norman motte-and-bailey style, and also the famed stone keep that formed the first manifestation of the Tower of London on the Thames River.

On his deathbed in 1087, William bequeathed his lands and wealth to his three sons: the eldest, Robert Curthose ("short boots"), received the richest prize, Normandy; William Rufus received England and would soon be crowned King William II (reigned 1087–1100); Henry, the youngest son, received no lands or property but five thousand pounds silver.

THE BAYEUX TAPESTRY

Our understanding of the events that took place during and prior to the battle of Hastings derives in part from one of the most extraordinary pieces of medieval material culture, the Bayeux Tapestry. A visual description of the prelude to and action of the battle, it consists of images made by sewing dyed wool onto a linen backing and measures 230 feet (70 m) in length and 20 inches (50 cm) tall. The events are described by Latin phrases running through the pictures. The work is physically incomplete, for after the death of Harold Godwinson the images trail off in a tattered fashion.

Almost every feature of the tapestry is heavily debated by historians, but most agree that it was commissioned to commemorate William's great victory in 1066. Its geographical origin remains highly controversial, however. The two dominant theories hold that it was produced either at Bayeux in Normandy, or at Canterbury in Kent, England, at the behest of Odo, William's half-brother, who was also both the Bishop of Bayeux and Earl of Kent. Other suggestions have surfaced in recent decades, the most persuasive of them suggesting that the tapestry was produced in the Loire Valley near Saumur. Whatever its provenance, the tapestry clearly shows a Norman bias and depicts King Harold as an oath-breaker who received his just deserts.

THE NORMANS IN ITALY

Normans also became involved in the politics and warfare of southern Italy. Their community arose from mercenaries operating in the region and by the 1050s was large enough to command significant influence. The Norman adventurer Robert Guiscard (*c.* 1015–1085) received the duchies of Calabria and Apulia directly from the papacy; thereafter, Norman magnates all swore oaths of loyalty to Rome. In 1130, the antipope Anacletus II (died 1138) created the Kingdom of Sicily through a papal privilege and crowned Robert's nephew Roger (1095–1154) King Roger II. During the eleventh and twelfth centuries, the Normans in Italy warred against Byzantium, Muslims, and, at the behest of Rome, the Holy Roman Empire.

NORMAN SUCCESSION

The reign of William I's son William Rufus as King William II of England was complicated by numerous military alliances with and against his brothers. The eldest, Robert, unable to win any lasting advantage against him, departed on the First Crusade in 1096. Indeed, it was in the East that Robert most distinguished himself, playing pivotal commanding roles at the Battle of Dorylaeum and the siege of Jerusalem.

In 1100, William Rufus was accidentally killed by an arrow while hunting in the New Forest in southern England. His other brother, Henry, who was with him at the time, immediately had himself crowned King Henry I (reigned 1100–35). Returning home to Normandy soon after, Robert raised an army to oppose Henry, but was decisively defeated at Tinchebrai in Normandy in 1106. Henry put his elder brother under house arrest in England, and seized the Duchy of Normandy, thus reuniting William the Conqueror's lands under one ruler.

Henry I was a bold warrior—more than once he escaped death in battle—but his reign was widely known for its

peacefulness. He achieved this through political rapprochement, pardoning those who had opposed him and making overtures to potential foes. Those that refused peace had their lands confiscated or, in very rare cases, were mutilated—to his medieval contemporaries, this was not cruelty but effective governance.

THE ANARCHY OF STEPHEN'S REIGN

With Henry's death in 1135 (after eating a surfeit of lampreys), stability in England came to an end. Henry had fathered dozens of illegitimate children but only one male heir, William Adelin, who had died in a tragic shipwreck in 1120. To provide for the succession, Henry's barons had sworn oaths that they would support as heir the first son

LEFT: A network of powerful connections bolstered Matilda's position. Daughter of Henry I, she had been married to the Holy Roman Emperor Henry V, a union that remained childless when Henry died in 1125.

ABOVE: *After Stephen's capture in 1141, his wife, also called Matilda, rallied supporters in London and pleaded for his release. Here, her pleas are rejected by her imperious namesake.*

of his daughter, Matilda. That boy, also called Henry, was born in 1133; after Henry I's death, however, many of the magnates broke their promise and supported the ambitions of Stephen, Count of Blois and Henry I's nephew, allowing him to claim the English throne.

King Stephen (reigned 1135–54) was at once faced with a daunting problem: while half of the nobles supported his rule, the other half backed Matilda. The so-called Angevin side (Matilda's husband Geoffrey Plantagenet was Count of Anjou) was led by the formidable Robert, Earl of Gloucester, one of Henry I's illegitimate sons and the most powerful magnate in England after Stephen. Following a few years of tense peace, war broke out in England in 1139. The conflict is often referred to as "the anarchy of Stephen's

RIGHT: *The dogged persistance of King Stephen, shown at left with a falcon, in battling to retain the English throne was ultimately insufficient to halt the advent of Angevin rule under Henry II, at right.*

reign," although it was hardly anarchical in nature. Rather, the wars featured a dizzying number of alliances and shifts in support on both sides, as nobles and church leaders repeatedly reconsidered their positions in the light of military developments. The building of private castles accelerated, and knightly contingents became strong bargaining chips when the English barons offered their loyalties.

TRIUMPH OF THE ANGEVINS

Matilda gained an early advantage when Robert of Gloucester defeated Stephen's armies at the Battle of Lincoln in February 1141. Ever the valiant knight, Stephen fought in the thick of the action and even when his army was routed continued fighting. Surrounded, the king defended himself with a two-headed ax and when it shattered fought on with his sword until he was finally captured. In the wake of the battle, Matilda moved to secure her coronation as queen but was frustrated by recalcitrant Stephen supporters and the citizens of London, who refused to support her financially and even attacked her retinue at Westminster. In September 1141, Robert of Gloucester was captured in battle, and to secure his freedom Matilda was forced to release King Stephen in exchange. The war dragged on for several more years but ultimately to the Angevins' benefit: while Stephen was preoccupied in England, Geoffrey Plantagenet invaded and conquered

RIGHT: *The dogged persistance of King Stephen, shown at left with a falcon, in battling to retain the English throne was ultimately insufficient to halt the advent of Angevin rule under Henry II, at right.*

Normandy and was invested as its duke in 1144. The Anglo-Norman realm had been divided once again.

After Robert of Gloucester's death in 1147, the Angevin cause found a new champion in Matilda's son, Henry Plantagenet. In two separate invasions of England in 1149 and 1153, the brash Henry brought a high profile, fresh troops, and a renewed vigor to Stephen's enemies. Through a series of sieges and skirmishes, Henry achieved substantial success and an increasing number of

magnates flocked to his side. As Stephen fell ill, his cause was prosecuted most forcefully by his eldest son Eustace, who warred against Henry not only in England but also in Normandy through his alliance with Louis VII of France. However, after Eustace's death in 1153, Stephen accepted the Treaty of Westminster, which recognized Henry as the legitimate heir to his throne. Stephen died in October 1154; two months later Henry was crowned King Henry II of England (reigned 1154–89).

CAPETIAN FRANCE

LEFT: *Led by mounted warriors like the one in this Norwegian tapestry, Norman forces were a thorn in the side of the Capetian rulers through the eleventh and twelfth centuries.*

For three centuries after the first millennium, the Capetian family occupied the throne of France. Their wars were fought principally to contain ambitious families, notably those of Normandy. In this they were not always successful: the extension of Norman control, beginning in 1051, to Maine and adjacent areas meant fewer revenues for the French crown and a reduction in its military resources.

In the eleventh century, most other internal conflicts in Capetian France were the result of disputes between barons. Increasingly powerful magnates with stables of mounted knights could range swiftly into neighboring areas, devastate the landscape, and force political concessions from rivals. Such activities led to numerous localized armed feuds, which in turn prevented the coalescence of France into a stable and dominant kingdom until two or three generations after England was unified under William the Conqueror.

By the eleventh century, the knight had taken up a central position in the military culture of France and, consequently, had acquired an elevated social status. Horseborne warriors were considered the primary element of an army, and most battles were fought by mounted knights and their attendants. This contrasted with contemporary England, where even after the Norman Conquest Anglo-Norman cavalry often preferred to dismount to fight. In neither country, however, could kings and nobles rely fully on levies of knights, so they made regular and extensive use of mercenaries or forced common folk into military service.

DEFENDING THE REALM

The Capetian kings of the twelfth century became renowned for their strong governance and knightly exploits. Louis VI (reigned 1108–37), also known as Louis the Fat, was a vigorous fighter who did not shy from entering the fray. He strived to maintain the territorial integrity of France in the face of the hostilities of Henry I of England, the Holy Roman Emperor Henry V (reigned 1111–25), and the counts of Blois and Champagne.

Louis managed to keep the Germans out of Lorraine, but the Anglo-Normans proved more difficult to counter. He backed William Clito, the grandson of William the Conqueror, in his attempt to supplant Henry I as Duke of Normandy. In 1119, however, Louis's army was crushed by Henry's forces at the Battle of Bremule. Although the king subsequently allied himself with the Count of Anjou and other

LOUIS THE FAT

King Louis VI of France was dubbed "the Fat," for he was reputedly so large that he could not scale a horse without the assistance of a mechanical winch. Yet once astride his mount, Louis was a fearsome presence and a deadly warrior. He personally charged into battle alongside his knights or dismounted to fight in the infantry ranks. Louis's knightly deeds were recalled in writing by the famous Suger, Abbot of St. Denis and royal advisor. Suger's dramatic flourishes make for exciting reading, as Louis swings "arms as powerful as Hector's" and launches "attacks worthy of a giant!"

LEFT: *Louis VI brought stability to France and reined in the country's feuding barons.*

lesser Normans, such efforts did little to improve his position and he was forced to accept Henry's lordship over Normandy. His successors, however, continually strived to limit the influence of their powerful neighbor, and in the remainder of the twelfth century French military activities sought to chip away at English control of Normandy and other areas on the Continent.

AN AGE OF COMPROMISE

Louis the Fat's son Louis VII (reigned 1137–80) had a scholarly upbringing. Nevertheless, he retained an enthusiasm for war, though he lacked an ability to plan for extended conflicts and was thus easily persuaded into diplomatic compromises. Along with Conrad III of Germany (reigned 1138–52), Louis was the principal commander of the Second Crusade (1147–49). In fact, French soldiers were ubiquitous on the crusades of the late eleventh and twelfth centuries, and it was the charge of French heavy cavalry that became the dominant image of Western warfare and was the crusaders' most effective weapon against their more lightly armed Muslim foes. Yet Louis's expedition was not a success: Conrad's army was destroyed before the French even arrived in the East, and Louis suffered a brutal defeat at the Battle of Latakia in 1148, although he distinguished himself in combat while trying to save his knights.

Louis also spent a great deal of time warring unsuccessfully against King Henry II of England on the Continent. He launched campaigns into Normandy, allied with Henry's sons and rebellious magnates in Brittany, and tried to check Henry's expansion in lands near to Aquitaine. In this last endeavor, Louis was relatively successful, but in general he was unable to forestall the massive territorial gains of his rival.

BELOW: *Jean-Baptiste Mauzaisse's 1840 painting shows Louis VII receiving the oriflamme, the battle standard of French kings, from Pope Eugene III in 1147. Louis's wife, Eleanor of Aquitaine, kneels on the right.*

HENRY II AND HIS QUEEN

As well as being descended from kings and counts, from early on Henry Plantagenet had powerful supporters—upon reaching the age of reason, he was knighted by King David I of Scotland (reigned 1124–53) and the Earl of Hereford. His marriage to Eleanor of Aquitaine (*c.* 1122–1204), former wife of French king Louis VII, in 1152, brought him further prestige, lands, and wealth. King of the English, Duke of Normandy and Aquitaine, Count of Anjou, and holder of several other titles, Henry II became one of medieval Europe's most powerful rulers.

BELOW: *A fortress existed at Dover in Anglo-Saxon times, but it was Henry II who built most of the modern-day structure, including its rectangular keep—the largest in Britain.*

RIGHT: *Though naturally stocky, as indicated by his tomb effigy in Fontevrault Abbey, France, shown here, Henry II was, by all accounts, very fit and an impressive horseman and fighter.*

KNIGHTS UNDER HENRY II

Henry's rule saw significant developments in knighthood and warfare. He ordered, in 1166, the *Cartae Baronum* (Barons' Certificates), an inquest, similar to the *Domesday Book* census, that sought to document the number of knights his barons commanded and thereby the size of his forces. This was followed, in 1181, by the Assize of Arms, which sought to ensure an armed citizenry by requiring that all citizens retain weapons and armor, those with higher means being expected to possess and maintain more elaborate arms.

Henry frequently sought *scutage* (also known as a shield tax), whereby knights were asked to make a financial payment in lieu of their serving in war personally. Henry spent these monies on mercenaries, whom he employed on multiple campaigns as skirmishers, besiegers, and infantry. The use of hired men had been

THE ASSIZE OF ARMS

Henry II's 1181 order setting out rules for the arming of the English citizenry provides an interesting and detailed snapshot of twelfth-century preparations for war. The assize states that every knight is to have "a shirt of mail, a helmet, a shield, and a lance"; in addition "all burgesses and the whole community of freemen shall [each] have a gambeson [padded surcoat], an iron cap, and a lance." The export of arms is forbidden. Horses and missile weapons are not mentioned, but they do appear in a similar assize Henry assigned to Normandy, which highlights the differences between English and Continental warfare.

widespread since the days of William the Conqueror, and Henry relied upon them heavily. His knights had little complaint about the mercenaries themselves, but rather Henry's frequent demands for monies to pay for them.

Henry II was also interested in tales of knightly deeds and commissioned the writer Walter Map to write a history of King Arthur, whose legend enjoyed a strong resurgence in the late twelfth century. Henry was not pleasantly disposed toward tournaments, however, and prohibited them in England.

As a commander of men, Henry was extremely active in the prosecution of warfare. He led dozens of campaigns, concluding most of them with either victory in battle and siege or treaties advantageous to his political purpose. Among the scores of castles he built were the sophisticated structures at Dover in Kent and Chinon in Touraine. Henry never went to Jerusalem, but he was an active financier of the Crusades, and his son Richard I would become, along with Louis IX of France (reigned 1226–70), the most famous crusader of all.

ELEANOR OF AQUITAINE
Although Henry's marriage to Eleanor of Aquitaine brought him further titles and lands, it also deepened the political struggle between England and France and ultimately weakened his rule, for Eleanor would ultimately connive with her rebellious sons against her husband.

Renowned for her relationships with four kings, Eleanor of Aquitaine is a figure more defined by legend than verifiable history. She was the granddaughter of the crusader and troubadour Duke William IX of Aquitaine (c. 1071–1126) and in 1137 married King Louis VII. This was, however, an unhappy match, did not produce a male heir, and, in March 1152 was annulled on the basis of consanguinity (that is, because the spouses were descended from the same ancestor). Two months later, Eleanor married Henry, giving England, to Louis's dismay, control of Aquitaine—much of southwestern France.

Little is known about Eleanor's life as queen. Her connections to contemporary writers are well documented, although her literary patronage as queen has been overstated. She appears in the chronicles only in climactic moments, as in the Great Revolt of 1173–74, when Henry's sons rebelled against him. Eleanor sided with her sons and even attempted, disguised, to slip out of England and join them in France. Caught by Henry's men, she was placed under house arrest and did not regain her liberty until after the king's death in 1189.

Much more is known about Eleanor the widow. She became a confidant and political ally to her son Richard I, fighting for his rights on the Continent. In England, she acted to suppress her youngest son John's ambitions while Richard was away on the Third Crusade (as documented in the popular but fictional *Robin Hood* stories). The accession of John to the English throne in 1199 marked the beginning of Eleanor's military career. She led a mercenary army on a campaign to Anjou and later assisted John during his wars against King Philip II Augustus of France (reigned 1179–1223) in 1202. Still a vital woman at the age of 78, she joined him on campaign and defended his estates against Breton attacks before dying in 1204.

BELOW: *Henry leads his wife, Eleanor (right) and Eleanor's daughter-in-law Isabella of Angoulême (left), into captivity following the Great Revolt, as depicted in a fresco in the chapel of Sainte Radegonde at Chinon in France.*

THE ANGEVIN EMPIRE

In the course of his reign, Henry II aquired large tracts of land stretching from southern France to Ireland, ultimately achieving the greatest territorial reach of any medieval English king. The lands ruled by Henry II and his heirs, Richard I and John, are often referred to as the Angevin Empire, a term of considerable historical debate over the years.

It is clear that Henry never thought of nor styled himself as an emperor. Moreover, there were neither political nor legal structures that operated consistently across the realms; rather, each county, duchy, and kingdom retained in large measure its local customs. Even so, there is no disputing that Henry carved out a huge dominion, and so language suggesting an empire is largely a convenient method of referring to his lands in a collective sense.

EXPANDING THE NORMAN REALM

The Angevin Empire extended far and wide across western Europe. It included lands inherited or acquired through marriage or custom. The core of the empire was the Anglo-Norman realm as it had been bequeathed by William the Conqueror to his sons Robert Curthose and William Rufus. Lands subjugated by the Anglo-Norman kings, such as eastern Brittany and the Scottish and Welsh marches were commonly construed as extensions of the realm.

To these lands, Henry added the French counties of Anjou and Maine, the latter of which was claimed by rights by the Counts of Anjou. Henry's performance of homage to the counts of Blois also earned him control over Touraine as a fief. Through his marriage to

Eleanor in 1152 Henry gained her rich Duchy of Aquitaine. Finally, the Duchy of Brittany came under Henry's sway in 1166 when he married his son Geoffrey into the Breton ducal house—Henry ruled as regent until his son came of age in 1181 and then regained the duchy upon Geoffrey's death in 1186.

The rest of Henry II's lands came by way of treaty or conquest. He claimed Nantes by defeating his brother Geoffrey, who was its count. Other successful military campaigns gained him Poitou and portions of Bordeaux, Gascony, Berry, and the Vexin (lands

The knights in their battle-array have / come forth from the town: some sixty / thousand of them and more than sixty / companies, and not one of them but / thinks himself the equal of a Welsh king.

CHRONICLER JORDAN FANTOSME DESCRIBING HENRY'S ARMY IN WALES (1175)

between Normandy and the Île-de-France), although these last two areas were regions of constant dispute right up until his death.

THE CONQUEST OF IRELAND

One of the most remarkable of Henry II's acquisitions was eastern Ireland, which he invaded and conquered in 1171. This was an innovation—the conquest of Ireland had not been attempted by the Romans or even the Anglo-Saxons, although warfare between the latter and the Irish Vikings did occur on occasion. Neither did the early Anglo-Normans give much thought to the Emerald Isle.

According to the English writer John of Salisbury, in 1155 Pope Adrian IV (reigned 1154–59) promulgated the papal bull *Laudabiliter*, giving Henry II approval to obtain and possess Ireland in order that he might set right certain perceived liturgical abuses of the Irish church. The legitimacy of the bull has been flatly denied by generations of Irish historians, for its text has not survived and neither Henry nor any successive popes mentioned it when discussing the Irish question.

Nevertheless, in October 1171, Henry sailed across the Irish Sea. He took with him an invasion fleet numbering between 240 and 400 ships and carrying a large number of knights,

archers, and men-at-arms. Henry's real cause was not church reform but the support of the Earl of Clare, Richard "Strongbow" FitzGilbert, who had, with Henry's blessing, taken Dublin, but had then lost it to O'Rouric, King of Meath. Together, Strongbow and Henry landed on the Irish shore and were met by the Irish lords, all of whom at once submitted to English rule. Henry proceeded to spend Christmas in Dublin—Ireland had been conquered without a fight.

THE BECKET AFFAIR

On the home front, however, Henry increasingly had trouble dealing with opponents and subordinates, which in turn impacted on the rule and extent of his empire. The most famous of his domestic disputes was the Becket Affair, the drama that unfolded between the king and the Archbishop of Canterbury, Thomas Becket (c. 1118–70). In his prior role of royal chancellor, Becket had raised revenues for Henry's wars and had even gone on campaign himself, leading some 1,900 mounted warriors across Aquitaine and into the Norman Vexin in 1159–61. Yet he and Henry had a falling-out over a legal issue: whether or not clergymen accused of murder ought to be tried in royal or ecclesiastical courts. The king and even his fellow bishops turned against Becket, who fled into exile in France in

RIGHT: *After the murder of Thomas Becket in Canterbury Cathedral in 1170, depicted in this French fifteenth-century manuscript illustration, Canterbury became a major center of pilgrimage.*

November 1164; when he finally returned to England in late 1170, he excommunicated his ecclesiastical rivals. In response, four of Henry's knights, dramatically compelled by their king's raw anger at Becket, sailed to Canterbury and murdered the archbishop in his own cathedral.

Although he had given no order for Becket's death, Henry II was fully implicated in the crime. Threatened

LEFT: *Following his capture by Henry II, King William I of Scotland was forced to accept English control of his realm. After Henry's death, however, he obtained independence for Scotland once more.*

by the papacy with interdict and excommunication, Henry bided his time until he was finally forced, in 1174, to agree to a penance for his role in what was by then known as the martyrdom of St. Thomas, Becket having been canonized in 1172. The agreement, the Compromise of Avranches, demanded, among other things, that Henry take the cross and go on crusade to either Spain or Jerusalem and provide monies to the Knights Templar for the maintenance of two hundred brothers. The king fulfilled only the second promise: he never went on crusade, but his financing as a result of the Compromise and later arrangements such as the Saladin Tithe of 1188, a tax that provided about sixty thousand marks for the Holy Land, had a demonstrable effect on the size and effectiveness of Christian armies operating in the East.

THE GREAT REVOLT

Henry was also forced to contend with a series of armed rebellions and wars. In 1173, his three elder sons, Henry the Younger, Geoffrey, and Richard, joined with King Louis VII, King William I of Scotland (1165–1214), and a host of other nobles in the Great Revolt. The war ranged across England, Normandy, and Brittany, and featured multiple town and castle sieges in Normandy and on the Anglo-Scottish border, as well as major battles at Fornham in Suffolk and Dol in Brittany. Both sides relied heavily upon mercenaries during the conflict, with thousands of Flemish soldiers reported at Fornham and the frequent use of Welsh archers and Brabançon infantry and cavalry by Henry II. Although landed knights played important roles and received attention and accolades for their deeds,

LEFT: *Scene of Henry II's capture of William I of Scotland, Alnwick Castle in Northumberland, England, was founded in the Norman era and extensively renovated in the eighteenth century.*

more often than not hired soldiers were the critical, if less flashy, components of Angevin armies.

A turning point occurred in July 1174, when a group of Henry's knights captured the Scottish king at the castle of Alnwick, in Northumberland. William had surrounded the castle and meant to starve it into surrender, but his own men had insufficient supplies. He therefore split his army, keeping a group of five hundred knights beside him and sending the rest to ravage the countryside. Soon after, a group of Henry's knights burst into the clearing where the Scots were taking breakfast, having removed their armor. In the subsequent pitched cavalry battle, the Scottish king was captured. The following month, Henry himself broke Louis's siege of Rouen, a victory that forced his enemies to come to terms.

TROUBLESOME OFFSPRING

Henry II's problems were not over, however, for his sons continued to rebel throughout the 1180s, supported by their mother. Henry the Younger and Geoffrey seized Limoges in 1182, forcing the king to besiege them within; young Henry died soon after from dysentery. Geoffrey made peace with his father, but in 1186 he died as well, trampled by a horse while competing in a tournament in France. Richard had remained loyal throughout, but in the midst of war with France he also betrayed his father— defecting in November 1188 to Philip Augustus, and by July of the next year they had together captured Tours and driven Henry and his seven hundred knights out of Le Mans by way of assault. Among Henry's retinue was the renowned soldier William Marshal, the epitome of a medieval chivalric knight. Marshal guarded his liege's retreat and even managed to unhorse Richard but spared his life, saying, "Let the devil kill you for I shall not!" On July 6, 1189, however, a weak, ill, and defeated Henry II died at Chinon.

ABOVE: *In this image painted around 1415, French soldiers under the command of Philip Augustus and Richard Plantagenet besiege Henry II's forces in northern France, during the summer of 1189.*

AN EXEMPLARY KNIGHT

William Marshal (1147–1219) was the Earl of Pembroke and one of the most famous knights in history. He served under the three Angevin kings—Henry II, Richard I, and John—and was renowned for his military skill (displayed in tournaments as well as in battle), chivalric ethics, and political influence. That we know so much about him is due to a poem written in Middle French, *L'Histoire de Guillaume le Maréchal (The History of William the Marshal)*, **nineteen thousand lines of rhymed verse that tell of his deeds and life.**

LEFT: *Befitting his legendary, heroic status, this imposing statue of King Richard I, by Italian sculptor Carlo Marochetti (1805–67), stands outside the Palace of Westminster in London.*

Once in the Holy Land, Richard became the only one among his peers to make headway: Frederick Barbarossa died on the outward journey, and Philip Augustus, claiming his crusading vow fulfilled, departed for home in the middle of the siege of Acre. It was left to Richard to retake that city in 1191 in what has been recognized as a triumph of siegecraft, and then defeat Saladin at the Battle of Arsuf in the same year.

The success of Richard's crusading activities is a heated subject, however. In the end, Jerusalem escaped his grasp; indeed, believing his forces too small he never even besieged the city, and none of his efforts prevented Saladin's jihad from retaking great swaths of territory. Nevertheless, Richard's valorous deeds, some fictional, were widely recorded. This led the poet-singer Ambroise to say that Richard had "the heart of a lion" within him, giving rise to the nickname *Lionheart*. Moreover, Richard's military skill and prowess as a knight was undeniable, and also amply chronicled.

On his way home from the Holy Land, Richard was kidnapped and only released after the payment of a huge ransom to the Holy Roman Emperor, Henry VI. Once back in England in 1194, he reinstituted the tournament, which his father had outlawed. His ordinance specified five tournament sites and a system of entrance fees determined by social rank—the lowliest knights paid the least, while earls paid the most.

By then, Richard's relationship with Philip Augustus had soured, and he had to spend much of his time in France trying to keep Angevin lands out of Philip's clutches. He died there in 1199, after a siege at Châlus in Aquitaine. Nearing his end, he had himself carried to Chinon, where his father had died.

RICHARD I AND JOHN

The deaths of the elder Plantagenets, Henry the Younger and Geoffrey, allowed Richard, Henry II's third son, to inherit the English throne, and even after his relatively short reign the monarchy remained in Plantagenet hands, under John, the youngest of the brothers. Keeping the realm together, however, proved a difficult proposition for both of them, and John's reign in particular would see the Angevin Empire shrink to a shell of its former self.

RICHARD THE LIONHEART

King Richard I (reigned 1189–99) ultimately spent little of his time in England, traveling overseas to fight in the Crusades or defend his holdings in Europe. Soon after his coronation, he emptied his father's treasury and sold off lands, titles, and even government positions to raise money for the Third Crusade, and in July 1190 he set off for the Holy Land, determined to retake Jerusalem from Saladin.

JOHN'S BLUNDERS

Most of Henry II's work was undone during the reign (1199–1216) of John. In a series of disastrous military and diplomatic blunders, John lost control of Normandy, Anjou, Aquitaine, Maine, and Brittany. By 1206, all that remained of the Angevin dominions on the Continent was Gascony, a small piece of Aquitaine, and the Channel Islands. To compound his difficulties, in 1209 John was excommunicated by Pope Innocent III (reigned 1198–1216) for refusing to appoint Stephen Langton as Archbishop of Canterbury, which prompted John's surrender of England to the pope in 1213 as penance, although the country was soon returned to him. Following the crushing of his ally Otto

BELOW: At Runnymede, in a meadow by the Thames River, on June 10, 1215, King John reluctantly attached his seal to Magna Carta, under the watchful eye of attendant barons.

RIGHT: Four copies of the original 1215 Magna Carta survive, along with various copies of the 1216, 1217, and 1225 charters. This is the 1225 version, issued by Henry III.

IV by Philip Augustus in July 1214 at the Battle of Bouvines, John found himself entirely isolated and without support.

Having seen their European holdings steadily eroded, despite paying the king huge sums in the form of scutage, John's barons decided enough was enough. On June 10, 1215, at Runnymede, Surrey, England, they compelled him to accept Magna Carta, a document that reiterated the traditional relationship between lord and subject and reasserted the duties and rights of knights. Under the charter, no man could be forced to fight longer than the terms of his estate required, the levying of scutage was forbidden without the consent of the barons, payments in lieu of performing castle guard were prohibited, and foreign mercenaries were expelled.

At Innocent III's insistence, the original Magna Carta was nullified on the basis that barons possessed no right to distrain a lawfully anointed king. Yet it was reissued in 1216, 1217, and 1225, and soon widely accepted. Three of its provisions remain effectual in English constitutional law, including the provision forbidding payments in lieu of soldierly service. Magna Carta did not directly influence the decrease of knightly obligations in England, but was indicative of thirteenth-century trends. Leaders were now relying heavily upon mounted sergeants, infantry, and missile troops, and some knights sought to avoid the obligation of wartime combat.

SOWING THE SEEDS OF WAR

Following John's death from dysentery in 1216, his son Henry III (1216–72) would unsuccessfully attempt to regain some of the territories his father had

lost by invading Brittany in 1230 and Poitou in 1241. But in 1259 he was forced by King Louis IX of France to accept the Treaty of Paris, under which he had to surrender his claim to the lost portions of the Angevin Empire in exchange for only Gascony. The subsequent dispute over the English ownership of that territory would be one of the principal causes of the Hundred Years' War (1337–1453).

The Crusades

The Crusades were always conceived as defensive wars on behalf of Christendom. Originally directed against the Muslims, with whom Christians had been continually at war since the initial Islamic invasions of the seventh century CE, they were later extended to other enemies of Christendom, including pagans and heretics.

The knights who went on the Crusades generally did not do so to increase their wealth or to enhance their prestige; in fact, after the First Crusade—the only truly successful campaign—it can be said that the continual failures of the crusaders were sometimes humiliating blows to their reputation and treasury. Warriors undertook the arduous journey involved in a crusade in order to place their professional military skills at the service of Christ and his church, rather than using them for cruel or unjust personal ends.

THE CONTEXT OF THE CRUSADES

The Crusades were the first significant Western Christian counterattack after centuries of Muslim attacks. In CE 634, two years after the death of the Islamic prophet Muhammad, Muslim-led Arab forces began serious incursions into Christian Byzantine territory in Syria. In 636, a Muslim army destroyed the primary Byzantine army in the east at the Battle of the Yarmuk, and in 638, Muslims besieged and took Jerusalem, a holy city for Jews and Christians alike and held by Christians ever since the fourth century CE.

By the early eighth century, Islamic armies had conquered Syria, Asia Minor, Egypt, North Africa, and Spain, stripping away more than half of the territory that had been Christian in 632 and inflicting a near-mortal blow on the late Roman world. The Byzantines managed to defend their capital city, Constantinople, through several sieges, but remained in a constant state of war with their Muslim enemies. During the tenth century, the Byzantines even launched a series of modest counterattacks, retaking Asia Minor up to the city of Antioch. The holy city of Jerusalem, however, lay completely beyond their grasp.

In the west, the Muslim invaders had been halted deep inside France at the Battle of Poitiers (also known as the Battle of Tours) in 732, by the Frankish war leader Charles Martel (c. 688–741). Each year thereafter, Muslim raiders were forced a little further south, out of Frankish territory and back into Spain. The great Frankish emperor Charlemagne (c. 742–814) led expeditions into Spain in the eighth and early ninth centuries to continue the process of repelling the Muslims, but with limited success.

MUSLIMS IN THE MEDITERRANEAN

Frustrated in the east by the Byzantines and in the west by the Franks, the Muslims turned their attention to the central Mediterranean in the ninth century, seizing the islands of Sicily, Sardinia, and Corsica, and in 846

LEFT: *A group of Muslims brandishing scimitars takes on a host of armor-clad crusading knights in this medieval illustration of an age-old conflict.*

they sacked the unwalled areas of Rome itself. Various Christian leaders—including the popes—beat them back.

By the early eleventh century, some Christian Italian powers were even beginning to mount small counterattacks across the Mediterranean, striking at the North African bases of their Muslim tormentors. On the Iberian Peninsula, the small Spanish kingdoms were beginning to extend their power southward against the Muslims. But the balance of power between Muslims and Christians in the Mediterranean in the year 1000 was approximately even. This was about to change, for several reasons.

WESTERN FRUSTRATION

In the early part of the eleventh century, the Muslim ruler of Jerusalem was a possibly mad and certainly unorthodox individual named Hakim (reigned 996–1021). He claimed personal divinity and persecuted Christians and Jews fiercely. In 1009 he ordered the destruction of the Church of the Holy

Sepulchre in Jerusalem, Christianity's most sacred church. Under Hakim, the Christian population of the Holy Land began to shrink steadily. Both the Byzantines and Western Christians were distressed by these problems.

Also in the mid-eleventh century, the Arab Muslim world of the Middle East was disrupted by a series of invasions by Turkish peoples from Central Asia. The caliph's city of Baghdad was taken over by Turks in 1055; thereafter, Turks replaced various Arab rulers. At first pagan, the Turks soon converted to Islam, leaving the region with a Muslim ruling class. But the political disorder engendered by these events left the Muslim Middle East in a weakened state for half a century or so. As a result of the Turkish incursions, as well as the earlier depredations of Hakim, Christian pilgrimage to the holy sites in Jerusalem and elsewhere became difficult, dangerous, and sometimes impossible. Western Christians, in particular, experienced growing frustration with the situation.

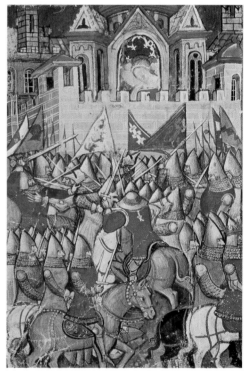

TOP: *Created by an Ottoman artist in the seventeenth century, this map shows the Crusades from the point of view of Islam.*
ABOVE: *Charlemagne's army attacked Pamplona in 778 during his battles with Spanish Muslims, as seen in this fourteenth-century image.*

RIGHT: *During the First Crusade, battles were fought with unique religious fervor. Mounted knights were unhorsed and killed, and there was plenty of hand-to-hand fighting. On the left of this late fifteenth-century image, a soldier wields a two-sided battle-ax known as a bipennis.*

Finally, in 1071 the Byzantines clashed with a large Turkish force in far eastern Asia Minor, in the Battle of Manzikert. The battle was a disaster for the Byzantines, who were driven back to Constantinople, losing all their hard-won reconquests in Asia Minor. They sent urgent appeals for help to the West, particularly to the pope, whom they viewed, not incorrectly, as the central authority of Western Christendom.

THE POPE FINALLY ACTS

Political and theological disputes between the various popes and German emperors at first prevented a coordinated response to the Byzantine appeals. Finally, in 1095, Pope Urban II (reigned 1088–99) arranged a series of church councils in which he allowed the Byzantines to make their case to Western leaders. After careful planning, Urban made a famous speech on November 27, 1095, in Clermont, France, in which he publicly urged Western warriors to "take the cross": to risk life and fortune by campaigning to the East, both to aid the Byzantine Christians and to regain control of the Christian holy sites in Palestine and Syria.

The response must have surprised even the pope. A very great number of people, both common and noble, answered the call, in what has become known as the First Crusade.

WHAT WERE THE CRUSADES?

Although the rules of crusading developed with, or sometimes after, the historical events, and may have varied from crusade to crusade, certain guiding principles were common to all of the campaigns. A crusade had to be

It is charity to risk your life for your brothers ...

POPE URBAN II (REIGNED 1088–99), PREACHING THE FIRST CRUSADE AT CLERMONT, NOVEMBER 27, 1095

called, in some form, by the pope; it was always conceived as a defensive operation (though it is not always easy to distinguish between defensive and offensive action once a conflict has begun); it was always seen as an exercise of love, following Jesus' statement that there was no greater form of love than to lay down one's life for one's friends; and it was not officially aimed at forcing conversion or conquering new territory (though occasionally this point became obscure in the heat of the moment).

The popes promised that death on a crusade—and later simply participating in a crusade—would remit the penance due for one's sins (though the sins still had to be properly confessed and repented for the remission of penance

to be valid). Crusading was often referred to as the "business of Christ" or even as a "pilgrimage"; it was, in short, an attempt to protect Christian territory, Christian individuals, and freedom of Christian worship from oppression by non-Christians, especially Muslims.

Crusading has, in the past, been described as an activity of restless younger sons, eager for adventure and greedy for gain, with little or no real religious content beyond a superficial glaze of piety. Closer study of the sources from the Middle Ages does not bear this view out, however—the majority of crusaders appear to have acted out of devotion, love, and self-sacrifice, although this of course does not preclude mixed motives in individuals, nor does it mean that all crusaders were equally pure-minded. But the older stereotype of the cynical, greedy, ignorant crusader has not withstood recent scholarly scrutiny.

Crusading was a continual process, from the beginning of the First Crusade in 1095 through to the seventeenth century. However, scholars typically recognize eight major crusades to the Holy Land, between 1095 and 1270.

THE EIGHT CRUSADES

Scholars recognize eight major crusades to the Holy Land. The First Crusade (1095–99) set out to capture Jerusalem, and was successful, while the Second Crusade (1146–48) was a failed attempt to reclaim the Christian County of Edessa, taken by the Muslims in 1144. Partially successful, the Third Crusade (1189–92) aimed to retake Jerusalem from Saladin; the Fourth Crusade (1202–4) was diverted to Constantinople. The Fifth Crusade (1218–21) tried in vain to relieve Jerusalem by attacking Egypt, while the Sixth Crusade (1228–29) was primarily involved in negotiations and had an ambiguous outcome. Targeting Egypt, the Seventh Crusade (1248–54) was ultimately unsuccessful, and the Eighth Crusade (1270) foundered in Tunisia before reaching the Holy Land.

LEFT: *A fourteenth-century illumination details a number of events that occurred during the First Crusade, including the Council of Clermont in 1095 and the capture of Jerusalem in 1099.*

The First Crusade struck the Muslim world in a moment of unique weakness after the earlier Turkish invasions, and it was the only one of the eight crusades to be entirely successful. It established four "crusader states," including the Kingdom of Jerusalem, which lasted from 1099 to 1187, when the city was captured again by the great Muslim Kurdish leader Saladin (1137/38–93). Two crusades—the Fourth and the Eighth—failed entirely to make it to the eastern Mediterranean, and the Fourth infamously disobeyed papal orders and involved itself in a Byzantine civil war. Twenty-one years after the Eighth Crusade of 1270, Muslim forces crushed the last Christian strongholds in Palestine and Syria and drove Christians, for the second time, from the Holy Land. No serious crusades to regain Jerusalem were mounted after that.

OTHER EUROPEAN CRUSADES

Crusading was not limited to the Holy Land, however. The expeditions to recover Spain, which had begun under Charlemagne, continued throughout the Middle Ages, and accomplished their goal in 1492 when Spanish monarchs Ferdinand and Isabella conquered Muslim Granada and drove the Muslims off the Iberian Peninsula. Attempts to pursue the Muslims back across North Africa and also to recover those provinces for Christendom quickly foundered, however, and the Spanish and Portuguese turned their attention elsewhere.

Crusades were also declared in the twelfth century to protect Christians from abuse by pagan authorities in the Baltic area, and in 1208 against the heretics of southern France. One late thirteenth-century pope even preached a crusade against some of his own cardinals during a heated dispute. The concept of crusade proved flexible enough to adapt to a wide variety of circumstances, but in theory, at least, it always remained a defensive action, undertaken out of charity for one's Christian neighbor.

LEFT: *Saladin, founder of the Ayyubid dynasty, enters Jerusalem in October 1187 after a 12-day siege, in this twentieth-century painting.*

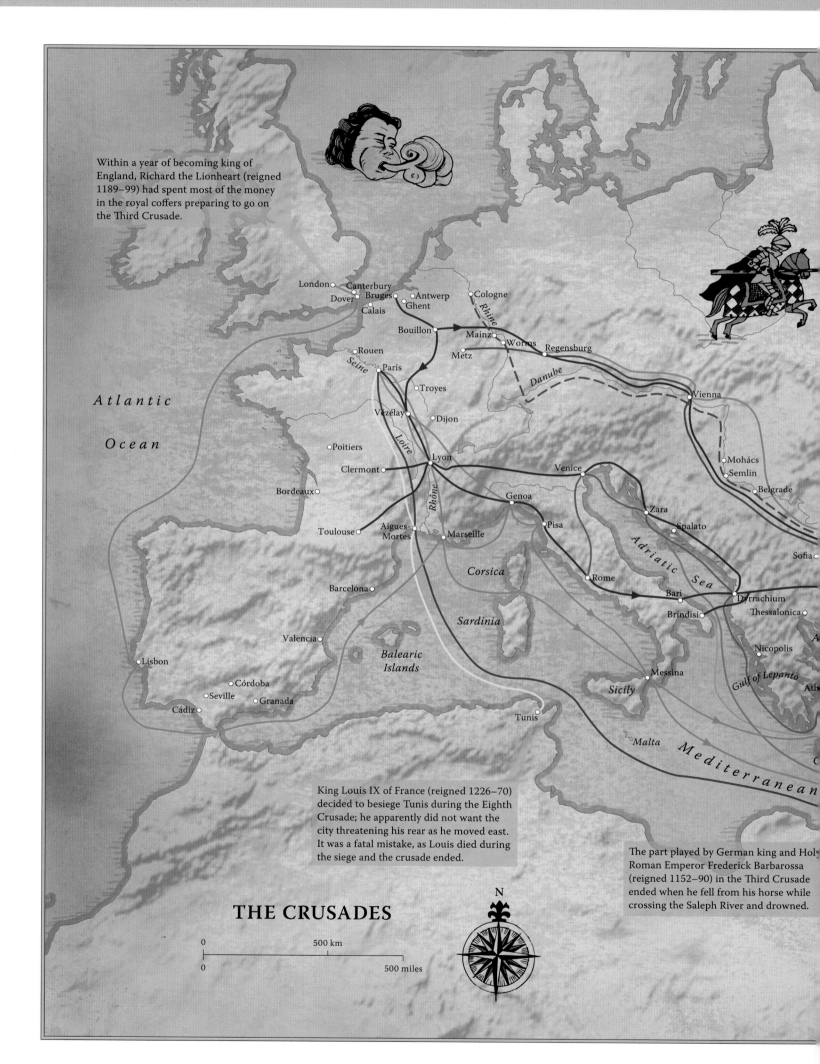

Within a year of becoming king of England, Richard the Lionheart (reigned 1189–99) had spent most of the money in the royal coffers preparing to go on the Third Crusade.

King Louis IX of France (reigned 1226–70) decided to besiege Tunis during the Eighth Crusade; he apparently did not want the city threatening his rear as he moved east. It was a fatal mistake, as Louis died during the siege and the crusade ended.

The part played by German king and Holy Roman Emperor Frederick Barbarossa (reigned 1152–90) in the Third Crusade ended when he fell from his horse while crossing the Saleph River and drowned.

THE CRUSADES

0 ——— 500 km

0 ——— 500 miles

N

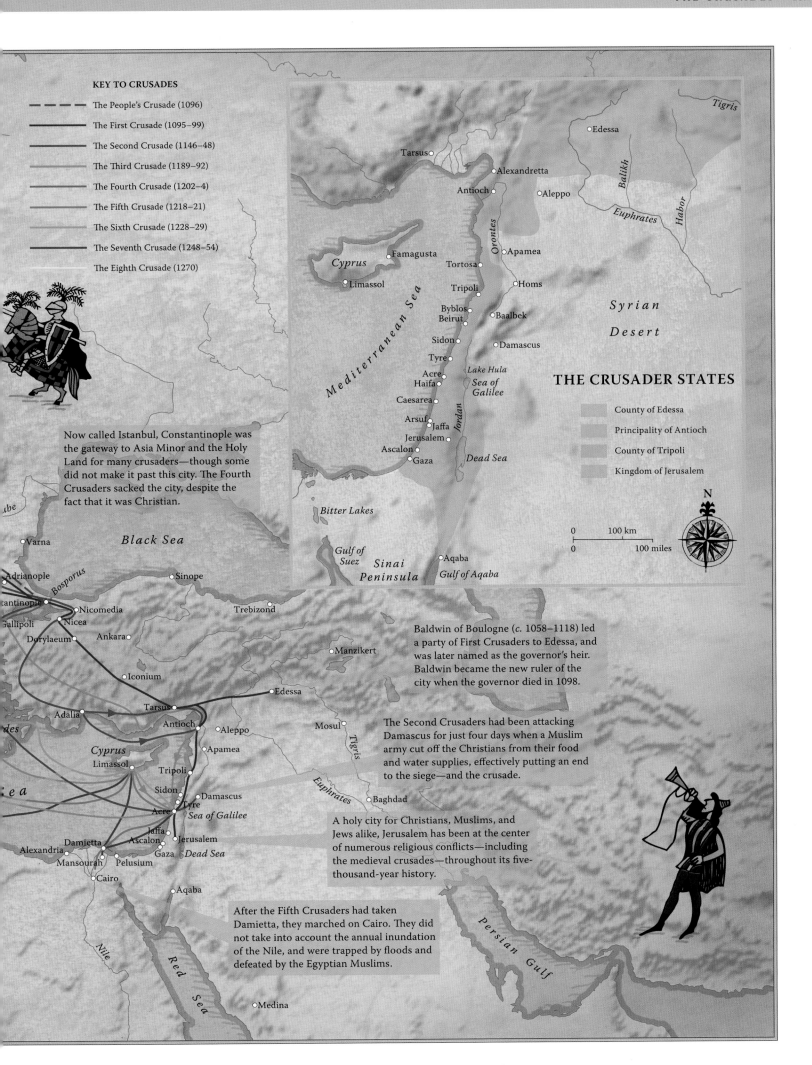

KEY TO CRUSADES

- – – – The People's Crusade (1096)
- ——— The First Crusade (1095–99)
- ——— The Second Crusade (1146–48)
- ——— The Third Crusade (1189–92)
- ——— The Fourth Crusade (1202–4)
- ——— The Fifth Crusade (1218–21)
- ——— The Sixth Crusade (1228–29)
- ——— The Seventh Crusade (1248–54)
- ——— The Eighth Crusade (1270)

THE CRUSADER STATES

- County of Edessa
- Principality of Antioch
- County of Tripoli
- Kingdom of Jerusalem

0   100 km
0   100 miles

Now called Istanbul, Constantinople was the gateway to Asia Minor and the Holy Land for many crusaders—though some did not make it past this city. The Fourth Crusaders sacked the city, despite the fact that it was Christian.

Baldwin of Boulogne (c. 1058–1118) led a party of First Crusaders to Edessa, and was later named as the governor's heir. Baldwin became the new ruler of the city when the governor died in 1098.

The Second Crusaders had been attacking Damascus for just four days when a Muslim army cut off the Christians from their food and water supplies, effectively putting an end to the siege—and the crusade.

A holy city for Christians, Muslims, and Jews alike, Jerusalem has been at the center of numerous religious conflicts—including the medieval crusades—throughout its five-thousand-year history.

After the Fifth Crusaders had taken Damietta, they marched on Cairo. They did not take into account the annual inundation of the Nile, and were trapped by floods and defeated by the Egyptian Muslims.

JOINING A CRUSADE

The most common way to join a crusade was to attend an event at which a priest or monk delivered a sermon describing the plight of the Holy Land and the duty of all Christians to come to its defense. At the end of such an event, volunteers were encouraged to come forward and "receive the cross," which usually involved accepting a cloth cross that was affixed to one's clothing to signify one's status, and making a public vow to go to the aid of the Holy Land. Volunteering for a crusade was optional, and, in general, going on a crusade had little effect on the standing of knights in their community.

Numerous legal complexities were involved in joining a crusade. Men were not generally allowed to take the cross without their wife's permission. Those who had taken prior vows, such as monks, were not allowed to participate unless they had received a dispensation from the original vows. The crusader's property and interests were placed under the protection of the church while he was away, and direct administration of his property had to be delegated to others (often his wife or mother).

Crusading was ruinously expensive. Fundraising, therefore, was of the utmost importance. Crusaders engaged in a variety of fundraising activities, including selling or mortgaging property to relatives, other noblemen, or the church itself. Loans might be obtained— or extorted—according to the credit-worthiness or prestige of the crusader, or the availability of credit.

THE INDULGENCE

Most important, from the point of view of medieval people, were the theological rewards involved in crusading. From the very beginning, crusaders were offered an indulgence. Often misunderstood, an indulgence involves remission of the temporal penalties for a person's sins.

The Catholic Church teaches that two kinds of penalties are imposed for sin: the spiritual and the temporal. The spiritual penalties of sin have to be dealt with by confession, repentance, and divine forgiveness. Temporal penalties, however, involve penitential activities on Earth (such as fasting) and time spent in purgatory in the next life. The church teaches that it has authority from Christ to impose or remit temporal penalties; indulgences carry partial or complete remission of them. Thus, if a crusader who had received a full indulgence died on a crusade, he was assured of going straight to the presence of Christ in heaven. Because most medieval people were more concerned about their eternal destination than modern people are, the prospect of an indulgence usually attracted favorable interest at that time.

There were many other theological complexities. Crusades have variously been considered "just wars" or "holy wars." A just war, according to Christian theology extant by at least the

RIGHT: A 1521 woodcut shows the pope selling indulgences. During the late Middle Ages, indulgences were often sold by "pardoners" to finance church projects.

LEFT: A lone crusader receives the symbol of the cross from a monk in this illustration from the fourteenth-century French manuscript Entry of Spain (Entrée d'Espagne).

fourth century CE, is carried out for a just cause (which may not include aggressive wars of conquest), under the proper authority (ideally a pope or emperor), and with the right intentions (this is difficult to prove, but basically requires that one act out of love for those in one's charge, not hatred of one's enemies). A holy war includes the previous criteria, but also assumes that those who wage it are fighting to establish an earthly order that will advance the agenda of the heavenly kingdom.

PLANNING A CRUSADE

Crusade leaders—usually noblemen (who might also be knights) or their deputies—had to stockpile food supplies, arrange transportation, choose routes, contact friendly and neutral

leaders along those routes, and plan strategies and tactics—a daunting task, and one not always successfully executed.

Once the immense resources—financial and otherwise—had been marshaled, crusaders had to face the very real dangers of the journey itself. Though statistics are difficult to come by, it is likely that more crusaders perished from disease, starvation, thirst, accidents, and numerous other hazards than from enemy action. During the First Crusade, the armies followed a

land route through the Balkans and across Asia Minor, pushing aside the disunited Muslim emirates that lay in their path. By the time the Second Crusade tried the same approach, however, the Muslims had become so strong again that the crusaders were unable to force their way through. Subsequent expeditions relied on the navies of Italian city-states such as Venice, Genoa, and Pisa to convey them to the East, leaving themselves vulnerable to the perils of medieval sea travel.

ABOVE: *Traversing the unpredictable Mediterranean was problematic for crusaders— as seen in this thirteenth-century illustration— and shipwrecks claimed the life of many knights.*

The conveyance of horses posed a particular problem. Modified galleys known as *tarides* served as horse transports. Horses are fragile animals that are easily injured in transport. They also cannot vomit, and so have no way of relieving the seasickness that inevitably occurred during journeys in small wooden vessels. Even if they arrived at their destination alive, they could not reasonably be expected to disembark and go straight into battle, but rather had to be fed and rested in safety for a time before being ready for action.

Far from being financially rewarding, crusading was so difficult, dangerous, and expensive that by the fourteenth century it had become almost impossible to recruit volunteers. Crusade leaders were forced to rely on mercenaries instead.

Why should one worry if the number of Christians is lessened in the world by deaths endured for God? By this kind of death people make their way to heaven who perhaps would never reach it by another road.

HUMBERT OF ROMANS (c. 1200–77), FIFTH MASTER GENERAL OF THE DOMINICAN ORDER, WRITING IN DEFENSE OF THE CRUSADES

THE EARLY CRUSADES

The first three official crusades were marked by a zealous enthusiasm for the cause, with large numbers of crusaders determined to come to the aid of the Christians of Jerusalem. Unfortunately, not all of the campaigns were fated to succeed.

BELOW: *The left-hand side of this fourteenth-century French illumination portrays the red-robed Pope Urban II arriving at the Council of Clermont in 1095, while on the right he is preaching the First Crusade.*

THE FIRST CRUSADE

Although both the pope and the Byzantine emperor had a professional military expedition in mind, the first volunteers to respond to Pope Urban's call for a crusade were from the lower classes. Led by people with no military training, sometimes misapplying the ideals of the crusade, and persecuting Jews along the way, this so-called People's Crusade came to grief in 1096 at various points between Hungary and western Asia Minor without accomplishing anything lasting.

The official First Crusade fared much differently. Led by a variety of nobles from western Europe—including brothers of the kings of France and England—and advised by a papal legate, the First Crusaders made their way in several large, well-organized groups to Constantinople, arriving shortly after the demise of the People's Crusade. There they received an ambivalent reception from the Byzantine emperor, Alexius I (reigned 1081–1118), who had hoped for easily controlled groups of Western mercenaries, and who was bemused and somewhat alarmed by the appearance of whole groups of knights, whom he considered crude and uncivilized, operating under the command of their own aristocrats. The crusaders in turn labeled the Byzantines as weak and foppish excuses for warriors. The mutual dislike set up a suspicious relationship between crusaders and Byzantines, which would later deteriorate into outright hostility.

ONWARD INTO ASIA MINOR AND BEYOND

The First Crusaders proceeded into Asia Minor and made their way east. One contingent left the main army and moved east to the city of Edessa, where it found a large population of Armenian Christians. These Christians welcomed the crusaders, and, with their help, the crusaders established the first of the crusader states, the County of Edessa.

The main body continued on to the city of Antioch, capturing it 1098 after a long and difficult siege—just in time to be besieged themselves by a late-coming Muslim relief army. The

LEFT: *The First Crusaders' siege of Antioch—depicted in this fourteenth-century image—took place from October 21, 1097, to June 2, 1098. The siege went on for so long that food supplies ran low, and many crusaders died of starvation.*

RIGHT: *Louis VII mostly traveled overland during the Second Crusade, but—despite being delayed by storms—he sailed from Adalia to Antioch to avoid an attack by the Turkish army, as shown in this 1499 hand-colored print.*

crusaders defeated this relief army in a highly unlikely action that they themselves considered miraculous. They established the second crusader state—the Principality of Antioch—and then continued on toward Jerusalem, battling some local Muslim rulers and being assisted by others. On July 15, 1099, after another arduous siege, they captured Jerusalem and established the third crusader state: the Kingdom of Jerusalem. A massacre resulted, though contrary to some later reports, it did not result in the deaths of all those inside the city nor did it exceed the usual slaughter that occurred in a city taken by storm.

Most of the crusaders then returned home, having discharged their vows. Their departure left the crusader states short of manpower, a condition that characterized their entire existence. The remaining crusaders set about building a new society in the Holy Land, creating states of remarkable flexibility and accommodation. Within ten years, one group of crusaders had established the fourth and final crusader state: the County of Tripoli, in modern Lebanon.

The crusader states were founded and led by noblemen, most of whom were also knights, as these men had the military knowledge to lead medieval kingdoms successfully. Some aristocrats gained fortune and prestige as rulers of crusader states, but most people involved in the crusades suffered a severe drain of financial and other resources. The Templars—created by a group of knights around 1120 to protect Christian pilgrims—were involved in the defense of the Kingdom of Jerusalem and other crusader states, as were the Hospitallers, who had begun as a hospital order in *c.* 1080 and had militarized by 1126.

THE SECOND CRUSADE

The Muslim world, distracted by its own problems, had not reacted to the capture of Jerusalem. As time went on, however, the disruptions of the eleventh century were overcome, and ambitious Muslim rulers began to assemble ever-larger holdings. As part of this, they began a jihad (holy war) against the crusader states, a movement known as the Counter-Crusade. On December 24, 1144, the Counter-Crusade scored its first success when Muslim forces seized the city of Edessa and slaughtered all the Western Christians within it.

The surviving Armenian Christians appealed to the Count of Edessa, who had not been present at the time, to come to their aid. He attempted to do so, but was also defeated. In retaliation, Muslim forces killed the Armenian Christians inside Edessa in 1146, and the county was permanently destroyed.

Western Christians, stunned by these events, reacted swiftly. Cistercian abbot Bernard of Clairvaux (1090–1153) and his student, Pope Eugenius III (reigned 1145–53), soon preached the Second Crusade. By 1147, King Louis VII of France (reigned 1137–80) and his German counterpart, King Conrad III

And among his hearers [the crusaders] were a few good men, / Many who were evil, / And most who were neither, / Like all men in all places.

T.S. ELIOT, "CHORUSES FROM THE ROCK" (1934)

(reigned 1138–52), were retracing the route of the First Crusade across southeastern Europe and into Asia Minor.

THE DOWNFALL OF THE SECOND CRUSADE

The Second Crusaders were not as successful as the First Crusaders, however. Both armies were, separately, ambushed and defeated. Conrad and some of his troops returned to Constantinople and sailed to the Holy Land. Louis took what ships he could find at Adalia, leaving most of his army to push on by land toward Antioch. Disease and Turkish attacks killed most of Louis's army.

What forces remained to the Second Crusaders assembled in the Holy Land and took counsel. It was now far too late to save Edessa, which was beyond restoration. For a variety of reasons now imperfectly understood, the crusaders decided to besiege Damascus. The siege failed, and the Second Crusaders returned home in disgrace in 1148, having accomplished nothing useful. Their failure soured Western Christians on crusading for a generation.

THE THIRD CRUSADE

Meanwhile, the Muslim Counter-Crusade continued to gain momentum. In the late 1160s, a young Kurdish officer named Saladin took over the government of Egypt, and he soon began to work himself into a unique position of power in the Muslim world. Picking up skillfully where other Counter-Crusaders had left off, Saladin soon had the Christian crusader states surrounded and badly outnumbered.

Saladin and his army invaded the Kingdom of Jerusalem repeatedly and tried to trap and destroy the kingdom's armies. For a time the Christians managed to evade this fate, and once or twice even defeated Saladin outright, a considerable achievement.

Then, in 1187, Saladin invaded once more. On July 4, the Christians made a tactical mistake, and Saladin trapped them on the Horns of Hattin, a mountain above the Sea of Galilee. Encircled, out of water, and choked by dust and smoke, the Christians were forced to surrender. Saladin's troops executed hundreds of members of the military orders, enslaved the common soldiers, and held most of the others for ransom. Saladin then moved almost unopposed throughout

LEFT: *The Second Crusaders, led by Baldwin III of Jerusalem, Conrad III of Germany, and Louis VII of France, besieged Damascus for just four days.*
BELOW: *In 1188, as he cut a swath through the Holy Land, Saladin laid siege to Krak des Chevaliers, in modern-day Syria—but he was unable to capture the crusader fortress.*

the Kingdom of Jerusalem, the County of Tripoli, and the Principality of Antioch, effortlessly capturing castles and cities. On October 2, after a short siege, the city of Jerusalem surrendered on terms, thereby avoiding a massacre of the sort that had occurred in 1099.

WESTERN CHRISTIANS GO ON THE OFFENSIVE

This disaster roused the West to action. In 1188, German Emperor Frederick Barbarossa (reigned 1152–90) took the cross; a few months later, English King Henry II (reigned 1154–89) and French King Philip II Augustus (reigned 1179–1223) followed suit. Henry died shortly thereafter, but was succeeded by his son Richard the Lionheart (reigned 1189–99), who had taken the cross even earlier.

Saladin was afraid of the German emperor and was dismayed when news of Frederick's advance reached him. His worries were unnecessary, however; Frederick drowned while crossing a river in Asia Minor in June 1190, and the German army that followed him dwindled to a few hundred knights,

who finally reached the Holy Land under the command of one of Frederick's sons.

The French and English kings had been slower to leave, as neither wished to leave before the other. They finally departed together in July 1190, reaching Sicily before splitting up. Richard captured Cyprus en route to the Holy Land, an act that would have long-term consequences for the survival of a Christian presence in the eastern Mediterranean; by July 1191, the Franco-English army, along with survivors from Frederick's crusade and from the Kingdom of Jerusalem, had retaken the important port city of Acre from the Muslims.

Philip returned home shortly thereafter, but Richard remained, desperate to recover Jerusalem for Christendom before he left. He campaigned down the

coast, with Saladin harassing him from inland, and eventually defeated Saladin at the Battle of Arsuf on September 6, 1191. Richard also recaptured Jaffa, another important port city, before turning inland to try to reach Jerusalem.

Weather, logistics, lack of manpower, and other factors conspired to prevent him from doing so, and in the end he had to retreat to the coast. Richard sailed for England in October 1192, vowing to return later and finish the job. On the way home, he was captured and held for ransom—at the encouragement of the French king. After finally being released, he plunged into battle in his mother's southern French duchy of Aquitaine. He died after a siege in Lorraine in 1199, without ever having returned to the Holy Land.

RIGHT: *Thirteenth-century tiles from Chertsey Abbey in England feature King Richard I (the Lionheart) opposite Saladin. Although they are depicted as if in close combat, the two rivals never met on the field of battle.*

THE LATER CRUSADES

The incomplete success of the Third Crusade left many Western Christians determined to keep trying until they recovered their holiest sites. Five more official crusades followed, but none came close to matching the achievements of the First Crusade.

THE FOURTH CRUSADE
In 1198, preparations began under Pope Innocent III (reigned 1198–1216) for a Fourth Crusade. Almost immediately, things began to go terribly wrong. Its leaders overestimated the number of participants, contracted with the Venetians for too many ships, and found themselves deeply in debt. The crusaders became involved in actions against fellow Christians, first by recapturing the Adriatic city of Zara for the Venetians as a down payment on their debt, and then by becoming entangled in a Byzantine civil war.

Deposed Byzantine prince Alexius IV (c. 1182–1204) promised the crusaders financial and military support if they reinstated him on his throne. Against Innocent's explicit instructions, the Fourth Crusade took Alexius back to Constantinople and recovered his throne for him—whereupon Alexius reneged

on his pledge, leaving the Fourth Crusade stranded. Having disobeyed the pope, and without any other options, the crusaders attacked and took Constantinople in 1204, setting up a Latin Empire of Constantinople. Few of the Fourth Crusaders ever reached the Holy Land.

THE FIFTH AND SIXTH CRUSADES
Undaunted, Western Christians began planning another expedition. In 1218, the Fifth Crusade landed in Egypt, captured the key city of Damietta, and made such progress that Egyptian Muslims, who controlled Jerusalem, offered to restore the city and other territory to the crusaders if they withdrew from Egypt. Friction between the military and ecclesiastical leadership of the crusade, however, coupled with the knowledge that Jerusalem could not be held permanently unless Christians controlled Egypt, led the Fifth Crusaders to decline the offer. Not long after this, the crusaders were defeated.

For many years, the papacy had been trying to induce Emperor Frederick II (reigned 1215–50) to mobilize the immense resources of the German empire in a crusade. Distrust between

AN EYEWITNESS ACCOUNT

Originally written in French by an unknown knight and historian serving in Cyprus sometime in the thirteenth and early fourteenth centuries, the *Templar of Tyre* contains the only eyewitness account of the fall of Acre in 1291: "Know … that no one could adequately recount the tears and grief of that day. The pitiful sight of the little children, tumbled about and disemboweled as the horses trampled them … I am sure that all Christian people who saw these things that day wept, because even some of the Saracens, as we learned afterward, had pity on these victims and wept."

papacy and empire, however, caused repeated delays. When Frederick finally set out on the Sixth Crusade in 1228, he was excommunicated—a peculiar way to commence an expedition legally under the direction of the papacy. Frederick was more inclined to negotiate than to fight, so he proposed a compromise: Jerusalem would revert to Christian administration, but could not be garrisoned or defended. Historians debate whether Frederick's expedition should even be called a crusade.

THE SEVENTH AND EIGHTH CRUSADES
In the summer of 1244, the Middle East suffered an incursion of Khwarezmians from the Central Asian Khwarezm-Shah

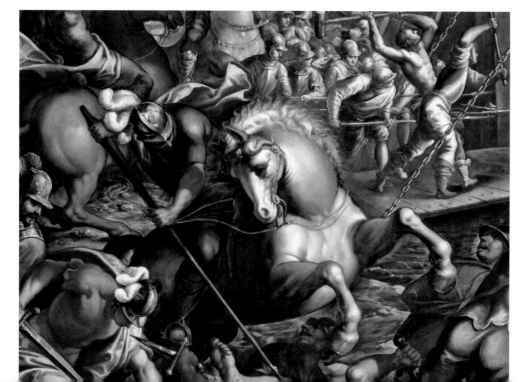

LEFT: *This painting by Andrea Vicentino (c. 1542–1617) re-creates the chaos surrounding the Fourth Crusaders' siege of Zara in 1202.*

LEFT: *During the Fifth Crusaders' siege of Damietta in Egypt, Francis of Assisi (1181/82– 1226) met the city's Ayyubid sultan and challenged him to a religious trial by fire. Giotto di Bondone painted this fresco c. 1297–1300.*

In the summer of 1270, Louis assembled one final crusade. This Eighth Crusade stopped off to secure its flank by besieging Tunis. Disease ravaged the camp, and Louis, along with many other members of the French royal family, died. Disillusioned, the crusaders returned home without accomplishing anything.

The situation of the remaining crusader states had become very grave. Muslim leaders picked off castles and fortified cities almost at will. Antioch fell in 1268 and Tripoli in 1289, with savage massacres and near total destruction of the cities. Acre, capital of the Kingdom of Jerusalem for the past century, suffered the same fate in 1291.

A number of other crusades were mounted in the following centuries, but Christians had been so badly defeated that none had as its immediate aim the recovery of Jerusalem. Rather, they sought either to cripple Muslim capability, or to slow a Muslim advance that soon reached into Europe itself.

dynasty; the Christians hastily rushed military forces into Jerusalem to try to defend it, but were swept aside. Churches and tombs were desecrated, and priests slain, ending Christian control over the city.

The Khwarezmians continued on their way toward Egypt, where they made common cause with the Muslim Mamluks. Alarmed, the Muslim government of Damascus allied with the Kingdom of Jerusalem. This odd combination of forces met in battle at La Forbie (near Gaza) on October 17, 1244. The Christian-Damascene side was utterly routed in a disaster equaling that of the Battle of Hattin in 1187.

Once again, the West rallied quickly in response. King Louis IX of France (reigned 1226–70) took the cross, and assembled a powerful French army for an expedition that cost six times the annual gross income of the crown. Following the route of the Fifth Crusade, this Seventh Crusade swiftly took Damietta. As they proceeded into the Nile delta,

however, one of Louis's brothers disobeyed a royal command at a critical moment, and Louis and most of his army were taken prisoner. Common soldiers were slaughtered like animals, while wealthier individuals were held for ransom. After being ransomed, Louis made his way from Egypt to the Kingdom of Jerusalem, where he remained from 1250 to 1254, providing much-needed leadership as he directed its defense and foreign policy.

BELOW: *A force of 15,000 men—including about 2,500 knights—led by King Louis IX of France captured Damietta in Egypt in 1249.*

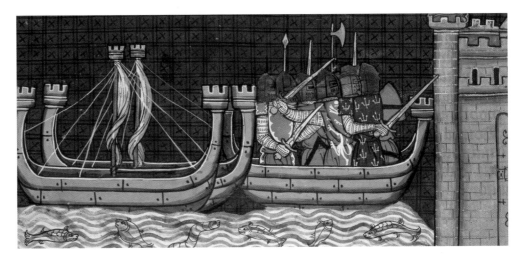

THE OTTOMAN EXPANSION

At about the time that the Muslim Mamluks were destroying the last of the crusader states, another Muslim power was rising in northwestern Asia Minor. During the last half of the thirteenth century, the Turks had steadily pushed the Byzantines back across Asia Minor, almost to the shores of the Bosporus. During the lull in conflict that followed, one minor Turkish chieftain, a semilegendary figure known as either Osman or Othman (1258–1324), sought ways to continue the jihad against the Christians, and thereby built up a faithful following around himself. By 1299, according to Turkish legend, he had declared himself independent. His supporters, taking his name, became the Ottoman Turks.

By 1330 the Ottomans had taken Nicea from the Byzantines, and in 1337 they took Nicomedia, depriving the Byzantines of their last main stronghold in Asia Minor. Incredibly,

RIGHT: *Osman (or Othman) was the emir first of Iconium and then of Anatolia, before founding the long-lasting Ottoman dynasty.*

the Byzantines then voluntarily involved the Ottomans in matters on the European side of the Bosporus: while still the regent, Emperor John VI Cantacuzenus (reigned 1347–54) employed them from 1342 to 1346 as mercenaries, and they were also used by Byzantine authorities in wars against the Christian Serbs from 1346 to 1350.

Having been brought into Europe, the Ottomans could not be removed. As early as 1359, they raided up to the walls of the mighty city of Constantinople, having acquired control over a considerable area of European territory, including the entry port of Gallipoli in the Dardanelles. A crusade led by Amadeus VI of Savoy (1334–83) recovered Gallipoli for the Byzantines in 1366, but the Byzantine emperor became a vassal of the Ottomans in 1371 and returned Gallipoli to their control in 1377. Meanwhile, in 1369, the Ottomans had captured the strategic city of Adrianople, which both blocked the road to Constantinople from the west, and also opened up the Balkans to attack.

In 1389, the Muslim Ottomans met the Christian Serbians at Kosovo; Serbia lost

the battle and was permanently crippled. In 1396, a lull in the Hundred Years' War released French knights for a crusade to try to blunt the Ottoman threat. Ambushed at Nicopolis, the crusade was completely smashed.

THE OTTOMANS SUFFER A SETBACK

These successes put the Ottomans on the verge of capturing Constantinople, something Muslim armies had sought to do since the seventh century CE. Fate intervened, however; the Central Asian horsemen of Tamerlane (1336–1405) burst into Asia Minor and, at the Battle of Ankara in 1402, shattered the Ottoman army. Tamerlane's triumphs were fleeting, and he established no permanent states as a result of them, but his incursion set Ottoman conquests back a generation, and gave Byzantine civilization a half-century respite.

By 1430, the Ottomans had recovered enough to take Thessalonica, the

LEFT: *A sixteenth-century fresco in Moldovita Monastery, Romania, illustrates the fall of Constantinople in 1453. Contrary to common belief, the city's name was not changed to Istanbul at that time; the Ottomans referred to it as Konstantiniyye.*

RIGHT: *Taken from the Ottoman manuscript* Hunername, *which is devoted to the military campaigns of the tenth sultan, Suleiman the Magnificent (c. 1494–1566), this illustration shows the Ottoman army capturing Belgrade from the Hungarians on August 29, 1521.*

second-largest Byzantine city, from its Venetian owners. In 1444, the Hungarians and the Knights Hospitaller combined forces to mount another crusade down the Danube valley to try to drive back the Ottomans and relieve the pressure on Constantinople. It came to grief at Varna, near the Black Sea.

THE FALL OF CONSTANTINOPLE

The failure of this "Crusade of Varna" sealed the fate of Constantinople. In 1453, Sultan Mehmet II (1432–81) battered his way into the city with the aid of massive cannon, and on May 29, it fell. The last Byzantine emperor, Constantine XI (reigned 1449–53), died fighting as a common soldier, unwilling to survive the destruction of his empire. A three-day massacre and sack followed. The destruction of the eastern half of Christendom was complete.

There was plenty of room for further conquests, however. In 1480, the Ottomans attempted to drive the Hospitallers off their island-state of Rhodes, but failed after a fierce siege. In 1509, the Ottomans lent aid to a Mamluk fleet that unsuccessfully sought to block Portuguese access to India in the Battle of Diu in the Indian Ocean. But these were only temporary setbacks. In 1517, the Ottomans destroyed Mamluk power and absorbed Egypt into their empire; in 1521, they took the strategic Balkan city of Belgrade; and, after a long siege, they were successful in expelling the Hospitallers from Rhodes on New Year's Day, 1523. In 1526, they met and defeated the Hungarian army at Mohács, imperiling that kingdom's survival.

MALTA, CYPRUS, LEPANTO ... AND VIENNA

A series of checks followed, however. In 1529, the Ottomans besieged Vienna, but were turned back. In 1565, the Ottoman army and navy besieged the Hospitallers on their new home of Malta; the Hospitallers resisted desperately and were finally rescued by a Spanish fleet. In 1571, the Ottomans captured Venetian-owned Cyprus, but were defeated in the same year by an allied Christian fleet off what is now known as the Gulf of Corinth, in the Battle of Lepanto. Historians have questioned if Lepanto was a critical turning point in the history of the Ottoman attempt to conquer Europe; it was certainly considered such at the time, and church bells in Protestant England rang to celebrate the victory. Yet the Ottomans returned to Europe in the seventeenth century, attacking Vienna as late as 1683; the city was relieved only by a joint Polish-German expedition that may reasonably be seen as the last crusade.

The Reconquista

In CE 711, the Iberian Peninsula was invaded by Muslims from North Africa. Within a decade, the Christian kingdom of the Visigoths that had previously controlled the length and breadth of the peninsula had been completely destroyed, and a Muslim state known as al-Andalus had emerged to take its place.

The Reconquista (the Spanish word for Reconquest) is the name given by modern historians to the centuries-long struggle by surviving peninsular Christians to expel the Muslims of al-Andalus and to restore Christian authority over Iberia, a process that was eventually completed in 1492.

ABOVE: *Created by Flemish artist Simon Bening (c. 1483–1561), this is a family tree of Spanish and Portuguese royalty up to the time of King Alfonso IV of Aragon (reigned 1327–36).*

THE IDEA OF RECONQUEST

Although the Muslim invasion of Iberia had taken place in the early years of the eighth century CE, it was probably around 150 years before peninsular Christians began to articulate clear notions of a reconquest. In the intervening period, those Christians who had survived the Muslim invasion had migrated to the northern reaches of the peninsula and had gradually established a series of independent regional polities, the most significant of which was the Kingdom of Asturias. It was here, most probably during the time of King Alfonso III (reigned 866–910), that the idea of reconquering the peninsula from its Muslim occupants was first established as a manifesto for military action. Alfonso and his chroniclers looked to the quasimythical Battle of Covadonga (722) as a source of inspiration for their efforts; as they saw it, this encounter in which the Christian Visigoths under Pelayo (reigned *c.* 718–37) routed the Muslims represented the first victory in the fight against the invaders, and it laid the foundations for future military initiatives.

Historians continue to debate how far the idea of "reconquest" consistently animated the actions of Christian kings and knights in medieval Iberia. Taking the long view, there was indeed a southward advance of the frontier between the Christian states of the north and the Muslim-held regions of the south in the Middle Ages, and there is clear evidence to show that at certain points in time Iberian rulers and their warrior aristocracy were attuned to the idea of a full peninsular reconquest. But there is also a good deal of evidence to show Christians and Muslims cooperating with one another in military alliances against their coreligionists, which complicates the picture somewhat: between 1069 and 1073, for example, King Sancho IV of Navarre (reigned 1054–76) swore to defend his Muslim neighbor, al-Muqtadir of Zaragoza (reigned 1046–81), from all aggressors, be they Christian or Muslim.

It is therefore difficult to know whether ideas of reconquest resonated with individual warriors at all points in medieval Iberian history; it seems likely that knights would just as often be fighting for more immediate and tangible concerns, such as a desire for booty, the acquisition of better pasture land, or perhaps even personal honor and glory. Nevertheless, ideas of reconquest were certainly used repeatedly, if not consistently, by secular and religious leaders alike to justify military action against the Muslims of al-Andalus.

> *The Christians now engage the Muslims
> in battle by day and by night, and they will clash
> with them daily until divine predestination decrees
> that they be cruelly expelled from here.*
>
> **THE IDEA OF RECONQUEST, AS RECORDED IN**
> ***THE CHRONICLE OF ALBELDA* (c. CE 883)**

LEFT: *King Ferdinand II of Aragon and Queen Isabella I of Castile are pictured with their oldest daughter and heiress, Joan (often called Joan the Mad), in this illustration from a late fifteenth-century Spanish manuscript.*

MILESTONES IN THE IBERIAN RECONQUEST

The southward advance of the frontier between the Christian states of the north and Muslim al-Andalus was a slow process, albeit one that was characterized by several landmark achievements. Of these, the reconquest of the former Visigothic capital of Toledo by King Alfonso VI of León-Castile (reigned 1065–1109) in 1085, the major victory over the Muslim forces at Las Navas de Tolosa by King Alfonso VIII of Castile (reigned 1158–1214) in 1212, and the capture of Seville by King Ferdinand III of Castile-León (reigned 1217–52) in 1248 can be numbered among the most significant.

There were also some notable setbacks for the Christians, such as the massive defeat at Sagrajas in 1086 and the rout at Alarcos in 1195. Nevertheless, by the middle of the thirteenth century, the Christians of the north had become so powerful and had taken back so much territory that it seemed possible they would soon emerge victorious in the war against peninsular Islam. However, it was not until the end of the fifteenth century that Christian rulers again reasserted complete control over the peninsula. As contemporaries saw it, one of the greatest achievements of King Ferdinand II of Aragon (reigned 1479–1516) and Queen Isabella I of Castile (reigned 1474–1504) was to fulfill the aspirations of their predecessors by expelling Islam from Iberia and restoring total Christian overlordship. In the minds of these "Catholic Monarchs," at least, their conquest of Granada in 1492 was the culmination of centuries of continuous campaigning against peninsular Muslims, which could justifiably be regarded as a single, uninterrupted endeavor: the Reconquista.

TOLEDO

RIGHT: *The conquest of Toledo in 1085 by King Alfonso VI of León-Castile—which brought to an end almost four centuries of Muslim control of the city—is celebrated in this tiled artwork.*

MUSLIM SPAIN

In the wake of the collapse of the Christian kingdom of the Visigoths after CE 711, the Muslim conquerors of Iberia established a new centralized state known as al-Andalus, from which the modern regional designation "Andalusia" is derived. While initially subject to the nominal authority of the Umayyad caliphs in Damascus, al-Andalus was ruled by a series of governors (in Arabic: *wali*) from the southern city of Córdoba. By 750, however, Umayyad authority over the Islamic world had been challenged, and the dynasty was replaced by that of the Abbasids, whose new capital was the city of Baghdad. One of the Umayyad refugees who fled from the struggles that surrounded this transfer of power, Abd al-Rahman I (reigned 756–88), traveled from Damascus to al-Andalus in 755 and quickly established control over Muslim Iberia as an independent Umayyad emirate.

At a local level, Umayyad al-Andalus was ruled by regional governors (in Arabic: *wazir*) based in cities such as Mérida, Toledo, and Zaragoza, but their loyalty to the central Córdoban administration was not always assured. By the tenth century, however, the authority of the Umayyads in al-Andalus had grown to the extent that in 929 the emir, Abd al-Rahman III (reigned 912–61), confidently pronounced himself caliph over all Sunni Muslims, be they in al-Andalus, North Africa, or further east. It was also during this period that international diplomatic relations were established between Córdoba and the Ottonian emperors

LEFT: *The Emir of Córdoba, Abd al-Rahman I —who famously fought the Frankish emperor Charlemagne—consults his courtiers in this fourteenth-century manuscript illustration.*

LEFT: Built during the 49-year reign of Abd al-Rahman III and later enlarged, the Mezquita in Córdoba became one of the biggest mosques in the Muslim world. When the Christians recaptured Córdoba in 1236, the mosque was reconsecrated as a cathedral.

tribute payments of gold and silver or other valued items, such as elaborate textiles or holy relics.

THE AFRICAN FUNDAMENTALISTS

The era of the *taifas* was brought to a swift end in the late 1080s by the invasion from North Africa of the Almoravids, an uncompromising sect of Islamic extremists. The Almoravids were committed to prosecuting holy war, or jihad, against nonbelievers such as the Christians of Iberia. Having inflicted a massive defeat on the armies of León-Castile in 1086, they took the opportunity to extend their power by removing the rulers of the *taifa* states and incorporating Muslim Spain into their transcontinental empire; in doing so, they restored political unity to al-Andalus. But Almoravid control over al-Andalus was to be challenged half a century later by another North African fundamentalist movement, the Almohads, who fought their coreligionists for political and spiritual control of Iberia and the Maghreb (a region of northwestern Africa). By *c.* 1150 the Almohads had begun to emerge as the victors in this conflict, and they proceeded to establish themselves as the new rulers of al-Andalus, basing themselves in a new capital city, Seville.

It was not until the 1220s and 1230s that Almohad rule in Iberia was to become seriously compromised. As had been the case some two centuries earlier, internecine power struggles for control of al-Andalus resulted in a fresh era of fragmentation and the emergence of new *taifa* city-states, many of which

of Germany and the Byzantine emperors of Constantinople. At the turn of the millennium, then, the caliphs of Córdoba were among the most important political players in the Mediterranean world.

FRAGMENTATION OF THE MUSLIM STATE

Yet within a generation of the death of the ferocious Muslim leader al-Mansur (*c.* 938–1002)—who died not long after being defeated by King Sancho III of Navarre (reigned 1000–1035) at the Battle of Calatañazor (1002)—the centralized control of the caliphate of Córdoba had been weakened beyond recovery by much infighting and factionalism. The outcome of this chaotic political strife was the fragmentation of al-Andalus and the emergence of a series of independent city-state principalities, known as the *taifas*.

During the *taifa* period (1031–86), the numerous Muslim rulers of the south were often more concerned with competing with one another than they were with offering a united front against the military advances of the Christian kings. On occasion, Christian armies from the north were even recruited to defend the interests and territories of the *taifa* principalities, in exchange for

EL CID

Rodrigo Díaz de Vivar (*c.* 1043–99) was a Castilian knight who fought as a mercenary warrior for both Christian and Muslim patrons in the eleventh century, and is remembered in particular for his conquest of Valencia in 1094. He is most commonly known as El Cid, a name that is said to derive from the Arabic word *sayyid* meaning "lord." The flexibility of Rodrigo's approach to cross-frontier conflict indicates the ease with which Christians and Muslims could fight alongside one another in the period before the Crusades. His actions took on a legendary quality in the famous medieval poem *Song of My Cid (El cantar de mio Cid, c.* 1140), where he is portrayed as a great Spanish hero.

BELOW: El Cid is celebrated in a large sculpture on St. Mary's Arch in Burgos, Spain; he is buried in the city's cathedral.

soon fell prey to the expansionist ambitions of the Christian north. Only one of these new *taifas*—the Nasrid emirate of Granada—was to remain completely independent until the close of the fifteenth century and the conclusion of the Reconquista itself.

RELIGIOUS CONVERSIONS

It is interesting to compare the two different periods of religious rule—Muslim and Christian—on the Iberian Peninsula, in particular the way the conquerors treated the vanquished with regard to religious freedom, and the varying attitudes to conversion held by the Muslims and Christians.

CHRISTIANS LIVING UNDER MUSLIM RULE

Although the population of al-Andalus was partly made up of the descendants of the original Muslim conquerors and the settlers who had followed in their wake, a significant number of the state's inhabitants were those vanquished Christians who had not fled to the northern regions of the Iberian Peninsula during the eighth century CE. Those individuals who retained their Christian faith despite living under Muslim rule were known as Mozarabs (derived from the Arabic *musta'rib*). At certain times, such as during the Almoravid period (1086–*c.* 1150), the Mozarabic communities of al-Andalus were subject to considerable persecution by their rulers, and many Mozarabs left their homes for the relative safety of the Christian kingdoms of León, Castile, Navarre, or Aragon.

Because of their shared Abrahamic heritage, Christians who lived under Muslim rule in al-Andalus were theoretically respected in Islamic law as "Peoples of the Book" (in Arabic: *dhimmis*). This meant that, although they had to pay a hefty annual poll tax (in Arabic: *jizya*), subjugated Christians were entitled to a degree of freedom in religious worship, although there were some restrictions on their more public religious activities, such as processions or the ringing of bells to call the faithful to Mass. Although there is very little evidence for any direct Muslim proselytization, conversion to Islam was certainly advantageous for the conquered peoples of al-Andalus, and it was a requirement for those who wished to pursue a career in the senior levels of Muslim public administration.

MUSLIMS LIVING UNDER CHRISTIAN RULE

As the Reconquista gathered momentum from the twelfth century onward, an increasingly large number of Muslim citizens fell under the rule of the Christian kings of Iberia. Although territorial conquest in al-Andalus was on occasion accompanied by ferocious massacres of the local Muslim population, such as that which took place at Palma on Majorca in 1229, such acts of religious violence were normally short lived. It is true to say that, in the aftermath of conquest, mosques were often reconsecrated as cathedrals (such as after the capture of Seville in 1248), and that vanquished Muslims—known as Mudejars—were frequently expelled from reconquered towns and cities or forced to live in urban ghettos known as *aljamas*. But some historians have argued that over the course of time conquest often gave way to a spirit of coexistence,

RIGHT: *The Visigothic-Mozarabic Bible of St. Isidore (CE 960) is a valuable manuscript that features over one hundred illustrations, including a representation of the temple of Jerusalem.*

known in Spanish as *convivencia*, between the Christian rulers and their new Muslim subject population. This pragmatic approach to interfaith contact was in part a response to circumstance: Christian rulers were initially the "ethnic minority" in the reconquered territories of the south, and they were thus reliant on the local Muslim farmers and other workers to maintain the agricultural and economic prosperity of the region.

Nevertheless, there was often a lingering paranoia that the Mudejars were working to overthrow their Christian masters—a paranoia that sometimes resulted in violent massacres, such as that which took place in reconquered Andalusia and Murcia in the 1260s. Consequently, as Christian energies turned from reconquest to resettlement from the mid-thirteenth century onward, a number of initiatives to encourage the Mudejars of southern Iberia to convert to Christianity were launched. Two of the Catholic Church's

ABOVE LEFT: *The Mudejar craftsman—probably from Toledo, Spain—who created this Islamic star-shaped stucco tile inserted the arms of his Christian lords in the shield shapes that formed at the star's intersections. The tile has letters of the Kufic script intertwined to produce a lobed arch.*
ABOVE: *This painting from the Cantigas of Alfonso X the Wise—a thirteenth-century parchment codex with illuminated miniatures and musical scores—depicts a variety of different Christians being herded into slavery, along with their livestock, after the Muslim conquest of Spain.*

Mendicant Orders—the Franciscans and the Dominicans—were instrumental in this process, either through the establishment of schools or colleges to train Catholic missionaries, through direct preaching, or through engaging in public theological debates with representatives from the Muslim community.

Indeed, in the wake of the reconquest of Granada in 1492, missionary activities were seen to be of such importance that the city's first Catholic archbishop, Hernando de Talavera (1428–1507), was even willing to perform religious services in Arabic rather than in Latin as a means of stimulating conversion. This approach was abandoned, however, as the influence of the hard-line Toledan archbishop Francisco Jiménez de Cisneros (1436–1517) increased on the "Catholic Monarchs" of Castile and Aragon. From 1499 onward, Cisneros advocated a more aggressive policy toward Spanish Muslims, and by 1502 the Mudejar communities of reconquered Granada were forced to choose between conversion to Christianity or expulsion from the peninsula. At the same time, many of the cultural remnants of the peninsula's Islamic past, including buildings, books, and traditions of Moorish dress, were targeted for obliteration—a late-medieval manifestation of what might crudely be termed "ethnic cleansing."

THE MARTYRS OF CÓRDOBA

Not all Mozarabs were content with the assimilation between the Christians and Muslims of al-Andalus. Between CE 851 and his death in 859, Mozarabic bishop Eulogius of Toledo led a movement of religious insurgency in and around Córdoba. He preached publicly against Islam and encouraged those who had converted to Islam to return to the Christian faith; in doing so, he incurred the wrath of the Muslim authorities. Although Eulogius and around 50 of his supporters were executed as Christian martyrs, the example they set was not followed by their contemporaries, and the insurgency soon died out.

CASTILE AND ARAGON

By the middle of the thirteenth century, Christians had retaken much of the Iberian Peninsula, and the Christian states of Iberia were more clearly defined than ever before. On the peninsula's western coastline lay the Kingdom of Portugal, which had

BELOW: *Accompanied by numerous knights, King Alfonso VII of León-Castile and his wife carry the royal coat of arms toward a cathedral (from a fourteenth-century manuscript).*

developed as an independent realm during the rule of King Afonso I Henriques (reigned 1139–85). He was a long-lived leader who had boldly conquered the city of Lisbon in 1147 with the assistance of a fleet of crusaders from northern Europe, and for whom ideas of reconquest had been of vital importance.

The Kingdom of Navarre, in the peninsula's northeastern corner, played an increasingly minor role in the Reconquista as the centuries wore on; unlike its neighbors, Navarre had not always

been able to capitalize on the opportunities for territorial expansion that the Reconquista had afforded. Indeed, by the late fifteenth century, in terms of their contribution to the war against the remaining Muslims of Iberia, Portugal and Navarre had both been eclipsed by two of their peninsular rivals: the Kingdoms of Castile and Aragon.

THE KINGDOM OF CASTILE

Castile was originally a county that was dependent on, and subject to, its northern neighbor, the Kingdom of León. The Castilian region was named after the numerous castles (in Latin: *castella*) that demarcated its southern frontier from that of the border with al-Andalus. By the early eleventh century Castile had been constituted as a distinct state in its own right: its counts had become kings, and they were no longer dependent on the rulers of León. Indeed, by the later Middle Ages, it was in fact Castile that had become the more important and powerful of the two kingdoms.

Although on occasion the two realms were united through the reign of a single

ABOVE: *Born in Troyes, King Theobald I (reigned 1234–53) was the first French king of Navarre. He appears, riding a white stallion, in the Zodiac Window of Chartres Cathedral.*

individual, such as took place during the time of King Ferdinand I (reigned 1035—65) and his great-grandson King Alfonso VII (reigned 1126—57), León and Castile theoretically remained independent of one another. It was not until the thirteenth century and the reign of King Ferdinand III that the Kingdom of León would become permanently united with its southern neighbor. From this time on, and in comparison to Iberia's other Christian states, it was the Castilians who could claim to be the most highly motivated by ideas of reconquest and who had the drive to reestablish Christian supremacy.

THE KINGDOM OF ARAGON

Aragon emerged as an independent state in 1035, but by 1150 it had merged with the neighboring County of Barcelona to form the quasifederal Corona de Aragon (Crown of Aragon). Aragon's rulers included some formidable military leaders who played crucial roles in the Reconquista. King Alfonso I (reigned 1104—34), who was widely known as El Batallador (the Battler), led campaigns against the Muslims of the Ebro valley for a period of almost 20 years, and in 1125—26 he led a daring raid deep into al-Andalus, returning to Aragon with several thousand Mozarab refugees. On his death in 1134, Alfonso bequeathed his kingdom to two of the recently founded military-religious orders, the Hospitallers and the Templars. Although the terms of his will were never fulfilled, his intentions are a striking indication of how far crusading ideas had impacted on the devotional horizons of the twelfth-century warrior aristocracy.

One of Alfonso's successors, King James I (reigned 1213—76), was also a great crusader. In the 1230s he successfully conquered the Balearic Islands and reestablished Christian control over Valencia, and he left a detailed account of his actions and ideas in an autobiographical text known as *The Book of Deeds (Llibre dels fets)*. It was also during

James's reign that the ruling classes of Aragon began to look to the east as well as to the south to satisfy their expansionist ambitions, and Aragonese commercial interests and political influence in the Mediterranean were given a significant boost by the conquest of Sicily in 1282 by King Peter III (reigned 1276—85), and by later gains, such as Sardinia (from 1323) and the Kingdom of Naples (by 1443).

KNIGHTS ON THE FRONTIER

As the frontiers of the Christian states of Iberia advanced ever further south, the rulers of Castile and Aragon required new settlers to colonize reconquered lands and defenders to ensure that they were secure from Muslim reprisals. Consequently, warriors who traveled south to protect and administer the newly acquired territories were offered

ABOVE: *The army of King James I of Aragon conquered the Muslim-held island of Majorca in 1229, after a three-month siege of the capital, Palma, as seen in this fourteenth-century mural.*

a number of incentives, including booty, tax breaks, and even opportunities for regional lordship. Among the greatest beneficiaries of this process were the national military-religious orders that were established in the second half of the twelfth century: Calatrava (1158), Évora (later Avis, 1166), Santiago (1170), and Alcántara (1176). These orders—which were modeled on their eastern counterparts, the Hospitallers and the Templars—consisted of organizations of knights who lived a quasimonastic life and who were devoted to fighting for the recovery and defense of the Iberian Peninsula from its Muslim occupants.

FERDINAND AND ISABELLA

On October 19, 1469, the heiress and heir to Iberia's two most powerful Christian states were married in a secret ceremony held at Valladolid. Ten years later, as Queen Isabella I of Castile and King Ferdinand II of Aragon, the two monarchs brought their respective kingdoms together in a personal and dynastic union. Many historians have often identified this union (perhaps somewhat romantically) as the birth of Spain as a unitary state that would hold sway over a vast extent of the Iberian Peninsula down to the modern era.

Isabella's accession to the throne of Castile in 1474 had not been without incident. She had been forced to fight off a rival claimant to her crown, the Infanta Joanna, who was married to King Afonso V of Portugal (reigned 1438–81) in 1475. The Infanta Joanna had the support of a considerable number of the Castilian nobility, who probably feared for their influence if and when

a unification with Aragon was to take place. It was in fact Isabella's Aragonese husband who dealt the decisive blow in the power struggle: Ferdinand overcame Joanna's supporters at the Battle of Toro in March 1476. Three years later, a peace treaty was agreed between Isabella and her opponents, and the Infanta Joanna was dispatched to a Portuguese nunnery. With Isabella's Castilian inheritance secure, and following Ferdinand's accession to the Aragonese throne after his father's death in 1479, the stage was finally set for a coming together of the two kingdoms.

To a large extent, however, the nature of the unification in the years that followed Ferdinand's accession was symbolic rather than having any real practical application. Although royal commands were issued in the names of both Ferdinand and Isabella, and the images of both individuals appeared on all Castilian and Aragonese coins that

were minted from 1479 onward, Isabella steadfastly remained the queen of Castile and Ferdinand the king of Aragon, each ruling over an autonomous state that maintained its legal, institutional, and fiscal independence.

RELIGIOUS UNIFICATION

Ferdinand and Isabella both saw themselves as pious Catholic rulers, and a greater sense of Iberian religious uniformity was high on the political agenda for their reigns. As with their earlier medieval predecessors, they ruled over a population that was made up of three faiths—as well as Christians, late medieval Castile and Aragon also included significant numbers of Muslims and Jews. The situation was further complicated by the presence of *conversos,* Jews who had officially converted to Catholicism but who were continually viewed with suspicion by their "Old Christian" neighbors. Partly in response to the growing doubts over the authenticity of the faith of the *conversos*, in 1478 Isabella gave orders for the establishment of the Inquisition in Castile—orders that were eventually extended to Aragon in 1484. In both kingdoms, the inquisitors were given the task of ensuring that all those individuals who claimed to have adopted Catholicism had in fact converted with all sincerity.

Concerns about Iberia's *conversos* and other religious minorities did not end there, however. In 1476, legislation

LEFT: *In this painting by Antonio Rodriguez (1765–1823), Muslim leaders of Granada pay tribute to Ferdinand and Isabella.*

had been enforced to ensure that Jews could be easily identified by the manner of their clothing, and four years later it was decreed that Jewish urban ghettos (aljamas) were to be walled off to prevent unnecessary contact with the neighboring Christian population. But these measures were just the tip of the iceberg, for in March 1492—just two months after they had celebrated the final victory over the Muslims of Granada—Ferdinand and Isabella ordered that all the Jews of Castile and Aragon were to choose between conversion to Christianity or expulsion from their realms. In doing so, they sought to impose a far greater degree of religious uniformity over their subjects than any Iberian ruler had done before them.

REPUTATION AND LEGACY

In 1494, the achievements of Ferdinand and Isabella as advocates for the Christian faith were recognized and praised by Pope Alexander VI (reigned 1492–1503), when he famously referred to the two monarchs as *Reyes Católicos*—"Catholic Monarchs." Ferdinand and Isabella were certainly keen to enhance their international status, as well as that of their Aragonese and Castilian kingdoms. Aside from their successful military conquests, one of the ways they did this was to secure a number of high-status dynastic marriages for their children. In 1501, for example, their daughter Catherine was married to Arthur Tudor, the heir to the English throne; after Arthur's sudden death in 1502, a subsequent (and more fateful) union was arranged with his younger brother, shortly after he had been crowned as King Henry VIII (reigned 1509–47).

Among their other claims to fame, of course, is the fact that Ferdinand and Isabella sponsored the Atlantic explorations of the Genoese sailor Christopher Columbus (1451–1506). It is a remarkable coincidence that in the same year that his patrons completed the Reconquista, Columbus himself "discovered" America and thus changed the course of Spanish history forever. Or perhaps it is not such a coincidence: after finally bringing the nearly eight-century-long Reconquista to a successful close, the Catholic Monarchs were looking for new worlds to conquer.

THE LAST MUSLIM STRONGHOLD

By the late fifteenth century, the Nasrid emirate of Granada was the last remaining Muslim state on the Iberian Peninsula. It had maintained its independence largely due to its rulers' successful attempts to secure treaties and alliances with the Christian kings of the north, who from *c.* 1250 onward were often more focused on fighting one another or competing for internal political security than they were on completing the Reconquista. The frequency of tribute payments to Castilian monarchs of gold and other precious items had once again become one of the most significant factors in determining the nature of cross-frontier relations.

MIGHTY MUSLIM FORTRESS

The rulers of the Nasrid emirate occupied the citadel of the Alhambra, which still stands on a hilltop above

BELOW: *In this detail from a sixteenth-century Flemish tapestry, a knight in the army of the Catholic Monarchs proudly stands ready to play his part in the siege of Granada.*

Granada and held an advantageous defensive position in the Middle Ages. Thick and imposing walls served to enclose a formidable military compound, which defied invaders for decades before the arrival of Ferdinand and Isabella's armies in the 1480s. At the Alhambra's western end was the citadel known as the Alcazaba (in Arabic: *al-Qasbah*), which housed the complex's barracks, armory, and dungeon.

The Alhambra was constructed and extended in various phases from the mid-thirteenth through to the mid-fifteenth century. Although it is difficult to trace the architectural development of the whole complex with great precision, the erection of certain sections can be located in time reasonably securely: for example, an inscription near the Alhambra's main entrance gateway, the Puerta de la Justicia, relates how it was built on the orders of Yusuf I (reigned 1333–54) in 1348. The complex's name was derived from its Arabic designation, *Qal'at al-Hamra*—literally meaning "the red fort," and named after the color of the clay of the surrounding terrain.

As well as being a monument to medieval Islamic military technology, the Alhambra was also filled with a wealth of artistic achievements, most of which survived the siege. The central palace area was adorned with fountains, pools, and gardens, and its walls were decorated with poetry by writers such

ABOVE: *After the fall of Granada, Nasrid emir Boabdil was exiled. He is said to have wept as he viewed the Alhambra for the last time.*

as Ibn Zamrak (1333–93), who served as chief minister during the rule of Muhammad V (reigned 1354–59 and 1362–91), and who eulogized the beauty of the Alhambra in verse. It was during Muhammad V's reign that much of the surviving construction and decoration of the palace—most notably, the Patio de los Leones—was completed.

After so much labor, expense, death, and shedding of blood, this kingdom of Granada, which was occupied for over seven hundred and eighty years by the infidels, has been conquered.

FERDINAND AND ISABELLA'S DECLARATION OF RECONQUEST (JANUARY 2, 1492)

THE RECONQUEST OF GRANADA

As Ferdinand and Isabella fought against the Muslims of Granada from 1481 onward, they tapped into a rich seam of militant Christian ideology. Ideas and privileges associated with the crusades had been a feature of the Iberian Reconquista ever since the late eleventh century. Like their predecessors, Ferdinand and Isabella—and those knights who fought in their service—expected to receive spiritual, material, and territorial rewards for their efforts. In this sense, the wars of the Reconquista were comparable to those military campaigns that had been fought for the recovery of Jerusalem and the Holy Land since Pope Urban II first started the crusading movement in 1095.

It was not difficult for Ferdinand and Isabella to find an immediate pretext for war against Granada. In December 1481, Muslim forces had attacked the Castilian frontier town of Zahara, which triggered fresh anxieties among Iberian Christians about the ever-present threat that was posed by the Muslim enclave on the peninsula's south coast. Following a successful response to the attack on Zahara in 1482, the armies of the Catholic Monarchs—which were made up of Iberian knights, members of the military-religious orders, and foreign mercenaries—prepared for the final phase of the Reconquista.

Riven with internal disputes, the Muslim ruling class of Granada was in no position to respond effectively to the oncoming Christian armies, who were more determined, better equipped, and better led; the Castilian "Great Captain," Gonzalo Fernández de Córdoba (1453–1515), was said to have been a formidable military tactician. The Muslim emirate fell to the Christians one city at a time: Ronda (1485), Malaga (1487), Guadix (1489), and Almería (1489) all eventually gave way to Castilian troops. By April 1491, the capital city of Granada itself was under siege,

ABOVE: *The Alhambra survived the siege of Granada relatively intact. It was added to the World Heritage List in 1984 due to its historical significance and architectural beauty.*

and its Muslim defenders surrendered on terms just seven months later.

Finally, on January 6, 1492, Ferdinand and Isabella led a triumphal procession into the city, and in a traditional act of great symbolism they ordered that the sign of the cross and a Castilian banner be lifted over the highest tower of the Alhambra—the extensive palace complex that served as both Granada's center of administrative activity and defensive stronghold in times of war. Their defeated Muslim opponent, Boabdil (reigned 1482–92), soon abandoned the peninsula for Morocco, taking an estimated two hundred thousand Muslims with him. After a period of almost eight hundred years, the Reconquista was complete.

The Albigensian Crusade

In January 1208, a papal legate was murdered beside the Rhône River. Pope Innocent III (reigned 1198–1216) accused the Count of Toulouse, Raimon VI (1156–1222), and the "heretics" within his lands of the murder.

The people accused of being heretics by the church belonged to a religious movement that flourished in the twelfth century in southern France and was also found in northern France and Italy. The subsequent crusade against them came to be known as the Albigensian Crusade, because in its early stages it was centered on the Albigeois, the region around the town of Albi in southern France; in turn, the heretics were dubbed "Albigensians." Later, historians called them "Cathars," a name deriving from the same root as the word *catharsis*, referring to cleansing or purification; but although some medieval heretics were known as Cathars, none in the lands of the Count of Toulouse was

ever thus named, either by choice or accusation, during the crusade. More commonly, they were known to themselves, and to their opponents, as the "good men" and "good women."

Broadly speaking, the good men and women believed that the material world was evil and the spiritual world good. Many medieval churchmen saw a clear link between these ideas and the Manichean heresy of the late Roman Empire. In any case, these beliefs put the good men and women at odds with orthodox Christianity, which held that the material world was not necessarily evil, as it, like the spiritual world, was God's creation.

The good men and good women led a life that they believed would free them from the taint of the material world and raise them to spiritual perfection. The good men in particular believed that they embodied a holy and honorable existence in which they resembled Christ through simple dress, diet, and behavior. They thought, too, that the version of Christianity followed by the popes and the rest of Europe had deviated from Jesus' true message and become too worldly.

THE PAPAL CALL TO ARMS

Innocent III saw these beliefs and practices as a threat to conventional Christianity. The murder of the papal

ABOVE: *During the Albigensian Crusade, the heretics of Orléans were gathered together and burned at the stake both as a punishment for their heresy and to purify their tainted souls, as illustrated in this c. 1880 woodcut.*
LEFT: *A seventeenth-century Italian fresco depicts the dramatic moment when papal legate Pierre de Castelnau is murdered by alleged followers of the Count of Toulouse, Raimon VI, on the banks of the Rhône River.*

RIGHT: *The fourteenth-century* Chroniques de France ou de Saint Denis *illustrates many medieval scenes, including knights attacking heretics during the Albigensian Crusade.*

RIGHT: *The fourteenth-century* Chroniques de France ou de Saint Denis *illustrates many medieval scenes, including knights attacking heretics during the Albigensian Crusade.*

legate, Pierre de Castelnau, gave him an opportunity to root out the heresy. Soon, he called upon all Christian knights to join a great crusade to exterminate all heretics between the Garonne and Rhône rivers. The Albigensian Crusade, the first holy war in which Christians were promised salvation for killing other Christians, would continue for 20 bloody years.

In his passionate promulgation of the crusade, Innocent III declared that all persons who had sworn an oath of allegiance to Raimon VI were freed from that bond by the pope's apostolic authority. The only proof Raimon could give of repentance for his crimes was to expunge heretics from his lands. Until that time, all those "signed with the cross," the *crucesignati,* must strenuously seek out faithless heretics and purify the lands of the Count of Toulouse. "Attack the followers of heresy more fearlessly than even the Saracens," proclaimed Innocent III, "since heretics are more evil!"

Although the heretics in the lands of the Count of Toulouse were an obsession among Latin Christian intellectuals before 1200, the idea of a grand exterminating holy war was the singular innovation of Innocent III. From a modern perspective, the idea of killing people for their faith is reprehensible. There were individuals in the thirteenth century who would have agreed. The predominant attitude, however, was that the heresy was a clear and present danger and must be addressed with extreme measures. For almost 50 years missionaries had been trying to talk the heretics of southern France out of their beliefs, without success. In the aftermath of the murder of his legate, Innocent III felt that the time for peaceful approaches had passed. Heresy was a cancer, he said, which must be cut

Forward then soldiers of Christ! Forward, brave recruits to the Christian army! Let the universal cry of grief of the Holy Church arouse you.

INNOCENT III (REIGNED 1198–1216)

out before it spread throughout the "body" of the Christian community.

Previous popes had sometimes allowed wars between Christians—for example, William the Conqueror had invaded England in 1066 with a papal blessing, because King Harold of England was an accused oath-breaker. But this was the first time that the language, symbolism, and indulgences associated with the crusades—the wars where knights took up the cross to combat those who were considered enemies of Christ—had been mustered against people who would have asserted that they were good Christians.

A CRUSADE TO SAVE CHRISTIANITY

Innocent III, "the vicar of Jesus Christ, the successor of Peter," considered himself in the middle between God and humanity, "below God but above man, less than God but greater than man, who judges all things but who no one judges." No pope had ever envisioned himself with so magnificent a mandate over the world, or so much responsibility for the Christians of his flock. He believed that the little foxes of heresy were, after centuries of concealment, poised to come out of hiding and destroy Christians. He claimed that these vulpine heretics, though scattered throughout the Lord's vineyard, swarmed in the lands of Raimon VI. Although the cancer of heresy was a malady always festering within the church, he feared that it had so feverishly escalated in recent memory that if it were not obliterated—immediately, swiftly—then all Christian existence would come to an end. As far as Innocent III was concerned, the crusade against heresy in the lands of the Count of Toulouse was a holy war for the very survival of Christendom.

THE LONG CAMPAIGN

In the stifling heat of early July 1209, a large, essentially northern French, crusading army mustered at Lyon on the Rhône River. It was an impressive gathering of three thousand horsemen, eight thousand foot soldiers, and ten thousand to twelve thousand other men, women, and children who had responded to the pope's call for a crusade. Only the First Crusade of 1095 managed to elicit a similar enthusiastic response from so many ordinary Christians. Although described at the time as a holy war, the Albigensian Crusade came to involve and impact upon the whole of southern French society, though, significantly, King Philip II Augustus—who reigned 1179–1223—played no part in the war.

A month before the muster at Lyon, Raimon VI had reconciled himself to the church and even "yielded to Christ" as a crusader. At this point, with the count no longer the target of the crusade, a decision was taken by the leading crusader nobles and ecclesiastics that they should invade, instead, the heresy-infected lands of the 24-year-old Raimon-Roger Trencavel (1185–1209), Viscount of Béziers, Carcassonne, Razès, and Albi, a youth whose overlord (as the Count of Barcelona) was King Peter II of Aragon (reigned 1196–1213) rather than Raimon VI.

THE SIEGE OF BÉZIERS

The crusaders reached Béziers on July 21, 1209. The next day—Raimon-Roger Trencavel having galloped away to Carcassonne—the men and women of Béziers refused to hand over any heretics. They were surprised when, in response to the death and dismemberment of a crusader by an inhabitant of the city, thousands of frenzied servant boys from the crusader army began leaping over defensive ditches and scrambling over ramparts.

After an hour or so, through sheer numbers, the boys finally succeeded in smashing open the city's gates. Once inside Béziers, they began to kill everyone they met, young and old, with wooden clubs. Amid the killing, a greedy search began for treasure, and it was only at this point that the crusading nobility rode in and stopped the rampaging youths. Béziers, its population butchered, was then burned to the ground.

Here and elsewhere, the crusaders, under their leader Simon, Count of Montfort l'Amaury (1160–1218), made little effort to distinguish between the

heretics and those who might have been perfectly orthodox Christians, fueling resentment among the wider populace. Even today, one should not make Simon de Montfort jokes in southern France.

CHARGING TOWARD CARCASSONNE

The crusaders, after resting for three days by the smoldering ruins of Béziers, marched through the valley of the Aude upon Carcassonne. They reached the city on August 1, 1209, and—unwilling to negotiate with Raimon-Roger Trencavel—they vigorously attacked at dawn three days later, storming the outer walls. The young viscount retreated with most of the inhabitants of Carcassonne into his citadel. Tormented by thirst, heat, fear, and the cries of the women and children, Trencavel finally surrendered his city, goods, and lands to the crusaders on August 15.

Simon de Montfort became, by common consent among the noble and ecclesiastical crusaders, the new Viscount of Béziers, Carcassonne, Razès, and Albi. He also became the new lay leader of the crusade, as many of the crusading nobility, such as the Duke of Burgundy and the Count of Nevers, left the army and returned north. Raimon-Roger Trencavel was imprisoned by the crusaders and died, probably from dysentery, on November 10, 1209.

In early September 1209, Raimon VI, having successfully diverted the crusaders away from his lands, was unexpectedly sent a delegation from Simon de Montfort and the monk Arnau Amalric (died 1225) demanding all suspected Toulousian heretics be handed over for judgment. The count refused. Once more, Raimon was threatened with excommunication;

once more, he appealed to Innocent III; he also complained to his liege-lords King Philip II Augustus and Emperor Otto IV of Brunswick. All this effort was wasted, and a new sentence of excommunication was placed upon him.

MONTFORT ON THE MOVE

After the siege of Carcassonne, Simon de Montfort spent the next year and a half campaigning aggressively, aided by an influx of new crusaders. Lavaur was taken by the crusaders on May 3, 1211, after a six-week siege. Following the victory, four hundred townspeople who had been condemned as heretics were gathered in a meadow and burned in a funeral pyre. As this massacre took place, 80 Lavaur knights were put to the sword, when the initial idea of a mass hanging—a humiliating death for a knight—failed because the gibbet toppled over.

Simon de Montfort now invaded the lands of the Count of Toulouse. The village of Les Cassés was occupied, and 60 supposed heretics were tossed into fires. Toulouse finally saw the crusaders when they camped before the southeastern walls on June 16, 1211. Simon de Montfort, lacking men and resources, vainly tried a number of sorties against the defenses of Toulouse but, achieving nothing, abandoned the siege on June 29. He retreated to Castelnaudary, and started to raid the possessions of Raimon Roger, Count of Foix.

THE MIGHTY KING OF ARAGON STEPS IN

King Peter II of Aragon, disturbed by the events north of the Pyrenees, intervened on behalf of Raimon VI. At first he met with sympathy from Innocent III, but nothing more was achieved.

In an ambitious move, the king accepted oaths of allegiance from Raimon VI and his son Raimon (1197–1249) on January 27, 1213. This theoretically sliced off the County of Toulouse from the Kingdom of France and effectively made Peter the ruler of all the territories occupied, or threatened, by the crusaders.

In August 1213, Peter crossed the Pyrenees intending to destroy Simon de Montfort. Outside the little village of Muret, 12 miles (20 km) from Toulouse, the king was joined by Raimon VI. The crusader army, going through one of its habitual shrinkages because a large number of knights had left after completing their 40-day crusading vow, was trapped inside Muret. Nevertheless, because of a perfectly timed cavalry charge into the Aragonese army, Simon was victorious. It was all over in less than an hour on the morning of September 12, 1213. Peter was dead, his five-year-old son James captured, and his knights either slaughtered in battle or drowned in the nearby Garonne River. A stunned Raimon VI simply rode away without unsheathing his sword, fleeing soon after to England. Simon de Montfort was named the new Count of Toulouse by Innocent III in November 1215.

TOULOUSE IS BESIEGED

Raimon VI, though stripped of all his possessions by the papacy, immediately began a vigorous resistance from his place of exile, largely undertaken by his

talented son Raimon; within a year, the two Raimons had retaken Avignon and Beaucaire. The old count even managed to sneak into Toulouse on September 13, 1217. The citizens, joyful at his return, now rebelled against the French crusaders.

Simon de Montfort rode back from the Rhône valley and assaulted the southern walls of Toulouse. As the people of Toulouse attacked the crusaders within the city, they themselves were being assailed by Simon and his army. The siege went on for nine months, each side reinforced by new recruits, especially mercenaries, and each side building trebuchets, mangonels, and other catapults. Simon de Montfort died on June 25, 1218, when a rock flung from a mangonel being worked by women crushed his skull. A month later the crusaders, after one more lackluster assault on Toulouse, retreated.

THE END OF THE CRUSADE

Aimery de Montfort, though acclaimed by his father's followers as the Count of Toulouse, lost all crusading conquests to the triumphant campaigning of Raimon VI and his son. In 1216 the new pope, Honorius III (reigned 1216–27), offered the French king, Philip II Augustus, half of all crusading tithes if he would go on crusade against the two Raimons; the king eventually sent his son, Prince Louis (later King Louis VIII, reigned 1223–26), who marched south in May 1219 and immediately captured the town of Marmande. Over five

RIGHT: *Created not long after the event, this manuscript illustration depicts the 1218 death of Simon de Montfort, who was originally buried in Carcassonne's Cathedral of Saint-Nazaire.*

LEFT: *Portrayed in this fourteenth-century French illuminated manuscript, Simon de Montfort's small army at the Battle of Muret included 270 skilled knights, which is one of the reasons he was able to defeat the much larger Aragonese army.*

thousand men, women, and children were hacked to pieces by the crusaders. After this massacre, the royal crusaders marched on Toulouse and started besieging it on June 16, 1219. After six weeks of inconclusive warfare, Louis, his 40-day crusading commitment over, abruptly ended the siege on August 1, 1219, and returned to northern France.

Three years later, in August 1222, Raimon VI—still an excommunicant—died at Toulouse. Aimery de Montfort endeavored throughout these years, in a number of truces with Raimon VII, to secure a peace. Nevertheless, in January 1224, Aimery fled north, abandoning his claims to the County of Toulouse. Raimon VII was excommunicated on November 30, 1225, and a continuation

LEFT: *As well as pursuing the Albigensian Crusade, Pope Honorius III was responsible for preaching the Fifth Crusade. Giotto di Bondone painted this fresco of the pope in 1297–1300.*

THE MASSACRE AT MONTSÉGUR

Even after the official end to the crusade, some heretics held out in castles on peaks in the foothills of the Pyrenees, perhaps most famously Montségur. Here, in 1243–44, heretic knights and their families held out for months against the French army. When the castle was finally taken, by having climbers scale the steep mountainside and castle walls at night, the attackers agreed to give the defenders—especially those with families—a week's head start to escape. But after a week, most were still there, ready to welcome death for their beliefs. The crusaders slaughtered men, women, and children in a massacre that turned many people in northern France against the crusade.

of the crusade proclaimed. The new papal legate to France, Romanus Frangipani, and Louis VIII captured Avignon in September 1226 after a three-month siege, and then proceeded to march toward Toulouse. However, Louis died on November 8, 1226, from an illness he caught during the siege of Avignon.

The death of Louis VIII did not end the crusade. The king's newly acquired lands were placed under the control of his cousin, Imbert de Beaujeu, and protected by five hundred French knights. The crusade, as undertaken by Imbert, became a war of attrition. Badly in debt, starved of resources, and fighting a losing battle against the French crown, Raimon VII was offered the chance for peace—which he gladly took in 1229.

On April 12, 1229, the Treaty of Paris officially ended the crusade, although periodic warfare against the heretics continued. Raimon VII swore submission to the church and to the young King Louis IX of France (reigned 1226–70). He forfeited to the French crown over two-thirds of his lands, which later became known as the lands of the "tongue [language] of oc" (because the local word for "yes" was *oc* rather than *oui*)—that is to say, Languedoc. The knights who had participated in the crusade were celebrated by an anonymous French cleric in 1226: "The good would never survive if the wicked did not fear knights." Christendom and France, "if there were only Saracens, Albigensians, Barbarians, and others

of evil faith," would never survive unless protected by the order of knighthood.

Although the Albigensian Crusade was over, its memory lingered long. An inquisition was set up, the first in Europe, to question ordinary men and women who were suspected of heretical beliefs (or who had been denounced by their neighbors). Resentment against northern France endured for a long time in Languedoc. Historians of the nineteenth century created a romantic vision of the heretics as brave freedom-fighters—proto-Protestants for British historians, anti-clerical idealists for the French—but in fact they had been a mix of knights, townspeople, and peasants who just believed they were following the true meaning of Christianity.

The Hundred Years' War

The Hundred Years' War was the most significant conflict of the later Middle Ages, shaping the national identities of both England and France. Even though at its heart the war was a struggle for the throne of France, it came to dominate politics and warfare across the whole of Europe.

Rather than lasting one hundred years, the Hundred Years' War is generally considered to cover the 116 years from 1337 to 1453. It was not actually a single conflict, but rather a series of campaigns that were later seen as part of a whole by military historians, and then named collectively. The war coincided with the formation of the exclusive orders of knighthood like the Order of the Garter in England (following the much-celebrated victory of the English at Crécy) and, shortly afterward, King John's Order of the Star in France. The body of rules that make up chivalry were institutionalized, for the first time, through this period. The line drawn between public and private warfare came into sharper focus as the central, royal control of violence became increasingly monopolized. At the same time it is widely perceived as the period in which the rules of war were challenged by numerous factors, such as the rise in the number of professional mercenaries who were not interested in the

"discipline of chivalry," and the increased use of various forms of archery.

CAUSES OF THE WAR

The war was a continuation of events that had been ongoing in Anglo-French relations for centuries. The causes of the conflict can be found in the different interpretations of rights and obligations between the English and French crowns.

King Edward III of England (reigned 1327–77) controlled the territory of Aquitaine in France, but, through this, he owed King Philip VI of France (reigned 1328–50) certain obligations, including military duty. It also meant that although Edward was a king in his own right, the citizens of Aquitaine could appeal over his head to the king of France when they did not like something. This interfered with the king of England's affairs and became intolerable. With Edward also having a claim on other territories in France, the only way of resolving the conflicting rights and duties, according to the English, was for Edward himself to become the king of France.

Edward had a claim to the French throne through his mother, but the huge challenge of asserting that claim meant that it was not publicly made until there was no other option available to him. For the French, the only way of solving the issue was to dispossess Edward completely from his holdings in France. Thus, in 1336 Edward renounced his homage to Philip for his French lands. A year later, he formally declared war and launched an invasion of France from neighboring Flanders—the Hundred Years' War had begun.

RIGHT: *William Bruges (c. 1375–1450), a member of the Order of the Garter, kneels before St. George and the dragon. The 26 founding knights of the Order of the Garter (1348) wore mantles bearing St. George's Cross.*

RIGHT: *A fourteenth-century illustration from Froissart's Chronicles depicts the Battle of Sluys (1340). The French had chained their ships together, which reduced their maneuverability.*
BELOW: *King Edward III of England spent 40 years of his long rule engaged in the sieges and battles of the Hundred Years' War.*

HOW THE WAR WAS FOUGHT

When not actually defending against the successive English invasions, the French long-term plan was to whittle away at the English holdings in France through campaigns of sieges and harassment. The English plan changed as time went on. To begin with, Edward organized raids called *chevauchées* into France. Rather than being seen as merely a mounted plundering expedition, a *chevauchée* should be thought of more as a procession. By moving unchallenged through an area, it demonstrated the French king's inability to defend his land and people. Therefore, a *chevauchée* could be used to call into question the legitimacy of the position of the impotent French king. The idea was to force the French king to the negotiating table to stop the destruction of his land and people. Once there, Edward hoped to persuade the French king to agree to a more accommodating position with regard to Aquitaine and to restore other lands in France that

had been lost. The acquisition of plunder was also a useful side effect of the strategy, allowing the English crown to distribute the loot among its followers and reward its supporters.

If a French army intercepted an English *chevauchée,* then a battle might result, but, due to the risks involved, battle was not a popular option for either side. It was widely accepted in the Middle Ages that, in a pitched battle, God would grant victory to the side that was most just. Such confrontations became ordeals, or trials by battle, where the result on the battlefield was also seen as the judgment of God. There was no guarantee that God would not choose to punish those involved for something else entirely, and, as no one was without sin, this meant that trial by battle was fraught with danger for both sides.

THE MAKEUP OF THE ARMIES

The English armies were generally raised through a system of indenture, whereby a captain (who was often a

lord) would agree to provide a certain number of knights and soldiers for a set amount of money. This system was well suited to overseas expeditions.

The French continued to rely upon the traditional military obligations due from its nobility and chivalrous class until near the end of the Hundred Years' War. Any infantrymen that were required were raised from the local area as militias. This meant that, while the French knights were just as capable as their English opponents, the other troops raised were often of variable quality. The French relied primarily upon Genoese crossbowmen to act as their missile troops.

KEY EVENTS IN THE WAR

Although Edward began with an attack into France from Flanders, the first major battle of the war was not actually on land at all. Edward won a convincing victory at sea off Sluys (now in the Netherlands), halting the counterthreat of a French invasion of England.

MILITARY REPUTATION

At the start of the war, the military reputation of the English was not actually that high. However, the combination of dismounted knights and flanking archers, developed against the Scots, proved to be successful in France. The number of archers employed in the English war machine grew steadily through the period until they outnumbered the knights. The experience of fighting against the Scots and the Irish had also led to the development of a very mobile force, with most soldiers mounted on horses, for travel if not necessarily for fighting.

RIGHT: *This illustration from a fifteenth-century manuscript of Froissart's Chronicles (c. 1369–1400) shows the English taking the town of Caen in Normandy in 1346. The English seized gold and valuables, kidnapped nobles for ransom, and killed approximately five thousand of the town's inhabitants.*

However, his subsequent siege of Tournai proved fruitless, and subsidizing his allies was expensive. Campaigns in Brittany in the early 1340s proved more profitable for the English and led to the *chevauchée* of 1346 that resulted in the taking of Caen and the famous victory at the Battle of Crécy. This defeat undermined Philip's authority at home, and it also led to Edward being able to capture Calais. Calais was important because it provided a strong base in France close to England, from which future attacks could be launched.

Trying to distract Edward, Philip persuaded King David II of Scotland (reigned 1329–71) to attack from the north. The Scots met an English army led by the Archbishop of York at Neville's Cross, where they were defeated. King David was captured and remained in captivity until 1358.

The war now ground to a temporary halt as the Black Death ravaged France. The respite also allowed English war coffers to recover from the enormous expense of continuous warfare. Edward III's son and heir, Edward of Woodstock (1330–76)—later known as the Black Prince—invaded France from Gascony in 1355 and again in 1356. He won a huge victory at Poitiers, capturing the new French king, John II (reigned 1350–64). John signed a truce with England, agreeing to pay a large ransom and to the annexation of a swath of western France. As the French government collapsed and the political and social upheaval known as the Jacquerie engulfed the land, the English found it impossible to enforce the agreement. Instead, they settled in 1360 for the Treaty of Brétigny, which recognized English holdings in Poitou, Gascony, Aquitaine, and Calais.

LEFT: *As shown in this fourteenth-century image, to bring the siege of Calais to an end, the city's burghers offered their lives to King Edward III if the besieged populace could be spared. The siege ended on August 3, 1347, and Edward did spare those who were left in the city, as well as the burghers.*

ABOVE: *With his marriage to Charles VI of France's daughter, Catherine, on June 2, 1420, King Henry V of England became heir apparent to the French throne. He had signed the Treaty of Troyes with Philip III, Duke of Burgundy (1396–1467), just 12 days beforehand.*

THE WAR BEGINS AGAIN

The accession of Charles V (reigned 1364–80) to the French throne again led to war, as both sides blamed each other for not meeting their treaty obligations. The English were less successful throughout this period. The French had learned not to offer battle, and the English found themselves gradually being pushed back through the effective strategy pursued by French knight Bertrand du Guesclin (c. 1320–80). The deaths of the Black Prince, King Edward III, and then du Guesclin led to the war winding down and a series of truces that were eventually extended until 1415.

After a long succession of militarily ineffective rulers, the accession of

Henry V (reigned 1413–22) to the English throne dramatically changed the course of the war. Just like Edward III before him, Henry began his campaign in 1415 with a siege (this time at Harfleur) and then a *chevauchée*. He was met by a large French army at Agincourt in October 1415, and, despite his inferiority in numbers, Henry's victory was overwhelming.

The strife within the French ruling house helped Henry, and his clear victory at Agincourt combined with the continuing threat of ongoing military operations led to the Treaty of Troyes in 1420. Henry married the daughter of King Charles VI of France (reigned 1380–1422), Princess Catherine, and it was agreed that their future son would

inherit the kingdom of France. Henry's untimely death two years later and the lack of a suitable heir (his son was only nine months old at the time) meant that the war continued after all. The English triumphed again at Cravant and Verneuil, but the tide of war began to move away from them.

The timely arrival of Joan of Arc (c. 1412–31) saved Orléans from the besieging English, and this marked a resurgence in French martial activity. The English were defeated at Patay and then at Formigny, and England's important ally of Burgundy made a separate peace with France. Although no formal peace treaty was signed, the French victory at Castillon in 1453 effectively marked the end of the war. Despite their successes on the battlefield, the English had lost everything except Calais by the end of the war.

DECISIVE BATTLES

Many of the histories written about warfare in the Middle Ages focus upon the dramatic battles. In doing so, they tend to overshadow the far more common activities of *chevauchées*, raids, attrition, and sieges. Pitched battles with the royal leaders of both sides present were relatively rare in the Middle Ages, but when they did occur—such as those at Crécy, Poitiers, and Agincourt during the Hundred Years' War—their impact on the course of European history was immense. Without a doubt, the Battle of Sluys was also an important engagement, made all the more interesting because it actually took place at sea.

SURPRISE ATTACK OFF SLUYS
At the very start of the Hundred Years' War, Philip VI threatened England with invasion. He had collected together about two hundred ships and amassed a huge number of knights and Genoese crossbowmen. Crossing the English Channel in his own, probably smaller fleet, Edward III surprised the French and their allies off Sluys (now in the Netherlands) in 1340.

Neither of the two French admirals, Quiéret and Béhuchet, were actually seamen, and the whole naval engagement was fought more like a land battle, with the French ships being chained together. This was supposed to allow the soldiers onboard to move easily around and reinforce any threatened points, but in reality it meant that the ships themselves had no maneuverability at all.

It was here that English longbows made their first impact on the Hundred Years' War. The archers were positioned, as on land, on the flanks of the knights

ABOVE: *King Philip VI holds a war council at Sluys before the infamous naval engagement with the forces of Edward III on June 24, 1340.*

who were positioned centrally. Following the initial barrage of arrows that swept the decks, the French ships were boarded. Unable to maneuver, the French ships were overwhelmed. Both French admirals were captured in the bitter hand-to-hand fighting that ensued, and they were executed. A total of 190 French and Genoese ships were captured, effectively handing control of the sea to England for the rest of the war.

THE CHAOS OF CRÉCY
The Crécy campaign of 1346 started with a surprise landing in Normandy of some fifteen thousand Englishmen,

Then the English archers stept forth one pace and let fly their arrows so wholly [together] and so thick, that it seemed like snow.

FRENCH CHRONICLER JEAN FROISSART (*c.* 1333–*c.* 1400), ON THE BATTLE OF CRÉCY

who planned to join up with a Flemish force that was advancing from Flanders. The city of Caen was stormed and sacked, but Rouen proved a harder nut to crack, and Edward's army was forced further upriver toward Paris. The English offered battle on several occasions, but it was not until Philip had assembled a force double the size of the English—and the English were seeking to return to friendly territory— that he felt confident enough to meet them on the field of battle.

The steep, terraced hillside at Crécy allowed Edward to deploy his archers to great effect around the dismounted knights. Trees protected the rear, and wagons were on the flanks. A windmill provided a command position for Edward. The French troops arrived at the battle-field and, due to their enthusiasm to get to grips with the English enemy, Philip lost control of their deployment. The Genoese crossbowmen were sent forward to exchange fire with the English longbowmen, but they were quickly

ABOVE: *A fourteenth-century image portrays Edward, the Black Prince, and Thomas de Beauchamp, the eleventh Earl of Warwick (c. 1313–69), fighting together against the French at the Battle of Crécy in 1346.*

beaten back. It is famously recorded that after their failure, the Count of Alençon charged the retreating crossbowmen, exclaiming "kill this riff-raff!"

In the search for scapegoats following the defeat, Philip ordered the massacre of the Genoese "traitors" wherever they could be found (although this order was countermanded once the king's temper had cooled). In fact, the poor crossbow-men had simply been out-ranged by their longbow-armed opponents, overwhelmed by their superior rate of fire, and prob-ably frightened by the use of an English cannon. If they had had their pavises (large shields used for shelter while reloading) and a sufficient supply of ammunition, then they might well have been able to acquit themselves more successfully. But as these vital supplies were still far behind with the slowly advancing main body of infantry, the crossbowmen had to make do with what they had, which clearly was not enough.

LEFT: *On August 24, 1346—two days before the Battle of Crécy—the English army met the French at Blanchetaque. The victorious English were able to ford the Somme River and head toward Crécy.*

THE WARRIOR KING

Henry V was a remarkable king, leader, and soldier. He was strong, decisive, athletic, energetic, pious, and, most importantly, successful. The son of Henry of Bolingbroke (later Henry IV), he was born in 1387 at Monmouth Castle in Wales. When he was born, it did not appear likely that he would ever take the throne, particularly after his father was exiled in 1398. However, he was made the Prince of Wales on the day of his father's coronation in 1399, also becoming the Earl of Chester, Duke of Cornwall, Duke of Lancaster, and Duke of Aquitaine.

AN EAGER YOUNG PRINCE

Henry saw military action at a young age, leading part of the English army against Owen Glendower in Wales and joining forces with his father in 1403 to fight rebels at Shrewsbury; he was wounded in this battle by an arrow. It was in these campaigns that he learned valuable lessons about command, military finance, and siege warfare, as well as how to deal with a rebellious people. This long apprenticeship served him well. When he took the throne in 1413, he was able to bring all his experience as Prince of Wales and apply it. He worked hard at reconciling political factions, placed great emphasis on justice and good governance, and was also personally involved in the government of his lands. Leading by example, he was a living symbol of knighthood and what it stood for.

When these talents and experiences were applied to war, Henry was equally effective. He prepared his war plans meticulously and could find a weakness in even the strongest of defenses. He understood the importance of logistics, ensuring that adequate supplies were shipped from England or bought from local merchants. While often commanding events himself, he was also willing

ABOVE: *This nineteenth-century portrait of a noble King Henry V by Benjamin Burnell reflects the esteem in which the monarch has been held for centuries. Shakespeare wrote a play about him in 1599, and Henry was voted one of the greatest British people of all time in 2002.*

to delegate power to his experienced commanders; however, Henry kept overall control of appointments at all times, and he always retained a keen interest in what was going on. He led from the front, and there is no doubt that he was the brains behind the successful strategies he pursued.

A CONTEMPORARY BIOGRAPHY

Written in Latin (and later translated into English) by an unknown author between 1416 and 1417, *The Deeds of Henry the Fifth (Gesta Henrici Quinti)* details the first three years of Henry V's reign in glowing terms: "Nor do our older men remember any prince having commanded his people on the march with more effort, bravery, or consideration, or having, with his own hand, performed greater feats of strength in the field. Nor, indeed, is evidence to be found in the chronicles or annals of kings ... that any king of England ever achieved so much in so short a time and returned home with so great and so glorious a triumph."

ABOVE: *Henry V woos the demure Catherine of Valois, in an 1873 engraving by W. Greatback. Henry and Catherine married on June 2, 1420, and—despite Henry's sudden death just two years later—they produced an heir, who became Henry VI (reigned 1422–61 and 1470–71).*

LEFT: *Returning home in late 1415, Henry V was greeted as a conquering hero, as depicted in Robert Alexander Hillingford's painting* England's Welcome to Henry V after Agincourt *(1880).*

CALLOUS OR CALCULATING?

The decision he took at Agincourt to kill his prisoners demonstrates his cool efficiency in war. While to modern eyes such an order seems to go against the whole idea of chivalry, the decision needs to be seen in the context of the battle itself. It was an attack on the English baggage carts late in the day that prompted the order. This was actually part of the original French plan: a small group of men-at-arms was to attack the rear of the English forces and their baggage train. It was the emergence of this sudden threat combined with the continued presence of the French rear guard—reforming, still outnumbering the English, and still displaying their banners—that persuaded the English king that it was necessary to begin executing his prisoners (the order must have been rescinded fairly quickly as the threat passed because many prisoners were taken back to England after the battle). Some modern observers have criticized this decision, but, at the time, any fault was seen to lie with the French, who attacked the English baggage carts when they had already lost the battle.

Henry's great success at Agincourt eventually led to the Treaty of Troyes in 1420, by which he was married to Princess Catherine of France and which was intended to bring lasting peace to the two nations after decades of war—the couple's firstborn was named as heir to the throne of France. However, Henry caught dysentery at the siege of Meaux and died in 1422 while his son was still an infant. This led to a power struggle and renewed hostilities.

Henry V was one of England's greatest kings. According to the standards by which his contemporaries judged him, he was a very successful leader. He had restored good governance to England. By war, he had achieved peace with France through the Treaty of Troyes and appeared to have settled the long-running problem of competing obligations that had led to the Hundred Years' War in the first place. Although all his gains were subsequently lost, it would take 27 years for the French to recover what Henry had achieved in less than 7 years. If Henry's reign had not been cut short, European history may have been quite different.

THE FEMALE KNIGHT

Joan of Arc was the daughter of peasants from eastern France. At the age of 13 she heard the voices of saints and believed she was required to become the savior of France, liberating the land from the English. It is hardly surprising that her requests for an audience with the local lord were initially dismissed. However, she persisted and eventually persuaded the local count to escort her through hostile territory to meet Charles VII (reigned 1422–61).

At the beginning of 1429, the military and political situation of France was dire. Nearly all of the north and parts of the southwest were under foreign rule. The English held Paris, while their allies, the Burgundians, controlled the city of Reims, the traditional site for royal coronations. Although he had claimed the French throne following the death of his father in 1422, Charles had not yet been crowned, and Henry V's son was his rival. After years of humiliating defeats, what little political leadership there was

in France was discredited and demoralized. Charles listened to Joan's claims and, after background checks had been made, agreed to send her to Orléans with a relief force. Joan offered a last chance to a desperate king without a throne.

ENTER THE FRENCH HEROINE

Situated on the Loire, Orléans marked the frontier between the English-held north of France, and the French lands controlled by Charles VII. It was the only remaining loyal French city north of the Loire, and its strategic position made it the last real obstacle to an English assault on the rest of France. The siege of Orléans had begun in 1428 under a force led by the Earl of Shrewsbury. Although he did not have enough men to besiege the city fully, the defenders were relatively passive and did not take the opportunity to go on the offensive. Lord Talbot took over command after the death of Shrewsbury, and he constructed a ring of forts around the city.

Until the last, she declared that her voices came from God and had not deceived her.

GUILLAUME MANCHON, THE COURT CLERK AT JOAN OF ARC'S TRIAL

Equipped with donated armor, a white horse, and a banner, Joan's stunning arrival at Orléans with the relief expedition proved to be a turning point not only in the siege, but also in the Hundred Years' War. She inspired the French forces and argued for an offensive attitude (against the advice of the local commanders). This led to a number of successful assaults against the English forts and the end of the siege; the victory gave Joan the nickname she still carries: "the Maid of Orléans."

Although unusual, it was not unheard of for women to take lead roles in war during the Middle Ages. For example, in the twelfth century, Matilda, the daughter of Henry I of England, led an army against Stephen of Blois in a bitter civil war. Of course, during a siege, everyone was expected to play their part. Jeanne Laisne was renamed Jeanne Hachette by her fellow citizens during the siege of Beauvais in 1472, due to her defense of the city with a hand ax.

THE MAID TRIUMPHS AGAIN

Joan was granted co-command of the French forces, and the relief of Orléans was followed by the capture of the English-held bridges across the Loire,

LEFT: *As this fifteenth-century German tapestry represents, Joan of Arc first met Charles VII at his residence, the château of Chinon.*

ABOVE: *The fiery colors of* Joan of Arc *(1882) by English painter Dante Gabriel Rossetti reflect the fervent and strong-willed character for which Joan is often remembered.*

RIGHT: *Joan of Arc was hailed as a heroine on her entrance into Orléans—as seen in this 1887 painting—because she had continued to fight despite being wounded during the siege.*

and the Battle of Patay. Here, encouraged by Joan, the French forces under the Duke of Alençon pursued the retreating English and engaged them. The English archers were surrounded, and Lord Talbot was captured. The only English field army in France had been routed, and it had also lost one of its most experienced captains. After the Burgundian-held city of Auxerre surrendered, a succession of French cities swapped allegiance back to Charles until Joan and the army arrived at Reims. The city opened its gates in July 1429. Joan insisted that Charles was crowned here to end any further arguments about his legitimacy.

Political bungling failed to make the most of these victories, although the English were by now on the defensive. Joan continued to fight the English wherever she could. She was attempting to relieve the siege of Compiègne in 1430 when she was captured by the Burgundians. Eventually, after several escape attempts, Joan was sold to the English, who decided to hold a show trial to have their revenge and to undermine

Charles's position. Charles himself had refused to bid for Joan against the English, feeling increasingly uneasy that the Maid was more popular than he was.

A FARCICAL TRIAL

Joan stood trial on a charge of heresy at Rouen, the seat of the English government in France. The entire proceedings were fixed from the outset, with Joan being denied counsel. There was no chance that anything other than a guilty verdict was going to be delivered by this partisan court. During the trial, Joan was asked if she knew whether or not she was in God's grace—a question that was meant to trick her into proving herself guilty, as church principles maintained that no one could be sure of being in God's grace. An affirmative

answer would have shown her to be a heretic, while an answer of "no" would be seen as a confession of guilt. The subtlety and cleverness of the answer she actually gave—"If I am not, may God put me there; and if I am, may God so keep me"—is a testament to her extraordinary intellect and strength of character. Despite this, she was found guilty and burned at the stake on May 30, 1431.

In 1456, a French court reversed the decision against Joan, and in the early twentieth century she was canonized to become St. Joan of Arc, the only Catholic saint to have been put to death as a heretic by the Catholic Church. Since then, Joan of Arc has become an icon for a variety of different groups, from French politicians and nationalists to feminists around the world.

THE FRENCH ARE VICTORIOUS

Despite the capture, trial, and execution of Joan of Arc by the English in 1431, the French noose around Paris tightened, and popular uprisings further undermined the English position. Henry VI (reigned 1422–61 and 1470–71) was brought to France and crowned in Paris, but it was a pale imitation of Charles's coronation in Reims. There were some English successes through this period, but in 1435, the Burgundians abandoned their English allies and made a separate treaty with France. Paris was lost and Calais besieged.

A CHANGE IN THE BALANCE OF POWER

The tactical superiority of the English remained, and when their armies could be used they were still very effective. For example, Lord Talbot (who had been released by France in 1433) routed French forces at Avranches in 1439.

However, the French largely chose to avoid pitched battle and instead concentrated on gradually reclaiming their lost territory through sieges. English ships were no longer in control of the Channel, and defensive war was far more expensive than offensive war

where one could expect to plunder and live off the land. The English effort was becoming exhausted, and there were divided opinions on how best to proceed and secure a peace that was acceptable. While no one in England wished to lose territories in France, and Henry VI was not willing to relinquish his claim to the French throne, it was obvious that concessions were required.

CHARLES VII MAKES HIS MARK

Under King Charles VII, the military organization of France began to be restructured, and he became a convincing military leader. Until the resurgence inspired by the events of 1429, the French crown had been forced to rely mainly upon mercenaries; as success started to ease manpower problems, Charles began to reorganize his forces. He started to rein in the military companies who served in his name but were fickle with their allegiances and were often damaging to the areas in which they operated. Effective political control allowed revenues to be raised. The French artillery began to be reorganized in the late 1430s, with ordnance companies being created. A militia of eight thousand free archers was created, and permanent companies of veteran knights and men-at-arms were established and stationed around the realm, giving Charles a nucleus of permanent military units to draw upon.

By 1449, the French had retaken the city of Rouen. When an English army of four thousand to five thousand men arrived in France to relieve Caen, two smaller French forces utterly defeated

---

Such was the end of this famous and renowned English leader who for so long had been one of the most formidable thorns in the side of the French, who regarded him with terror and dismay.

MATTHEW D'ESCOURCY, FRENCH CHRONICLER, ON THE DEATH OF LORD TALBOT AT CASTILLON IN 1453

LEFT: *This late-fifteenth-century French illumination portrays the coronation of the young King Henry VI of England as the king of France on December 16, 1431.*

them. Bayeux and Caen resisted bombardment for over a fortnight, but then surrendered to the vastly superior French forces. Cherbourg fell in 1450, followed by Bordeaux and Bayonne the next year.

The last English effort in the war was an attempt led by Talbot to retake Gascony in 1453. In order to destroy one of the French columns closing in on Bordeaux, he tried to storm an entrenched French position at Castillon. The French were well supported by artillery; Talbot was killed, and his army was annihilated.

Charles's attention to the financing and organization of war had given him an overwhelming superiority in men and artillery at the same time as the English war effort was collapsing from within. His refusal to meet the English on the field of battle—where the English had traditionally surpassed the French in tactical superiority—took away their last advantage. Although no formal peace was signed, this was the end of the Hundred Years' War. England had lost everything in France

except Calais, which was to remain English for only another hundred years.

THE IMPACT OF THE WAR ON KNIGHTHOOD

By the end of the Hundred Years' War, knights were still considered to be the most important actors on the battlefield, but only when their skills and training justified it. Increasingly, it was a knight's

ABOVE: *An illustration from* Chroniques de l'Angleterre *by Jehan de Wavrin (died c. 1474) depicts the English garrisons of Cherbourg at war with the French. On August 12, 1450, Cherbourg surrendered, ending English rule in Normandy.*
LEFT: *Charles VII was known as Charles le Victorieux (the Victorious) due to his numerous triumphs over the English in the latter stages of the Hundred Years' War.*

competence, professionalism, and effectiveness as a military commander that saw his continued presence in the armies of the mid-fifteenth century onward.

Written not long after the end of the Hundred Years' War, Jean de Bueil's fifteenth-century manual of knighthood, *Le Jouvencel*, advised knights to develop a practical approach to the changes occurring within knighthood and chivalry at that time. According to de Bueil, the greater a knight's rank, the greater should be his professional pride, and therefore the less he should object to being placed under the command of a captain of inferior rank but of superior experience.

Knighthood in Decline

A combination of shifts in tactics, new technologies, and economics conspired in the late Middle Ages to topple the knight from his vaunted place in the battlefield to a position of equality with other soldiers. This process was not quick, taking over two centuries to transpire.

On the afternoon of July 11, 1302, an army of Flemish urban militia, armed with long metal pikes called *goedendags*, met a French army led by 2,500 mounted knights outside the castle of Courtrai in Flanders. Contrary to the dominant military philosophy of the day, the militiamen did not flee the field. Instead, they lined up in disciplined formations, pointed their *goedendags* in the direction of the assembling French knights, and awaited the expected cavalry charge. The knights had little regard for these commoner soldiers, with their simple weapons and infantry tactics—so they attacked. By the time the carnage was over, more than a thousand French knights lay dead on the battlefield, their golden spurs taken by the Flemish militiamen as victory trophies. Within the next dozen years or so, two more battles—Bannockburn in Scotland (1314) and Morgarten in the Swiss Alps (1315)—confirmed the results of Courtrai. The age during which the mounted knight had reigned supreme in the European battlefield was coming to a close.

IMPROVEMENT IN INFANTRY

The victorious infantry at Courtrai and Bannockburn fought in tight phalanxlike formations designed to withstand and ultimately defeat the cavalry charge. Armed with long weapons such as pikes and halberds, these infantry units were densely packed, sometimes up to a dozen rows deep. If a man fell, the man behind him quickly took his place without the formation losing cohesion. When all the pikes pointed outward, the phalanx resembled a porcupine. As time went on, archers, crossbowmen, and eventually firearms came to augment the infantry phalanx. Even dismounted knights became part of these new combined-arms tactics.

During the Hundred Years' War, as well as in battles played out on the Iberian Peninsula, the English became masters of these strategies, relying on infantry formations supported by thousands of archers. At battles like Crécy (1346), Poitiers (1356), and Nájera (1367), dismounted English knights and their allies joined the infantry to slaughter thousands of French knights and their allies, but only after these had been weakened by torrential volleys of arrows from the archers.

These battles, which often pitted the skill and training of aristocratic knights against that of the commoner infantry and archers, were also becoming much bloodier than had traditionally been the case. In the battles of the twelfth and thirteenth centuries, it was common for casualties among the knights to be

RIGHT: Portrayed in this fourteenth-century illustration, the Battle of Courtrai (1302) is also known as the Battle of the Golden Spurs. Many of the French spurs seized by the Flemish fighters were exhibited in the Church of Our Lady at Courtrai (now called Kortrijk) after the battle.

RIGHT: *The fourteenth-century Holkham Bible depicts the Battle of Bannockburn (1314), where Robert the Bruce's Scots defeated the English under King Edward II (reigned 1307–27).*

FAR RIGHT: *King Matthias of Hungary (also known as Mátyás Corvin) was an educated and well-read man. He was eager for his armies to be at the cutting edge of firearms technology.*

quite low, perhaps only a few dozen at most. This was not so with the new style of warfare that developed in the fourteenth and fifteenth centuries. In the major engagements of this period, the knights died by the thousands. Not only were they losing their military supremacy, but they were also being exterminated as a social group.

By the fifteenth century, moreover, soldiers wielding powerful firearms—notably arquebuses—joined the companies of archers in increasing the destructive ability of ranged weapons in any given army. By the end of the century, the armies of King Matthias of Hungary (reigned 1458–90) boasted infantry formations in which one out of every five infantrymen was equipped with an arquebus. On the Iberian Peninsula, during the last phase of the Reconquista in the 1480s and early 1490s, the Christian armies of Ferdinand and Isabella may have fielded close to 1,500 firearms, many of them handguns, but also a significant number of cannon.

> *A knyght ther was, and that a worthy man, / That fro the tyme that he first bigan / To riden out, he loved chivalrie, / Trouthe and honour, fredom and curteisie.*
>
> **GEOFFREY CHAUCER, "GENERAL PROLOGUE," *THE CANTERBURY TALES* (c. 1387–1400)**

THE KNIGHTS RALLY

In order to counter these changes, the knightly class responded with ever heavier and more intricate body armor. Plate armor kept the knight and his horse (which was also increasingly protected by armor) safe from the thrusts of pikes and the hails of arrows. But it was not very effective against firearms, and it was becoming very expensive. This was a cost that few knights could bear, and, as time went on, very few monarchs were willing to subsidize the knights, especially when there were relatively cheap and effective infantry, archers, and arquebusiers available.

By the end of the fifteenth century, the armies of France fielded the most extensive artillery corps in Europe, and it is in the armies of France that the decline of the knight as the dominant force in the battlefield becomes most obvious. At the Battle of Courtrai, many of the French knights were actually very happy to see the Flemish infantry preparing to offer battle. Few enemies did so at that time, so fearful were they of the overwhelming power of the mounted knight. Within two hundred years, in the French armies that marched into Italy in 1494, artillery was supreme. The mounted soldiers, many of them still drawn from the knightly or aristocratic classes, still had a role to play (the importance of cavalry would continue up to the twentieth century), but it was now a complementary function working in conjunction with infantry, ranged weapons, and artillery. The days of the mounted knight dominating the battlefield had come to an end.

NEW TECHNOLOGIES

One of the leading causes for the decline of the knight in the medieval battlefield was the advent of new weapon technologies between the fourteenth and sixteenth centuries. The first such weapons were the pikes, halberds, and other pole arms that limited the effectiveness of mounted knights and allowed infantry formations to withstand the shock of a cavalry charge. The second important innovation was the longbow, which disrupted and harassed cavalry charges before they could form effectively. And finally came the gunpowder weapons, including cannon and handguns, which would prove lethal to knights, even in their heavy armor. It would ultimately be the foot soldier, equipped with a handgun, who supplanted the mounted knight as the dominant warrior in European combat.

THE POWER OF THE PIKE

The advent of long, thrusting infantry weapons in the medieval battlefield can be traced to the late thirteenth century, when Scottish troops in their destructive wars with the English typically found themselves with much smaller cavalry forces than their adversaries. The Scots opted to equip their infantry with pikes, some of them up to 10 feet (3 m) in length. These foot soldiers fought in formations known as *schiltrons,* massed several ranks deep.

Following the example of the Scots, the Swiss perfected the use of pikes over the course of the fourteenth and fifteenth centuries, and they covered themselves with glory at battles like Morgarten (1315), Sempach (1386), Montlhéry (1465), and Nancy (1477). As a result, Swiss pikemen became the elite infantry units of the later Middle Ages, eventually hiring themselves out as mercenaries. The Swiss pikemen were highly trained and fought in well-disciplined infantry formations. Their squares (a type of formation) were extremely successful against cavalry charges. Moreover, their level of training was such that they also became a very effective offensive force, capable of charging other infantry formations as well as cavalry as it formed and prepared to charge. Today the Vatican is still guarded by Swiss pikemen, who wear late medieval garb.

ALONG CAME THE LONGBOW

The widespread use of the longbow was another element that helped to accelerate the decline of knightly supremacy on the battlefield. Emerging as an important weapon at the same time as the pike, the longbow was instrumental in English victories against the Scots at Dupplin Moor (1332) and Halidon Hill (1333), and against the French at Crécy (1346), Poitiers (1356), and Agincourt (1415).

For a long time, historians believed that the longbow alone was responsible for the slaughter of thousands of French knights during their wars with the English in the fourteenth and fifteenth centuries. More recently, the scholarship suggests that arrows fired from longbows would have had a difficult time penetrating the improved armor that knights began to use in the later Middle Ages. Yet, while the lethality of the longbow is now debated, its usefulness as a revolutionary weapon in medieval combat remains unquestioned. Even when arrows did not penetrate armor, the volleys launched by English archers were capable of disrupting cavalry charges and funneling them

SOLDIERS WITH CLOUT

The archers that marched with the English armies into France were highly skilled and well-paid professional soldiers. Drawn from the yeomanry, archers began their training very early in life. The archer needed this lifetime of preparation in order to learn his craft well, but more importantly to develop the extensive upper body musculature needed to draw the powerful weapon and to sustain the high rate of fire that gave the longbow its fearsome reputation. English monarchs viewed archery practice as a matter of national security and sometimes banned the playing of football (soccer) and golf to ensure that archers kept up their skills without distractions.

RIGHT: *Researchers have theorized that it would have taken 500 to 800 newtons of force to draw back the string of a medieval longbow; English archers would have needed exceptional strength to fire arrows for any length of time.*

ABOVE: *The devastating impact of pikes is seen in this* c. *1860 illustration portraying the Battle of Sempach, which occurred on July 9, 1386, between the Swiss Confederation and the forces of Leopold III, Duke of Austria (1351–86).*
RIGHT: *The siege of Avray in 1364 was one of the first medieval engagements where handguns and cannon came to the fore. In this 1477 image, the pikemen and mounted knights stand idle while the gunpowder weapons wreak havoc.*

into the deadly pikes and halberds of the awaiting infantry lines. This combination of archers and pikemen accounted for huge numbers of casualties.

TECHNOLOGICAL EXPLOSION

The third major innovation that altered the balance of power on the medieval battlefield was gunpowder, beginning in the 1340s. At Crécy, for example, the English had brought along a few small cannon, to cause panic among the French forces. As the fourteenth century wore on, gunpowder weapons were used for decidedly more deadly purposes. By the early fifteenth century, almost every major European army had cannon. Moreover, these armies also included large numbers of soldiers with

handguns. In the armies of Ferdinand and Isabella of Spain in the late fifteenth century, around 20 percent of the infantrymen were handgunners—a regiment of 6,000 men would have included about 1,200 handgunners.

The massed firepower that these soldiers could bring to the battlefield was devastating, piercing plate armor and decimating cavalry formations in a way that arrows simply could not.

As an example, during the Battle of Pavia (1525) in Italy, the Spanish forces—which included about seven thousand arquebusiers—met a larger French force dominated by cavalry and Swiss pikemen. The massed fire of the gunners severely disrupted the cavalry charge and obliterated the advancing Swiss squares. A new age in warfare, dominated by gunpowder weapons, had clearly arrived.

FROM CASTLE TO FORT

The emergence of gunpowder weapons, and in particular the cannon, did not immediately render the medieval castle obsolete. Throughout its existence, the castle had been continually adapted to counter technological advances in siege weaponry, and the threat posed by cannon was addressed during the fourteenth and fifteenth centuries. Indeed, rather than threaten the castle, the manufacture of bombards and cannon in the later 1300s actually strengthened its defensive capability, as the weight and immobility of these early guns were more suited to the static defense of a fortification. Edward III (reigned 1327–77) provided the most important English coastal castles with bombards, six being sent to Dover in 1371, and in 1365 his new castle of Queenborough on the Isle of Sheppey received two great guns as well as nine small guns.

Effective incorporation into the defenses led to the construction of gun ports in castle walls, and it was not unusual for arrow slits to be modified for this purpose, the gun port most commonly taking the form of a large "keyhole" that allowed the gun barrel to be traversed. In the 1380s, Carisbrooke Castle on the Isle of Wight was one of the first castles to have gun ports built specially into its walls, and during the fifteenth century new castles at Caister in Norfolk and Kirby Muxloe in Leicestershire were built with gun ports forming an integral defensive feature. When Raglan Castle in Wales was rebuilt during the early fifteenth century, its formidable new *donjon,* the Yellow Tower, possessed both arrow slits and gun ports.

DEVISING CREATIVE COUNTERMEASURES

Castles continued to be built in the fourteenth and fifteenth centuries, and it was during the later fifteenth century that the destructive capability of gunpowder weapons became ominously efficient. The rapid French reconquest of Normandy in 1449–50 was largely achieved by extensive employment of artillery against English-held castles, and the highly mobile artillery train of Charles VIII (reigned 1483–98) facilitated the French conquest of the Kingdom of Naples in 1494–95.

During this period the castle suddenly appeared alarmingly vulnerable. The height of its walls, once the principal strength of a castle, had now become a fatal weakness. The relatively flat trajectory of guns allowed missile fire to be concentrated on the lower, weight-bearing sections of a wall, thereby exploiting its height to the advantage of the attacker. By 1519, philosopher and politician Niccolò Machiavelli (1469–1527) believed that "No wall exists, however thick, that artillery cannot destroy in a few days." Yet this was not true of all castles. The medieval keep at Coucy in Picardy was a massive structure, with stone walls more than

ABOVE: *Niccolò Machiavelli, a Florentine philosopher, statesman, and writer, was the author of* The Art of War *(Dell'arte della guerra, 1521), a treatise on military science. In 1509, he led a group of Florentine citizen-soldiers into battle against Pisa and emerged victorious.*

23 feet (7 m) thick, and its masonry proved resistant to artillery even in the seventeenth century. During the sixteenth-century Wars of Religion, the curtain walls of Angers were adapted into artillery galleries, the medieval masonry sufficient to withstand enemy fire.

Adding extra thickness to existing castle walls was a fundamental response to gunpowder artillery; the walls of Ham in Picardy were increased to a thickness of up to a massive 43 feet (13 m) in the later 1400s. The castle of Fougères in Brittany was strengthened in the late fifteenth century by the building of two immense D-shaped towers that projected forward from the curtain wall, the masonry at their base 23 feet (7 m) thick.

LEFT: *The numerous gun ports—located directly below the arrow slits—in the base of the Yellow Tower at Raglan Castle in Wales are round in shape, ideal for accommodating the circular barrels of small cannon.*

IMPROVED RENAISSANCE FORTIFICATIONS

It was the early sixteenth century that witnessed the development of an entirely new fortification that successfully countered artillery. Modifications of the previous century had included the lowering of existing curtain walls and towers, the reinforcing and thickening of masonry, the filling of the lower levels of exposed towers with packed earth, as well as the building of substantial round or D-shaped towers as impact-absorbing platforms for defensive cannon. These underlying principles culminated in a new fortification, the *trace italienne,* which first appeared in Italy during the early 1500s. The walls of these fortresses were built thick and low, the lack of height offset by several projecting angular artillery bastions,

with a series of bastions providing all-round protective fire. A further network of fortifications—ditches, casements, hornworks, and ravelins—extended outward. By the mid-sixteenth century, the offensive capability of gunpowder artillery had effectively been countered by the bastion fort.

The cost of such a fort was enormous, and only the wealthiest of rulers could afford to construct a fortification network. Henry VIII of England (reigned 1509–47) famously built a series of sixteenth-century artillery fortresses—his fort at Sandgate in Kent is especially noteworthy, as it contains embrasures for 60 artillery pieces and 65 handguns—although Henry's 28 forts were not angled bastions, comprising a less effective concentric hollow keep with semicircular bastions.

ABOVE: *The fortress of Deal Castle in Kent was commissioned by Henry VIII in around 1540, and features 145 embrasures (flared openings) for firearms.*

The artillery fort bore scant resemblance to the castle in appearance or function. Built, maintained, and garrisoned by a ruler such as a king or a duke, rather than an individual baron or knight, the fort was purely military, and a residence only for the paid troops manning its defenses. Originating as a product of medieval society, the castle had essentially been a private fortification; it had a military function, but it was also the residence and home of a lord or knight. The fort signaled the end of the castle as a residence and private fortification; knights generally built grand houses instead.

THE RISE OF URBAN POWER

The development of cities and urban institutions gave commoners a military role they had never enjoyed before and made them a force to be reckoned with on the medieval battlefield. As these urban dwellers became more effective in war due to their own military skill, their ability to hire mercenaries to help with urban defense, and the great protective walls their wealth allowed them to build, they began to chip away at the military dominance of the knightly class.

GROWTH AND REVOLUTION

Starting in the eleventh century, medieval Europe had experienced a dramatic recovery. This recovery manifested itself in numerous ways, including an agricultural revolution, extensive demographic growth, a renaissance of knowledge and culture, an economic boom, and an explosion of urban growth. All of these changes helped to alter the social structures of medieval society, and, although some of these changes would take decades and in some cases centuries to develop, their impact was profound.

The growth of cities and towns in particular, as well as their emergence as important political and economic centers, would ultimately contribute to the decline of the knightly class. The interests of the merchants, artisans, craftsmen, and numerous other burghers who inhabited these cities were often at odds with those of the church, the aristocracy, and the crown, and these urban populations would later emerge as a powerful counterweight to the entrenched elites.

By the fourteenth century, various parts of Europe boasted large urban populations. The two most important regions were Flanders (now parts of modern-day Belgium, France, and the Netherlands) and Italy, especially the part of the peninsula that lies to the north of Rome. Flanders was home to a thriving cloth trade, importing wool from England, producing finished textiles in cities like Ghent and Bruges, and then exporting the cloth to the rest of Europe. Italy was also a critical manufacturer of textiles, with cities like Florence leading the way. In addition,

ABOVE: *In 1337, Italian artist Ambrogio Lorenzetti (c. 1290–1348) decorated the side walls of the Council Room (Sala dei Nove) of Siena's City Hall (Palazzo Pubblico) with frescoes on the subject of good and bad government and the consequences of each for cities and towns.*

Italian city-states such as Genoa, Pisa, and Venice benefited from a geographic position that gave them easy access to the vital markets of the Byzantine Empire, the Muslim world, and later the Indian Ocean and East Asia—so that, by the year 1300, Italians were the dominant commercial powers in the Mediterranean. Additionally, the Italian city-states, led again by Florence, were also important financial centers, which only served to add to their economic and political power.

FREEDOM TO SELF-RULE

The defining characteristic of these urban centers was their freedom, at least in comparison to the obligations owed by those who lived and toiled in the countryside. Townsmen and women considered themselves to be free, and they zealously guarded the rights and privileges of urban living. They considered any effort by the local prince or nobility to infringe upon their commercial activities or to impose dues or taxes an affront to their way of life, and they resisted these attempts.

The degree to which cities were able to exercise autonomous rule varied from one part of Europe to another. By the late twelfth century, the autonomy of the Italian city-states from princely rule was close to absolute. The Holy Roman (German) Emperors sometimes tried to assert their rights to govern over them, but these attempts typically ended in complete failure, as the cities would band together and form military alliances that proved more than a match for the invading German forces.

Throughout Flanders, independence from seigneurial rule would be slower to arrive, but by the early fourteenth century, the Flemish cities were assiduously asserting their independence, resorting to arms when necessary to defend their rights. Other areas of Europe such as the Rhineland, parts of France, Castile, and Aragon also gained a degree of independence from seigneurial interference by buying rights and privileges with money or service to their lord or sometimes, more dearly, with blood.

FEARSOME URBAN MILITIAS

When the cities and towns went to war, they had significant military resources at their disposal. One important resource was their population reserves. In times of conflict, the cities were capable of fielding large militia forces to defend themselves. And although at first the

citizen-soldiers were often poorly trained and tended to come off badly against knights in combat, over time their fighting abilities improved; by the fourteenth century the urban cohorts were actually beginning to win battles against mounted knights. Moreover, the cities, with their economic power, were also able to hire large groups of mercenaries when they felt threatened. Finally, their wealth allowed urban communities to build large walls and prepare stout defenses. By retreating behind their walls and forcing their enemies to lay

siege to them, city residents negated the advantage of shock and power that the knights enjoyed in pitched battles.

Among the most effective of all urban militias in Europe were those of the Iberian Peninsula. In the Spanish kingdoms, warfare was not limited to the aristocracy as was typically the case in other regions of Europe. Faced with Muslim kingdoms with which they were often at war, the Christian kingdoms of Castile and Aragon depended extensively on their urban cohorts to shoulder much of the weight of the Reconquista. And these militias did not disappoint, acquitting themselves reasonably well in numerous battles against Muslim armies, most notably during the critical Battle of Las Navas de Tolosa (1212) in which the Christians were victorious.

RIGHT: *Francisco de Paula van Halen's (died 1887) detailed oil painting depicts the mix of knights, soldiers, and urban militia that fought for the Christian kings of Spain and Portugal against the Muslim Almohads during the Battle of Las Navas de Tolosa (1212).*

> *Mercenaries and auxiliaries are useless and dangerous ...*
> *for they are disunited, ambitious, and without discipline,*
> *unfaithful, valiant before friends, cowardly before enemies;*
> *they have neither the fear of God nor fidelity to men.*
>
> NICCOLÒ MACHIAVELLI, *THE PRINCE (IL PRINCIPE,* 1513)

The militias in Italy also performed well, first during the incursions by the German emperor and later in wars fought among the city-states themselves. In northern Europe, it took a little longer for the militias to become effective military forces, but when they did emerge, they posed a serious threat to knightly domination in combat. The city-states of Flanders proved their mettle at the Battle of Courtrai (1302), and the Swiss cantons with their pikemen squares proved decisively that citizen-soldiers when properly trained and motivated could be just as effective as squadrons of knights on horseback.

MERCENARIES MAKE THEIR MARK

Besides their own native troops, cities could use their economic resources to hire mercenaries. The widest use of mercenaries by city-states occurred in Italy. Driven by its thriving economy, the Italians turned to paid military service quite early on. By the fourteenth century, the mercenary was a staple in Italian warfare, with captains known as *condottieri* leading companies of soldiers for hire from one contract to the next. A few of these mercenary companies, such as the Catalan Company, formed during the wars that followed the Sicilian Vespers of 1282, and the White Company led by English knight Sir John Hawkwood became rightly famous and highly sought after by potential employers.

The Hundred Years' War between France and England (which began in

1337) led to an ever wider use of mercenary troops as both sides relied extensively on paid soldiers. These mercenary companies employed professional soldiers, most of whom came from non-noble backgrounds. Their martial skills, honed to a fine edge by a lifetime of experience, made them foes to be feared in battle. In many late medieval armies, they supplanted the knights, who often lacked the discipline and unit cohesion of the professional mercenary soldier. Moreover, not being

ABOVE: *The fortification of cities led to a rise in siege warfare, with armies using a variety of weapons and techniques to breech the formidable defenses, as depicted in this fifteenth-century image.*
LEFT: *Although hired by Italian city-states,* condottieri *like the unknown captain seen here were not necessarily Italian—John Hawkwood was English, while Walter VI of Brienne was French.*

of an aristocratic background, they seldom felt bound by the ideas of chivalry embraced by many knights. Whereas knights fought for their own personal honor and the glory that came from capturing their enemies in combat, mercenary soldiers fought for pay and saw little profit in allowing their enemies to survive. The growing importance of mercenaries (as well as urban militias) in late medieval warfare made the battlefield a much more dangerous place for knights.

THE FORTIFICATION OF CITIES

The development of cities and towns as physical structures in which people could seek safety and from where garrisons could rally to engage invaders made their capture an important goal in late medieval warfare. The countryside was relatively easy to conquer, but it was very difficult to hold if castles and towns in the vicinity remained in the hands of the enemy. As such, sieges of castles and urban strongholds became a critical aspect of contemporary military strategy. This was particularly true of warfare in France during the Hundred Years' War. Almost as soon as the war started in the late 1330s, both sides began to fortify the towns under their control so that they could withstand long sieges. It was during this period that towns such as Caen, Rouen, Avignon, and Reims constructed their impressive fortifications, some of which survive to this day.

The fortifications were very expensive, and some towns spent over a quarter of their annual budget in building and maintaining them. It was only because of their economic wealth that towns were able to afford the expenses associated with fortifications. The impressive walls made towns very difficult to take by siege, and those towns that fell did so only after protracted investment. It was only when new and improved forms of artillery arrived on the scene in the fifteenth century that fortified cities and strongholds began to lose some of their military importance.

Massive cannon, which could lob projectiles weighing over 1,500 pounds (680 kg), could make quick work of walls and towers. Thus, the physical growth of cities would lead to two significant military trends, both of which helped to limit the effectiveness of knighthood. First, the importance of cities as military objectives made sieges a much more

ABOVE: *A fourteenth-century image of Rome shows the city wall at that time. Rome has been protected by a number of city walls during its long history, each built by an emperor or pope to contain the ever-increasing urban population.*

common occurrence than pitched battles, relegating the latter and the knights that gloried in them to secondary importance. Secondly, the most destructive weapons against fortifications were the cannon, elevating artillery over cavalry in terms of military value. Thus, whether it was due to their demographics, which allowed them to field growing numbers of well-trained and motivated militia; their economic power, which enabled them to hire professional mercenary companies to defend their interests; or their fortifications, which limited the value of the knight and raised that of artillery, cities and towns slowly but surely contributed to the decline of knighthood.

THE DEMISE OF CHIVALRY

The period *c*. 1400–1700 saw the rise of professional standing armies employed in the service of the state, with the heavily armored mounted warrior no longer the supreme battle winner. Noblemen's enthusiasm for war diminished, and some no longer wanted to be dubbed knights.

From the mid-fifteenth century onward, men called knights increasingly tended to be mercenaries from a lower social rank, or wealthy noncombatants enhancing their social standing by purchasing titles. The warrior-knight who honored the ideals of chivalry as they had evolved in the Middle Ages—even if he did not live up to them—disappeared. His social place was taken by both the gentleman-courtier and the professional military officer. The knight as a brave and courteous warrior obliged to protect the weak evolved into the European gentleman, fitted by birth and education to govern and lead.

However, the appeal of chivalry lived on long after the traditional knight became

BELOW: *Tournaments of the fifteenth century, such as the one depicted in this c. 1455–65 painting, were little more than pageants. Rather than the all-in melees of previous centuries, tournaments of the later Middle Ages predominantly focused on the one-on-one joust.*

effectively obsolete. Tournaments, which had once been training grounds for battle, became courtly spectacles by the fifteenth century, a time when idealization of the traditional knight was in part an attempt to reinvigorate and reform the living actuality of knights. By the seventeenth century, interest in chivalry was nostalgic and academic.

SECULARIZATION, CRITICS, AND REFORMERS

By the fourteenth and fifteenth centuries, wars between Christian states were endemic, and the idea of an international brotherhood-in-arms engaged in a common Christian cause had been eroded by a growing nationalism throughout Europe; the new orders of chivalry, such as the Order of the Garter, were national ones intended in the main to bind recipients to the sovereign. When, in the sixteenth century, all vestiges of a united Christendom disappeared with the Reformation, Christians were even more engaged in fighting other Christians.

Debasement of the concept of "just war" from a religiously motivated and authorized crusade against infidels to recover the Holy Land to wars fought between Christian nations for entirely secular reasons contributed to knighthood's declining prestige. Heterodox

thinkers such as Cathars and Lollards reiterated the early church's uncompromisingly pacifist stance, condemning all wars as unchristian. John Wycliffe (*c*. 1330–84), denouncing the English wars in France, said hangmen and butchers should be praised more than knights because they killed with more justice and compassion.

UNCHIVALRIC CONDUCT

From its origins, the gap between the ideals and the reality of knighthood had been a target for satirists and reformers. But changes in the nature and purpose of wars did increase the incidence of what was called "mortal war" (where inhumane conduct was tolerated or even sometimes prescribed) as distinct from "honorable war," fought according to "the discipline of chivalry."

Even though protection of the lives and property of noncombatants was (historically speaking) fundamental to chivalry, civilians were almost always the chief victims of war throughout the Middle Ages. But political ambitions and nationalist animus encouraged kings and their armies toward total war. Systematic devastation of the countryside for strategic purposes became a feature of fourteenth- and fifteenth-century wars. The killing of captured Christian knights had earlier precedents, but the

RIGHT: *While civilians were often the unwitting victims of medieval warfare, during the fifteenth century unchivalrous soldiers—sometimes knights—could be seen attacking peasants.*
BELOW: *John Wycliffe was one of the first theologians to challenge Catholic supremacy. So that the Bible could be read by the average man, he translated it into English in 1382.*

massacres of prisoners perpetrated by the English in France were on a far greater scale than ever seen before.

Wars were increasingly fought by men who, unlike the aristocracy, felt no need to pay even lip service to the ideals of honor and chivalry. Mercenary "knights," who lived off the spoils of war, also ravaged the land, savagely robbing and killing civilians. Communes massacred vanquished knights, refusing offers of ransom because they regarded it as cowardly and liable to lead to deception. Such experiences led to a retaliatory loss of chivalric restraint on the part of traditional knights.

Even from its beginnings, chivalry was regarded as being in a state of decline, as there were always good knights as well as bad. The most famously chivalric of English knights, William Marshal (1147–1219) can be compared with Bertrand du Guesclin (c. 1320–80), whose relatively pragmatic attitude to soldiering foreshadowed the professional soldier of later centuries. Although the chivalrous knight and his traditional role on the battlefield were eventually superseded, the institution endures to this day in honorific orders and remains alive in various forms of art and literature.

AN ADVOCATE FOR CHIVALRIC IDEALS

Philippe de Mézières (c. 1327–1405) was a French nobleman who tried to revive crusader idealism. He called upon the warring kings and knights of England and France to repent the "wrongs they had perpetrated and cruelly carried out against God and their neighbors," and to join together to form a new order of chivalry to recover the Holy Land. But the crusade organized by the king of Hungary, Sigismund of Luxemburg (reigned 1387–1437), that followed also ended in defeat, with Nicopolis (in modern-day Bulgaria) being lost in 1396 through the same individualistic bravado that Mézières deplored.

Part Four

The Cultural Legacy

Knights in Literature

For more than a thousand years, knights, or characters embodying the chivalrous ideals of knighthood, have been depicted, glorified, debunked, and idealized in works ranging from medieval songs and Romantic poems to modern novels and, most famously, the great narrative romances of the Middle Ages.

LEFT: *Stories linked with the mythical English ruler King Arthur, portrayed here by Charles Ernest Butler (1903), have been a major inspiration for works about knights.*

The heroic knight of medieval legend has clearly identifiable predecessors in some of the protagonists of Classical literature, such as Odysseus, hero of Homer's *Odyssey*, and Aeneas, portrayed in Virgil's *Aeneid*—inspiring figures who fought courageously in single combat, overcame physical and supernatural obstacles, and battled bravely for just causes. But he makes his first appearance in his more typical and recognizable form in stories that were recounted in song by minstrels at medieval courts, most notably in France, and later recorded in verse in a genre now known as the *epic*.

Medieval nobles delighted in hearing the exploits of illustrious forebears, particularly if it helped bolster the prestige of their own lineage. Most of what we know about the original meaning of chivalry comes to us from literature that both inspired and was inspired by knightly ideals. The ethos of chivalry became increasingly prominent in knightly tales— evidence of its importance to the nobles, who were the patrons of the composers of these stories.

UPHOLDERS OF VIRTUE

A major influence on the development of the heroic image of the knight in literature was the advent of the Crusades. In calling on nobles to protect the Holy Land, the Church gave knights the official role of defenders of the faith and upholders of virtue, and sanctioned the use of force to achieve this. The period between the First Crusade (1095–99), and the Third Crusade (1189–92) saw increasing glorification in literature of the knights who fought for Christianity in the Holy Land. Many literary works highlighted the chivalric ideals of these knights and even those of their enemies, describing the mutual regard expressed by adversaries such as Saladin and Richard the Lionheart.

As ideals of chivalry took root, there was a great flourishing of knightly literature, most notably of narrative verses, or *romances*, many of them inspired by early medieval myths and legends. These gave rise to the most powerful and enduring stories of this genre, those of King Arthur, which were soon disseminated throughout Europe, inspiring innumerable variations on the original stories, in a range of languages.

Chivalry! Why, maiden, she is the nurse of pure and high affection ... the stay of the oppressed, the redresser of grievances, the curb of the power of the tyrant. Nobility were but an empty name without her.

SIR WALTER SCOTT,
IVANHOE **(1819)**

DECLINE AND RENAISSANCE

Such stories not only idealized the knight as an upholder of Christian virtue, a defender of justice, and a protector of the weak, but also portrayed him as a pillar of feudal society. From the fourteenth century onward, however, the image of the knight in literature went into decline. By the late sixteenth cen-

RIGHT: *With his vivid historical novels, notably* Ivanhoe *(1819), Sir Walter Scott reignited interest in knights during the Romantic era.*

tury, the ideals of knighthood were being depicted as outmoded, impractical and even irrational, most famously in Miguel de Cervantes's novel *Don Quixote*.

However, with the rediscovery and revival of interest in medieval manuscripts that began in the nineteenth century, knights and the ideals of chivalry were again seen in a more positive light, especially by the poets and novelists of the Romantic era. Legends, epics, and romances were exhumed, printed, and translated into modern languages. They inspired and were adapted by authors such as Sir Walter Scott and Alfred, Lord Tennyson, who imposed a Romantic sensibility on their versions. At the same time, other scholars sought out the origins of medieval texts.

Enthusiasm for knightly literature endured in the twentieth century,

inspiring popular works such as those of C.S. Lewis, J.R.R. Tolkien, and T.H. White. Even today, tales of knights continue to be retold in literary and popular fiction, demonstrating that the fascination for the figure of the chevalier, bold in battle and generous in spirit, is as strong as it was a millennium ago.

BELOW: *Miguel de Cervantes's satire on chivalrous ideals,* Don Quixote, *published in two parts (1605, 1615), gained a wide readership and was quickly translated into many languages.*

MEDIEVAL SONG AND VERSE

The medieval verse epics emerged in France, where they were known as *chansons de geste*, meaning "songs of deeds." Originally composed in Old French and sung at royal courts by traveling minstrels, or *jongleurs*, they ultimately developed into song cycles made up of dozens of verses, and began to be written down in the twelfth century. Most were about the heroic deeds of famous figures from French history, particularly Charlemagne (*c.* CE 742–814) and his family, and drew on an established body of stories and legends known as the *Matter of France (Matière de France)*.

Unlike the romances, the *chansons de geste* are largely devoid of mysticism and fantasy. They focus on the achievements of the Franks in establishing and expanding their empire and defending it against external threats and traitors from within, and highlight the personal qualities of loyalty, solidarity,

ABOVE: *This illustration from a thirteenth-century manuscript of* The Song of Roland, *shows Roland, surrrounded by slaughtered Frankish troops, sounding the alarm on his horn.*

courage, and boldness. The works are divided into three groups: the *Geste du Roi (Deeds of the King)*, the *Geste de Garin de Monglane*, and the *Geste de Doon de Mayence*, the last two named after barons. The first group concerns Charlemagne's campaigns against pagans and infidels such as the Saxons and Saracens, and includes probably the oldest and certainly the most famous of all the *chansons de geste*, The Song of Roland (*La chanson de Roland, c.* 1100). The second group recounts how Charlemagne and his kinsmen secured their marches and kingdoms, and includes one of the most prolific works, the *William of Orange Cycle (Cycle de Guillaume d'Orange)*; the third, named after a rebellious baron, describes uprisings among the nobility and how they were put down.

LEFT: *Songs recited by minstrels, seen here regaling their king, were the starting point for many medieval verse epics.*

THE SONG OF ROLAND

The Song of Roland recounts the story of the Battle of Roncesvalles, which took place in the Pyrenees in CE 778, during Charlemagne's campaigns against the Muslims of northern Spain, then ruled by the Saracen King of Saragossa, Marsile. Over the next few centuries, the details of the story were recounted and embellished in various oral accounts, before being written down around 1100.

Early in the story, Charlemagne's paladins discuss sending an envoy to negotiate peace, and Roland, one of the king's favorite knights, nominates his stepfather, Ganelon. This is seen by Ganelon, who is jealous of Roland, as a ruse to send him away from the court. Infuriated, Ganelon meets with Marsile in Saragossa, and together they plan to destroy Charlemagne's rear guard as it leaves Spain under Roland's leadership.

Subsequently attacked by a huge Saracen army at the pass of Roncesvalles, Roland obstinately refuses to blow his signal horn, Olifant, to call reinforcements, because he thinks that to do so would be an act of cowardice, and fights on until everyone has been killed and he is mortally wounded. Finally, he sounds his horn, but dies with the effort. Charlemagne arrives to find Roland dead and, with divine assistance keeping the sun motionless in the sky to allow him more time, pursues and defeats the Saracens. He then invades Saragossa, defeats Marsile, subdues the populace, and has Ganelon tried for treason.

Many elements and lessons of the story, such as never fleeing in the face of the enemy and fighting to the death to protect the king and the greater good, were viewed by contemporary audiences as noble ideals and were subsequently alluded to in almost every piece of chivalric literature. Today, *The Song of Roland* remains the oldest known work of French literature, and still has great significance in both modern France and Germany as a model of solidarity from a time when there was unity in empire.

NOBLE ADVERSARIES

The knights in the medieval epics are often seen fighting against Muslims or Saracen foes. However, the depiction of these Arabic knights varies widely and is frequently benevolent, reflecting respect for noble adversaries. In the *William of Orange Cycle*, for example, after William has won the heart and hand (and lands) of the Saracen Queen Guiborc, many of Guiborc's kinsmen attempt to take revenge on him. These knights, many of them kings, are portrayed with all of the chivalric qualities then expected of a Christian knight, such as courtliness, generosity, bravery, and loyalty.

THE SPREAD OF THE EPIC

Many of the *chansons de geste* were translated into, reworked, and emulated in other languages, and received enthusiastically. In Spain, the recent history of the Reconquista gave rise to a local version, the *cantar de gesta*. The best known of these, the *Song of My Cid* (*El cantar de mio Cid*, c. 1140), written down in the twelfth century, tells the story of the Castilian knight Rodrigo Díaz de Vivar, also known as El Cid (1043–99). Banished from the kingdom of Castile and Leon on a false accusation, he fights the Muslims to regain his honor, and helps reunite Spain.

The outstanding work of the genre in medieval Germany is the *Song of the Nibelungs* (*Nibelungenlied*, c. 1200), by an unknown poet of the Passau region. Comprising both historical and mythological material, it recounts the heroic exploits of a prince, Siegfried, prior to and during his attempts to woo a princess, Kriemhild, and, following Siegfried's murder by jealous in-laws, the story of Kriemhild's marriage to Attila, king of the Huns, and her revenge on her own brothers. The Siegfried of the *Nibelungenlied* is the epitome of the epic knight, and the fundamental theme of the story is unswerving loyalty and devotion, the ancient Germanic *triuwe*, which drives the story even after Siegfried's death.

BELOW: *Still regarded by many in Spain as a national hero, the Castilian leader El Cid is commemorated by this bronze statue in Seville.*

THE GOLDEN AGE OF ROMANCE

As verse epics were adapted and rewritten, new values deriving from the growing interest in chivalry were incorporated—such as mercy for the defeated, veneration of and service to the feminine sex, and attention to the knight's spiritual and moral development—along with, in some cases, supernatural elements such as sorcery and spirits. At the same time another type of verse, the love poetry of the troubadours, became increasingly influential. Together, these developments and influences gave rise to a new genre: the romance.

Romance works typically depicted the physical, mental, and spiritual journey of a knight seeking to attain chivalric perfection. Some had a didactic purpose, but others were humorous or even satirical, showing knights struggling to reconcile their natural inclinations with the demands of chivalry. Increasingly in this kind of literature, it was acknowledged that the courtly ethos, like human nature, was intrinsically corruptible.

BELOW: *A renowned patron of literature, Eleanor of Aquitaine was laid to rest in a tomb in Fontevrault Abbey, in Anjou, France, next to her husband, Henry II, and son, Richard I.*

A CRUCIBLE OF LITERATURE

The love poetry of the troubadours flourished between the eleventh and thirteenth centuries. These works typically describe a knight or noble man wooing a lady of the court, often from afar, while extolling feminine beauty and grace. Among the most famous authors of the genre was Duke William IX of Aquitaine (c. 1071–1126), and troubadour poetry and ideals of chivalry flourished especially at his court. William's granddaughter Eleanor (c. 1122–1204), wife of Louis VII of France and later of Henry II of England and mother to Richard the Lionheart, also enjoyed verse and was a patron of the famous late-twelfth-century troubadour Bernard de Ventadour.

Moreover, Eleanor displayed a keen interest in a well-known body of legends and stories from Britain, the so-called *Matter of Britain* (*Matière de Bretagne*), which centered on the exploits of King Arthur. These stories were popularized by Geoffrey of Monmouth's *History of the Kings of Britain* (*Historia regum Britanniae*), published between 1135 and 1139 in England. It in turn was translated into French and rewritten in a more courtly and romantic tone by an Anglo-Norman poet, Robert Wace, as the *Roman de Brut*. Possibly commissioned by Henry II of England, this work was presented to Eleanor in about 1155.

Eleanor's daughter, Marie, Countess of Champagne (1145–98), upheld the family tradition at her court in northern France, promoting literature and

ABOVE: *The knight, poet-musician, and celebrated author of the Arthurian romance* Parzival *(c. 1210),* Wolfram von Eschenbach, *is shown here preparing for a tournament.*

supporting writers and poets. Among them probably was André Le Chapelain (Andreas Capellanus), who wrote *De Amore* (c. 1185). Inspired by the Roman poet Ovid, it describes relations between the sexes, the rules of love, and how disputes in matters of love could be settled by a so-called court of love. The work, now thought to be a satire, emphasizes that men need to woo women thoughtfully and wittily. Undoubtedly, it reflects the widespread interest in romantic love at the time, even though most of the women in it repulse their would-be lovers, and André ends by warning that too much interest in love can send one to hell.

THE FIRST ARTHURIAN TALES

Thought to have been another of Marie's poets, Chrétien de Troyes (flourished 1165–80) used Wace's *Roman de Brut* as

RIGHT: *In this illustration from a fifteenth-century manuscript of the works of Chrétien de Troyes, the Knights of the Round Table bid farewell to their ladies.*

the inspiration for his hugely influential series of poems based on the Arthurian legend, including *Erec*; *Cligès*; *Yvain, or The Knight of the Lion (Yvain, ou Le chevalier au lion)*; *Lancelot, or The Knight of the Cart (Lancelot, ou Le chevalier de la charrette)*, and *Perceval, or The Knight of the Grail (Perceval, ou Le conte du Graal).* Incorporating ideals of chivalry, these poems firmly established the Knights of the Round Table as leading characters of the romance genre and popularized many of the mystical elements of the Celtic legends, including the Holy Grail, the Round Table, the enchanted swords, and the magic fountains.

The Arthurian material also became popular across the Rhine, where writers combined it with tales from German myth and history, such as the legend of Siegfried, and stories from classical literature. Hartmann von Aue composed his *Iwein* (c. 1200), retelling the story of Yvain; Gottfried von Strassburg wrote his *Tristan and Isolde* (c. 1210), reworking Chrétien's version of the legend; and Wolfram von Eschenbach used *Perceval* to create his *Parzival* (c. 1210), a masterful retelling of the quest for the Holy Grail in which Perceval is the favored knight.

Another German author, Heinrich von Veldeke, gained renown for his romance of Aeneas, *Eineit* (c. 1187–89), modeled after a French version of the story rather than that of Virgil, and one of the great works of the Middle High German era—indeed, the creation of all these works helped standardize and refine the Middle High German language. Elsewhere, too, writers began to combine the Arthurian stories and *chanson de geste* traditions, a notable example being the *Gwigalois*, by Wirnt von Grafenberg (c. 1210–20).

LEGENDS IN PROSE

French prose versions of the Arthurian stories, such as the *Prose Lancelot* and the *Vulgate Cycle*, were written in the thirteenth century and were refashioned soon after in what has come to be called the *Post-vulgate Cycle*. These works were a major influence on the fifteenth-century English author, Sir Thomas Malory, who published the first English prose account of the legend, *Le Morte Darthur* (1485), the source for many later Arthurian works in English.

I think my sense of right and wrong, my feeling of noblesse oblige, and any thought I may have against the oppressor and for the oppressed, came from this secret book.

JOHN STEINBECK (1902–68) ON MALORY'S *LE MORTE DARTHUR*

THE LEGEND OF ARTHUR

The legend that has contributed the most to the enduring fame of the knight in literature is that of Arthur and his Knights of the Round Table. The historical origins of the legend have long been sought, but there is no evidence to associate it with any one figure. Arthur first appears in orally transmitted Breton and Celtic legends as a heroic leader who defends his land

BELOW: *The lack of historical detail in the legend allowed artists to give free rein to their imaginations, as in this fourteenth-century illustration of Arthur and his knights in battle.*

against both temporal and supernatural enemies, and is present in various forms in Welsh verse dating from the seventh to the twelfth centuries. But it was the work of Geoffrey of Monmouth, Robert Wace, and Chrétien de Troyes, and the interest of Angevin patrons such as Eleanor of Aquitaine, that raised the Arthurian legend to prominence and ensured its enduring popularity.

STAPLE THEMES

Mystical elements from the orally transmitted legend were incorporated into early romances, and, after Chrétien, the story of the quest for the Grail became almost synonymous with the Arthurian world. While some later stories linked the Grail to a magic cauldron in Welsh legend, the association with Biblical stories gradually became stronger. In Robert de Boron's thirteenth-century trilogy of poems, *Josephe d'Arimathe*, *Merlin*, and *Perceval* (c. 1200), the Grail became the cup used by Christ at the Last Supper and by Joseph of Arimathea to catch the last drops of blood from the dying Christ.

Other elements of the legend that became staples of the romance genre are the Grail Castle and the Fisher King. Resident of the castle and steward of the Grail, the Fisher King suffers from a wound that can only be healed by the arrival of a predestined and pure knight. Until then, he suffers terribly and, as a consequence, his kingdom is a

My knights, my servants, and my faithful sons who have attained to the spiritual life whilst in the flesh, you who have sought me so diligently that ... it is right you should see some part of my secrets and my mysteries ...

CHRIST ADDRESSING KNIGHTS, *QUEST FOR THE HOLY GRAIL* (*QUESTE DEL SAINT GRAAL*, THIRTEENTH CENTURY)

wasteland. Many Arthurian stories also feature a broken sword, whose rupture and repair occur in different ways, but are always symbolic.

In the Arthurian romances, knights have to display certain chivalric, super-human qualities to attain a place at the Round Table. They are expected to be chaste and impervious to seduction, and to provide service in return for the love and devotion of a lady. To have any hope of finding and understanding the mysteries of the Grail, they must display spiritual fortitude and introspection, humility, and a capacity to show mercy. Many of the Knights of the Round Table are portrayed as flawed, either giving in to love, jealousy, or disloyalty, and therefore incapable of completing the Grail quest. A very few surmount all these obstacles to complete their quest.

LANCELOT, A VERY HUMAN KNIGHT

One of the most famous knights in Arthurian tradition, but one who seems to have been an invention of Chrétien, is Sir Lancelot. Lancelot appears in three of Chrétien's tales (*Erec*, *Cligès*, and *The Knight of the Cart*) and became a main character in the *Prose Lancelot* and *Vulgate Cycle*. Among his most famous exploits is the conquest of the castle of Joyeuse Gard, which has been placed under a curse that can only be lifted by killing the 20 knights guarding its walls and then defeating its king in single combat. Though many knights have already died attempting this, Lancelot is undaunted and after many days, much fighting, and, with the aid of magical shields sent by the "Lady of the Lake," succeeds. In the castle, he discovers his own gravestone, revealing the place of his future death.

Yet Lancelot's fatal flaw, his love for Queen Guinevere, wife of King Arthur, ultimately prevents him from finding the Grail—Malory, indeed, shows Lancelot's affair with Guinevere leading to the destruction of Arthur's kingdom, after which Lancelot retires to a monastery. In spite of or perhaps due to his very human failings, and Chrétien's skilled composition and characterization, Lancelot's stories became some of the most popular adaptations of the genre.

THE EDUCATION OF PERCEVAL

In Chrétien's unfinished *Perceval* and Wolfram von Eschenbach's more complete *Parzival*, Perceval is the knight who locates the Grail. He is raised by his

ABOVE: *King Arthur and his knights gather at the Round Table in this French illuminated manuscript dating from 1470. At the center of the table, two angels raise the Holy Grail, the focus of the Arthurian knights' questing.*

BELOW: *Glastonbury Tor in Somerset, England, has been linked with the mythical Arthurian Isle of Avalon since 1190, when monks claimed to have found the bodies of Arthur and Guinevere there—a claim dismissed by modern historians.*

LEFT: *In the thirteenth century, Galahad, a pure and devout character, shown here bearing a shield with a cross, was introduced to Arthurian stories to emphasize the spiritual and religious significance of the quest for the Holy Grail.*

procession involving certain symbolic items—a bleeding lance representing the wound of the king that must be healed, two golden chandeliers, and a golden chalice carried by a young and beautiful girl, which contains food to sustain the king—and sees the Grail itself, a dish in Chrétien's story and a mystical stone in Wolfram's tale. Perceval is the knight the Fisher King has been waiting for, but remembering his teacher's advice not to be too curious, Perceval fails to ask any questions, leaving the king in pain and despair.

Upon his return to Camelot, Perceval learns that the Fisher King is really his uncle and is accused of being unworthy of the Grail. Unable to understand, Perceval embarks on a quest that entails years of introspection and humility. The hermit Trevrezant is instrumental in his spiritual development and helps him understand the true significance of the Grail: it is the only means by which a knight, pure of heart, can gain unity with God.

In Wolfram's version, Perceval next encounters an unknown knight with

mother in the woods, where, by keeping him ignorant of chivalry, she hopes to prevent him from becoming a knight and thereby avoid the fate of his father, a knight who died in a faraway land. As a youth, however, Perceval meets some traveling knights, and, intrigued, decides to set forth to Arthur's court to become one. His mother, still seeking to thwart his ambitions, dresses him in fool's clothing and gives him advice sure to lead to failure. Consequently, he offends several people in the court, even unwittingly insulting Arthur. Realizing what he has done, he leaves, disenchanted, but then meets a knight, called Gornemant in Chrétien's story and Gurnemanz in Wolfram's version, who undertakes to educate him. The knight stresses good measure and self-control, warning the young Perceval about being too curious.

THE PLIGHT OF
THE FISHER KING

Later, Perceval meets the Fisher King (Anfortas in Wolfram), and is taken to his castle, where he witnesses a Grail

SUPPORTING ROLES

Other knights in the Arthurian romances exemplify good or bad behavior and its consequences. In Chrétien's *Erec*, Erec falls in love with and marries Enide, but spends so much time in bed with his new wife that the court accuses him of neglecting his duties as a knight. To prove his courage and chivalry, he embarks on an adventure with Enide, the pair overcoming many obstacles before returning to the court. The hero of Chrétien's *Yvain* overcomes jealousy and other obstacles to win the hand of Laudine; then, after a long absence, has to relearn humility and proper courtly conduct to regain her love. Bors, a cousin of Lancelot, is depicted in Malory and later stories as being pious enough to reach the Grail alongside Galahad.

whom he fights; finding that they are equally matched, they call a halt to the contest then discover that they are half-brothers. Together Perceval and the knight, Feirefiz, arrive at the Grail Castle, where Perceval frees Anfortas from his wound and restores the kingdom to prosperity.

GAWAIN, THE FLAWED FIGHTER

Gawain appears in the Perceval stories as Perceval's companion. In Wolfram's version, the adventures Gawain has when he is separated from Perceval seem designed to demonstrate the different trials by which a knight was to learn how to conduct himself properly and how to reconcile chivalry with love.

Famed for his courage and courtly ways, Gawain is attractive to many seductresses, but as a fighter he is flawed in that his strength subsides as the sun wanes after noon. In later versions of the Grail story, he becomes the hero of the quest, but the character never became as famous in literature as Perceval, though Malory portrays him as an adviser to Arthur near the end of his story.

GALAHAD, THE PUREST KNIGHT

In the thirteenth-century *Quest for the Holy Grail (Queste del Saint Graal)*, part of the *Vulgate Cycle*, and in Malory's *Le Morte Darthur*, it is Galahad, rather than Perceval, who is chosen to learn the mysteries of the Grail. Galahad is the son of Lancelot and Elaine, the daughter of one of the keepers of the Grail, who seduced Lancelot with magic. After being knighted by his father, Galahad sets off for Camelot.

Arriving at King Arthur's court, Galahad takes his place at the Round Table and unwittingly occupies the "Siege Perilous," a mystical chair that, tradition has it, belongs to the knight most likely to succeed in the quest for the Grail. Seeing this omen, Arthur asks Galahad to pull a sword (called

MAGNUS ARTURUS REX POTENTISSIMUS ANGLIAE ✿ DOMINUS L. UNCELOT DU LAC EQUES INVICTUS ✿

Excalibur in some stories) from a magical stone in order to confirm his status as the long-awaited hero of the Grail. Galahad does this easily and is then told of the quest.

Being pure, entirely chaste, and without sin in body or mind, Galahad surmounts every obstacle, physical and fantastical, and accomplishes the task of finding the Holy Grail and unlocking its mysteries. At the Grail Castle, he repairs the broken sword and receives instruction from Christ, who also tells him to take the Grail away from Britain to a spiritual and mystical palace, where the Christian faith will be restored. Galahad then spends his last years in pious contemplation and prayer, before being taken up into heaven along with the Grail and mystical bleeding lance.

TOP: *English artist and author of romance proses William Morris crafted these stained-glass images of King Arthur and Sir Lancelot in 1862.*
ABOVE: *In some versions of the Arthurian legend, including Malory's* Le Morte Darthur *(1485), Arthur proves he is the "true king" by pulling a sword, Excalibur, from a stone.*

MODERN LITERATURE

Although the aristocracy had completely dominated the culture of Europe in the eleventh and twelfth centuries, the towns that grew rapidly during this period in many parts of the continent began to produce extremely wealthy townsmen, who in some cases were more than an economic match for the nobles—especially those knights who had overspent on Crusades and castle-building. Some of these townsmen attempted to emulate the glamor of knighthood and chivalry themselves, and others patronized religious institutions as aristocrats had previously done almost exclusively. This growing class soon became an audience for a new form of literature that directly critiqued courtly knights.

CRITIQUE AND SATIRE

As early as the thirteenth and fourteenth centuries, the French *Fabliaux*, a series of satirical short stories, portrayed knights and clergymen failing to live up to the high standards of courtly etiquette, in turn implying that such ideals were by then unrealistic, not to mention unprofitable. French poet and author Christine de Pisan (1364– c. 1430) wrote a series of works in which the woman played the central

ABOVE: *Based on an episode in Ariosto's* Orlando furioso, *Jean-Auguste-Dominique Ingres's* Ruggiero Rescuing Angelica *(1819) in turn inspired a sonnet by Dante Gabriel Rossetti.*

role while the knight was conspicuous by his absence in affairs of consequence.

Although it is better known for its fantasy elements, Italian poet Ludovico Ariosto's *Orlando furioso* (1516), itself a continuation of Matteo Boiardo's unfinished *Orlando innamorato* (1483), also satirized knightly ideals. But it was Miguel de Cervantes's *Don Quixote*, published in two parts, in 1605 and

1615, and considered by many to be the first modern novel, that most eloquently delineated the rupture that had come to exist between the ideal of chivalry and the realities of the modern world.

THE KNIGHT OF LA MANCHA

The protagonist of Cervantes's novel, Alonso Quixano, is a country gentleman who becomes so obsessed with the knights he reads about in books that he begins to imagine himself living in the past, where courtly manners and the rules of chivalry still hold sway. Hoping to emulate the exploits of El Cid and the great songs of deeds, he renames himself Don Quixote de la Mancha and embarks upon a farcical series of misadventures in which he frequently mistakes ordinary people and objects for characters and elements of a classic romance tale. He imagines mystical knights and magic potions, and sees windmills as giants that must be killed.

On his quest, Quixote is accompanied by his neighbor, Sancho Panza, who has agreed to play his squire. To keep his master content, Sancho fuels his fantasies and concocts elaborate scenarios, though at the same time he is hurt when others poke fun at his master. Eventually, Quixote recovers from his madness and renounces chivalry, but he dies disillusioned and heartbroken.

As well as mirroring the waning of chivalric ideals, *Don Quixote* reflects an increasing trend in literature to depict the psychology of human relationships and to portray human failings and weaknesses in a more sympathetic light, in order to promote understanding. Quixote's journey and his impact on other characters deftly demonstrates the complexity of personalities and relationships, as well as the perennial

problem of reconciling ideals with reality. As a result, the novel is still widely read and continues to inspire adaptations in literature, art, and music.

THE ROMANTIC REVIVAL

In the late eighteenth century, many medieval manuscripts were rediscovered and read for their own intrinsic value, reviving interest in knights and chivalry among scholars. This in turn inspired literary writers to incorporate such themes in their works. One of the most successful was Sir Walter Scott's novel *Ivanhoe*, published in 1819, about a knight in twelfth-century England, which incorporated numerous romantic

figures and events of the Middle Ages, including Richard the Lionheart and the Third Crusade, the Knights Templar, and Robin Hood.

The enthusiasm of the public for these tales was in part a reaction to recent philosophical developments and historical events. The austerity of Enlightenment thinking, the rise of Nationalism, the violence of the Napoleonic Wars and the return to conservatism under the Congress of Vienna, the beginnings of the Industrial Revolution and the introduction of major social reforms—all of this contributed to a widespread desire to return to a bygone era of etiquette, of courage

RIGHT: *Characters from chivalric romances swarm the imagination of Don Quixote in this engraving by artist Gustave Doré for a French edition of Cervantes's novel issued in 1863.*

in combat, of fighting for what was right and good, and of loyalty and solidarity.

Diverse Romantic authors took the knight as subject and chivalry as a theme, and new versions of the romance tales proliferated. Prominent English poets produced a variety of works featuring knights, such as Keats's "La Belle Dame sans Merci." These later prompted numerous paintings by Pre-Raphaelite artists, whose Romantic renderings in turn inspired later poets such as Algernon Charles Swinburne (1837–1909), author of works such as "Tristram of Lyonesse."

One of the most influential knightly works of the nineteenth century was the series of poems published by Alfred, Lord Tennyson over a nearly thirty-year period (1859–85), and collectively known as *The Idylls of the King*. These 12 Arthurian poems retell episodes of Malory's *Le Morte Darthur*, culminating with the destruction of Camelot, the perfect kingdom that cannot survive. The elegiac sadness of these poems is usually taken as a response to the rapid socioeconomic changes of the period. Modern retellings of the story of Arthur, including the musical *Camelot* (1960), are usually based on Malory's plots as mediated by Tennyson's sense of tragic loss.

NATIONALIST LEANINGS

In Germany, prominent figures such as Richard Wagner, the philologist Karl Lachmann, and the Brothers Grimm took a strong interest in medieval manuscripts previously disregarded as folk literature. Wagner sought out medieval sources to trace the origins of legends, which he used for his libretti, even employing Old German alliterative verse and incorporating early Germanic stories from the *Nibelungenlied*. Wagner was also instrumental in adapting the romances of the medieval German poets to suit the tastes of an increasingly nationalist public, portraying the heroes of these works as the embodiment of all that was best in German culture.

In France, too, rising nationalist sentiments increased interest in romance literature, as well as in the compilation of manuscripts of the *Matter of France* and the *Matter of Britain*, which highlighted the French origins of chivalry. Alexandre Dumas's hugely popular *The Three Musketeers* (1844) transferred the romance to early-seventeenth-century France. With their catchcall of solidarity, their stoic adherence to personal

BELOW: *John Keats's poem "La Belle Dame sans Merci" (1819), about a knight who falls under the spell of a mysterious lady, is the subject of this 1902 painting of the same name by the English Pre-Raphaelite artist Sir Frank Dicksee.*

LEFT: *This wash drawing by Gustave Doré comes from an 1875 edition of Tennyson's* The Idylls of the King. *Tennyson called the Arthurian legend "the greatest of all poetical subjects."*

honor, and their firm belief that this honor was sacrosanct and superior and required defending, even in duels, the musketeers epitomized the knights of old and had a strong influence on Romantic notions of chivalry.

THE IDEALS OF THE INKLINGS

Romanticism suffered a serious setback with World War I. Thousands of young men, inspired by ideals of courage and noble sacrifice, rushed off to war, only to find that modern industrialized warfare had no place for chivalry. After World War II, the mid-century Modern movement embraced progress and novelty, most literature stressed realism, and medieval knights seemed to have no place in culture.

Yet interest in chivalry never died out entirely. In the 1930s, the so-called Inklings, an informal literary group made up mainly of medieval scholars working at the University of Oxford, England, deplored industrialization and the loss of chivalric values and began writing works to keep these ideals alive. What are now the most famous of these works appeared in the 1950s: J.R.R. Tolkien's *The Lord of the Rings* (1954), and C.S. Lewis's *Chronicles of Narnia* (1950–56). Tolkien's work was set in a semimedieval world of knights and swords, but his central theme was the strength of ordinary men, in a context of the loss of simple rural beauty and values, and was inspired by his experiences in World War I. A series of seven novels, the *Chronicles of Narnia* was written for children rather than adults and told of English children who accidentally enter an alternate magical world where even the young can learn and apply chivalric values, including (significantly for Lewis) Christianity.

THE FANTASY GENRE

These books had only a small following for a dozen years, but in the late 1960s and especially in the 1970s there was a surge of interest in this type of writing, which came to be known as *fantasy literature*. Like the Romanticism of the nineteenth century, fantasy began as a reaction to the failures of modernism and a desire for a world where good and evil were more clearly delineated. Originally characterized as "fairy tales for grownups," fantasy is generally set in a world inspired by the Middle Ages, or at least the literature of the Middle Ages, with kings, medieval weaponry, and wizards. In the early days, fantasy was heavily influenced by Tolkien and Lewis and was viewed as a subgenre of science fiction. By the end of the twentieth century, however, it had been become not only a separate genre but also one of the most popular genres in adult fiction in English (behind romance and mystery), and *the* most popular genre for teenage readers. And it is not just in English that fantasy literature flourishes: Cornelia Funke's acclaimed *Inkworld* series (2003–), for instance, was written and first published in German.

The knights of fantasy literature are used by their authors to make points about modern society. For example, Tamora Pierce suggests that girls as well as boys can grow up to be chivalric knights in *Lady Knight* (2002), the culmination of her *Protector of the Small* series for teens. George R.R. Martin's enormously popular *Song of Ice and Fire* series of novels, which began with *A Game of Thrones* (1996), has plenty of fearless, loyal knights; however, many of them are from nonaristocratic backgrounds, and even the noblest, truest, and bravest may be betrayed and killed.

RIGHT: *With* The Lord of the Rings, *British writer J.R.R. Tolkien, shown here in his study at Merton College, Oxford, in 1956, helped launch the modern genre known as fantasy literature.*

KNIGHTS ON FILM

Many of the qualities by which a knight demonstrated his worth—honor, loyalty, skill, strength, power, courage, endurance, honesty, generosity, and polite courtliness—are still valued today. Makers of medievally inspired films aim to present these qualities of knighthood in such a way that the audience is able to sympathize with knightly heroes by relating their various attributes to the modern world.

Filmmakers also use a selection of standard items and settings (known as *realia*) to conjure up the medieval world for the viewing public. The most important of these are armor and weapons—swords in particular—but they also include horses, colorful clothing, jewels, crowns, and all the other trappings of wealth. The primary setting is the castle, and the most significant events are tournaments and feasts.

The image of knights in film has changed considerably over the years. In early Hollywood films, such as those by D.W. Griffith, the horse riding of the knights bore a close resemblance to that seen in westerns. Before World War II, cinematic sword fighting was little more than fencing; the two main stars of *The Adventures of Robin Hood* (USA, 1938), Errol Flynn and Basil Rathbone, were both expert fencers. Since the 1940s, great advances in camera technology, sound, color, special effects, and computer-generated imagery (CGI) have combined to produce a higher demand for spectacle and "medieval atmosphere" in films. Filmmakers must cater for an increasingly cinematically aware audience who want to feel that they have seen "real knights," leading to the more frequent employment of historical specialists in set and costume design, and in fight choreography.

THE KNIGHT AS A WARRIOR

One of the most unpalatable facts about medieval knights for filmmakers seeking to make them sympathetic for a modern audience is that they were warriors, trained to maim and kill their enemies. To get around this, many films try to temper the potential violence inherent in knighthood with incisive humor. A very perceptive look at the medieval world, *Monty Python and the Holy Grail* (UK, 1975) was inspired by the Grail Quest in Sir Thomas Malory's medieval work *Le Morte Darthur*. In one scene, Sir Lancelot slaughters almost everyone at a wedding in order to save a "damsel in distress," who turns out to be an effeminate young man. In another scene, the Black Knight demands lethal combat from all comers, despite the fact that, as King Arthur points out, they could "just go round." Like *Monty Python and the Holy Grail*, Jean-Marie Poiré's *Les Visiteurs* (France, 1993) is played for laughs. A twelfth-century knight and his squire are projected by magic into the twentieth century, where they come face to face with their descendants. Their bad medieval hygiene causes

RIGHT: *In* Kingdom of Heaven *(UK/Spain/USA/Germany, 2005), computer-generated imagery was used to great effect during battle scenes, filling the screen with thousands of knights, foot soldiers, standard bearers, and other combatants.*

ST. JOAN CAPTURED ON CELLULOID

One of the first historical subjects in early filmmaking was Joan of Arc. French director Georges Méliès made a series of films about Joan, beginning as early as 1899; *Joan the Woman* (USA, 1917) was one of Cecil B. DeMille's first epics; and Carl Theodor Dreyer's *The Passion of Joan of Arc* (France, 1928) remains one of the most iconic films ever made about Joan's life. DeMille presents Joan as a matriarchal warrior and national savior, Dreyer as a saint and martyr. A German film by Gustav Ucicky, *Das Mädchen Johanna* (1935) linked Joan's career from peasant to savior with Nazi ideals of an Aryan peasant race and the recovery of Lorraine.

RIGHT: *Angela Salloker stars as Joan in* Das Mädchen Johanna *(Germany, 1935).*

problems, but most destructive is their rapid recourse to violence when confronted with the unknown and (to them) unexplained. On seeing a car for the first time, they attack and smash it.

Other filmmakers aim to glorify knighthood in a serious and reverent way by linking the warrior to a good cause, such as fighting for the freedom or salvation of a nation, religious body, or ethnic group. The protagonist in *El Cid* (Italy/USA/UK, 1961) leads the ethnically diverse peoples of medieval Spain to victory against the Moorish invaders, while the heroes of *Alexander Nevsky* (Soviet Union, 1938) and *Black Cross* (Poland, 1960) lead a successful campaign against the invasion of Russia and Poland, respectively.

In many cases, personal motives come before the hero's conversion to more altruistic ones. Rodrigo in *El Cid* is acting to prevent his father's dishonor when he becomes the king's champion.

Balian in *Kingdom of Heaven* (UK/Spain/USA/Germany, 2005) begins the film seeking relief from the guilt and pain he suffers over the suicide of his wife, and ends by saving the people of Jerusalem from death at the hands of Saladin's forces. Robin Hood initially seeks revenge for his father's death in *Robin Hood: Prince of Thieves* (USA, 1991); it is while achieving this aim that he accepts responsibility for protecting the peasantry from the evil Sheriff of Nottingham.

LEFT: Monty Python and the Holy Grail *(UK, 1975) parodied many aspects of knighthood seen in earlier films, including the quest, horse travel, clothing, weaponry, and chivalry.*

Robert Bresson's *Lancelot of the Lake* (France/Italy, 1974) represents a carapace that, when donned, turns the knight into a brutal killing machine. This violence and inhumanity is always beneath the surface in the film, and the audience is reminded of this by the constant clanking and scraping of the knights' sabatons (metal shoes) as the men move around.

In many films based on the Robin Hood tale, Robin is presented as a dispossessed earl with the great fighting skills usually associated with someone of his noble birth. However, in *Robin and Marian* (USA, 1976), director Richard Lester has chosen to make Robin Hood of a lower status than his enemy, the Sheriff of Nottingham. This is done visually through the armor (or lack thereof): Robin fights with bare legs and a leather breastplate and cap, while the Sheriff is in full chain mail. Despite the differences in attire, Robin is shown to display the qualities of knighthood better than those who are recognized as knights, whose espousal of an evil cause turns their chivalry to oppression.

How did the nobles become noble in the first place? They took it at the tip of a sword.

WILLIAM THATCHER (HEATH LEDGER),
A KNIGHT'S TALE **(USA, 2001)**

THE KNIGHT'S ARMOR

Armor is often used in film to divulge the nature of the wearer to the audience. In *A Knight's Tale* (USA, 2001), the Nike swoosh seen on William Thatcher's new armor indicates that he is a new type of knight, representing merit over birth, companionate marriage over societal compulsion, friendship over hierarchical obedience, enterprise over acceptance.

Thatcher's suit of armor is the mark of a knight who has won his honor, rather than a pretender in someone else's clothing, and its silver sheen tells the audience that he is the hero, while the villain's armor is black (associated with evil). The armor in

THE KNIGHT'S SWORD

As in medieval romance, the sword is the knight's most iconic weapon in medievally inspired films. In the hands of filmmakers, swords are transformed from simple weapons to powerful symbols of strength and religious righteousness. In *Kingdom of Heaven*, Balian is recognized on his arrival in Palestine

LEFT: *In* King Arthur *(USA/UK/Ireland, 2004)—which attempted to place the legendary king in a historical context—Arthur's strangely hybrid armor reveals the mixed Romano-British ethnicity that results in his divided loyalties.*
RIGHT: *Starring Nigel Terry as King Arthur,* Excalibur *(USA/UK, 1981) follows the journey of this mythical sword from Uther Pendragon to the stone in which it was embedded, and from Arthur to its final resting place with the Lady of the Lake.*

by his father's sword. In *El Cid*, the sword is used both as weapon and as a form of the cross, which King Sancho kisses as he dies. In *Robin and Marian*, Robin and the Sheriff kneel to pray before fighting their final duel, holding their upright swords in front of them like crosses.

The resonance of the knightly sword can be transposed onto other genres of film, such as the "magical" swords in the martial arts epics *Hero* (Hong Kong/China, 2002) and *Crouching Tiger, Hidden Dragon* (Taiwan/Hong Kong/USA/China, 2000), and in fantasies such as *Highlander* (USA/UK, 1986). The Jedi lightsabers of *Star Wars* (USA, 1977) are futuristic reinterpretations of knights' swords, and require as much training and skill to wield successfully as their medieval predecessors.

THE KNIGHT'S SETTING

Traditionally, the knight's castle represents his wealth, his power, and his security. Filmmakers have played with the idea of the castle, using parody, allusion, and juxtaposition to great effect. In *Monty Python and the Holy Grail*, Camelot is referred to as "a silly place" and "only a model." In *Lancelot of the Lake*, the castle is a prison in which the king and his knights are trapped, a place where the chivalric community finally implodes due to mutual suspicion and infighting. The castles in *Perceval le Gallois*

(France/Italy/West Germany, 1978) are merely representations of gatehouses, but they are enough to signify the whole.

The security and wealth of the castle is often inverted in outlaw stories, and the castle becomes a symbol of oppression, a threat to security, and a source of fear for those who live inside it. In *The Adventures of Robin Hood*, the great hall of Nottingham Castle, in which Prince John holds his feast, is contrasted with the warm sunshine of Sherwood Forest. While the seating in the hall is hierarchically arranged, and the atmosphere is one of Norman dominance, the forest feast is shown to have all sorts and conditions of people jostling happily and eating and drinking their fill. The wealth of the castle, the property of the Norman ruling classes and evidenced by expensive jewels, gold plates, and rich clothing, is subverted by positive images of the wealth of Nature, freely provided to all, regardless of race or class.

DUELS AND TOURNAMENTS

The knights' duels, in the form of jousts, usually take place in front of the castle, and often mark stages in the knight's development both as a fighter and as a man (as seen in *Perceval le Gallois*). More frequently portrayed in film is the judicial duel, in which God grants victory to the deserving party, and in which life or freedom is at stake. The most famous judicial duel in Arthurian films is that fought by Lancelot to save the life of Guinevere, but the hero also fights a climactic duel at the end

LEFT: *The dingy great hall seen in* The Adventures of Robin Hood *(USA, 1938) is juxtaposed with the bright forest scenes. As the film was shot in California, the producers had to add native English plants to the forest, and paint the grass green.*

of cinematic versions of *Ivanhoe*, where the life of Rebecca the Jewess is at stake.

A Knight's Tale shows tournaments in an informal way, presenting them as major social, recreational, and political events taking place over long periods of time, and including other forms of fighting besides jousting. The film creates an interesting link between tournament culture and the culture of modern sports such as NFL (American football) and soccer (European football), envisioning the Smithfield lists in medieval London as the counterparts of the US Superbowl and the FA Cup at Wembley Stadium.

THE QUESTING KNIGHT

The quest or journey, with one or a series of trials, is a popular subject in many film genres, particularly in the form of a descent into some type of personal and/or physical "hell," a process known by the Classical Greek term *katabasis*. The challenge that begins the quest may be delivered by an individual in words, as in *Gawain and the Green Knight* (UK, 1973) and Hrothgar's speech in *Beowulf* (USA, 2007), or in a physical act such as throwing down a gauntlet (*El Cid*). The challenge may be the persecution or murder of a loved one, as in *Braveheart* (USA, 1995) or *Black Cross*. In order to be a valid test of the hero's knightly qualities, the challenge must always be very difficult, even apparently impossible.

ABOVE: Perceval le Gallois *(France/Italy/ West Germany, 1978) features theatrical sets, basic props, a chorus of singers, and rhyming dialog, all of which disassociate the story and its characters from history.*
BELOW: *Created with computer-generated imagery, Beowulf (USA, 2007) is a classic quest tale in which the warrior hero must overcome a number of obstacles in order to kill a demon that has been terrorizing his people.*

MONSTERS, BOTH FRIEND AND FOE

Fantasy creatures—especially dragons—captured the imagination of medieval audiences, and they remain popular subjects for films today. Depending on the film's plot, these creatures can be likable or loathsome—and they inevitably serve to aid or hinder the hero. This is exploited in "family" films such as *Dragonheart* (USA, 1996) and *Dragonslayer* (USA, 1981), in which the monsters are dangerous but sympathetic, whereas in *Beowulf* (USA, 2007) the dragon is fearsome and deadly. Sometimes there is more to the dragon than meets the eye—in *Star Knight* (Spain, 1985), the dragon is actually an alien in a spaceship.

BELOW: *In* Dragonheart, *Draco the dragon helps the hero (Dennis Quaid) fight an evil king.*

The quest involves not only a corporeal trial, but also a mental journey of self-discovery. The physical and psychological *katabasis* narrative is well represented by Beowulf's expedition to the bottom of the lake to kill Grendel's mother, and his combat with the dragon. In *The War Lord* (USA, 1965), the hero believes that his challenge is to save the people of the Frisian village over which he is lord from their pagan customs. Instead, he discovers the destructive nature of his own prejudice and achieves personal redemption, although at the cost of his own life.

The great Swedish director Ingmar Bergman's two medievally inspired films are also based on this type of *katabasis* narrative. In *The Seventh Seal* (Sweden, 1957), a returning crusader, who has already experienced the "hell" of what he thought was a God-ordained cause, challenges Death to extend his life for the duration of a chess game. During this time he attempts to find both God and a purpose for life by performing "one meaningful act." He accomplishes this by saving a young couple and their baby from Death, before being taken away himself—significantly, the couple are named Mary and Joseph. The knight in *The Virgin Spring* (Sweden, 1960) is, unusually, presented in his secular role as lord and patriarch. He must overcome the spiritual and psychological crisis of his young daughter's rape and murder in order to find personal redemption.

Modern anxieties about life's struggle and the basic need to find one's personal identity are echoed in the challenge, quest, and trial stories. Knights on screen also provide spectacle, violence, and romance, and can act as a mirror for contemporary public debates.

TELEVISION KNIGHTS

While film portrayals of knights regularly focus on the visual spectacle, television often takes the time to fully explore the historic roots of legendary knights such as King Arthur and Ivanhoe. Television knights can appear as heroic defenders of the poor and champions of good, but also as comedic imbeciles who need women to guide their way or as seedy fools who seek only their own glory (as seen in the first season of the 1980s' UK series *The Black Adder*). In the past, television executives have favored storylines in which the lowly born becomes a knight through a quirk of fate, with frequent comedic implications, but modern portrayals tend to depict medieval ideals of chivalry in a realistic setting.

KING ARTHUR

The many tales involving King Arthur are ideal fodder for television producers, as they feature discrete yet dynamic events that join together to form the Arthurian legend. Arthurian myth evolved from Celtic lore, and the producers of *Arthur of the Britons* (UK, 1972–73) attempted to capture the essence of early Arthurian legend. Here Arthur is simply the Welsh pagan leader of a small band of warriors, not the grandiose and Christian king of Camelot who had at his service the Knights of the Round Table. This Arthur is unfamiliar to most audiences, and more fantastical portrayals appear in the miniseries *Merlin* (USA/UK, 1998), which depicts elements of Celtic legend but also the full-blown medieval version of the Arthurian saga. Just as medieval legend blended several Arthurian sources, the miniseries conflates the various legends of Arthur's swords and female figures such as Merlin's love, Nimue.

The Mists of Avalon (Czech Republic/Germany/USA, 2001) presents a feminist perspective on the pagan origins of the Arthurian legend. It questions the extent to which the coming of Christianity was a positive thing for women, and rethinks the interpretation of some of the nefarious female figures in the Arthurian saga. Pagan deities were often depicted as women, and the miniseries suggests that their contributions were supplanted by a male-dominated religion. Arthurian television portrayals have also commented on modern ethnic issues; in *Merlin*, a 2008 UK series, young Merlin and Arthur ahistorically cavort with black actors, highlighting the fact that such figures do not appear in medieval texts.

ROBIN HOOD

One of the most popular medieval subjects on television is the story of Robin Hood. As the character has little basis in fact—being first mentioned in William Langland's allegorical poem *Piers Plowman* (1377) and later appearing in medieval ballads—television producers have a wide scope in which to explore Robin and his life. In early literary versions Robin Hood is a yeoman farmer, a fairly wealthy peasant but not a noble. Later, he is a knight who returns from the crusades only to find that the evil Sheriff of Nottingham has stolen his family lands. By the sixteenth century Robin is the Earl of Huntingdon. The reasons why

LEFT: *Julianna Margulies plays Morgaine, the antagonistic half-sister of King Arthur, in* The Mists of Avalon *(Czech Republic/Germany/USA, 2001).*

RIGHT: *The adventures of Ivanhoe have made their way onto television screens numerous times. The 1982 television movie starred Anthony Andrews (center) as Ivanhoe, and Sam Neill (left) as de Bois-Guilbert.*

Robin becomes an outlaw are unclear, but he famously fights for the rights of the poor, is a protector of women, and often criticizes church officials.

Television producers often blend together the various identities of Robin Hood found in literature for dramatic effect. In *The Adventures of Robin Hood* (UK, 1955–60), noble Robin is almost a communist who redistributes goods from the rich to the poor. Several of the show's writers were blacklisted for Communist affiliations in the McCarthy era, and both Robin and the show's writers faced the constant danger of exposure. In *The Legend of Robin Hood* (UK, 1975), Robin believes he is the son of John Hood, a peasant, but he soon discovers that he is actually the son of the Earl of Huntingdon. In *Robin of Sherwood* (UK, 1984–86), Robin of Loxley dies and is replaced by Robin of Huntingdon, so that "Robin Hood" is really two different people. The UK series *Robin Hood* (2006–) portrays Robin as a knight returning from the Third Crusade to find that his life can never go back to normal.

The story of Robin Hood is a perennial favorite that easily crosses cultural and time barriers. Shinto beliefs permeate a Sherwood Forest with mystical powers in the Japanese animated *Robin Hood no daibôken* (1990). Robin timeshifts to the year 3000 in *Rocket Robin Hood* (Canada, 1966), and in a 1991 *Star Trek: The Next Generation* episode, the quirky Q zaps the *Enterprise* crew into the Robin Hood myth.

RIGHT: *A short-lived 1953 series from the UK became the first television show to feature the character of Robin Hood, who was ably portrayed by Patrick Troughton.*

IVANHOE

A literary creation of Sir Walter Scott in the nineteenth century, Ivanhoe is a Saxon knight who fought for King Richard the Lionheart in the Third Crusade. His story has at its heart the struggle to unite two very different groups of people, the Saxons and the Normans. Scott was from Scotland, which historically had been subjugated by the English, and so the story reflected a conflict in his own heritage.

The dramatic events and compelling relationships within Ivanhoe have inspired television producers for years. A&E Television Networks produced a lavish miniseries based on *Ivanhoe* in 1997. Ivanhoe is oddly absent for a good portion of the action, but when he is there, he defeats many knights at once,

single-handedly. The series focuses on the evil knights, providing interesting character studies. In 1982, a made-for-television movie transformed Ivanhoe's enemy, the Templar Knight Sir Brian de Bois-Guilbert, into a compassionate hero and chivalrous knight, thereby departing from the original text.

SCIENCE FICTION KNIGHTS

Modern science fiction portrayals of knights often focus on high-tech weaponry and warfare. Whereas medieval knights valued their metal swords, science fiction knights fight with swords of light. Medieval knights fought on horseback, but modern science fiction knights ride in space-ships or cars with artificial intelligence. While medieval knights fought for the church, among other things, science fiction knights often battle the dark forces of the universe, seeking to unite all peoples in a realm of peace. Medieval knights and science fiction knights may use different technology, but their aims and ideals are similar.

STAR WARS AND THE JEDI KNIGHTS

The most famous examples of knights in science fiction are the Jedi from

Star Wars (USA, 1977) and its sequels and prequels. Much like their historic counterparts, Jedi Knights fight for good against evil, have a wide array of special battle techniques and weapons, and emphasize codes of honor that resemble the medieval European ideals of chivalry or the Japanese code of *bushido*.

Similar to medieval knights, Jedi Knights progress through various stages of training. Children who display a special affinity for the Force (described by Jedi Obi-Wan Kenobi as "an energy field created by all living things … [that] binds the galaxy together") train at the Jedi Temple on the planet Coruscant. Upon their graduation, they become a Padawan (apprentice) serving under a Jedi; after the completion of a series of trials, Padawans become Jedi Knights. The most skilled Jedi Knights rise to the rank of Master.

ABOVE: *As in all of the* Star Wars *films, the lightsabers in* Star Wars Episode II: Attack of the Clones *(USA, 2002) are not just deadly weapons—they also help their Jedi owners to concentrate on and channel the Force.*

Jedi Knights have at their disposal a number of special weapons and combat abilities. They fight with lightsabers—futuristic reinterpretations of the sword—and use their special awareness of the Force to predict the movements of their enemies. Most famously, the hero of *Star Wars*, Luke Skywalker, skillfully fires a proton torpedo into an inaccessible exhaust port on evil Darth Vader's space station, the Death Star, by relying on the Force rather than on visual signals to guide him. The Jedi's ability to concentrate resembles the Buddhist meditative techniques practiced by Japanese *samurai*.

The central conflict within the extensive *Star Wars* universe is between those who embrace the Light (good) Side or the Dark (evil) Side of the Force. The Jedi Knights champion a code of honor that advocates love, courage, and loyalty; they know that straying toward anger, fear, and hate leads to the Dark Side, from which it is almost impossible to return. In battling mal-evolent enemies such as Darth Vader and the Sith, the Jedi seek to bring harmony to the galaxy, in which all races can live in peace.

LEFT: *The character of Lennier (played by Bill Mumy) in* Babylon 5 *(USA, 1994–98) is a member of the Minbari race, and becomes one of the Rangers known for their staunch bravery and unique fighting skills.*

THE RANGERS OF *BABYLON 5*

The Rangers of television's *Babylon 5* (USA, 1994–98) were not explicitly called knights, but they featured many knightlike qualities. A class of warriors created to stand up for the alliance against an evil race called the Shadows, the Rangers wore black and gray robes with a medallion that had two heads on it, representing the union between the human and alien races. Rangers were forbidden to retreat from a fight, and their motto was: "We walk in the dark places no others will enter. We stand on the bridge and no one may pass. We live for the One, we die for the One." Although similar in many ways to European knights, these science fiction war-riors did one thing that their medieval counterparts never managed to do: they united all living beings in their quest to eliminate the dark forces that threatened to imperil the peace of their domain.

FIGHTING FOR JUSTICE AND REDEMPTION

There are numerous other instances of memorable figures that function as knights in science fiction films and television shows. For example, the complex character of Batman in *The Dark Knight* (USA, 2008) is an enlight-ened crusader for justice whose painful childhood memories make him both vulnerable and strong.

Knight Rider (made into two US television series: 1982–86 and 2008–) features a policeman who is rescued from a near-fatal wound to his face. He is re-created as Michael Knight to fight crime with a high-tech super car, known as KITT, whose artificial intelligence makes for a far more useful companion than the horses of medieval knights.

Medieval texts often portray historic knights as ruffians who were encouraged by the church to do penance. Inspired by this, the television series *Forever Knight* (Canada/West Germany, 1986–96) features a vampire from the thirteenth century fighting crime for the police in modern Toronto, Canada, in order to achieve redemption for his past sins.

LEFT: *Christian Bale's brooding interpretation of Batman in* The Dark Knight *(USA, 2008) reflects the character's constant struggle between living a normal life (as Bruce Wayne) and fighting against evil and injustice.*

War Games

Perhaps aspiring to emulate the valor and chivalry of an earlier romantic age, or possibly to highlight and encourage what still remains of such virtues, later generations have understandably sought to recreate knightly ideals and the heroic deeds of medieval champions in the games they play.

Recreational games were well known to the knights of the Middle Ages, who used jousting to practice the sword and lance skills they needed for survival in war. Medieval tournaments and mock battles, still enacted to this day, were also a popular means of capturing the pageantry of military action and commemorating past victories.

Fascination with knightly deeds has not diminished over the years, and games based on the exploits of knights have always been popular. Knights have been represented in many kinds of games, from simple toy soldiers through to board games and complex role-playing games. Modern computer simulations are now able to recreate the exploits of individual heroes or the maneuvers of entire medieval armies across vast battlefields.

CHESS AND MEDIEVAL LIFE

Chess is probably the oldest and certainly the best-known board game based on medieval life. It was introduced to Europe in the ninth and tenth centuries, though its origins stretch further back, to sixth-century India. In Europe, chess was most commonly played by the educated nobility, but variations on it, and similar games, such as checkers (draughts), were also played by the other social classes for recreation.

The first chess pieces were modeled on the infantry, elephants, chariots, and cavalry of Indian armies, but the modern form of the game reflects life and combat in medieval Europe. Essentially it is an abstract representation of the tactics and broader strategy employed by medieval leaders to protect and expand their domains, and in this respect it provides a fascinating insight into how the social order was structured in the Middle Ages. As it was in medieval society, supreme power in chess is represented by the kings and queens, with threats to either delivering a potentially mortal blow. The central role of the church is reflected by the bishops, and two highly maneuverable knights protect the royal families. Castles, or rooks, simulate the

LEFT: *Still a dramatic spectacle, jousting tournaments are regularly held today at medieval fairs and festivals. The lances are usually made of soft wood so that they break easily.*

*The game's afoot. /
Follow your spirit,
and upon this charge. /
Cry "God for Harry!
England and Saint George!"*

WILLIAM SHAKESPEARE,
HENRY V, **ACT 3, SCENE 1**
LINES 32–34 (1599)

fortifications of the age, with the defensive "castling" move suggesting a harassed king's retreat behind strong walls. Pawns, of course, represent foot soldiers, serfs, or peasants, and they are often sacrificed in the game in much the same way that they were in real life.

MINIATURE WAR GAMES

Popular though chess has remained throughout history, less abstract representations of medieval warfare have also gained strong followings. The most obvious and common are the games played by many children using toy soldiers—often with marbles and rubber-band catapults—to recreate knightly deeds and magnificent victories. Though plastic figures fill the toy-shop shelves today, in times past they might have been made of lead or tin, or even ivory or silver.

Similar but more sophisticated war games are played by history enthusiasts using beautifully crafted and painted figurines, a hugely popular pastime that has given rise to a strong figurine industry and inspired thousands of so-called miniature war-gaming groups and collectors around the world. Guided by comprehensive and historically accurate rules, these tabletop war games recreate entire battles from the Middle Ages, with each knight's offensive and defensive ratings usually determined by attributes such as armored protection, previous victories, and displays of valor, courage, or skill at arms.

Miniature war games of this kind have not only been a longstanding form of recreation but also, throughout history, an important means of demonstrating tactics to soldiers and aspiring leaders, in military schools and in the field, all over the world. The French Army, for example, long taught its officers about strategy using scale models of famous engagements; some of these models are still on display in the museum in Les Invalides in Paris.

RIGHT: *Plastic replicas of knights have fired imaginations for decades. Gaming enthusiasts demand precise detail in their figurines.*

ABOVE: *The Lewis Chessmen were discovered in 1831 on the Isle of Lewis, Scotland. Numbering 78 in all, they were carved out of walrus ivory in the twelfth century, probably in Norway.*

MODERN BOARD AND ROLE-PLAYING GAMES

Those lacking the skills and patience needed to paint or the resources needed to acquire historically accurate figurines have still been able to experience medieval battles in return for an investment of only a few dollars. Reaching a peak of popularity in the 1970s and 1980s, just prior to the advent of personal computers, board war games allow individuals and small groups to take the roles of medieval knights and rulers seeking territorial conquest and battlefield victories. Avalon Hill's *Kingmaker* (1974) and *Barons' War* (2004) from Clash of Arms are two well-known examples of the genre. Despite lacking the lifelike figures and color of miniature war games,

LEFT: *The board game* Dungeons and Dragons *has inspired software spin-offs, including this 1996 arcade game,* Shadow over Mystara.

board games still manage to recreate the excitement and challenges of medieval warfare, often using complex rules and charts to enhance realism. Some releases, such as Hans im Glück's *Carcassonne* (2000) have successfully evolved from board games into equally popular computer and console titles.

Players seeking a more personal experience often participate in role-playing games, which became remarkably popular toward the end of the last century. Perhaps best represented by the *Dungeons and Dragons* phenomenon of the 1970s and 1980s, which still survives today, role-playing games almost always include knightly characters who epitomize virtue and the age of chivalry. In *Dungeons and Dragons*, participants choose characters to role-play, after

which the group sets off on a virtual adventure under the direction of a designated Dungeon Master, who acts as both storyteller and guardian of the rules. As they gain points through successful quests, players advance through the levels of the game and acquire a range of abilities and powers. The Paladin character especially upholds the ideals of righteousness, justice, honesty, and chivalry. He is well protected by armor and a master of hand-to-hand fighting with the long sword. His presence in a fight gives confidence to other members of his group—much as a famous medieval knight might have done when his standard was unfurled on the battlefield.

VIRTUAL KNIGHTS

The development of personal computers created a whole new medium for medieval war games. Ranging from simple text-based games, in which players type responses to questions as they complete quests, to exciting programs that allow

the player or players to engage in hand-to-hand fighting against knights, dragons, and demons, computer games offer a romantic insight into life in the Middle Ages and unparalleled ways to recreate key events and battles. When sophisticated computer-modeling techniques and modern processing power are combined, medieval computer games can create incredibly

TASTING THE GLORY OF VICTORY

The popular computer game *Medieval: Total War* (2002) allows players to take the roles of great kings or generals, refighting key battles such as Hastings or Agincourt while pushing the boundaries of their empires in fictional or historically based attempts to conquer their adversaries. Recreating different categories of troops, such as knights, archers, and light cavalry, *Medieval: Total War* places thousands of soldiers on the screen at one time, forming an impressive military spectacle. Yet a battle can still be won or lost by a single maneuver, such as a final and ferocious charge of a small group of elite knights led by their king. As well as winning battlefield glory, players can experience other elements of life in the Middle Ages, such as economic management, diplomacy, and the raising and training of recruits.

realistic game environments, including virtual cities, fortifications, inhabitants, and weather conditions. Even the glint of armor, flash of steel weapons, and the sounds of battle can be recreated, adding to the sense of realism. Sega's *Medieval: Total War* series (2002) and Firefly Studios' *Stronghold* (2001) are very popular examples of the medieval computer war game.

MULTIPLAYER GAMES

The Internet has opened up even more possibilities for interactive gaming, both by individuals and, especially, groups. Battles can now be fought by players in different zip codes or even different countries, and the remarkable growth of Internet access and online communities ensures that new experiences, scenarios, and environments become available almost daily. Virtual armor and weapons can even be purchased from the wide range of supply sites that has grown up around the most popular games.

The possibilities of Internet play are best illustrated by the growth in Massively Multiplayer Online Role-playing Games (MMORPG), in which players assume a character and join a group of geographically dispersed companions to explore online realms. Just as in the earlier role-playing games, knightly virtues and skills are at a premium in the virtual world and players aspire to advance the level of their character by completing quests and defeating enemies. Blizzard Entertainment's *World of Warcraft* is a leader in this genre, offering a world that has all the hallmarks and trappings of the real and mythical Middle Ages and is populated by more than 11 million registered online players. Swords and sorcery abound throughout the game, and entire mythical realms and kingdoms are there for the conquering. Just like the knights of old, players must make ethical and moral decisions as they proceed, often having to choose to advance their position through virtue or vice. Twenty-first century processing power has ensured that the age of chivalry has not yet passed.

Currently limited by the physical restrictions of computer or videogame screens, the future of such games probably lies in virtual reality and the increasing capacity of hardware and software to simulate medieval life. New virtual champions will emerge to take the place of the famous knights of old, and it might not be too long before we can all feel the thrust of a sword or the blunt shock of a well-placed lance in a tournament.

LEFT: *Enthusiasts play* World of Warcraft, *a leading example of a Massively Multiplayer Online Role-playing Game, at the annual Games Convention trade fair in Leipzig, Germany.*

MODERN MEDIEVAL EXPERIENCES

Many history enthusiasts want to go beyond recreating the world of knights in tabletop and computer games and experience it firsthand. This has given rise to modern medieval societies and an array of commercial organizations offering a host of medieval experiences, ranging from banquets, theater, and fairs to role-playing games. Today you can choose to explore the world of knights over dinner or, if you prefer, for an entire week in a medieval-style battle encampment. Because so much of this activity is paid for by barter, with, for example, a weaver exchanging a set of clothes for a blacksmith's weapons, or put on for free by folk artists, it is impossible to tell how much money is spent on these activities, but based on the financial reporting of the companies involved it generates hundreds of millions of dollars in the United States alone. Clearly, a lot of people don't just want to learn about knights; they want to be them.

MEDIEVAL BANQUETS

One way to satisfy an interest in medieval life is to attend a medieval dinner or banquet. These events, often family-friendly, try to provide a brief immersion in the world of the Middle Ages. Often the buildings in which they are held are constructed or decorated to

LEFT: *Historically accurate foods, tableware, songs, and costumes help bring the medieval feast to life.*

resemble castles and usually the people serving (often termed "serfs" or even "wenches") are dressed in period costume. Customers are normally treated as lords and ladies and, to maintain authenticity, required to eat with their fingers (though concessions to modernity, such as vegetarian fare, are available).

Many medieval dinners involve a show of some type. Often a narrative frames contests between groups of knights. Opposing sides may be distinguished by their colors and the spectators encouraged to cheer for their favorite knight. Even though the outcome of the competition is usually planned so that good always triumphs over evil, the performances of the knights can be very real and include impressive feats of horsemanship, weaponry, falconry, and so on. In many ways it is like professional wrestling: the outcome is "rigged," but the athleticism of the knights is genuine.

FAIRES AND FESTIVALS

If a single night of dinner theater does not suffice as an experience of the days of knights, a more prolonged immersion in medieval life can be enjoyed at a wide range of medieval festivals, such as those known in the United States as Renaissance Faires. Medieval festivals usually gather vendors and entertainers in an outdoor setting, sometimes a castle, and customers come to buy merchandise, watch medieval-themed shows, and experience aspects of medieval life. Visitors may be simple observers or, as at most Renaissance Faires, dress in medieval costume and participate in the action. Some even dress as knights, though brandishing a real sword will most likely get you expelled! Many festivals are run by local history groups, others by large commercial organizations; some are annual events, while others operate more or less continuously throughout the year, the flavor of the festival changing with the seasons.

BELOW: *Performances by appropriately attired musicians are a feature of the many Renaissance Faires that take place in the United States.*

Naturally, knights are an important part of any medieval festival. Jousting and other tournaments are usually staged, often several times per day. While some of these tournaments have a loose storyline, like the dinner theater, others are real competitions between professional jousters. Whether they have a narrative or not, the knightly tournaments generally draw the largest crowds of the day, and few visitors would consider a trip to a medieval fair complete without witnessing knightly prowess.

CLUBS AND SOCIETIES

Some devotees of real knights want to go even further, however, and make such experiences a regular part of their lives. One way to do this is to join a medieval club or society. These groups, usually run by knowledgeable history buffs and sometimes even academics, get together regularly for discussions, lectures, and performances, as well as reenactments in which members can participate. Members may also learn medieval skills such as weaving, blacksmithing, and dancing.

The largest and best-known modern medieval society is the Society for Creative Anachronism (SCA), whose Web-site tagline is "Welcome to the Current Middle Ages." Formed in 1966 following an outdoor tournament in Berkeley, California, by hobbyists interested in medieval and Renaissance life, it grew quickly and soon spread across North America, Europe, and beyond. Today it has more than thirty thousand members all over the world. Participants take on the role of someone who would have lived in the past, with a name that has to be approved by the society's heraldry experts. Appropriate medieval clothing—referred to as "garb" rather than costuming—must be worn to all events. Even newcomers are required to dress properly, though local organizations ("shires" and "baronies") will lend out appropriate garb. Everyone must be part of the recreation.

For many in the SCA, the main draw is armed combat. Members (whether male or female) who are interested in being a knight can train for and compete in tournaments. Generally they will use real-but-blunted weapons and padded armor. Marshals oversee the training and competition to ensure safety as much as possible. Though the SCA does put on demonstrations at other times, these tournaments are not for show—they are real competitions. Indeed, monarchs are not elected; they win their title by feat of arms in actual competition.

ABOVE: *Many festivals in Europe, such as this carnival at Santu Lussurgiu, near Nuoro, Sardinia, Italy, allow participants to enjoy medieval spectacles in their original settings.*

REINED IN BY CHIVALRY

ABOVE: *Two members of the Society for Creative Anachronism participate in a competitive sword fight at a medieval gathering in California. Such contests are governed by strict rules.*

The modern-day knights of the Society for Creative Anachronism (SCA) primarily maintain their safety through their own chivalric behavior. One of their three peerages is the Order of Chivalry, and fighters who attain this level are expected to exemplify knightly chivalry. The chivalric virtues such as honor and prowess are not part of a show; they are taken very seriously as an integral part of combat in the SCA. Indeed, regardless of skill, a fighter who shows little honor on or off the field of battle is unlikely to progress through the ranks.

BATTLE REENACTMENTS

In the modern imagination, the knight is most closely connected with his martial skills, symbolized by armor and sword. It is not surprising therefore that one of the central activities of modern medieval societies is reenacting armed combat and full-scale battles. How these reenactments are conducted depends to some extent on what is important about knighthood to those involved. Some emphasize the romance of literary knights, others their fanciful place in the modern imagination; yet others aim to recreate a historical event accurately.

THE REVIVAL OF THE TOURNAMENT

As social and technological innovations through the Renaissance and early modern era made knights obsolete,

the idea of the tournament changed, from being an opportunity for a knight to hone his martial skills and showcase his prowess to a display of pageantry and tradition. Eventually, the tournament more or less died out. Then, at the beginning of the nineteenth century, interest in tournaments was sparked by the romantic portrayal of knights in the works of writers such as Sir Walter Scott and Alfred, Lord Tennyson.

The medieval tournament was resurrected for real at Eglinton Castle, in Ayrshire, Scotland, in August 1839. The event was planned by Archibald Montgomerie, thirteenth Earl of Eglinton, and his family as a reminder of the importance of tradition and political conservatism. The plan was to have an enormous procession,

ABOVE: *Competitors gather for the Eglinton Tournament on August 30, 1839. It turned out to be a much wetter day than shown here.*

followed by a tournament with dozens of knights, all played out before the general public. Only the elite of Scotland, and elite guests from other countries, were asked to participate, which was just as well because the immense cost of outfitting a knight and his entourage was so great that only the wealthiest could even think of it.

For all the planning, though, the tournament was a disaster. After the procession, it began raining so hard that everyone fled indoors, and the competitions had to be postponed until the next day. By that time, comical images of knights cowering beneath umbrellas were already being bandied about by the press (and the Earl of Eglinton's political enemies) and became fixed in the public imagination. Indeed, the embarrassment of the fiasco, combined with the immense cost of the event, began the decline of the Montgomerie family, and in a few generations Castle Eglinton was abandoned.

"Chivalry," said Lycion, glancing carelessly over the leaves. "Don't you remember what an absurd thing that Eglinton Tournament was?"

EDWARD FITZGERALD, *EUPHRANOR* (1851)

Yet, the event was successful in that it resurrected interest in tournaments, inspiring events in the United States and elsewhere. Perhaps the greatest vindication for the Earl of Eglinton occurred in 1989, when Eglinton Country Park, site of the castle, hosted a reenactment for the tournament's one-hundred-and-fiftieth anniversary. What greater praise can there be than when one's reenactment is reenacted?

HISTORICAL ACCURACY

Many reenactments are less about reviving a lost way of life, and more about commemorating a particular battle. For example, Battle Abbey in Sussex, England, hosts an annual reenactment of the Battle of Hastings of 1066. However, few battles are of such importance that they garner annual performances, and most are reenacted only on special anniversaries.

Unlike many other forms of reenactment, historical reenactments typically have no competitive element, though often the participants are experienced reenactors who could demonstrate a great deal of prowess. Generally, the events consist of large battle scenes, rather than tournaments, and often have an educational purpose. Thus the side that won historically is the side that must win in the reenactment.

However, some historically accurate tournaments do have a competitive element. Rather than reenacting a particular battle, these adhere to authentic historical rules of tournaments, and have no set outcome. For example, the American Jousting Alliance is an organization of competitive jousters who compete in events such as ring spearing, spear throwing, and shield-quatrain hitting. The International Jousting Championships take place in California, and groups such as the International Jousting Association hold Australasian and European events. Europe has its own tournaments, most notably the Kaltenberger Ritterturnier in Germany.

GOING INTO BATTLE

Five major annual "wars," drawing thousands of competitors from around the world, are hosted by the Society for Creative Anachronism (SCA). The biggest is Pennsic, held in or near Pennsylvania in late summer. Given the size of these events, nearly every type of knightly combat can be seen. Unlike historical reenactments, however, these wars are set within the SCA's own system of kingdoms and baronies.

Other ways of joining the fray include live-action role-playing games (LARPs), in which players act out the role of a character in a fantasy setting. While some LARPs are diplomatic affairs, with players talking and negotiating with one another, one particular subcategory is the *boffer LARP*, in which the characters do real battle with each other using heavily padded weapons. Though most LARPing groups are small, some can be quite large. The Darkon Wargaming Club in the Washington–Baltimore area is a boffer LARP that takes place in a setting incorporating knights, magic, and elves, and draws up to three hundred participants per event. It was the subject of a documentary film, *Darkon* (2006).

BELOW: *The annual reenactment of the Battle of Hastings at Battle in Sussex, England, involves up to two thousand participants.*

TEAM AND BRAND NAMES

It is not just writers of historical romances who have learned that knights sell; many other savvy marketers have figured this out, too. The sheer number of organizations and companies that use knights and concepts associated with knights to promote their image or sell their wares is staggering: knight-related marketing ranges from everything from an "Excalibur" line of food dehydrators to the rapper Sir Mix-a-Lot.

Knight-related names tend to have two different functions. In some cases, such as in the names of sports teams, they are employed to evoke the idea of chivalric virtue. In others, especially where the names derive from the legends of King Arthur, they evoke a sense of romance, wealth, and tradition.

CHIVALRY ON THE SPORTS FIELD

Probably the least surprising of all knightly brands are the names of sports teams. After all, prowess is a chivalric virtue, and teams want to promote their own athletic prowess on the field; they also like to be seen to champion the chivalric ideal of fair play. Branding a sports team with a knightly name simultaneously communicates that this is a heroically athletic team and that it will never repay its fans' loyalty with deceit or dishonor.

Some team names are explicitly knightly, such as that of the Newcastle Knights, an Australian rugby league team. With a plumed helmet as their logo, the Newcastle Knights call upon their fans to "Defend Your Kingdom" by buying a ticketed membership, thus suggesting that fans, too, are knights of the realm, whether they actually play in the matches or not. The name and marketing campaign seem designed to evoke the image of the knight as the defender of the realm while at home, and as the questing knight at away matches.

COLLEGIATE KNIGHTS

American college football teams in particular seem to favor knightly names, perhaps because the helmets and padding worn by the players evoke the image of a modern-day knight. Examples include the University of Central Florida Golden Knights, the Rutgers Scarlet Knights, or the West Point Army Black Knights. Knightly brands and mascots are even found in a range of sports at high school level, with more than one high school using a name such as "Warriors" and associated imagery to make the connection to knights.

It is not only sports clubs that use knights for branding, however: universities and schools themselves often incorporate knights and related images in their marketing. Lynn University in Florida, for example, uses the name "Fighting Knights" as its brand. The

ABOVE: *A medieval helmet and green crest adorn the uniform of the London Knights ice hockey team, based in Ontario, Canada.*

logo is a knight in a plumed helmet, but instead of wielding a sword he has his fists raised as if he were in a boxing match, the image suggesting a bellicose knight, but one who is involved in nonlethal combat.

ARTHURIAN IDENTITIES

King Arthur and his Knights of the Round Table have a pronounced place in brand names and marketing. Though the word *knight* and the names of Arthurian knights may be used, the legends are often simply alluded to in names such as Camelot, Excalibur, Lancelot, or even King Arthur.

The use of Arthurian place-names such as Camelot and Avalon is often a way of evoking a sense of the wealth and tradition associated with knights. Ironically, these brand names tend to be used for places at the lower end of the socioeconomic scale, such as cheap apartments or trailer parks, rather than

LEFT: *A player from the Rutgers Scarlet Knights college football team raises a replica long sword alongside the club mascot, a knight in red armor.*

for upper-class neighborhoods. Someone moving into, say, "Camelot Villa Mobile Home Community" will not reasonably expect that they are entering a community of luxurious mansions, but the association with knightly wealth might in some ways make the move a more appealing prospect. In addition to making such a community sound more affluent, the use of the name *Camelot* also creates a sense of personal safety, as if one lives in a fortified castle protected by knights. This sense of safety can be an important selling point.

THE ONE AND ONLY

Excalibur, the name of the most famous weapon of the most famous knight, has been used to market everything from electronics to fireplace accessories, but just as often it is used to refer to one specific product sold by a company,

often the top-of-the-line model. In this case, marketers are playing up the exclusivity of the product—just as there was only one Excalibur sword, so these items are few and far between and available only to special customers—and, often, that it is part of a grand tradition. Excalibur automobiles, for example, introduced in Milwaukee, Wisconsin, in 1963 and produced

until 1990, were designed to reflect the styles of earlier eras, thus ensuring that their products were both classic and unique—like Excalibur itself.

The Excalibur Hotel in Las Vegas taps into this sense of uniqueness, while also attempting to create a medieval environment by hosting events such as a "Tournament of Kings" and incorporating knight-themed attractions such as the Roundtable Buffet, Canterbury Wedding Chapel, and Sherwood Forest Café. Of course in this context the name *Excalibur* is also meant to evoke the wealth of the knights of Camelot—and perhaps hint at the riches gamblers might win at the hotel's gaming tables.

BELOW: *The architecture of the Excalibur Hotel in Las Vegas blends Modernism with faux-medieval features such as turrets and crenellations.*

Honorific Orders

With the decline of the military role of the knight from the fifteenth century on, the title of knight *came to refer to a nonhereditary grade of the nobility conferred by a monarch. Today it is used mainly as a state honor rewarding distinguished service.*

Since around 1100, when European kings, princes, and nobles began to have it conferred on their sons when they came of age, knighthood has been regarded as an honorable status. This honorable character was enhanced around 1250 when the title of *knight* was restricted to men of noble birth. However, the functional military status of knighthood began to be eroded by the subsequent conferral of knighthood on men who were primarily judges, civil servants, or rich merchants, and when changes in military technology and organization implemented from about 1430 removed the military distinction between knights and squires, knighthood became principally an honorific status, even for men who pursued a traditional knightly career. This situation was recognized by the reduction of the dubbing or *arming* ceremony to its final action, the *accolade*, or blow with the flat of a sword. In most countries even that ritual fell into disuse after 1500, though it has been preserved in Britain to this day.

MONARCHICAL ORDERS

In the British realms, simple knighthood was converted after 1600 into an honor conferred by the monarch in recognition of loyal service or exceptional achievements by men who were not rich or powerful enough to be raised to the peerage. In most of the other countries of Europe, however, conferrable knighthood came, by 1600, to be associated exclusively with membership of a secular order of knighthood of the monarchical type, attached to the throne of its royal or princely founder. The earliest such orders—the Castilian Order of the Band and the English Order of the Garter—had been founded in

LEFT: *Roger Mortimer, second Earl of March, shown in this fifteenth-century portrait, was a founder member of the Order of the Garter.*

ABOVE: *The star (top) and collar (bottom) of a knight or dame grand cross of the military division of the British Order of the Bath both incorporate an eight-pointed Maltese cross.*

1330 and 1348–49, and the latter had become the principal model for all of the later foundations.

The Order of the Garter was established by Edward III as a successor to the fictional Arthurian fellowship of the Round Table, supposed to have been made up of the best knights in the world, and to have promoted the highest standards of chivalry. As the organization of the Round Table had never been clearly described in the romances, Edward had adopted as a constitutional model the contemporary devotional confraternity (of the type that included most merchant and craft guilds), modified to suit his peculiar purposes. Like most of its imitators, the Order of the Garter was founded in part to promote the chivalrous image—and therefore the honor—of its founder and his heirs, and in part to reward the past and secure the future loyalty and service of the most renowned and important of his subjects and allies.

By 1380, the Order of the Garter had inspired the foundation of at least one monarchical order in the court of almost every kingdom of Latin Europe. A second wave of foundations was inspired by the creation in 1430 of the Burgundian Order of the Golden Fleece, closely modeled on the Garter, but introducing a livery collar as a form of insignia that by 1495 would be characteristic of all monarchical orders.

By about 1520, however, only four such monarchical orders survived: those of the Garter, the Collar of Savoy or Annunciate One, the Golden Fleece, and St. Michael of France. These four very similar orders would all survive to at least 1830, and serve as the direct models for a succession of newer orders founded over the next three centuries in Europe. Prominent among the new orders were the Scottish Order of the Thistle (abortively proclaimed by James II in 1687 and effectively established by his daughter Anne in 1703), and the British Order of the Bath (founded by King George I in 1725).

THE MONASTIC MODEL

In the meantime, the secularization and royal annexation of the Iberian monastic orders of knighthood in the sixteenth century had provided another model for honorific monarchical orders, distinguished by a larger membership, division into a hierarchy of administrative grades including *grand cross* and *commander*, a president with the title of *grand master*, and a badge in the form of a cross. This model—also preserved in the handful of semimonastic orders

THE ORDER OF THE GARTER

ABOVE: *The services of the Order of the Garter are held in St. George's Chapel at Windsor Castle, England, depicted here on the occasion of an 1838 service attended by Queen Victoria.*

Dedicated to St. George, patron of knighthood, the Order of the Garter was limited to 25 knights called *companions* **and the king as** *sovereign***, all of whom wore a badge in the form of a miniature knightly belt, and a mantle like those of the crusading orders, charged with a shield bearing the cross of St. George. The order was given a magnificent hall and chapel (where each knight was assigned a stall) in Windsor Castle. There the companions held (and still hold) their annual business meeting, banquet, and celebratory and commemorative services—performed by the order's canons—near their patron's feast-day.**

with roots in the twelfth century, notably that of the Hospital of St. John based on Malta—was first fully emulated in 1693 by Louis XIV of France. His Order of St Louis was the

first strictly secular order with more than a single grade—specifically, the three grades of *knight*, *knight commander*, and *knight grand cross*. Each grade was marked by a special form of the order's

ABOVE: *Members of the modern Order of Malta, based in Rome, wear a badge and habit, bearing a Maltese cross, on ceremonial occasions. The order has about 12,500 knights and dames.*
RIGHT: *Napoléon Bonaparte awards the first cross of the Legion of Honor, on July 14, 1804, at the church of Les Invalides in Paris, as painted in 1812 by Jean-Baptiste Debret.*

badge: an eight-pointed, or Maltese, cross of the type first used by the Knights of St. John.

Although the Order of St. Louis was thus given the outward appearance of a monastic order, it was in fact the first of the new type of state order now called the *order of merit*, designed to reward a large number of persons for services to the state of varying degrees of importance below those recognized in the monarchical orders. Eleven orders of this type—usually with two or three grades under a grand master, and a form of Maltese cross as a badge—were founded in continental Europe between 1748 and 1797. However, it was only after the foundation in 1802 by the then First Consul of France, Napoléon Bonaparte, of the Legion of Honor— the first unrestricted order of merit, organized first in four and then (in 1805) five grades—that this became normal for new foundations.

This period also saw the creation of a growing number of such orders designed to reward services or achievements of particular types, in Britain beginning in 1815 with the reorganization of the Order of the Bath into three grades designed to reward the service of military and naval officers, and culminating in the foundation of the Order of the British Empire in 1917, with five grades in two divisions (civil and military) to reward all manner of services.

MODERN FORMS OF KNIGHTHOOD

After 1805, the title of *knight* was attached to the lowest grade in all of the Continental orders, so that all of their members have been titular knights. Because knighthood had become a relatively select honor in Britain, however, only the members of the two highest grades of the multigrade British orders (usually called *knight grand cross* and *knight commander*, in descending order)

When I was young, I asked fortune to allow me,
more than anything else, the Order of Saint Michael, as it was
the extreme mark of honor of the French nobility.

MICHEL DE MONTAIGNE, *ESSAYS (ESSAIS, 1580–88)*

were knighted, excluding from the traditional dignity the evermore numerous members of the lower grades (usually called *commander*, *officer*, and *member*). This laid the groundwork for the foundation of a growing number of other orders—beginning with the Distinguished Service Order in 1878—whose members, whether of one or three grades (as in the Order of Canada founded in 1967), were not knighted. Meanwhile, women were first admitted to the knightly grades of a British order in 1917, with the new title of *dame* (thus, *dame grand cross* or *dame commander*)—which also replaced the masculine *sir* as an honorific prefix. They were also admitted with the same titles to other multigrade orders later in the century.

The only orders existing today that maintain even the basic forms of classic knighthood are the British royal orders that include a knightly grade; the other monarchical orders of the confraternal and secularized-monastic types maintained by some European and Asian monarchies, including the papacy; and the handful of secularized military monastic orders not under state control. Most of the last group are detached branches of the great Order of the Hospital, including the Venerable Order of St. John of Jerusalem in the British Realm, revived in 1831 and both officially recognized and privately attached to the British Crown in 1888. In addition, a large number of orders of this class were illicitly revived in the twentieth century, the best known

being that of St. Lazarus, now a major charitable fraternity. Both membership and rank in most of these orders is conferred by a process involving local nomination and vetting at higher levels of the order's hierarchy, culminating in formal approval by the grand master.

KNIGHTS IN NAME ONLY

Finally, since around 1860 a substantial number of charitable, religious, and political fraternities have been founded in many countries whose members call themselves knights without any claim whatever to that title, simply because their founders wished to associate themselves with the prestige and glamor

traditionally associated with knighthood. Notable among these are the Knights of Pythias (founded in Washington, D.C., in 1864), the Knights of Labor (founded in Philadelphia, Pennsylvania, in 1869), the Knights of the Maccabees (founded in London, Ontario, Canada, in 1878), and the Knights of Columbus (founded in New Haven, Connecticut, in 1882). Most of these societies were inspired by Freemasonry, which took its modern form in England in 1717, and came itself to claim a (wholly unfounded) connection to the long-suppressed monastic Order of the Temple—a claim formally embodied in the Masonic societies whose members actually call themselves "Knights Templar." The fact that such bodies still flourish and even multiply today testifies to the continuing prestige of the knightly title and the ideals associated with it.

BELOW: *The dubbing ceremony used today in the United Kingdom still involves a gentle tap with a sword, seen here in the knighting of Sir Garth Morrison by Queen Elizabeth II.*

Part Five

Reference

Timeline

CE 481	Clovis becomes king of the Franks; he is later considered the first king of France
622	Beginning of the rise and spread of Islam
711	Muslim kingdom of al-Andalus established in Spain
722	Battle of Covadonga, traditionally seen as the start of the Spanish Reconquista
732	Charles Martel defeats Muslims at the Battle of Poitiers (Tours)
751	Pepin the Short becomes king of the Franks, beginning the Carolingian dynasty
793	First Viking raids into England, at Lindisfarne
800	Charlemagne crowned Roman Emperor by Pope Leo III
911	Vikings settle in Duchy of Normandy
955	Magyars defeated by dukes of Saxony at the Battle of Lechfeld
c. 980	First knights and first castles begin to appear in historical records
987	Hugh Capet becomes king of France, beginning the Capetian dynasty
990	Peace of God movement begins
c. 1020	First fiefs begin to appear in historical records
c. 1024	Truce of God movement begins
1040	Death of Count Fulk Nerra of Anjou, first great castle builder
1066	Norman Conquest of England
c. 1080	French nobles begin to characterize themselves as "knights"
1095	First Crusade launched at Council of Clermont
1099	Death of El Cid
1100	Establishment of the Christian Kingdom of Jerusalem
c. 1100	Composition of *The Song of Roland*
c. 1120	Foundation of the first crusading orders, the Hospitallers and Templars
1137	Eleanor of Aquitaine marries Louis VII of France
1146	Second Crusade launched
1152	Eleanor of Aquitaine marries Henry II of England
c. 1180	Chrétien de Troyes writes first Arthurian romances
1185	Foundation of the first shogunate in Japan
1187	Fall of Jerusalem to Saladin
1188	Third Crusade launched
1204	Fourth Crusade sacks Constantinople
1209	Albigensian Crusade begins
1214	England loses Normandy at the Battle of Bouvines
1215	King John of England signs Magna Carta; Pope Innocent III holds Fourth Lateran Council
1218	Fifth Crusade launched

1219	Death of William Marshal, considered the quintessential knight
1228	Sixth Crusade launched
1248	Seventh Crusade launched
1270	Eighth Crusade takes place
c. 1280	Edward I of England builds series of castles along Welsh coast
1291	Acre falls to the Muslims, effectively ending the Crusades
c. 1300	New infantry tactics begin to change the face of warfare
1315/16	Death of Ramon Lull, author of *The Book of the Order of Chivalry*
1328	Philip VI becomes king of France, beginning the Valois dynasty
1337	Hundred Years' War begins
1340	English defeat the French at the naval Battle of Sluys
c. 1345	First cannon used in battle
1346	English armies defeat the French at the Battle of Crécy
1347	First outbreak of the Black Death
1348	Establishment of the chivalric Order of the Garter
1350	Geoffrey of Charny writes his *Book of Chivalry*
1356	English armies defeat the French at the Battle of Poitiers
c. 1380	The arquebus becomes a common military weapon
1400	Death of Geoffrey Chaucer, author of *The Canterbury Tales*
1415	English armies defeat the French at the Battle of Agincourt
1420	Treaty of Troyes unsuccessfully tries to end the Hundred Years' War through a royal marriage
1429	Joan of Arc turns tide of Hundred Years' War with victory at Orléans
1431	Joan of Arc burned at the stake
1453	Hundred Years' War ends with French victory; fall of Constantinople to the Turks
1455	Wars of the Roses break out in England
1469	Marriage of Ferdinand of Aragon and Isabella of Castile unites Spain
1478	Establishment of the Spanish Inquisition
1485	Wars of the Roses end with accession of Henry VII; publication of Thomas Malory's *Le Morte Darthur*
1492	Muslims and Jews driven out of Spain, completing the Reconquista; Christopher Columbus reaches North America, effectively ending the Middle Ages
1527	Death of Niccolò Machiavelli, author of *The Prince*
1616	Death of Miguel de Cervantes, author of *Don Quixote*
1819	Sir Walter Scott publishes *Ivanhoe*, reviving interest in knighthood
1954	Publication of J.R.R. Tolkien's *The Lord of the Rings,* beginning modern fantasy genre

ABOVE: *The coronation of Harold Godwinson as Harold II of England, on January 5, 1066, prompted William of Normandy, who claimed he was the rightful heir to the English throne, to invade England later that year.*

Medieval Monarchs

KINGS OF FRANCE

Charlemagne, CE 768–814

Louis I the Pious, 814–40

Charles II the Bald, 840–77

Louis II the Stammerer, 877–79

Louis III, 879–82

Carloman, 882–84

Charles the Fat of Germany, 884–87

Odo, 888–93

Charles III the Simple, 893–922

Robert I, 922–23

Raoul, 923–36

Louis IV d'Outremer, 936–54

Lothair, 954–86

Louis V, 986–87

Hugh Capet, 987–96

Robert II the Pious, 996–1031

Henry I, 1031–60

Philip I, 1060–1108

Louis VI, 1108–37

Louis VII, 1137–80

Philip II Augustus, 1179–1223

Louis VIII, 1223–26

Louis IX Saint, 1226–70

Philip III, 1270–85

Philip IV the Fair, 1285–1314

Louis X, 1314–16

John I, 1316

Philip V, 1316–22

Charles IV, 1322–28

Philip VI Valois, 1328–50

John II the Good, 1350–64

Charles V, 1364–80

Charles VI, 1380–1422

Charles VII, 1422–61

Louis XI the Spider, 1461–83

Charles VIII, 1483–98

Louis XII, 1498–1515

KINGS OF GERMANY (AND, AFTER 960, EMPERORS)

Charlemagne, CE 768–814

Louis I the Pious, 814–40

Louis II the German, 840–76

Charles II the Fat, 876–87

Arnulf, 887–99

Louis III the Child, 899–911

Conrad I, 911–18

Henry I the Fowler, 919–36

Otto I, 936–73

Otto II, 973–83

Otto III, 983–1002

Henry II, 1002–24

Conrad II, 1024–39

Henry III, 1039–56

Henry IV, 1056–1106

Henry V, 1106–25

Lothar III, 1125–37

Conrad III, 1138–52

Frederick I Barbarossa, 1152–90

Henry VI, 1190–97

Otto IV of Brunswick, 1197–1215

Frederick II, 1215–50

Conrad IV, 1250–54

Great Interregnum, 1254–73

Rudolph of Hapsburg, 1273–91

Adolf of Nassau, 1292–98

Albert I of Austria, 1298–1308

Henry VII of Luxembourg, 1308–13

Louis IV of Bavaria, 1314–47

Charles IV, 1347–78

Wencelas, 1378–1400

Rupert, 1400–10

Sigismund, 1410–37

Albert II of Austria, 1438–39

Frederick III, 1440–93

Maximilian I, 1493–1519

KINGS OF ENGLAND

Ethelred II the Unready, 978–1016

Edmund II Ironside, 1016

Canute, 1016–35

Harold I Harefoot, 1035–40

Hardecanute, 1040–42

Edward the Confessor, 1042–66

Harold II, 1066

William I the Conqueror, 1066–87

William II Rufus, 1087–1100

Henry I, 1100–35

Stephen, 1135–54

Henry II, 1154–89

Richard I the Lionheart, 1189–99

John, 1199–1216

Henry III, 1216–72

Edward I, 1272–1307

Edward II, 1307–1327

Edward III, 1327–77

Richard II, 1377–99

Henry IV, 1399–1413

Henry V, 1413–22

Henry VI, 1422–61, 1470–71

Edward IV, 1461–70, 1471–83

Edward V, 1483

Richard III, 1483–85

Henry VII, 1485–1509

Henry VIII, 1509–47

ABOVE: *Already king of the Franks, Charlemagne was crowned as "Emperor of the Romans" by Pope Leo III, in Rome, in December CE 800.*

TOP RIGHT: *Louis IX of France arrives in Tunisia during the Eighth Crusade. Louis's death there led to his canonization, in 1297.*

Further Reading

THE LIFE OF A KNIGHT

Knighthood and Medieval Society

Baldwin, John W. *The Language of Sex: Five Voices from Northern France Around 1200.* Chicago: University of Chicago Press, 1994.

Bisson, Thomas N., ed. *Cultures of Power: Lordship, Status, and Process in Twelfth-Century Europe.* Philadelphia: University of Pennsylvania Press, 1995.

Bouchard, Constance Brittain. *"Every Valley Shall Be Exalted": The Discourse of Opposites in Twelfth-Century Thought.* Ithaca: Cornell University Press, 2003.

Bumke, Joachim. *The Concept of Knighthood in the Middle Ages.* Translated by W.T.H. Jackson and Erika Jackson. New York: AMS, 1982.

Evergates, Theodore. *Aristocracy in the County of Champagne, 1100–1300.* Philadelphia: University of Pennsylvania Press, 2007.

———, ed. *Aristocratic Women in Medieval France.* Philadelphia: University of Pennsylvania Press, 1999.

———. *Feudal Society in the Bailliage of Troyes Under the Counts of Champagne, 1152–1284.* Baltimore: Johns Hopkins University Press, 1975.

Hopkins, Andrea. *Knights: The Complete Story of the Age of Chivalry from Historical Fact to Tales of Romance and Poetry.* London: Collins and Brown, 1990.

Jaeger, C. Stephen. *The Origins of Courtliness: Civilizing Trends and the Formation of Courtly Ideals, 939–1210.* Philadelphia: University of Pennsylvania Press, 1985.

Karras, Ruth Mazo. *From Boys to Men: Formations of Masculinity in Late Medieval Europe.* Philadelphia: University of Pennsylvania Press, 2003.

Martindale, Jane. "The French Aristocracy in the Early Middle Ages: A Reappraisal." *Past and Present,* 75 (1977): 5–45.

Reynolds, Susan. *Fiefs and Vassals: The Medieval Evidence Reinterpreted.* Oxford: Oxford University Press, 1994.

Robertson, D.W. "The Concept of Courtly Love as an Impediment to the Understanding of Medieval Texts." In *The Meaning of Courtly Love,* edited by F.X. Newman. Albany: State University of New York Press, 1968.

Chivalry

Anglo, Sydney, ed. *Chivalry in the Renaissance.* Woodbridge: Boydell Press, 1990.

Barber, Richard. *The Knight and Chivalry.* Woodbridge: Boydell Press, 1995.

Bouchard, Constance Brittain. *"Strong of Body, Brave and Noble": Chivalry and Society in Medieval France.* Ithaca: Cornell University Press, 1998.

Chickering, Howell, and Thomas H. Seiler, eds. *The Study of Chivalry.* Kalamazoo: Medieval Institute, 1988.

Duby, Georges. *The Chivalrous Society.* Translated by Cynthia Postan. Berkeley and Los Angeles: University of California Press, 1977.

Flori, Jean. *L'essor de la chevalerie, XIe–XIIe siècles.* Geneva: Droz, 1986.

Kaeuper, Richard W. *Chivalry and Violence in Medieval Europe.* Oxford: Oxford University Press, 2001.

Keen, Maurice. *Chivalry.* New Haven and London: Yale University Press, 1984.

Painter, Sidney. *French Chivalry.* Baltimore: Johns Hopkins University Press, 1940.

Rudorff, Raymond. *Knights and the Age of Chivalry.* New York: Viking Press, 1974.

Scaglione, Aldo. *Knights at Court: Courtliness, Chivalry, and Courtesy from Ottonian Germany to the Italian Renaissance.* Berkeley and Los Angeles: University of California Press, 1991.

Strickland, Matthew. *War and Chivalry.* Cambridge: Cambridge University Press, 1996.

Trim, D.J.B., ed. *The Chivalric Ethos and the Development of Military Professionalism.* Leiden and Boston: Brill, 2003.

Vale, Malcolm. *War and Chivalry: War and Aristocratic Culture in England, France, and Burgundy at the end of the Middle Ages.* London: Duckworth, 1981.

Castles

Cruden, S. *The Scottish Castle.* Edinburgh: Nelson, 1960.

Gillingham, John. "An Age of Expansion, c. 1020–1204." In *Medieval Warfare: A History,* edited by Maurice Keen. Oxford: Oxford University Press, 1999.

Jones, R.L.C. "Fortifications and Sieges in Western Europe, c. 800–1450." In *Medieval Warfare: A History,* edited by Maurice Keen. Oxford: Oxford University Press, 1999.

Prestwich, Michael. "English Castles in the Reign of Edward II." *Journal of Medieval History,* 8 (1982): 159–78.

Smail, R.C. *Crusading Warfare, 1097–1193.* Cambridge: Cambridge University Press, 2008.

Taylor, Arnold. *The Welsh Castles of Edward I.* London: Hambledon Continuum, 1984.

Armor, Weapons, and Horses

Ayton, Andrew. *Knights and Warhorses.* Woodbridge: Boydell Press, 1994.

Byam, M. *Eyewitness Arms and Armour.* London: Dorling Kindersley, 2003.

DeVries, Kelly. *Medieval Military Technology.* Peterborough: Broadview Press, 1992.

DeVries, Kelly, and Robert D. Smith. *Medieval Weapons: An Illustrated History of Their Impact.* Santa Barbara: ABC-CLIO, Inc., 2007.

Hyland, Ann. *The Medieval Warhorse.* Conshohocken: Combined Book, 1996.

Oakeshot, Ewart. *Records of the Medieval Sword.* Woodbridge: Boydell Press, 1991.

Talhoffer, Hans. *Medieval Combat: A Fifteenth-Century Illustrated Manual of Swordfighting and Close-Quarter Combat.* Translated and edited by Mark Rector. London: Greenhill Books, 2004.

Windsor, Guy. *The Swordsman's Companion: A Modern Training Manual for the Medieval Longsword.* Texas: The Chivalry Bookshelf, 2004.

Warfare

Contamine, Philippe. *War in the Middle Ages.* Translated by Michael Jones. Oxford and New York: Blackwell, 1984.

Delbrück, Hans. *Medieval Warfare.* Translated by Walter Renfroe, Jr. Lincoln: University of Nebraska Press, 1982.

France, John. *Western Warfare in the Age of the Crusades.* Ithaca: Cornell University Press, 1999.

Hale, J.R. *War and Society in Renaissance Europe, 1450–1620.* New York: St. Martin's Press, 1985.

Jones, Terry. *Chaucer's Knight: The Portrait of a Medieval Mercenary.* London: Eyre Methuen, 1980.

Keen, Maurice, ed. *Medieval Warfare: A History.* Oxford: Oxford University Press, 1999.

Mallet, Michael E. "The Art of War." In *Handbook of European History: Late Middle Ages, Renaissance and Reformation,* edited by Thomas A. Brady, Heiko Oberman, and James D. Tracy, 535–62. Grand Rapids: William B. Eerdmans Publishing Company, 1994.

Morillo, Stephen, Jeremy Black, and Paul Lococo. *War in World History: Society, Technology and War from Ancient Times to the Present,* Vol. 1. New York: McGraw Hill, 2009.

Whetham, David. *Just Wars and Moral Victories: Surprise, Deception and the Normative Framework of European War in the Later Middle Ages.* Leiden: Brill, 2009.

Heraldry

Beddoe, Alan. *Beddoe's Canadian Heraldry.* Revised by Strome Galloway. Belleville: Mika Publishing, 1981.

Boutell, Charles. *Boutell's Heraldry.* Revised by J. P. Brooke-Little. London: Frederick Warne Publishers, Ltd, 1983.

Burnett, Charles and Mark D. Dennis. *Scotland's Heraldic Heritage: The Lion Rejoicing.* Edinburgh: Mercat Press, 1997.

Fox-Davies, Arthur Charles. *Complete Guide to Heraldry.* London: 1909; London: Wordsworth Editions, 1996; New York: Skyhorse Publishing, 2007.

Friar, Stephen, and John Ferguson. *Basic Heraldry.* London: A & C Black, 1999.

Friar, Stephen, ed. *A Dictionary of Heraldry.* Sherborne and New York: Harmony Books, 1987.

Innes of Learney, Sir Thomas. *Scots Heraldry.* Revised by Sir Malcolm Innes of Edingight. Edinburgh: Johnston & Bacon, 1978.

Neubecker, Ottfried. *Heraldry: Sources, Symbols, and Meanings.* London: Macdonald and Jane's, 1976.

Von Volborth, Alexander. *Heraldry: Customs, Rules, and Styles.* London: New Orchard Editions, 1991.

Woodcock, Thomas, and John Martin Robinson. *The Oxford Guide to Heraldry.* Oxford: Oxford University Press, 2001.

Zieber, Eugene. *Heraldry in America.* Mineola: Dover Publications, 2006.

Crusading Orders and the Church

Barber, Malcolm. *The New Knighthood: A History of the Order of the Temple.* Cambridge: Cambridge University Press, 1995.

————. *The Trial of the Templars.* Cambridge: Cambridge University Press, 2006.

Barber, Malcolm, and Keith Bate. *The Templars: Selected Sources Translated and Annotated.* Manchester: Manchester University Press, 2002.

Bouchard, Constance Brittain. *Holy Entrepreneurs: Cistercians, Knights, and Economic Exchange in Twelfth-Century Burgundy.* Ithaca: Cornell University Press, 1991.

————. *Sword, Miter, and Cloister: Nobility and the Church in Burgundy, 980–1198.* Ithaca: Cornell University Press, 1987.

Boulton, D'Arcy Jonathan Dacre. *The Knights of the Crown: The Monarchical Orders of Knighthood in Later Medieval Europe, 1325–1520.* Woodbridge: Boydell Press, 2000.

Bradford, Ernle. *The Shield and the Sword: The Knights of St. John in Jerusalem, Rhodes, and Malta.* London: Penguin, 2002.

Marcombe, David. *Leper Knights: The Order of St Lazarus of Jerusalem in England, c. 1150–1544.* Woodbridge: Boydell Press, 2003.

Riley-Smith, Jonathan. *The Knights of St John in Jerusalem and Cyprus 1050–1310.* London: Palgrave Macmillan, 1967.

Rosenwein, Barbara H. *Rhinoceros Bound: Cluny in the Tenth Century.* Philadelphia: University of Pennsylvania Press, 1982.

Seward, Desmond. *The Monks of War.* Revised edition. London: Penguin, 1995.

Sire, H.J.A. *The Knights of Malta.* New Haven and London: Yale University Press, 1994.

Asian Knights

Bartusis, Mark C. *The Late Byzantine Army. Arms and Society, 1204–1453.* Philadelphia: University of Pennsylvania Press, 1992.

Friday, Karl. *Samurai, Warfare and the State in Early Medieval Japan.* London: Routledge, 2004.

Graff, David A. *Medieval Chinese Warfare, 300–900.* London and New York: Routledge, 2002.

Graff, David A., and Robin Higham, eds. *A Military History of China.* Boulder: Westview, 2001.

Jackson, Peter. *The Delhi Sultanate: A Political and Military History.* Cambridge: Cambridge University Press, 1999.

Kar, H.C. *Military History of India.* Calcutta: Firma KLM, 1980.

Lewis, Mark Edward. *Sanctioned Violence in Early China.* Albany: SUNY University Press, 1992.

Lyons, Malcolm, and D.E.P. Jackson. *Saladin: The Politics of the Holy War.* Cambridge: Cambridge University Press, 1997.

Morgan, David. *The Mongols.* Cambridge: Cambridge University Press, 1990.

Turnbull, Stephen. *The Samurai. A Military History.* London: RoutledgeCurzon, 2002.

Van de Ven, Hans, ed. *Warfare in Chinese History.* Leiden: Brill, 2000.

Varley, Paul. *Warriors of Japan as Portrayed in the War Tales.* Honolulu: Hawaii University Press, 1994.

THE KNIGHT IN HISTORY

The Rise of Knights

Bachrach, Bernard S. *Early Carolingian Warfare: Prelude to Empire.* Philadelphia: University of Pennsylvania Press, 2001.

Becher, Matthias. *Charlemagne.* Translated by David S. Backrach. New Haven: Yale University Press, 2003.

Collins, Roger. *Charlemagne.* Toronto: University of Toronto Press, 1998.

Head, Thomas, and Richard Landes, eds. *The Peace of God: Social Violence and Religious Response in France Around the Year 1000.* Ithaca: Cornell University Press, 1992.

McKitterick, Rosamond. *Charlemagne: The Formation of a European Identity.* Cambridge: Cambridge University Press, 2008.

The Norman Era

Abels, Richard P., and Bernard S. Bachrach, eds. *The Normans and their Adversaries at War: Essays in Memory of C. Warren Hollister.* Woodbridge: Boydell Press, 2001.

Aird, William M. *Robert Curthose, Duke of Normandy (c. 1050–1134).* Woodbridge: Boydell Press, 2008.

Corvisier, André, and Philippe Contamine, et al. *Histoire militaire de la France, 1: dès origines à 1715.* Paris: Quadrige/Presses Universitaires de France, 1992.

Crouch, David. *William Marshal: Knighthood, War and Chivalry, 1147–1219.* Edinburgh: Pearson Education, 2002.

Hollister, C. Warren. *The Military Organization of Norman England.* Oxford: Oxford University Press, 1965.

Hunt, Tony. "The Emergence of the Knight in France and England, 1000–1200." *Forum for Modern Language Studies,* 17 (1981): 93–114.

Keen, Maurice. *Nobles, Knights and Men-At-Arms in the Middle Ages.* London: Hambledon Press, 1996.

Morillo, Stephen. *Warfare under the Anglo-Norman Kings, 1066–1135.* Woodbridge: Boydell Press, 1994.

————. *The Battle of Hastings: Sources and Interpretations.* Woodbridge: Boydell Press, 1995.

Musset, Lucien. *The Bayeux Tapestry.* Woodbridge and New York: Boydell Press, 2005.

Prestwich, J.O. *The Place of War in English History, 1066–1214.* Edited by Michael Prestwich. Woodbridge: Boydell Press, 2004.

Prestwich, Michael. *Armies and Warfare in the Middle Ages: The English Experience.* New Haven: Yale University Press, 1996.

Strickland, Matthew. *War and Chivalry: The Conduct and Perception of War in England and Normandy, 1066–1217.* Cambridge: Cambridge University Press, 2005.

————, ed. *Anglo-Norman Warfare.* Woodbridge: Boydell Press, 1992.

The Crusades

Christiansen, Eric. *The Northern Crusades.* London: Penguin, 1997.

Crawford, Paul, ed. *The "Templar of Tyre": Part III of the "Deeds of the Cypriots".* Translated by Paul Crawford. Aldershot: Ashgate, 2003.

France, John. *Victory in the East: A Military History of the First Crusade.* Cambridge: Cambridge University Press, 1997.

————. *Western Warfare in the Age of the Crusades.* Ithaca: Cornell University Press, 1999.

Gabrieli, Francesco. *Arab Historians of the Crusades.* Berkeley: University of California Press, 1984.

Kennedy, Hugh. *Crusader Castles.* Cambridge: Cambridge University Press, 1994.

Madden, Thomas. *A New Concise History of the Crusades.* Lanham: Rowman & Littlefield, 2005.

Peters, Edward, ed. *The First Crusade: "The Chronicler of Fulcher of Chartres" and Other Source Materials.* Philadelphia: University of Pennsylvania Press, 1998.

Riley-Smith, Jonathan. *The Crusades.* New Haven: Yale University Press, 2005.

————. *The First Crusaders, 1095–1131.* Cambridge: Cambridge University Press, 2008.

————. *What Were the Crusades?* London: Macmillan, 2009.

————. "Crusading as an Act of Love." *History* 65 (1980): 177–92.

Setton, Kenneth, ed. *A History of the Crusades.* 6 vols. Madison: University of Wisconsin Press, 1969–89.

Ye'or, Bat. *The Dhimmi: Jews and Christians under Islam.* Madison: Fairleigh Dickinson University Press, 1985.

The Reconquista

Barton, Simon. *A History of Spain.* Basingstoke: Palgrave Macmillan, 2004.

Fletcher, Richard. *Moorish Spain.* Berkeley: University of California Press, 2006.

Lomax, Derek W. *The Reconquest of Spain.* London and New York: Longman, 1978.

MacKay, Angus. *Spain in the Middle Ages: From Frontier to Empire, 1000–1500.* Basingstoke: Palgrave Macmillan, 1977.

O'Callaghan, Joseph F. *Reconquest and Crusade in Medieval Spain.* Philadelphia: University of Pennsylvania Press, 2003.

The Albigensian Crusade

Barber, Malcolm. "The Albigensian Crusades: Wars Like Any Other?" In *Dei gesta per Francos: Crusade Studies in Honour of Jean Richard,* edited by Michel Balard, Benjanim Z. Kedar, and Jonathan Riley-Smith, 45–56. Aldershot: Ashgate, 2001.

Marvin, Laurence W. *The Occitan War: A Military and Political History of the Albigensian Crusade, 1209–1218.* Cambridge: Cambridge University Press, 2008.

Pegg, Mark Gregory. *A Most Holy War: The Albigensian Crusade and the Battle for Christendom.* New York: Oxford University Press, 2007.

Strayer, Joseph R. *The Albigensian Crusades.* With a New Epilogue by Carol Lansing. Ann Arbor: University of Michigan Press, 1992.

Sumption, Jonathan. *The Albigensian Crusade.* London: Faber and Faber, 1978.

Wakefield, Walter L. *Heresy, Crusade and Inquisition in Southern France, 1100–1250.* London: George Allen & Unwin, 1974.

The Hundred Years' War

Allmand, Christopher. *The Hundred Years War: England and France at War, c. 1300–c. 1450.* Cambridge: Cambridge University Press, 1989.

Ayton, Andrew and Philip Preston, eds. *The Battle of Crécy, 1346.* Woodbridge: Boydell Press, 2007.

Curry, Anne, ed. *Agincourt 1415.* Stroud: Tempus, 2000.

Hooper, Nicholas, and Matthew Bennett, *Cambridge Illustrated Atlas of Warfare: The Middle Ages.* Cambridge: Cambridge University Press, 1996.

Rogers, Clifford J. *War Cruel and Sharp: English Strategy Under Edward III, 1327–1360.* Woodbridge: Boydell Press, 2000.

Sumption, Jonathan. *The Hundred Years War: Trial by Battle.* London: Faber & Faber, 1990.

———. *The Hundred Years War: Trial by Fire.* London: Faber & Faber, 1999.

Knighthood in Decline

Allmand, Christopher. "War." In *The New Cambridge Medieval History VII, c. 1415–c. 1500,* edited by C. Allmand. Cambridge: Cambridge University Press, 1998.

Ferguson, Arthur B. *The Indian Summer of Chivalry: Studies in the Decline and Transformation of Chivalric Idealism.* Durham: Duke University Press, 1960.

Keen, Maurice. "The Changing Scene: Guns, Gunpowder, and Permanent Armies." In *Medieval Warfare: A History,* edited by Maurice Keen. Oxford: Oxford University Press, 1999.

McNeill, William H. *The Pursuit of Power: Technology, Armed Force, and Society Since A.D. 1000.* Chicago: University of Chicago Press, 1982.

O'Neil, Bryan Hugh St. John. *Castles and Cannon: A Study of Early Artillery Fortification in England.* Oxford: Clarendon Press, 1960.

Parker, Geoffrey. *The Military Revolution: Military Innovation and the Rise of the West, 1500–1800.* Cambridge: Cambridge University Press, 1996.

———. "The Gunpowder Revolution, 1300–1500." In *The Cambridge Illustrated History of Warfare,* edited by G. Parker. Cambridge: Cambridge University Press, 1995.

THE CULTURAL LEGACY

Knights in Literature

Bumke, Joachim. *Courtly Culture: Literature and Society in the High Middle Ages.* Translated by Thomas Dunlap. Berkeley and Los Angeles: University of California Press, 1991.

Capellanus, Andreas. *The Art of Courtly Love.* Translated by John Jay Parry, edited by W.T.H. Jackson. New York: W.W. Norton, 1969.

Chrétien de Troyes. *Arthurian Romances.* Translated by W.W. Kibler. London: Penguin, 1991.

Cooper, Helen. *The English Romance in Time: Transforming Motifs from Geoffrey of Monmouth to the Death of Shakespeare.* Oxford: Oxford University Press, 2004.

Ferrante, Joan M., trans. *Guillaume d'Orange: Four Twelfth-Century Epics.* New York: Columbia University Press, 2001.

Matarasso, P.M., trans. *The Quest of the Holy Grail.* London: Penguin, 2005.

Owen, D.D.R. *Noble Lovers.* London: Phaidon Press Limited, 1975.

Pearsall, Derek Albert. *Arthurian Romance: A Short Introduction.* Oxford: Blackwell, 2003.

Spiegel, Gabrielle M. *Romancing the Past: The Rise of Vernacular Prose Historiography in Thirteenth-Century France.* Berkeley and Los Angeles: University of California Press, 1993.

Von Eschenbach, Wolfram. *Parzival.* Translated by A.T. Hatto. London: Penguin, 2004.

Film and Television

Aberth, John. *A Knight at the Movies: Medieval History on Film.* New York and London: Routledge, 2003.

Aronstein, Susan. *Hollywood Knights: Arthurian Cinema and the Politics of Nostalgia.* Houndmills: Palgrave Macmillan, 2005.

Burt, Richard. *Medieval and Early Modern Film and Media.* Houndmills: Palgrave Macmillan, 2008.

Driver, Martha, and Sidney Ray, eds. *The Medieval Hero on Screen: Representations from Beowulf to Buffy.* Houndmills: Palgrave Macmillan, 2004.

Harty, Kevin J. *The Reel Middle Ages. American, Western and Eastern European, Middle Eastern and Asian Films about Medieval Europe.* Jefferson: McFarland, 1999.

———, ed. *Cinema Arthuriana. Essays on Arthurian Film.* New York: Garland, 1991.

———, ed. *King Arthur on Film. New Essays on Arthurian Cinema.* Jefferson: McFarland, 1999.

Haydock, Nickolas. *Movie Medievalism.* Jefferson: McFarland, 2008.

Knight, Stephen. "A Garland of Robin Hood Films." *Film and History,* 29.3–4 (1999): 34–44.

Nollen, Scott Allen. *Robin Hood: A Cinematic History of the English Outlaw and His Scottish Counterparts.* Jefferson: McFarland, 1999.

Olton, Bert. *Arthurian Legends on Film and Television.* Jefferson: McFarland, 2008.

Ramey, Lynn, and Tison Pugh. *Race, Class and Gender in "Medieval" Cinema.* Houndmills: Palgrave Macmillan, 2007.

Rosenstone, Robert. *Visions of the Past: The Challenge of Film to Our Idea of History.* Cambridge: Harvard University Press, 1995.

Sorlin, Pierre. *The Film in History: Restaging the Past.* Oxford: Blackwell, 1980.

Taves, Brian. *The Romance of Adventure. The Genre of Historical Adventure Movies.* Jackson: University Press of Mississippi, 1993.

War Games

Girouard, Mark. *The Return to Camelot: Chivalry and the English Country Gentleman.* New Haven: Yale University Press, 1985.

Marshall, David W., ed. *Mass Market Medieval: Essays on the Middle Ages in Popular Culture.* Jefferson: McFarland and Co., 2007.

Sklar, Elizabeth S. and Donald L. Hoffman, eds. *King Arthur in Popular Culture.* Jefferson: McFarland and Co., 2002.

Honorific Orders

Bergent, Peter J., and Hubert Chesshyre. *The Most Noble Order of the Garter: 650 Years.* London: Spink & Son, 1999.

Boalt, Gunnar, Robert Ericson, Harry Glück, and Herman Lantz. *The European Orders of Chivalry.* Stockholm: Norstedts, 1971.

Boulton, D'Arcy Jonathan Dacre. *The Knights of the Crown: The Monarchical Orders of Knighthood in Later Medieval Europe 1325–1520.* Woodbridge: Boydell Press, 2000.

Collins, Hugh E.L. *The Order of the Garter 1348–1461: Chivalry and Politics in Late Medieval England.* Oxford: Oxford University Press, 2000.

Galloway, Peter. *The Most Illustrious Order: The Order of Saint Patrick and its Knights.* London: Unicorn Press, 2002.

———. *The Order of the British Empire.* London: Spink & Son, 1996.

Matikkala, Antti. *The Orders of Knighthood and the Formation of the British Honours System, 1660–1760.* Woodbridge: Boydell Press, 2008.

Glossary

aketon A quilted garment worn underneath chain mail and body armor to prevent the armor rubbing on the skin and to help absorb the shock of blows from weapons.

antipope A pope elected or appointed in opposition to the incumbent Bishop of Rome. If a split in the college of cardinals, or the intervention of the Holy Roman Emperor or another temporal ruler, led to the election of more than one pope, the one later determined not to have been the true pope became known as the antipope.

arms A distinctive emblem used to identify a knight, which often appeared on his shield, banner, and clothing. By the late Middle Ages, the arms became widely known in English as the *coat of arms*.

bailey The area of ground enclosed by the main defensive walls of a castle, especially in the earliest motte-and-bailey castles. In later stone castles, the bailey was often called the *ward*.

barbican A defensive outerwork, consisting of walls and towers, which surrounded a castle gate and was designed to protect it.

bastion fort A low, thick-walled fort designed to withstand cannon fire. Such structures proliferated in the late Middle Ages, following the advent of gunpowder and cannon. In place of the towers common in earlier castles, these fortifications incorporated low, projecting structures known as bastions.

bohort A form of tournament fighting, in which groups of mounted knights, without armor and using blunted weapons, attempted to unhorse each other. The bohort was often fought as a prelude to a tournament proper.

buckler A small, round shield, often covered with leather.

byrnie A leather jacket or vest onto which metal rings were sewn; a simpler version of the hauberk.

caparison A cloth covering placed over a knight's horse to protect it and/or its armor. Caparisons often bore heraldic emblems that identified the rider.

castellan The lord of a castle. In some cases, the castellan (or his ancestors) built the castle himself; in others he (or his ancestors) was given it to hold by a count or duke.

chain mail Armor made by linking thousands of metal rings. Flexible and relatively inexpensive, it was the most common form of medieval armor.

chanson de geste In medieval literature, an epic tale of knightly deeds, set in an imagined past and originally recounted in song. The first great *chanson de geste* was *The Song of Roland* (*La chanson de Roland, c.* 1100).

chevauchée In war, a pillaging raid made by a group of knights on enemy territory. Designed to terrorize the local population, it often involved looting and the destruction of crops.

ABOVE: *Tournaments of the late Middle Ages, like the one illustrated in this English engraving, were a focus of social life among the nobility.*

charger A warhorse, strong enough to carry a man in armor and trained for use in tournament or battle.

coat of arms The term adopted in English in the late Middle Ages for the distinctive emblem of a knight or noble family, originally known simply as the *arms*.

coif A hood made of chain mail, worn under the helmet and designed to cover the neck and provide additional protection to the head.

condottiere The leader of a band of mercenaries, particularly in Italy in the late Middle Ages and Renaissance.

crusade A war conducted by Christians against Muslims, pagans, or heretics. The modern English word comes from the same root as the word *cross*; the medieval term was *peregrinatio,* the same word used to mean "pilgrimage."

curtain wall The outer wall of a castle, which by the late twelfth century usually incorporated multiple towers, and into which were built, on the inner side, such structures as stables, storehouses, and sleeping quarters.

demesne The lands on which the lord of a manor grew food for his own household or to sell at market. These lands were worked by his tenants as part of their rental agreement.

dubbing The ceremony by which a young man was declared a knight. The dubbing would normally be carried out by an older knight—in the epics and romances, usually King Arthur or Charlemagne.

enfeoff To grant a fief to someone, thereby accepting him (or, occasionally, her) as a vassal.

epic A story of knightly deeds told in the Middle Ages, usually in the vernacular, and often involving semilegendary figures such as Charlemagne.

escutcheon A representation of a shield, within which a knight's arms were commonly depicted when they appeared on a banner or clothing.

falconry Hunting birds with hawks, especially falcons. Falconry was considered a uniquely aristocratic activity; the term also refers to the complex art of training the hawk to kill and retrieve game birds.

fief A piece of property which one noble or knight—known as the lord of the property—granted to another noble or knight to hold for his lifetime, in return for his loyalty. The person who received the fief was known as the *vassal* of the lord who granted it.

garderobe A latrine in a castle, usually a small room built on an upper story, projecting over a wall. The term was a euphemism, meaning "a place to keep clothing" or "closet."

greave A piece of plate armor designed to protect a knight's lower leg.

halberd A weapon consisting of a spear with a sharp point, and an ax mounted on one side near the tip. It was used effectively by foot

soldiers in the late Middle Ages both to impale and to slash.

hauberk A chain-mail shirt, with or without sleeves, usually made of rings linked together. The hauberk was the basic item of body armor throughout the Middle Ages.

helm A helm or helmet was armor designed to protect the head. Originally not much more than an inverted bowl with a nosepiece, it became quite elaborate by the late Middle Ages, often having a hinged visor over the eyes and a crest mounted on the top.

herald A court official with a range of roles, including proclaimer, messenger, and master of ceremonies. In particular, heralds recorded the arms of knights and, from the late Middle Ages, were in charge of the granting of arms to those recognized as noble. Heralds also presided over tournaments, enforcing the rules, keeping track of those who fought, and publicizing the winners.

heraldry Strictly speaking, the activities of a herald; since the early seventeenth century, however, the term has also been used to refer to the creation of the emblems used as a means of identification by knights and, later, noble families. The rules governing this practice became complex, with only specific color combinations and symbols being allowed and restrictions being placed on the transfer of emblems to heirs.

hoarding A wooden structure built out from the top of a castle wall, designed to provide defenders with a vantage point, from which they could shoot down on or drop objects onto enemy soldiers below. Also known as *brattices*, hoardings were later made of stone.

homage To pay homage to someone was literally to declare oneself the *homo* (Latin for "man") of that person. Such a declaration usually involved a ceremony, at which the "man" promised lifelong loyalty in return for a fief.

joust A formal contest at a tournament, in which two mounted knights, each armed with a long lance, charged toward each other and attempted to unhorse the opponent with a blow from the point of the lance. Sometimes also called a *tilt*.

keep A large, and usually the first, stone tower built inside a castle; also called a *donjon*. Even when castles were expanded and rebuilt, as they were nearly every generation, a castellan usually preserved his keep as a final line of defense.

livery A distinctive outfit, usually of a certain color and often bearing heraldic emblems, in which a late medieval lord might dress his household.

lord A noble, king, or other landholder who granted fiefs to vassals, often knights. Also used to refer to a landholder with peasant tenants.

mace A weapon consisting of a spiked ball on the end of a long handle, which could either be used by a foot soldier or a mounted man. Its purpose was to crush an opponent's helmet or other armor.

mangonel A form of catapult used to fire missiles at castle walls. It usually incorporated a wooden arm, with a bucketlike container at one end, a counterweight at the other, and a winch in the middle. A missile would be placed in the container, and the arm winched back. When it was released, the counterweight would propel the missile with great force.

melee At a tournament, a pitched battle between two large groups of knights. It was carried on with little organization and few rules, other than that the knights were supposed to capture rather than intentionally kill each other.

moat A ditch that might be dug around a castle when it was not protected by a natural waterway. When flooded, the moat provided an extra layer of defense.

motte A mound or artificial hill, on which a tower was built. The first castles, in the eleventh century, were usually built around a central motte and its tower, and are called *motte-and-bailey* castles.

mural tower A tower built into the outer wall of a castle, from which the defenders would be able to sight along the outside of the wall and shoot at attackers.

order A group of knights selected for their honor and skill and all dedicated to a common purpose. The first military orders emerged during the Crusades and were created to defend and spread Christianity. In the late medieval period, honorific orders, such as the Order of the Golden Fleece, were formed to commemorate fading chivalric ideals; these are echoed today in certain civic associations such as the Knights of Columbus.

page A youth just beginning his knighthood training. Pages served at table and were expected to work at gaining a good education, as well as learning to fight.

phalanx A line or lines of foot soldiers standing close together, usually with their shields arranged in a wall and spears pointing outward.

pike A long wooden shaft with a sharp spearhead at the end. Foot soldiers armed with pikes played a major part in medieval battles, even in the heyday of knights.

poleax A form of battleax, mounted on a long shaft. The head consisted of an ax blade on one side and a spike or hook on the other.

portcullis An iron grate, usually with spikes at the bottom, that could be lowered into a castle gateway to close it off and aid defense.

postern gate A small gate or doorway in a castle, just big enough for one person to pass through at a time. It allowed people to enter or exit even when the main gates were shut.

quintain A target, often consisting of a shield or mail shirt, which a knight would use to practice his jousting.

rampart A parapet or walkway just inside the top of a castle wall. The top edge of the wall usually alternated higher masonry with openings, called *embrasures*, through which a defender could look or fire.

Reconquista Following the Muslim conquest of the Iberian Peninsula in the eighth century, the long, slow process by which the Christian armies of the peninsula reclaimed it, which culminated with the final expulsion of the Moors in 1492.

romance In medieval literature, a story about knights and ladies, usually incorporating themes of love and/or religion. The first Arthurian romances were written by French poet Chrétien de Troyes in the late twelfth century.

samurai The dependents and retainers of the warlords of medieval Japan, usually treated as analogous to Europe's knights.

shell-keep castle A castle with a relatively thin stone outer wall surrounding its central tower and outbuildings. Such castles appeared in the eleventh century, when castellans began to replace their wooden palisades with stone structures.

service knight A knight of non-noble status who served as a retainer in the households of a castellan. Even as nobles began to define themselves by their knightly attributes, service knights continued to flourish—while striving to emulate their lords or to marry their daughters.

squire A youth well along in his knightly training. Squires typically assisted knights in battle or at tournaments. A nobleman would remain a squire until his formal knighting ceremony.

tabard A usually sleeveless garment worn over armor. Typically, it was decorated with the bearer's coat of arms or, in the case of a crusader, a cross. Also known as a surcoat.

tournament An event consisting of a series of mock fights and battles, which allowed knights to demonstrate their skills without actually killing anyone. The first tournaments took place in the late eleventh century.

trebuchet A heavy catapult, used in sieges to hurl stones against an enemy castle. See also *mangonel*.

vassal A person who swore loyalty to a lord in return for a fief. Normally the vassal would hold the fief for his lifetime, as long as he remained loyal. To be a vassal became one of the markers of knighthood by the thirteenth century.

Index

Plain page numbers refer to the main body text, italic page numbers to illustrations or illustration captions, and bold numbers to text within feature boxes.

ABOVE: *Hunting wild animals, as depicted in this c. 1450 German illustration, was seen as ideal training for young knights.*

Acknowledgments

The Publisher would like to thank Sophia Oravecz and Dannielle Viera for their help during the conceptualization process prior to production, as well as Rochelle Deighton for her help in the early stages of the book's production.

ABOVE: *This 1513 engraving,* The Knight, Death, and the Devil, *was created by the renowned German artist Albrecht Dürer.*

CAPTIONS FOR PRELIMINARY PAGES AND OPENERS

Page 1: This image of a mounted knight is from a French medieval manuscript now in the Bibliothèque de l'Arsenal, Paris.

Page 2: In *St. George and the Dragon*, German artist Lucas Cranach the Elder (1472–1553) depicted the saint as a medieval knight rather than the Roman soldier of religious tradition.

Page 4: Reenactors dressed as medieval knights parade at the Kaltenberg tournament at Kaltenberg, Germany.

Page 6: Ornate statues of knights adorn the building facades surrounding the Grand Place in Brussels, Belgium.

Page 8: *Top:* This stained-glass image of Charlemagne (c. 742–814) is displayed in the Musée de l'Oeuvre de Notre Dame, Strasbourg, France. *Center:* The foundation of the Cistercian Abbey of Zwettl, Austria, in 1137, was recorded in this medieval manuscript. *Bottom:* These ornate sculptures of knights decorate the throne used by the reigning monarch in the United Kingdom's House of Lords during the annual State Opening of Parliament ceremony.

Page 9: *Top:* The prominent role of horseborne warriors in the Norman force that invaded England in 1066, shown here in a section of the Bayeux Tapestry, prefigured the widespread military use of units of mounted knights from the eleventh century onward. *Center:* King Richard I of England (reigned 1189–1199), also known as Richard the Lionheart, has come to be seen as the epitome of the chivalrous knight. *Bottom:* Robust doors and a portcullis still protect the entrance to Bodiam Castle in Sussex, England, which dates from 1385.

Page 11: Edmund Blair Leighton's painting *The Accolade* (1901) is a romanticized depiction of the dubbing ceremony, by which a squire became a knight. It is unlikely, however, that a woman would have ever carried out this ritual.

Page 12: Frank Topham's painting *The Queen of the Tournament* illustrates a famous scene from Walter Scott's novel *Ivanhoe* (1819), in which Ivanhoe, having been declared champion of a tournament

at Ashby-de-la-Zouche in England, is allowed to choose its queen.

Page 26: This colorful French medieval manuscript illustration depicts a domestic scene from the thirteenth-century romance *Maugis of Aigremont*, a work that originally derived from the twelfth-century Doon de Mayence cycle of *chansons de geste*.

Page 148: *Ptolemais Given to Philip Augustus and Richard the Lionheart*, by Merry-Joseph Blondel (1781–1853), shows Muslims departing the town of Acre—known in Classical times as Ptolemais—after the crusader siege of 1191, as the victorious Christian kings and their knights look on.

Page 244: *The Temptation of Sir Percival* (1894), by Arthur Hacker, is one of numerous English Pre-Raphaelite–style paintings inspired by Arthurian legend.

Page 286: The walls of the Ferrande Tower near the town of Pernes-les-Fontaines in Provence, France, are adorned with thirteenth-century frescoes, including this one showing combat between an Angevin king and Manfred, king of Sicily.

PHOTOGRAPHIC CREDITS

Front Cover CB, **Endpapers** Shutterstock,
Back cover t AA, ct AA, cb AA, b AA.
1 GI, 2 GI, 5 GI, 6 GI, 8b GI, c GI, t GI,
9b GI, c GI, t GI, 11 GI, 12–13 GI, 14b
IMP, 15tl PL, tr PL, 16t CB, 17b IMP, 18b
AA, 19c PL, t GI, 20b AA, t AA, 21b PL,
22c PL, 23b AA, t AA, 24b GI, 25c AA,
t CB, 26–27 GI, 28b CB, 29b AA, t AA,
30b AA, t GI, 31t GI, 32l AA, r IMP, 33b
AKG/British Library, 34b PL, 35b AA,
t AA, 36b IMP, t AA, 37t AA, 38t GI, 39b
AA, t AA, 40b AA, t AA, 41t PL, 42b PL,
t AA, 43t AA, 44b PL, 45tl AA, tr AA,
46b PL, 47tl AA, tr AA, 48t AA, 49b AA,
t AA, 50c AA, 51b AA, t AA, 52b AA, 53t
AA, 54t AA, 55b AA, 56bl AA, br AA, 57t
AA, 58b AKG/akg-images, 59c AA, t AA,
60b IMP, 61b PL, t IMP, 62t IMP, 63b GI,
t PL, 64t PL, 65b PL, t GI, 66b CB, 67t
AA, 68t CB, 69b PL, c AA, 70b PL, 71t
IMP, 72br IMP, cl AA, 73b CB, 74bl AA,
tr IMP, 75t AA, 76b CB, 77t IMP, 78br
CB, tl CB, 79r IMP, 80b IMP, t IMP, 81cr
IMP, t AA, 82b AKG/Jérôme da Cunha,
83b AKG/Erich Lessing, t IMP, 84c IMP,
85t IMP, 86t AA, 87b AKG/Werner
Forman, t IMP, 88b IMP, t AA, 89b IMP,
t CB, 90b CB, 91l GI, r CB, 92t IMP, 93b
IMP, t AA, 94bl PL, c PL, 95b IMP, t PL,

96b PL, 97c CB, t GI, 98t IMP, 99b IMP,
100c AA, 101c AA, 102b IMP, 103b PL,
t IMP, 104t AA, 105t AA, 106t IMP, 107bl
PL, br AA, 108b IMP, 109b GI, t AA,
110bl AA, tr IMP, 111b AA, 112l AA,
r AA, 113b IMP, 114t GI, 115b IMP, t IMP,
116l AA, r IMP, 117t IMP, 118t IMP, 119b
IMP, t IMP, 120–121t PL, 120b PL, 121r
AKG/akg-images, 122b AA, 123l IMP,
r IMP, 124t AA, 125b IMP, t AA, 126l AA,
127 AA, 128b AKG/akg-images, 129b AA,
l PL, 130t College of Arms, London, reference: MS. 1 M.5, ff. 18v-19, description:
shields from the Hyghalmen Roll, 131b
College of Arms, London, reference:
Westminster Tournament Roll, description:
"Le Roy desarmey", t AA, 132–133b GI,
132l AA, 133t AA, 134l CB, r GI, 135r GI,
136r GI, t AA, 137t CB, 138t PL, 139l GI,
t CB, 140l AA, r AA, 141t AA, 142t PL,
143b AKG/akg-images, t AA, 144l AKG/
British Library, 145l AKG/akg-images,
r IMP, 146b AA, 147l AA, r AKG/François
Guenet, 148–149 GI, 150b CB, t PL, 151r
AA, 152b AA, t CB, 153t PL, 154t AA,
155b AA, t AA, 156l AA, 157l AA, r AA,
158c GI, 159b PL, t IMP, 160b PL, 161r
AKG/akg-images, 162b AA, t IMP, 163l
PL, 164t AKG/Erich Lessing, 165l IMP,
r AKG/Erich Lessing, 166l PL, r AA, 167b
PL, 168b PL, t GI , 169 AA, 170–171t AA,
170b PL, 172b IMP, t IMP, 173r IMP, 174b
PL , t PL, 175b AA, 176b CB, t CB, 177b
AA, 178t AA, 179b AA, 180b PL, t PL,
181r IMP, 182l PL, 183l AKG/akg-images,
r GI, 184b CB, 185b AA, t AA, 186t IMP,
187b AA, t IMP, 190b AA, t AA, 191t CB,

192b IMP, t AKG/Erich Lessing, 193t PL,
194–195b GI, l IMP, 195r IMP, 196b GI,
197b IMP, t AA, 198b AA, t AA, 199r AA,
200l AA, 201b AA, t AA, 202–203t IMP,
202b AA, 203r AA, 204b AA, 205l CB,
r AA, 206l AA, r AKG/Jean-Paul
Dumontier, 207t AA, 208b CB, 209l GI,
r AA, 210b AKG/Gilles Mermet, t GI,
211t GI, 212l AKG/Tristan Lafranchis,
r AKG/akg-images, 213t IMP, 214b AA,
t CB, 215t IMP, 216b AA, t AKG/British
Library, 217l AA, 218b IMP, 219l AA,
r AA, 220b AA, 221l AA, r AKG/
VISIOARS, 222t AA, 223b AA, t AA,
224b AA, t PL, 225l CB, 226–227 PL,
226l PL, 227r AA, 228b AA, 229l CB,
r AA, 230b AKG/Jerome da Cunha, 231b
IMP, t AA, 232b IMP, 233l AA, r AA,
234b GI, 235b GI, t AKG/akg-images,
236b PL, t GI, 237t CB, 238t IMP, 239b
PL, t CB, 240–241 IMP, 240l IMP, 241r
IMP, 242b AA, 243l AA, r IMP, 244–245
GI, 246l GI, 247b PL, t PL, 248b GI, t AA,
249r PL, 250b AKG/Erich Lessing, t AA,
251r AA, 252–253 GI, 252l PL, 253r PL,
254l AA, 255b IMP, t GI, 256l PL, 257r
PL, 258b GI, 259b GI, t AA, 260t CB,
261b KC, t KC, 262b KC, 263t KC, 264b
KC, t KC, 265 CB, 266–267t KC, 266b
KC, 267b KC, tr KC, 268l KC, 269b CB,
t KC, 270t KC, 271b KC, t KC, 272l GI,
273b GI, t AKG/akg-images, 274–275 GI,
274t PL, 276b CB, t CB, 277b CB, t GI,
278t IMP, 279b CB, 280b GI, t GI, 281b
PL, 282l IMP, r AA, 283t IMP, 284l PL,
r AA, 285b GI, 286–287 GI, 288–289 GI,
290t GI, 291t GI, 294t GI, 303t GI.